Italian Fashion

Italian Fashion

From Anti-Fashion
to Stylism

Electa
Rizzoli, New York

Design
Pierluigi Cerri

Translation
Christopher Huw Evans

© Copyright 1987
by Electa Spa., Milano

Distributed exclusively in the United States and Canada by
RIZZOLI INTERNATIONAL PUBLICATIONS, INC.
597 Fifth Avenue, New York, NY 10017

ISBN 0-8478-0890-4
LC 87-63256

Printed and bound in Italy

Italian Fashion

From Anti-Fashion to Stylism

Edited by
Grazietta Butazzi
Alessandra Mottola Molfino

Contributions by
Nicoletta Bocca
Marzia Cataldi Gallo
Carla Cavelli Traverso
Elisa Coppola
Federica Di Castro
Gianfranco Ferré
Chiara Giannelli Buss
Alessandra Gnecchi Ruscone
Giovanna Grignaffini
Rietta Messina
Massimo Mininni
Enrica Morini
Elisabetta Pagani
Rosanna Pavoni
Lamberto Pignotti
Gerardo Rangone
Stefania Ricci
Emilio Tadini

Editorial Coordination
Francesco Porzio

Over the last forty years a striking change of direction has taken place in the world of Italian fashion: from post-war deprovincialization, but one that coincided with dependence on French fashion, and the "outside fashion" production of the ready-to-wear clothing manufacturers, to the international success of stylism, which has taken the exclusive right to the invention of fashion away from the realm of haute couture and released into the boundless territory of ready-to-wear clothing. From clothing as a precise, even rigid, connotation of social class to clothing, first as anti-fashion and then as personal playfulness and free performance.

Developments in Italian fashion after the boom of the fifties and the crisis that overtook some aspects of this process during the following decade (specific ones like the sales of high fashion, or ones linked to delays in interpretation of and planning for the market in the ready-to-wear clothing industry) were taken up and responded to, often in an original way and one that in any case achieved almost immediate success, in the phenomenon of stylism. In an investigation of the motives underlying the success of this phenomenon, it is difficult to separate the creative aspects from suitability of entrepreneurial strategies and, at all events, the constant interest in research and experimentation.

As always in the history of Italian figurative culture the success of a visual formula depends on a combination of factors such as the demands of clients, economic gains and social promotion. All this in a "polis" (In this case Milan, but in the past Urbino or Venice or Rome or Florence) which supplies the background of taste and aesthetical and political traditions, becoming a national and international crossroads for people and values. When this occurs, in Italy, there also come into play experiences that seem to stretch far back into the past: the modest and artisan production of many generations; the minor and provincial centres; the immemorial social stratifications; the economic model and organization of labour in which the workshop of Renaissance tradition and the cottage industries of the "urban" countryside have coexisted for centuries with major industries on the Anglo-Saxon pattern, with artistic and entrepreneurial talents always ready to flower. In this case, that figure typical of Italian visual culture that is the designer, whether of furnishings, clothes or motor-cars.

In the second volume of the work an attempt has been made to put this fundamental factor in the development of contemporary fashion into perspective, investigating its effects on modes of social conduct as well, as they are expressed, for example, in the different responses of consumers or the emblematic value of cinematographic images. Hence we feel that useful or usable connotations at every level of research have emerged from the analysis of a social choice of deep-rooted tradition such as "classic" men's tailoring, and its underlying motivations, when confronted with the wide range of stylistic proposals whose innovative content is based on a more openly self-critical interpretation of masculine nostalgia. Or when the early "off-fashion" events staged on the premises of the companies promoting them are seen in relation to new and unusual kinds of interior decoration that brought about important changes in the mentality and behaviour of young people. Or when a research and a methodology that is a concrete manifestation of a relationship, even in spatial terms, between form and body is associated with the reflections of those who have interpreted this relationship in a work of art.

The difficulty of tracing documentary materials – from the articles themselves to the historical information that links them together –, although somewhat reduced in comparison with the often insurmountable ones encountered during the compilation of the first volume, still demonstrate the lack of an institution dedicated to the collection, preservation and study of the results of a phenomenon with as vast a range of implications not only for the field of economics but also for the possibility of understating some of the most striking social and psychological manifestations of our time. The absence of a museum and a historical archive of Italian fashion is something that makes itself more and more widely felt with the passing of time.

Where specimens have been preserved or tracked down there is often a grave shortage of information concerning the history of a particular element, especially when it was "taken in" after the phase of presentation in fashion shows or shops. Equally common is the need to make do with information passed down by oral tradition instead of reliable and documented facts. At this point, when dispersion of the historical and documentary heritage, even with regard to the contemporary output of Italian fashion, has almost become an accomplished fact, it is vital to seek out the missing data and organize it into a systematic scheme that will take account of the complete "journey" of the element, from production to consumption. Vanished or converted companies, items of clothing thrown away as leftovers from an era that people want to forget, from a style of which they are ashamed, from events that occurred barely 8 or 10 years ago. Tracking down the clothes put together and photographed for this volume, for instance, has been a labour of what amounts to archaeology. Especially as far as the neglected and modest ready-made clothing industry of the sixties is concerned, despite the fact that it lay the foundations for the more successful organization of production in the late seventies.

Two major, and indispensable, sources for the research have been the specialized press and women's magazines on the one hand (all too often ignored by the public libraries) and the surviving documents in company archives on the other (that we hope will be preserved in a more rational manner in future). These latter documentary materials, together with the testimonies of those directly involved, have allowed us to reconstruct biographies and economic histories of people, firms and companies which went to make up the culture medium put of which emerged, and flowered, contemporary Italian fashion.

As in the first volume, the method of inquiry for the chapters specifically devoted to the production and creation of fashion in clothing is linked to structural analysis of individual materials. This constitutes the ground for any further discussion aimed at providing a picture of the historical development of production itself and a critical commentary on the work of individual personalities. Examination of the clothes, even when entrusted to different researchers, is given methodological unity in a distinct framework that makes it possible to see these objects in the perspective of their constituent and formal characteristics and of the variety of decorative idioms that distinguish them. Thus, for example, the article of clothing of greatest structural complexity – the suit – is given substance through the researcher's examination of a

series of precise features, in identical sequence. The description, moving from top to bottom, from the chest to the lower part of the body, picks out, as for any object of applied art, all the typical aspects of execution and decoration, immediately identifying it as representative of a particular historical period and as expression of a particular creative direction. The measurements, which relate "vital" cuts to technical solutions, complete the analysis since they are not limited to a list of details or a mere reconstruction of manufacturing data. Analysis and description of the textiles (external and internal) and ornamentation, by establishing a series of corroborations and proposals of origin and date and a necessary verification of economic and productive factors, also throws light on experimentation in clothing design, one of whose most important aspects is research into materials. The article of clothing also has to be looked at and analyzed on the historical level in order to discover the contents and meanings that determine its historical identity within a logic of creativity or production, as well as its social and behavioural influences.

The original cataloguing of the garments reproduced in photographs in this volume, which it has only been possible to give in part for reasons of space, offers, in our view, the most significant results for a method of potential application to contemporary fashion, at least as far as the primary requirement of safeguarding collections and standardizing historical and analytical data is concerned.

The files relating to all the materials examined during the compilation of both volumes of this work will be made available to the public in their entirety by the Commune of Milan. It is our hope that this initiative will eventually constitute the nucleus of an archive of contemporary Italian fashion, by now the only possible way to avoid the gradual disappearance of any record of the past.

Quite apart, then, from the many declarations, including those by figures with authority, comparing fashion to art but which have remained on the level of intentions as far as historiography is concerned, we have set out in this research to promote practically (as well as philologically) the fashion object as historical and historico-artistic material, as a testimony to the history of taste and outlook.

Grazietta Butazzi   Alessandra Mottola Molfino

Contents

Garment descriptions and biographical notes were edited by:

A.B. Adriano Benvenuto
N.B. Nicoletta Bocca
M.C.G. Marzia Cataldi Gallo
C.C.T. Carla Cavelli Traverso
E.C. Elisa Coppola
C.G.B. Chiara Giannelli Buss
A.G.R. Alessandra Gnecchi Ruscone
M.M. Massimo Mininni
E.M. Enrica Morini
M.L.R. Maria Luisa Rizzini
M.C.V. Maria Cristina Vimercati

THE INFLUENCE OF "NOVELTY," "DISTINCTION" AND "QUALITY" ON CONSUMPTION

Gerardo Rangone

The interest in new products, the demands of status and the hankering after well-being constitute the three basic motives underlying consumption. All forms of consumption that have emerged so far in industrial societies have always been driven by pressures and motivations of this kind. What, perhaps, has made them different is the different weight exerted, in each of them, by these three factors. From this point of view one can speak of consumption based on "novelty" when, the interest in new products has a greater influence than concerns about status and aspirations after well-being; of a consumption of "distinction" when it is the requirements of status that prevail over the other two factors; lastly, of "quality" when it is the quality of daily life that shapes patterns of consumption. With a little bit of effort, the "profiles" of consumer society worked out by Katona a few years ago can be fairly easily identified with the three types described above.[1] It also needs to be pointed out that not only have different national forms of consumption been distinguished in the past by the different make-up of this "mix" of motivations and values, but that the history of each of them has often been marked by phases, periods that are characterized by different combinations of the three factors.

What is the dominant sequence of the three types of consumption in a process of economic development and the way in which shifts take place from one pattern to another are theoretical problems that we are not concerned with here. What does interest us, however, is whether this "three-phase" model can also be used to interpret – at least in broad outline – the evolution of consumption in Italy since the war, or more precisely from the moment of effective take-off of the Italian economy in the fifties up until the present day.

The Years of Novelty

If the fifties – taken up, as is well known, by post-war reconstruction – are excluded, then it can safely be asserted that the first impact of modern patterns of consumption on Italian society was both violent and traumatic. Violent, because the cultural penetration of the "American way of life" was rapid and comprehensive, in the sense that it did not in practice spare any sphere of daily life. Traumatic because the new life style that emerged out of North American society broke with many ancient customs and rooted habits, with the result that, at least in

Fiorucci advertising sticker.

the early stages, Italian families put up a fair amount of "resistance" to the new consumer goods that were appearing on the market. Yet once they had overcome their doubts and suspicions about the new world of consumption and prosperity, Italians did not hang back from changing their life style and began not only to acquire the new consumer products with remarkable enthusiasm but also to reject, without too many regrets, the cultural framework on which their customs and habits had previously been based.

What whetted the appetite of new consumers in those days was primarily the "new" product, the commercial novelty: anything, in other words that appeared different from the old consumer goods and traditional ways of life. What Pizzorno defined as "innovatory consumption" was the true impetus behind domestic demand in the early years of the transformation of Italian society.[2] In particular, the frame of reference for the selection of these new consumer goods was the American way of life, i.e. that of processed foods, the motor-car, domestic gadgets and plastic articles, all things that were completely new with respect to habits of consumption in traditional Italy. The later were based around the concept of the "domestic hearth," and involved natural foods, hand-crafted products, etc. Faced with this avalanche of new objects and products, the behaviour of the Italian consumer appears almost infantile, made up in part of curiosity about the new goods and in part of plain greediness and possessivity, something very close to the "hoarding tendency" of Fromm's theories. This probably derived from an old tradition of economizing combined with a still older condition of poverty, at least for a large part of the country. The fact remains that Italians approached the new products of mass society from a position of weakness and subordination: they were fascinated and seduced by this world of new objects and products, rich, among other things, in promises of happiness and pleasure.

But the new was also desired because it permitted integration into the new urban industrial society. The possession of certain goods was a guarantee of a new status; those who lacked them remained on the margins of the new society or were even excluded from it. Alberoni defined the new forms of consumption as "consumption of citizenship" to underline just this fact that the new status of citizenship was ensured primarily by the ownership of new goods. "The new goods," wrote Alberoni, "born out of technological progress and produced in great quantity through the process of industrial growth are... bearers of new meanings, correspond to new needs and enter as premises within new systems of action and experience, i.e. they are an indistinguishable component of the modern urban social system."[3]

That this interest in everything that was new constituted the underlying motivation for patterns of consumption in the early years of Italian economic development is further demonstrated by the growing attention paid by consumers to so-called luxury products over this period. At the time there was even talk of a distortion of consumption, with reference to the fact that, as family incomes increased, the expenditure on "non-essential" goods went up faster than that on "essential" ones.[4] The truth is that the "new" was largely to be found among the first type of products, while innovation in the sector of basic consumer goods was far slower, or even virtually non-existent.

So the most characteristic trait of consumption during this period was undoubtedly the obsession with novelty. New products were preferred both because they satisfied the curiosity of consumers and because they secured integration into the new social system. In short, as long as they were new, goods were desired and acquired, even when they were not very useful and did not assign any prestige to their owner.

Styles of dress did not escape this rule, even though it may seem strange to define as characteristic of a period what is the very essence of fashion, that is to say "novelty." But in this particular case, it is a question of qualifying the aspiration for the "new." In the realm of fashion, in fact, preference for newness can be based on a need for social distinction, on requirements of practicality and convenience and, lastly, on a need for a more broadly based social identification. The latter was the situation in the fashion of the fifties and early sixties. For both men and women the primary task of the new garments and styles was to testify to the end of wartime and post-war penury. As has been rightly pointed out, "... the novelty of Dior was accepted as a reconquest of femininity, as a mark or a hope of prosperity..."[5]

But the new clothes – just like other products – also served to bear witness to the wearer's membership of urban industrial society. To follow fashion in those years meant, in fact, to make a decided break with tradition, to go over to the side of the affluent society. A clear sign of this was the decline of interest, among women, in underwear, with strong preferences being shown for outer garments.

"In the field of clothing, it was observed, there has been a reversal of expenditure between 'underwear' and 'outwear'; the traditional concentration in the sector of underwear has given way to an equivalent concentration in the sector of *public* clothing, that which

is seen and which permits identification and comparisons."[6]

The Years of "Distinction"

It was towards the beginning of the sixties, however, that this frame of reference for the pattern of consumption began to slowly change, in fashion just as in other sectors of industrial production. The consumer was more mature and had more money to spend at his discretion. Above all, he was beginning to be selective about the new products and to appraise the advantage to be gained from them in terms of social prestige and position in the new hierarchies of status. Thus the consumption of "novelties" was replaced by a new kind, that of "distinction," i.e. social competition through consumer goods, status expenditure and conspicuous consumption. The demand for goods became more complex and differentiated. It began to divide into many segments, as if to satisfy the requirements of a society that, having reached a respectable level of prosperity and established a new framework of values, was starting to tackle the problem of putting everyone in his right place, of defining the new borders of class and rank. And, in some ways, life was growing more complicated for the production system and for advertising itself. For the incentive to consumption was now the desire for status, and to sell new products it was no longer sufficient to arouse the curiosity or the acquisitiveness of consumers. The new system of social stratification had to be taken into account; a system, moreover, that was far more complex than the fairly linear hierarchies to be found in more typically consumer societies, such as that of North America. However, what concerns us here is the fact that, unlike in the previous period, consumer goods were now strongly desired when they conferred prestige on the purchaser, even when they were neither new nor useful.

It was in this period that, for the first time, luxurious styles of clothing began to appear on the mass market. To use a term coined by Hirsch, "positional" factors began to play an important role in fashion.[7] Up until then, in fact, luxury in dress had been confined solely to the upper classes. That is to say, expensive items of clothing and original designs had circulated only at the highest levels of the social strata. The other levels were either dominated by traditional styles of dress, as in the countryside, or made do with cheap imitations of what was presumed to be in fashion among the well-to-do-élite. In the years of the economic boom, however, extravagance in dress started to become a reasonable objective for broad strata of the population. Hence all the features of distinction that had been confined to the élite up until a few years earlier, now began to interest a much wider public. The prime consequence of this was an acceleration in the rate of innovation in fashion.

The different styles and cuts that character-

ized the boom years and that to some extent prepared the ground for the great transformation of the seventies, are not of much concern. What matters is that in fashion, as in other areas, the requirements of social distinction became the main impetus behind the demand for products. The reason – it is worth repeating – was a structural one. The major economic recovery of the mid-sixties, like all periods of strong economic growth, entailed a reshuffling of the system of social stratification, and in particular its extension. What this meant was an increase, at every level of society, in the availability of social positions, of spaces to be occupied: more places among the petite bourgeoisie and the proletariat, more spaces among the middle classes and so on, up to an expansion of the privileged élite itself. As a consequence of this increase in the supply of social positions, everyone was induced to take a few steps up, to gain a better position. But this very process of social reorganization brought with it an accentuation in the symbolization of status. In fact, in order to be socially recognized and ratified, shifts in status required exhibition of proof.

Thus "marks of recognition" became important and this explains why during such phases of economic expansion, not only does status-oriented consumption take on particular value but the "positional" component increases at all of the various levels of consumption. While in the previous period the main goal of individuals was integration into urban industrial society, and consumer goods were selected on the basis of this particular aim, now the main goal was social mobility, the achievement of a higher social rank in the new and enlarged system of stratification.

Consequently, products were selected on the basis of this other aim. It is in this sense that one can speak of a consumption of "distinction" during these years, a type of consumption very different from that based on "novelty" or "integration."

Just as there was a growing demand for high status consumer goods on the part of individuals and families, the social system adjusted to provide an increase in the supply of such goods. All that had been the preserve of the dominant élite in the past was now made available for consumption by larger numbers of people.

In other words, the sixties can be described as the years of a democratization of high-class consumption in almost every sector of the market, from clothing to furniture, and from holidays to motor-cars. In the fashion sector, for example, the fur made its appearance in middle-class wardrobes, while in that of furnishings the antique began to take its place among the "functional" pieces of furniture of the ordinary house. Tennis and skiing, traditional symbols of conspicuous affluence among the upper classes, spread to other levels of society with surprising speed, just as among automobiles, the aristocratic line of the coupé or the sports-car was made avail-

Fiorucci shopping bag with cowgirl and advertising stickers.

able at all ranges of power (Bianchi even produced a luxury two-seater version of the cheapest of all cars, the Fiat 500).

So the consumption of the sixties was dominated by the phenomena of "distinction," which does not mean that there were no other motivations for consumption; just that social acknowledgement of the standard of living attained had become the major concern of those who were benefitting from a process of upward mobility.

A Variant of "Distinction": The Strategies of Conspicuous Underconsumption in the Seventies

If we wish to interpret this third period in terms of "positional economy" and "positional competition" (Hirsch), emphasis must be laid on the fact that at the very moment when the majority of the middle-class had managed to acquire a "good dress" (as well as a "good drawing-room," etc.), fashion went through a

frustration in a large part of the population and clearing the way for the generation gap that was to be a mark of the whole of the seventies. What had in fact been the dream of an entire generation – to dress like the "rich" – went up in smoke when the "rich" changed the rules of the game and began to dress as "poor." Thus good, tidy, pressed, clean, respectable clothing gave way, over the span of a few years, to old, wrinkled, poor, shabby, worn, untidy

Fashion show at Tivioli, 1985-86.

In any case it was a phenomenon of more than considerable proportions, to the point where some traditional barriers of class and rank began to fade.

But then came a surprisingly violent jolt which was to profoundly alter the system of stratification that had been formed as a result of the economic boom, radically modifying the habits, consumption and customs of the Italian people.

radical change and, under the impetus of the notorious social and political upheavals of those years, churlishly introduced "bad dress": a type of clothing, in other words, from which every trace of the formal rigidity that had been typical of the styles of the preceding period was rigorously eliminated. It was a move that left the new petite bourgeoisie and the emerging middle classes stranded high and dry, provoking a considerable amount of resentment and

and incongruous clothes. But it was not just a question of dress. It was the entire pattern of behaviour, the "look" that changed radically. To be in fashion now meant in practice repudiating all the canons of bourgeois respectability and adopting a tone of ostentatious slovenliness and visible contempt for the obligations and rules of traditional middle-class life. The new marks of fashionableness for men, and the symbols of a new social status, were the full beard, the shoulder-bag, sneakers, jeans, corduroy and the parka. Among women, the famous sequence "mini-midi-maxi" was just the start of an unlimited series of innovations and inventions in dress, in which practically everything that could reasonably occur actually did.

Young people and the various élites were the earliest protagonists of this abrupt shift in clothing styles, while adults and the lower classes remained confined, at least at the beginning, to the tidy world of bourgeois respectability. Thus there was an alliance between "classes and generations," as Alberoni would put it, that, from its playful origins in the fashion world, rapidly extended to every other kind of consumption, eventually producing significant changes in the behaviour, opinions and attitudes of a large section of the Italian population. In fact it was not just clothing that was humble, sloppy and eventually "casual." The same thing happened with furnishings: an aesthetics developed that was based on old things, of little value, arranged in any old order and with flaunted indifference. But the "poor" house became fashionable too and so the preferences of the new consumers shifted towards historic city centres, where a combination of "poverty" and tradition could be found. And the same was true for the car: in vogue were old, cheap, spartan and technologically simple cars (explaining the success of the "beetle"), in contrast to the new, shiny, well-kept cars, crammed with "optionals," preferred by those who still believed in the dream of affluence and plenty. Lastly there was leisure and tourism where, in tune with the ideology of under-consumption, the traditional aristocratic and bourgeois holiday resorts were totally neglected in favour of pilgrimages to poor areas and the underdeveloped Third World.

From more to less, in short, from rich to poor, from the cult of affluence to that of poverty, from order to disorder, from stability to precariousness. Such a radical shift had never occurred before and it is clear that it too derived from structural changes. Referring to men's wear, Alberoni points out that "... the bourgeois uniform came under threat only when something in the system of political, economic and cultural relationships of capitalist society had changed. And this change came gradually with the development of technology, along with the expansion of the bureaucratic proletariat (office-workers) and the technico-bureaucratic proletariat (technicians), which has brought a new role for the family, an increase in leisure and an increase in the level of mass education."[8] This is undoubtedly true, but it is also true that the new patterns of partiality that emerged in 1968 led in practice to a reclassification of the entire population, giving rise to new social classes and strata. But the very fact that this was yet another process of social reclassification meant that the symbolic elements of consumption based on "distinction"

remained dominant. As has been said, essentially what happened in the preceding period was a quantitative transformation of the system of social stratification, while the mechanisms of social differentiation and "distinction" remained unchanged. This time, however, the transformation of social stratification was of a qualitative nature: the positions available did not increase in number (indeed, in some areas, such as that of employment, they began to diminish), while what changed was, so to speak, their arrangement, their positioning within the social hierarchy. This is why the rules of the game were profoundly altered, were in fact turned upside down. The traditional social logic of upward movement through accumulation and ostentation was replaced by movement based on underconsumption. Reminding us that contemporary consumption rests essentially on a system of marks and differences, rather than on real objects, Baudrillard points out that "... only this allows us to explain the paradox of underconsumption or inconspicuous consumption, i.e. the paradox of a differentiation of levels of prestige that is no longer made manifest through Veblen's conspicuous ostentation, but through discretion, renunciation and modesty, which amount to nothing more than another luxury, a surplus of ostentation that turns into its opposite, and is therefore a more subtle difference. Differentiation can then take the form of a rejection of objects, a rejection of consumption that is in reality the highest refinement of consumption."[9]

So from the viewpoint of consumption and social stratification, the seventies – or perhaps to be more accurate the period from 1968 to 1975 – were still years of "distinction," even though the profound changes in life styles and the inversion of the rules and the symbolic codes on which status is based that occurred during this period were to prepare the ground for a third type of consumption. This type, profoundly different from the other two, was that based on the "quality of life."

The Years of "Quality"

It was around the middle of the seventies that the cultural pattern of "distinction" – in both the versions examined – began to fade away. For a whole range of reasons, partly economic and partly social and cultural, social prestige ceased to represent the prime motivation for consumption and a new cultural framework was set up in its place. This was founded on the aspiration for well-being and on the desire to live in a qualitatively meaningful manner. If, in other words, during the first period of our model the consumer acquired objects because he was seduced by their "novelty," while in the second he was obsessed by questions of status, he now calmed down and returned to ordinary life, concerning himself with basics and spending his money mainly on living better, feeling good and quietly enjoying the pros-

perity he had achieved. This does not mean that no more useless things were sold in this period, or that prestige had ceased to be a motivation for consumption. It just means that these were no longer the main factors determining trends in consumption. The principal factor, the dominant incentive to consumption was something else now: the desire to live well, to feel good, to be healthy and, if possible, beautiful. In short, to enjoy life without being carried away by "new" products and without worrying too much about the requirements of status. What Alberoni has recently described as the "gracious way of life." In terms of our discussion so far, it could be said that as long as they were useful, products were desired and acquired, even when neither new nor prestigious. Yet this new sort of consumption, probably more mature than its forerunners, was initially interpreted in negative terms as a "withdrawal" and "return to the private sphere." To many people it looked as if a great deal of the social and political goals attained in previous years would be lost as a consequence of this renewed interest in private life and comfort, and of a certain amount of "disillusionment" – as Hirschman would put it – with regard to participation in public life. Such an attitude is of disconcerting naivety, to say the least, for in practice it denies what has been the most significant change of the last twenty or thirty years, that is to say the transfer of private consumption into the "public" sphere. In the seventies, the years of great conflict, participation had undoubtedly been greater, but consumption – understood here in the more general sense of custom and ways of life – remained, despite everything, an exclusively private matter, and in addition much concerned with show. In this most recent pattern of Italian consumption political involvement has without doubt been reduced – at least in the spectacular forms that were typical of the so-called "hot" years – but in exchange consumption acquired those public, collective or, if you will, civil connotations whose absence had always been criticized by Marxists and Catholics. In short people participated less but were demanding different things to make up for it: useful products, efficient services, an unpolluted environment. This signified a notable reduction in the position of subordination to the requirements of production in which consumption had found itself in previous periods. Hence the naivety and blindness of the "theory of withdrawal," incapable of recognizing that the "private sphere" which has gained the upper hand in recent years is something profoundly different from the "private concerns" that had been a mark of earlier Italian history.

Just what is it that is different about this "private sphere" of the eighties, this concern with what has been described as the "quality of life?" To start with, as has already been said, it is a "private sphere" that maintains a close relationship with the "public" one and with public

*Kimono jacket in chamoise leather with
attached fringes of Persian lamb, Matti
1984.*

consumption. In order to grasp this change it is necessary to look at the relationship between public and private consumption in the history of Italian economic development. It is sufficient to recall here that up until the mid-seventies each of these two types of consumption had in practice been growing independently of the other, and that this was made possible by the influence of individualistic cultural attitudes on the formation of demand. In fact the consumption of "novelty" and of "distinction" were largely taken up with the individual and with his personal and family circumstances. When on the other hand consumer spending is motivated by a desire for a qualitatively better life, the problem of products has to be dealt with simultaneously with that of the environment: not only objects and goods, but also a suitable setting for their use or consumption. The great innovation that took place in consumption during the eighties consists in the fact that the majority of products desired by people imply the presence of a favourable habitat, in other words of an environmental and territorial context able to guarantee the activity of consumption itself. This is precisely because the new consumption based on the "quality of life" is made up of products, objects and services that have more connections with the environment outside the home than with that inside it, while the reverse was true in earlier periods. Necessarily, the exaltation of well-being, whether material or non-material, that is inherent in the ideology of the "quality of life," subordinates private consumption to collective resources. It is in this way that private consumption has begun to acquire public and collective connotations. It requires a regularization, an ecological guarantee. Gratifications and satisfactions in terms of "quality of life" are unthinkable within the walls of the home, whereas the latter is ideally suited for the growth and consolidation – as in fact happened – of interest in "innovatory" products or of a certain lust for conspicuous consumption. The fact is, today's consumer is more mature, aware and balanced than he was in the previous phases of economic development, having adopted a cultural model that is largely concerned with making the best out of himself and his own life. As a result his demand has become more complex, being not just a demand for goods and products, but also a demand for conditions, for requisites for the use and consumption of these things. This is why private consumption is gradually becoming less subordinate to production and more subordinate to public consumption, and it is also why the "private sphere" of the eighties is very different from that of earlier periods.

In fashion, for instance, this bias towards "quality" is extremely evident. The factors of practicalness and comfort have never been as important in the assembly of a wardrobe, whether for men or for women, as in this period. Jeans have become loose, shoes comfortable, shirts practical and full. But above all everyone dresses more or less how they like, playing with fashion, freely combining different styles and shapes, the old and the new, the modern and the post-modern. And this is true for a good many consumer goods, just as recent signs of a move away from the big cities should be seen against this background. There seems to be a new preference for middle-sized urban centres, which can offer better conditions for urban life than those which are to be found nowadays in the great metropolitan areas.

On the one hand, then, this new private realm, in virtue of its qualitative connotations, acquires a more social, more collective dimension, and therefore a more public one. On the other – but once again as a result of this first characteristic – it has very little effect on changes in status. That is, the status element of products vanishes, or is highly reduced, in this third type of consumption. In a sense, consumption has become "neutral" with respect to social mobility. Within certain limits, one can possess what one likes without this altering one's position in the social hierarchy in the slightest. The boat, the cross-country vehicle, the holiday in the Maldives, the designer clothes: these are all things that no longer help the individual to improve his social position. This is particularly true in fashion. Indeed it could be said that the great fashion boom of the eighties, the fashion, that is, of the stylists, has been possible precisely because it no longer compromises the system of social stratification. It is the one extraordinary thing about the fashion of this period: it no longer affects positions of status. It is pure playfulness, spectacle, amusement and pleasure.

Let us not forget that the main function of fashion in the past was to distinguish individuals, groups and classes within society. Hence it was something that people took very seriously. Those who followed fashion did it with diligence and stringency, knowing that an error of dress could have not inconsiderable consequences. Today, however, this function of fashion as a status symbol has gone or, at least, has been much diminished. Those who follow fashion now do it in a different spirit and with a different attitude, in the sense that they are fully aware that their choices in this field will not have any effect on their position in society. This is a new phenomenon. People have many reasons for wanting to be in fashion, but hardly ever any longer to display their status. And this may also explain why so many of the proposals put forward by major fashion designers over the last ten years seem to have a great deal to do with "dressing up."

Once again, what is true of the fashion sector holds true in other areas as well. What is, however, certain is that the return to the "private sphere" that began around the middle of the seventies is far from a withdrawal. On the contrary, it is a new cultural attitude, marked by an ideology of the "quality of life" which, in its individual and collective implications, is a sure sign of a shift towards maturity in the history of consumption and custom in Italy.

1. G. Katona, B. Strumpel, E. Zahn, *Il comportamento economico della famiglia. Un'analisi comparata Europa-USA*, Etas Kompass, 1972.
2. A. Pizzorno, "Materiali per una sociologia dei consumi," in *Passato e presente*, 1958, no. 2.
3. F. Alberoni, *Consumi e società*, Bologna 1964, p. 37.
4. A. Graziani, "Lo sviluppo di un'economia aperta," in Var. Auts., *Lo sviluppo di un'economia aperta: aspetti teorici e strutturali*, Portici 1967.
5. M. Contini, "L'abbigliamento: la moda come consumo e come costume," in *Sbiprauno*, 1967, no. 2, p. 54.
6. L. Gallino, "La famiglia e i modelli di consumo," in *Siprauno*, 1967, no. 1, pp. 43, 44.
7. F. Hirsch, *I limiti sociali dello sviluppo*, Milan 1981.
8. F. Alberoni, "Osservazioni sociologiche sull'abbigliamento maschile," in Var. Auts., *Psicologia del vestire*, Milan 1972.
9. J. Baudrillard, *La società dei consumi*, Bologna 1976, pp. 118, 119.

A QUESTION OF PERFORMANCE

Giovanna Grignaffini

The division of phenomena into periods obeys, as always, a perverse sort of logic: it requires a search for events, situations and inaugural and conclusive texts that can be used as a cage to imprison the actual subject of investigation. Still more perverse are those divisions which, independently of any factual criterion or reference, chop up history into decades, each one endowed with a "poetics" of its own, an internal consistency and homogeneity. These are purely "operative" divisions whose principal purpose is to offer relatively limited units for analysis, making possible an examination at closer range. Obviously what is lost in this kind of approach are the "long-term effects," that set of factors which are actively at work in the period under consideration, but whose causes and motivations are much more remote and whose consequences extend much further in time.

Such considerations become even more valid when one considers the subject of our investigation: the relations between Fashion and the Media from the seventies up to the present day. A subject whose definition involves both the internal forces at play within each of the various related components (the changes that have occurred within the realms of Fashion, Cinema, Television, Advertising, etc.) and the different – and rapidly changing – forms that their relationships have taken at different times. Hence we have opted for a partial integration of the two approaches: that of close-up analysis and that of a more general survey, sacrificing (given the limited space available as well) some analysis of detail and some attempts at speculation and explanation. Let us start by trying to delimit in operative terms our field of analysis by establishing some terms of reference. In other words, to pick out from a fairly undifferentiated situation some "symptoms" that may be worthy of investigation.

What is the distance that separates Michelangelo Antonioni's *Blow-Up* (1966) from Carlo Vanzina's *Sotto il vestito niente* (1985), the only two Italian films made since the sixties that have explicitly used the world of fashion as a background? It is a distance that cannot be explained merely in terms of the difference in the aesthetic qualities and breadth of artistic and cultural vision of the two directors. Primarily, it concerns the different ways in which the world of fashion is treated and utilized on the narrative plane. In particular, the way in which Antonioni regards it as an ideal setting for an

Eleonora Giorgi, model for the Postalmarket catalogue Spring-Summer 1986.

examination of the *problem of vision* and the enlargement of reality, while for Vanzina it is a spectacular location – on the scenographic and narrative plane – as well as a *mark of attraction.*

And again. What is the bumpy road that, from the almost total absence of news about the world of fashion which was typical of the television some years ago, has led to the current boom in features, interviews and programmes that stamp the palimpsests of public and private broadcasting with the trade-mark of fashion? Culminating in that *Serata d'onore* (Benefit performance, March 1986, Rai Uno, early Saturday evening) in which Pippo Baudo introduced a parade of the major Italian stylists, as part of a series of monographic programmes devoted to the "world of art." It is a boom that cannot be explained merely by the international success of Made in Italy fashion.

Finally. What profound changes have taken place in the idea of clothing as *image de marque* on the one hand, and the idea of *serialization* that characterizes the television film or miniserial on the other, to have produced the alliance in which the actors of *Miami Vice* wear Armani clothes and in which the dresses worn by Joan Collins and Marisa Berenson in the serial *Sins* were designed by Valentino?

A few references to the most glaring examples of the problems that beset the subject of our investigation have been sufficient to convey the theoretical, as well as historical complexity of the frame of reference in which we are obliged to operate. Yet it appears that all these questions turn on a crucial point that could be defined for the moment as the collapse of the film star system. A collapse that was heralded by the end of the Hollywood star system (and especially by the deaths of James Dean and Marilyn Monroe) and that went hand in hand with the political and social ferment of the sixties, but one that was finally confirmed, in *mediological* terms, right at the start of the seventies. A brief discussion of this collapse is required since it was precisely on the relationship between film stars and the big names of international haute couture (in this connection it is enough to mention some of the most famous alliances, such as Tierney-Cassini, Hepburn-Givenchy, Gardner-Sorelle Fontana) that the links between fashion and the media were based up until the end of the sixties.

To say that the collapse of the film star system was confirmed in mediological terms essentially means asserting two things. One is that over the course of the seventies (with a delay of about ten years with respect to the situation in America) an integrated system of media dominated by the *primacy of the medium of television* was established in Italy too. The other is that this very supremacy of television resulted in several significant modifications in the status of the star.[1]

In fact one often hears it stated, putting the question in banal terms, that the changes under course of the sixties, reaching its nadir with the antistars of the seventies. Without denying the validity of such a version of the events, the concept that we are trying to get across here is another one: that the seventies marked an "ontological" mutation in the status of the star, a mutation that has nothing to do with the change in models, which in fact can only be a consequence of the former. In fact the *mythical aura* that nourishes the film star, that "hybrid being" as Morin describes it,[2] because of the is set in motion by the "meaningful fiction" which is specific to cinema,[4] bound up with its ritual character and the "quest that characterizes going to the cinema,"[5] driven home by the "segregation of spaces" in the cinema hall, the regression and sinking into the dark that goes along with viewing the film. Well it is just these elements that feed the mythical and evocative substance on which the star in turn feeds; a substance that has been burned up in its entirety by the absence of the imaginary

Moschino fashion parade staged for Carlo Vanzina's film Sotto il vestito niente.

way in the film star system are basically dependent on the changing patterns and models produced by the cultural and behavioural system of any historical era, and that they can therefore be analyzed on the basis of the sociology of public tastes. According to this scheme, a graph of the status of the film star would register an ascending curve until it reached the point of maximum *mythical aura* in the period between the thirties and fifties and would then descend steeply to the zero level of "realism" and of intrusion into everyday matters over the indissoluble marriage between actor and personality, a creature eternally teetering between presence and absence, made real by the impression of reality produced by the cinematographic image and at the same time projected against an imaginary background by the game of make-believe, is nothing but the result of the cinematographic device itself.[3]

By device is not meant the definition of cinema as a machine for the production of "dreams more real than reality," but the material nature of the process of viewing itself. A process that and by the everyday realism that accompanies our domestic, fragmented and distracted consumption of television.

Let it be said then that the supremacy of television over the course of the seventies was asserted on the one hand as a capacity to impose and export its own structural, iconographic and behavioural models (and in this sense the popularity of a vast legion of antistars in the cinema owes much to the influence that television has been able to exercise over the tastes of the public, models that gave rise to a "personality cult of neutral bias," as it has been described on more than one occasion,[6] and that are profoundly mixed up with the daily life of the television viewer and unable to draw on any dimension of myth or merely separate from the sphere of gestures and habits that mark the consumption of television programmes. On the other, this dominance is expressed in the ability to "televisionize" the products of other media as well, in particular that of the cinema.

success and exportation of the models imposed by television: anonymous and interchangeable bodies and faces that are seen every day, bodies and faces that could belong to any of us. The second fact concerns the change in the criteria by which the star system is defined, starting out with the collapse of the star system in the cinema as a fundamental parameter of reference. The criteria defining the film star were essentially based on the face and the

Now what does all this mean? It means that the star produced by the cinematographic device was merely required to *appear* (it was not important whether he or she knew how to act *as well*) whereas the new star has to justify his own status on the basis of a precise principle of performance. In fact the most successful actors in the cinema of the seventies were those whose fame derived from their gift for interpretation. Good examples of this are Robert De

Catherine Deneuve, Liv Ulmann and Giuliano Gemma in Mino Monicelli's film Speriamo che sia femmina. *Deneuve's clothes are designed by Giorgio Armani.*

For years now the latter has been the source on which the palimpsests of television prefer to draw, which has had the effect of deritualizing and demythicizing the stars of cinema themselves, filtered as they are by the small screen.

We have made a long digression, and it is time to get back to the question that we started with, examining it in the light of some of the facts that derive directly from the situation described above. The first of these concerns the

body, seen in terms of their capacity to reveal a genuine landscape of the soul, independent of any principle of performance except one in which being and appearance were indissolubly linked. On the other hand the new kind of film star that began to dominate from the seventies onwards is paradoxically a star whose face and body have been pushed aside, leaving the task of revealing the soul entirely to the actor's skills of *technical and stylistic performance*.

Niro and Meryl Streep, no longer "masks" and archetypes who put in basically identical appearances in every film, but mobile forms that are incessantly changing, bodies and faces devoid of any identity apart from that of the various characters they play. In these roles their imitative faculty appears to be total, thanks to their extraordinary acting performances.

Yet once the principle by which consacration as

Silvana Mangano, photographed by
Elisabetta Catalano on the set of the film
Gruppo di famiglia in un interno *by Luchino*
Visconti, wearing a mink coat by Fendi.

a star could be divorced from the physical appearance revered by a system of make-believe, then it was no longer just actors and actresses who could gain access to the realm of the gods. It was open to all those who operate at a high level of quality in the field of the various arts, crafts and professions: in all those fields, in short, dominated by the principle of *technical and stylistic performance* as the single criterion of value. Thus the seventies have

Sylvester Stallone can be seen merely as the product of a principle of physical and athletic performance.

Hence it can be said that the star status assigned to stylists has been made possible by a cultural and mediological transformation that has made this status strictly dependent on the kind of technical and stylistic performance that he is capable of putting out. And ever since their entry into stardom, stylists too have had

above all, and necessarily, all the allure and the almost morbid curiosity that surrounds the "world in which the star lives."

At this point it remains to make a few brief remarks about the changes that are taking place in the logic of production of telefilms and serials, whose leads are increasingly obviously dressed in clothes designed by top names. Changes that derive, once again, from that principle of *technical and stylistic performance*

*Stefania Sandrelli and Sergio Castellitto in
Luciano Odorisio's film* Magic Moments.
The clothes are designed by Enrico Coveri.

seen the ranks of the stars augmented not only by film directors, but also by set-designers, directors of photography and creators of special effects. And, above all, the cult of personality has been extended in the seventies to cover nearly every sector of human activity: stars are made out of sports champions, politicians, managers, scientists, economists, conductors, journalists and stylists. From this perspective, even the superstar status of someone like

to submit to the ordeal of total visibility and the multimedia exposure that regulates it: the star is obliged to offer his fans not only his work, but his whole life, subjected to the thousand and one intrusions of the interview, the anecdote, the biography, the report and the *Benefit Performance*. So, when the world of fashion makes its way into that of fiction (television, literature or cinema, as in the case of *Sotto il vestito niente*), it will bring with it

that has been discussed at length. Television films and serials are in fact the most successful and original genres produced by the television medium. At the same time there is a slow but steady trend towards contamination between the various genres, leading eventually to those true forms of calculated mixture and hybridization that are the "container" programmes.[7] This process has now become so far-reaching that it is beginning to affect not only the most easily "contaminable" of television genres, such as news, quiz programmes and variety, but also those that are apparently less accessible, including the telefilm and the serial. In fact the latter seem increasingly disposed to lose their original character as "serialized stories" in order to take on the form of "miniature containers."

And what is the structural principle on which the container programme as a genre is organized? That of the accumulation of attractions, the paratactical juxtaposition of talents and the complication of technical and stylistic performances. This is the very structural principle to be found at the heart of telefilms like *Miami Vice* or *Sins*.

On the basis of these general trends that have regulated the relations between Fashion and the Media from the seventies up to the present, it is possible to draw up a map of events, data and situations that will provide a closer view of these hybridizations, concordances and affinities. It is a highly confused map, and one that can be viewed from several different perspectives. The first of these perspectives concerns the question of influences, which obliges us to venture onto slippery, often impalpable terrain. Occasionally it is possible to indicate very precise relationships, especially where these have been directly mentioned by the stylists themselves.[8] With the added complication of always looking like a two-faced Janus, since for every Missoni who admits using particular historical films (especially *L'armata Brancaleone* and *Decameron*) as a source for the study of materials to be employed in his creations, there is a Krizia who just barely anticipated the cult of thirties gangsters, sanctioned by the appearance of films like Arthur Penn's *Gangster Story*. Yet, with the notable exception of the films directed by Kurosawa, whose exotic blend of geometrical patterns, fabrics and colours has had a direct influence on the collections of a number of Italian stylists during the eighties (or the "thunderbolts" produced by a film like *A Passage to India* which has had much the same effect on the fashion world as had *Doctor Zivago* in the sixties), the cinema has almost totally lost the role of a primary source of inspiration for fashion designers that it used to play in the past.

The fact is that Italian cinema and the fashion world entered the seventies profoundly separated from one another by the internal changes to which each had been subjected over the course of the sixties. This gap was widened further by the definitive consecration of prêt-à-porter on the one hand, and by the progressive deterioration of the one successful genre on which the vitality of Italian cinema had been based, the comedy, on the other. Against this background, what managed to survive, apart from the isolated works of a few exceptional directors, were the films on political and civil subjects that imbued much of the seventies with the drab grey worn by politicians and

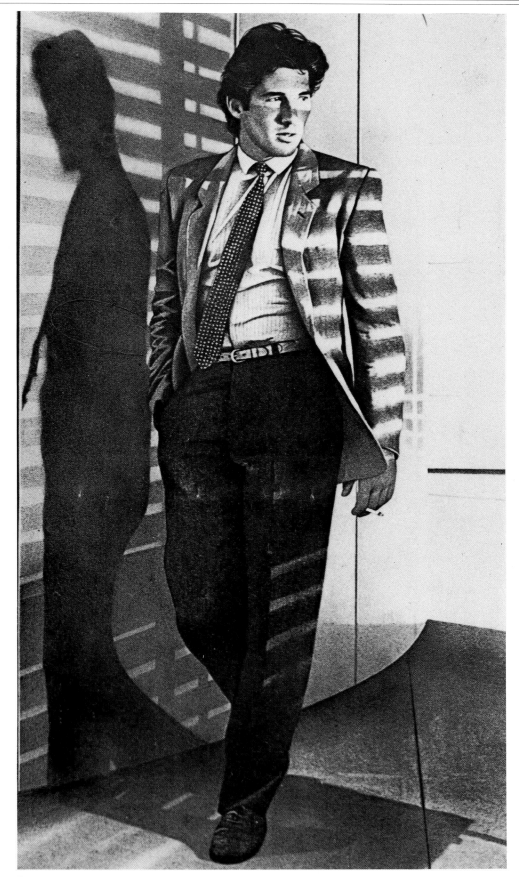

Richard Gere, whose clothes were designed by Giorgio Armani, in Paul Schrader's film American Gigolò.

21

magistrates (although the delicacy and precision of the work of the costume designer Franco Garretti, who specialized in this sort of film, deserves more than mere commendation). And alongside them, an output of very low budget serials, whose poverty of costumes did not even come close to the high levels of elaboration achieved by the "poor" materials of a casual designer like Fiorucci.

It is undeniable, however, that there were two genres of Italian cinema in the seventies that were capable of influencing, if not directly the creations of the fashion world, at least the patterns of consumption that were bound up with them. These were the genres of *erotic* and of *backward-looking* films. As far as the former

ence point of history. A nostalgia that, although applied with particular insistence to the period of the thirties – has ended up by not sparing any of the recent or remote past. And it has been the circulation on a mass level of this affectionate view of the past that has created the necessary affinity and familiarity for the success of the many creations inspired by the styles of another day. We have referred to *Il conformista*, and we cannot at this point fail to mention Gitt Magrini, whose premature death deprived Italy of one of its greatest costume designers. Her collaboration with Antonioni during the sixties and with Bertolucci in the seventies has allowed us to see some of the most beautiful "pictures" ever painted on the

on subsequent punk imagery; carrying on with the elegant whiteness of the costumes for *Barry Lyndon* (1975), again by Kubrick, which anticipated the look of new-romantic dandyism; and ending with the splendid costumes for Francis Ford Coppola's *Cotton Club* (1984), which Enrico Coveri explicitly used as an inspiration for his 1985-86 collection.

At this point, however, two closely interdependent premises need to be stated: the first of a historical nature and the second a structural one. The first concerns the fact that the artistic contributions made by stylists to film costumes are overwhelmingly concentrated in the eighties. The second, the fact that these contributions were not made in terms of *ad hoc*

Michael Peré in Walter Hill's film Streets of Fire. *The costumes are by Giorgio Armani.*

Mickey Rourke and Ariane, wearing clothes designed by Giorgio Armani, in Michael Cimino's film The Year of the Dragon.

– which can be set in an ideal sequence inaugurated by Salvatore Samperi's *Malizia* (1972) and brought to the pinnacle of success with Tinto Brass's *La chiave* (1984) – is concerned, we are dealing with a complex phenomenon of mores, but its effect on the subject we are investigating can be gauged in terms of a major revival on a mass level of the fashion in underwear, no longer seen as mere instruments of seduction but as specific sexual lures.

With regard to the latter genre – which can also be summed up in an ideal sequence beginning with Bernardo Bertolucci's *Il conformista* (1971) and culminating in Liliana Cavani's *Interno berlinese* (1985) – one can speak of a genuine feeling of nostalgia for the lost refer-

Italian cinema screen. Her legacy includes the only two costume designs for the Italian cinema of the seventies that have created fashions: Jean-Louis Trintignant's hat in *Il conformista* and Marlon Brando's shabby camel-hair overcoat in *Last Tango in Paris*.

But this digression on the subject of Italian costume designers would not be complete without a mention of Milena Canonero. Although she has never worked in Italy, she has been responsible for some of the costumes which have had a direct affect on trends in fashion. Starting with those for Stanley Kubrick's *A Clockwork Orange* (1971), whose futuristic, redundant and excessive artificiality, contorted by the use of masks, had a profound influence

creations, but in those of the utilization of previous designs. But let us take things in order and mention two glaring exceptions, over the course of the seventies, to the rule of the mutual indifference of fashion and cinema: the clothes designed by the Fendis for Silvana Mangano in *Gruppo di famiglia in un interno* (1975, directed by Luchino Visconti) and the ones designed by Pino Lancetti for Jill Clayburgh in *La luna* (1979, directed by Bernardo Bertolucci). The two cases were very similar, both because they involved directors very attentive to detail in the "realism" of their costumes and sets, and above all because the costumes were being used to denote the life style and culture of the characters who wore them. Thus the highly sophisticated and old-fashioned costumes designed for Mangano by the Fendis were nothing more than supplementary indications of an upper-middle class and nobility condemned to look like outdated fossils in the contemporary world. And Lancetti's magican and theatrical creations were no more than additional hints at a way of life in which the scenic splendour of the opera house was dragged into everyday life as well. In short they were two fine examples of how "realism" need not sacrifice anything to "stylization." On the contrary, one integrated the other, projecting it into that nebulous zone where poetic creation takes place.

But this rule governing the contribution of stylists to fashion design broke down at the end of the seventies, at the very moment when designer clothes made their triumphal entry into Italian cinema. To give just a few examples: Mila Schön's clothes used in the film *Nessuno è perfetto*, those of Regina Schrecker for *Vacanza di Natale* and *Una spina nel cuore*, those of Missoni for *Caro Michele* and *Nudo di donna*, those of Fiorucci for *Cipria*, Coveri for *Magic Moments*, Ferré for *Bingo Bongo*, *La piovra* and *L'attenzione* and Armani for *Speriamo che sia femmina* and *Diavolo in corpo*. Many more such examples could be found.

What needs to be emphasized, though, is that the collaboration of stylists did not become part of the active process of creation and definition of the various characters, but was confined to the insertion of a cunningly arranged signal intended to strengthen the impression of *verisimilitude* that all these films tried to put across. This is the reason why the *already-created*, the item of clothing that is immediately identifiable and recognizable because its multi-media exposure has already turned it into an *image de marque*, has become much more serviceable than the *ad hoc* creation. In fact its role is simply that of not contradicting a fact of contemporary society: that the designer garment – at least one – is now part of the wardrobe of all those who are required to be mirrored in the interchangeable faces that now saturate the cinema and television screens.

A question of cinema: increasingly constructed under the shelter of the television model, which is in turn increasingly obsessed with the attempt to transform itself into an exact copy of a reality that by now only takes place "live."

A question of fashion: by now increasingly likely to be seen as an indispensable "phase in the mirror" in every quest for individual and collective identity.

But also, *a question of special performance:* by now the accepted manner in which to handle the appearance of the various actors on the scene of the entertainment world.

At this point, the work of Giorgio Armani deserves a brief mention. Among the stylists, he is undoubtedly the one with the most long-standing and least "biased" relationship with the world of the cinema. In fact Armani has not

Carla Gravina wearing an original by Gianfranco Ferré, in Amica, *no. 33, 1984.*

Elsa Martinelli wearing an original by Gianni Versace, in Donna, *no. 63, 1986.*

limited himself to a number of "indirect" forms of collaboration (Deneuve's clothes in *Speriamo che sia femmina*, those of Marutschka Detmers in *Diavolo in corpo*, of Richard Gere in *American Gigolo*, of Nathalie Baye in *Rive Droite, Rive Gauche* and of Ariane in *The Year of the Dragon*) but was directly responsible for the costumes in Dario Argento's film *Phenomena* (1984) and Walter Hill's *Streets of Fire* (1984). Now, as far as his "indirect" collaborations are concerned, as well as his contribution to Dario Argento's film, the observations made above remain valid: the factor of the recognizability of the clothing and the trade-mark dominates over that of the construction of the character. Yet the results have been different from those obtained in other such experiences, and there are two reasons for this. One is that the clothes designed by Armani, unquestionably the most "original" of our stylists, do not just represent themselves as items of "designer clothing" but simultaneously a realm of values and a life style that turn on the notion of *informality*. The second is that, in *American Gigolo* and *The Year of the Dragon* for instance, this realm of values coincides perfectly with the one inhabited by the characters of the two films. This means that they can bring it onto the scene through the clothes they are wearing. *Streets of Fire*, on the other hand, a metropolitan western built around the rhythms of rock opera, leaves us no reason to lament the contributions of the great costume designers of the screen. In fact, within a narrative and scenographic structure ideally suited to the repertoire of designs on which Armani's work is habitually based, the stylist has produced a visual symphony in which the contrasts of colour, form and material constitute the principal indication as to the nature of the characters and the shifts that occur in their stories. With the overalls of chamois-leather and the braces worn by Michael Paré immediately spilling over onto the social scene.

The last perspective to be tackled is the one that could be described as the "exchange of services" between the fashion world and that of the media. It is a perspective that combines a wide variety of patterns (ranging from Moschino's design of the collection for the fashion show in *Sotto il vestito niente* to Dario Argento's staging on the presentation of the Trussardi Spring 1986 collection and Zeffirelli's direction of the commercial for Annabella furs; from top models who become actresses – like Carole Bouquet – to actresses who become top models – like Isabella Rossellini – or who just pose in the clothes from some collection or other) and which it is difficult to arrange in an orderly fashion. The one fact that does stand out is that this complex system of relationships (of which we are limited to pointing out only the most striking) is destined to become a systematic form of mutual cooperation between the world of fashion and the media. This is not just the outcome of the policy by which fashion shows have been turned into events and forms of entertainment, nor merely of the tendency towards the superimposition of marks of recognition that we have been looking at; rather the reason is bound up with the rules governing the functioning of integrated multi-media information. Rules that, while they encourage a *specialization of information* on the one hand (this is what lies behind the recent boom in fashion magazines and fashion photography, the two channels that have been preferred up to now), require a *differentiation of channels* on the other and this also means a multiplication of the vehicles of communication.

And what is left of the faces and the bodies of the film actresses who at one time represented the only means by which the message of fashion could be conveyed to those not involved in the work? They still speak to us. From the pages of magazines and from the screens of our televisions. But the words are no longer the same. In fact they now speak to us of a domain that must be shared with a thousand other protagonists, generated not by the silence of the camera obscura but by the flood lights and the clamour of social success.

They speak to us now of a distance that has been established between themselves and the clothes they wear. A distance that leads them to flit from one garment to another with the same sure nimbleness that they use to flit from one character to another. And they remind us above all that clothing no longer exists as form indivisible from the substance that animates it, but only as the thousand possible identities that can be put on for our daily performances.

Tre pezzi, tre materiali diversi: blazer in suede, gonna in nappa, blusa in seta operata. Il risultato e raffinatissimo. Tutto di Trussardi. Orecchini Bianca e Blu.

GIULIANA DE SIO

Giuliana De Sio wearing an original by Trussardi, in Donna, *no. 53, 1985.*

* The research for the illustrations in this text was conducted by Sylvana Vialli.

1. For a broader background to this argument the reader is referred to G. Grignaffini, *Star. Tre passi nel divismo*, Modena 1981.
2. In this connection, cf. E. Morin, *I divi*, Milan 1977, pp. 37-68.
3. For the concepts of "impression of reality" and "cinematographic device," cf. C. Metz, *Il significante immaginario*, Venice 1980.
4. C. Metz, op. cit.
5. On ritual character and quest, cf. R. Barthes, "En sortant du cinéma," in *Communications*, no. 23, 1977.
6. See in particular G. Bettetini, *La conversazione audiovisiva*, Milan 1984, pp. 43-47.
7. For a more wide-ranging discussion of the question of television genres and container programmes, cf. M. Wolf (editor), *Tra informazione ed evasione. I programmi televisivi di intrattenimento*, Rome 1983, and Costa-Grignaffini-Quaresima, *Lo spettacolo degli italiani. Strategie d'immagine e identità nazionale nella scena televisiva*, Rome 1985.
8. In this connection see the large collection of interviews and documentation in G. Grossini, *Firme in passerella*, Bari 1986,
9. Indicative in this connection is the Iceberg campaign entitled "The contemporaries" in which actresses, stylists, sports champions, artists, singers and various other kinds of successful people pose without a break.

ITALIAN WOMEN'S WEAR:
A SUCCESSFUL INDUSTRIAL PRODUCT

Rietta Messina

A Phenomenon of Industrial Design

The volume of business generated by the industrial production of clothing in Italy was 12,300 billion lire in 1985. Millions of garments were exported all over the world to a total value of 4,900 billion, creating a surplus in the balance of payments of 3,900 billion.[1] Between 1961 and 1978 clothing exports have seen uninterrupted growth by an average of 17.8% a year, and from 1977 to 1983 by 21.3%. The share of total Italian exports provided by exports of clothing has risen from 1.5% in 1973 to 3.1% in 1983. Since 1970 Italy has held the highest share of the total of clothing exports from the industrialized countries, 25%, as compared with 13% for Germany, 10% for France, 7% for the U.S.A. and 3% for Japan.

Massive industrial development of the sector has made it possible to increase the level of investment in pioneering technology and, at the same time, to safeguard hundreds of thousands of jobs. At the end of the war 25,000 people were employed in the clothing industry, 107,000 in 1961, 217,000 in 1971 and 330,000 in 1981, 207,000 of whom worked in companies with more than 20 employees.[2]

Although aesthetic, artistic and sartorial tradition, along with new techniques of promotion and distribution, have all played a decisive role in the worldwide popularity of the Italian look, its success is rooted in the phenomenon of Italian industrial design and in the distinctive ability of Italian manufacturers to bring about a fruitful encounter between design and high technology, together with the fact that they are able to rely on a whole range of small-scale concerns specializing in the realization of prototypes and open to innovation.

Even more than in the fields of furnishing and design, the clothing industry in Italy is engaged every day in the solving of problems of design and planning for mass production.

This situation has been created thanks to a mix with a high potential for success: a large and varied supply of quality fabrics, the foreign-oriented incentives of a scattered and uncontrolled distribution system free to expand vertiginously, the succession of unifying promotional initiatives putting across a powerful image, the sensitivity to changes in process and product, the development of new sectors such as sportswear, casuals and leather, a unique care taken over industrial production. This has meant that Italy has had a head start in learning to handle both the diversification of production and the

new fragmentation of consumption that is emerging in Western markets.[3]

The Birth of the Italian Market

And yet as recently as 1959 the Italian ready-to-wear industry was underdeveloped in comparison with that of the rest of Europe. As far as women's wear is concerned, Italy was producing a mere million and a half dresses and women's costumes, while much smaller Holland was turning out four million, France twenty and Germany as many as twenty-seven.[4]

During the fifties the not very large number of clothing manufacturers in Italy catered almost exclusively to a limited section of the national market, which continued to be dominated, throughout the decade, by grand couturiers, tailors and dressmakers. Once the war was over, the internal demand for clothes saw a sharp upturn as well. Clothes made-to-measure took the lion's share: in 1955 still no more than 22% of garments sold were produced by the ready-to-wear manufacturers.[5]

Italian clothing manufacturers, often assisted by experts on production from the United States, copied American models, patterns of distribution and levels of quality in manufacturing, shifting their target and making the prices more competitive.

These early and somewhat rigid garments, for the most part made out of not very good materials, cost a third as much as those made to measure and quickly attracted the attention of the masses who were steadily becoming more urbanized as a result of industrial reconstruction.

It is no coincidence that the first major centres of the clothing industry developed in close proximity to the large markets of Milan, Turin, Genoa and Bologna, which cities provided 31.4% of all those employed in the sector in 1961.

The city gave a great boost to clothing purchases: with shops, display windows and department stores offering everything immediately. Clothing stores for men, women and children, which numbered nearly 2,800 in 1951 multiplied, and by 1961 they totalled 5,000. Department stores with clothing sections grew from 163 to 289.[6]

But the great challenge for the fledgling industry was women's taste and fashion. In the lowest segments of the market, the difficulties in producing a range of sizes, technological rigidity and the containment of costs clashed with the sort of clothing required by the female

body. On the other hand, even the most highly qualified firms, who catered to more demanding consumers, came into conflict with the imperatives of fashion. Fashion, dictated in those years by the couturiers, seemed to be resisting the spectre of industrialization by turning out collections of close-fitting and lavish garments designed to hug the abundant endowments of the fifties woman.

At the end of the fifties the strongest sector of the women's clothing industry was still represented by that of coats, overcoats and raincoats. A full million and a half industrially manufactured coats were produced, as opposed to a mere three hundred thousand women's costumes.

Right from the outset the situation in women's prêt-à-porter was a highly differentiated one in business terms. Apart from the APEM, which supplied La Rinascente, the first steps were taken by major industrial concerns like Hettermarks and Vestebene and by more quality brands such as Confit, Juvenilia, Rosier, Conber, Spagnoli, Krizia and Max Mara.

In spite of the vague confines of this panorama, manufacturers began to promote the mass-produced product as well. The device settled on was that of the large-scale trade fair, which led to the staging of the SAMIA (International Clothing Market and Show) in Turin in 1954.

The concern for quality and the industry's interest in the "fashion content" of mass-produced clothing are demonstrated by an important step taken by the Italian Association of Clothing Manufacturers (A.I.I.A.): the setting up in Milan in 1958 of a Fashion Board of Clothing Manufacturers. The Board was intended to conduct research into the possibilities of forecasting colours and fabrics. The ready-to-wear industry had to deal more and more seriously with new, and more exacting, sections of the market, and had to cater to them and/or attempt to shape their tastes.

Although the export market for clothing was still largely the province of the great craftsmen, women's wear helped the Italian style to begin to make an impact on foreign markets. Between 1955 and 1965 the sales of women's clothing abroad increased constantly, outdistancing men's wear by all of seven hundred million lire out of a total of five and a half billion.

Mass-Production and the Economic Boom

In the sixties Italy was overtaken by the unexpected fortune of the economic boom and as

Gulp fashion show at a boxing ring, 1966.
Models with lurex minidresses and colored
spots. Gulp archives.

a new industrial power set out to overcome the age-old backwardness of a traditionally rural country.

The decisive factor in the development of the clothing industry was the fact that the couturier could no longer cope with both the new and the old bourgeoisie. In the wake of the successes of knitwear and thanks to the transformation of a number of traditional and sportswear stores, the cities began to fill up with high class outlets for ready-to-wear clothing: Pirovano and Bardelli

thing industry found room to diversify, improve in quality and grow in scale: the disdain for mass-produced garments was eroded year after year and by 1965 the industry managed to cover 56% of national consumption.

The decade from 1960 to 1970 saw a rapid expansion in women's prêt-à-porter: the number of costumes produced by the industry went up from 390,000 to two million, the number of coats from one million seven hundred thousand to over three million.

Beatles, Dongie Milling, to create a line for teenagers.

New Patterns of Behaviour and Industrial Fashion

While the clothing trade carried on its linear expansion through a quest for quality and a growth in scale, Italy also saw the spread of those avant-garde social and cultural phenomena which were to reach revolutionary heights in the seventies. Thanks to the combined effect of

Gianfranco Ferré, fashion show at Milano Collezioni in October 1985 for the 1986 Spring-Summer collection.

in Milan, Duca d'Aosta and Elite in Venice and Padua, Principe and Neuberg in Florence and Lietta Show, For You and Mademoiselle in Rome. They sold luxury and ready-to-wear, with many English products for men and French ones for women.

Although Italian prêt-à-porter was making gigantic strides, its backwardness showed up not so much in terms of the market as in those of image. Yet, in spite of the monoculture of the classic and formal bon ton, the Italian clo-

The business panorama underwent diversification at higher levels. The ranks of the industrial giants in the sixties were joined by new companies and brands that concentrated on style: Guido Ruggeri, Genny, Cidat, Maska, Selene, Zama Sport, Cori and Gibò.

On another flank, the eruption of youth culture led Italian industry to try and ride the tiger of adolescent fashion. In 1965 the GFT inaugurated its Ventanni (Twenty) line and in 1967 McQueen commissioned the manager of the

new socio-cultural developments, ready-to-wear clothing became predominant: in 1970 it accounted for 75% of national consumption.

The sexual revolution and emancipation had changed femininity too. In imitation of the slender forms of Elsa Martinelli and Audrey Hepburn, the skinny ones of models like Jean Shrimpton and the almost androgynous one of Veruschka, Italian women too learned to squeeze themselves into tight and flat clothes, with no sign of a waist. The new feminine ideals were futuristic beings in spatial mini-skirts, trouser suits, hot-pants and ankle-length coats.

The prêt-à-porter industry was in a good position to guide the new aspects of behaviour: the effect of the changes on fashion was perfectly suited to the requirements of the industry. Straight lines and spatial or spartan models implied less complex manufacturing processes, less need for finishing touches carried out by hand and faster rates of production.

The garment finished in an industrial way was no longer at a disadvantage, both because it had a more fashionable and up-to-date appearance and because a certain kind of look, a certain manner in which clothes hung on the body, could only be achieved through industrial design and manufacture.

The introduction of "fusing" was decisive in the success of industrially made coats and jackets: on the one hand it led to a simplification on the operations of cutting and assembly and on the other it permitted a qualitative leap in the wearability of the garments produced. The form of the jacket, even of the lightweight summer type, became impeccable.

The complexity of the market, with an increasingly diversified range of outlets, the elevation of prêt-à-porter to the level of fashion and the consequent expansion of many companies turning out quality clothing necessitated changes in promotional structures.

In 1969 the SAMIA expired: an undifferentiated supply aimed at all sectors and every kind of consumer neither satisfied the needs nor helped the work of the new distribution system.

The role of "testifying" to women's fashion shifted to Florence. From 1966 onwards the Sala Bianca in Palazzo Pitti was joined by a variety of other events organized in Florence by companies producing women's ready-to-wear fashion, first at Palazzo Strozzi and then in a number of hotels, until the fashion shows staged by the Centro Moda found a permanent site at the Palazzo degli Affari and the new name of Pitti Donna in 1975.

From Contradictions to Success

The period of social revolt from 1970 onwards had a profound effect on the Italian clothing industry, since it threw into question everything with which it was concerned, from industrial relations in the factories to patterns of consumption, and therefore the very substance of its products.

Between 1970 and 1975 small, medium and large companies came to grief in Italy.[7] Industrial unrest was pregnant with consequences. At the precise moment of a halt in the growth of domestic consumption, with the saturation of that share of the market which could be transferred from tailoring and couture to industry, the acceleration in the rate of increase in labour costs quickly brought a crisis in mass production. The competitiveness of Italian products declined rapidly at the same time as competition from the developing countries was on the rise.

Favoured by the new bias towards folk styles in young people's clothing, these very low cost imports wrought havoc in some sectors, especially among shirt manufacturers and at the lowest levels of the Italian and European market. In order to compensate for the increase in labour costs, manufacturers were forced to aim their products at higher levels of the market, stimulate consumption with new products and, to maintain the required level of production, export consistently and no longer in a haphazard fashion.

On the other hand, in order to get round increases in the rigidity of the organization of labour, the result of a change in the balance of power with the unions, the kind of growth adopted by the manufacturers was polycentric and the manufacture decentralized. The model of development was no longer along the lines of the large-scale vertically integrated company, but a type of organization based on a system of satellites, with companies in charge of strategic coordination operating at the centre to control the activities of the production units.

Year by year Italian manufacturers learned how to adapt to the new market with its vast range of choice, organizing their production on the basis of increasingly small batches, with a growing number of variants and paying more and more attention to finishing touches in the manufacturing phase.

Since they assumed the fragmentation and variability of the market to be an unavoidable constraint. Italian entrepreneurs often had to renounce commercial and organizational economies.

When investment was resumed between 1975 and 1980, out of the innovations available were chosen those that came either before or after the actual stage of manufacture. In particular, they were adopted during the pressing stage, with the introduction of automatic presses and "Transfert" systems, as well as in those of packaging and storage.

In the organization of work, block processing was adopted and ways of optimizing lay-outs and mechanizing internal transport were studied. The introduction of information processing turned out to be the most significant innovation for the larger-sized companies, which were able to make use of the computer to calculate sizes and to design pieces for cutting. The latter was carried out automatically with the Gerber Cutter or the Hughes Laser.

While there were only five companies that utilized computerized systems (CAD-CAM) in 1976, it has been estimated that there were almost two hundred and fifty by 1985.[8]

The difficult balance between costs, quality of the product and market potential involved paying increasingly careful attention to marketing: commercialization, promotion, advertising and image projection.

So, if in the sixties the Italian Look emerged out of high fashion, while German and American buyers chased after increasingly large quantities of Italian but unbranded products, in the seventies the businessmen organized themselves to promote the quality image of Italian clothing by concentrating on brands and on the names of stylists.

Product Research

What was created, in the first place, was an Italian Fashion System, an organic and integrated relationship between the various components of production and services, in the textile sector as well as in that of clothing and knitwear, which made it possible to cut down on the time required to bring in innovations, to expand the choice of materials and to increase the range of products.

In the second place, the industry has established more flexible links with stylists and investors. In particular, large companies specializing in women's prêt-à-porter have developed commercial and manufacturing partnerships with a number of prestigious names: Basile, first with Albini and then with Soprani; the Girombelli group with Versace for Genny, with Montana for Complice and with Keith Warty and Alan Cleaver for Byblos. These firms have made a strategy of exclusively promoting their brands, just as have Max Mara, Les Copains and Callaghan, achieving a reputation comparable to that of the collections produced by the same stylists under their own names.

One of the most important examples of the new trend, for its scale and the allure that surrounds it, is that of the Gruppo Finanziario Tessile. In fact, the dimensions and level of success of Armani and Valentino are closely bound up with the efficiency of the production, organizational and marketing system made available to them through their association with the GFT since 1975, with agreements covering both their own collections and their second lines, like Mani and Miss V. Since then, however, the GFT has come out with new brands of women's wear like Mix & Match (1975) and Solo Donna (1978), on a more up-to-date basis and with a higher fashion content.

The same degree of attention paid to their own brands and company strategies has brought other names into the limelight in recent years: Mariella Burani and Donna Luna of Selene, Ginocchietti, Oacks, Touche and Pancaldi.

The strongest feature of the whole system has been an innovative approach to the product.

If the social rebellion had brought about a crisis in classical styles of dress, heavily reducing the domestic consumption of coats and jackets for instance, the stylists, with their expertise in industrial design and grasp of quality and wearability, have changed the industrial conception of coats and jackets for men and women. The rigid features of the jacket have been eliminated, transforming it into a less structured blazer.

A bridge has been established between classic and casual, with creaseless trousers, raincoats, loden and loose jackets.

With regard to women's fashion, the severe appearance of the fitted costume and trouser suit has been revolutionized with more refined and/or contrasting lines, fabrics and colours. Between 1970 and 1980 the output of women's suits, jackets and coats tripled.

Even the production of blouses, under direct threat by importation from the developing countries, has shown a decisive shift towards research and sophistication. As a result exports have gradually risen from less than two million

Italian sportswear has acquired an international reputation with its output of casuals, sportswear and leather garments, Italian prêt-à-porter has achieved a pole position on the international market.

Although in 1970 no more than 2 million pairs of jeans were sold in Italy, and almost all of these were foreign brands, the country has specialized in the production of jeans, casual trousers and informal jackets.

The impetus has come from exports, which

Allegri and Ball. Italian fashion has created a boom in sportswear and leisure wear that contrasts strongly with the dullness of ordinary white-collar dress, unleashing a flood of so-called safari trousers, dungarees, overalls in the style of filling-station attendants or Formula 1 track technicians, down jackets, wind-cheaters and anoracks. It was in the seventies, in fact, that Italy made a breakthrough into the world of sport and reaped success in the sector of "active wear."

Fashion book gallery, Modit, March 1986.

items in 1975 to four and a half in 1983.

This new capacity to create fashion is due not only to injections of style but also to a more deeply-rooted Italian phenomenon, that is the development on the part of Italian industry of genuinely new modes of dress. Gambling that the fashions of the young will turn out to be lasting styles of dress, previously uncommon types of clothing were produced, introducing a fashion content into the revolution in casual and informal wear.

accounted for 25% of turnover in 1975, 31% in 1980 and 38.5% in 1985.

In 1984 Italy produced forty million pairs of jeans and women's slacks, four times the level of production in France and Germany. Of these, 11 million were exported. Names with an international standing have mounted the tiger of emancipated women's wear: not just Benetton and Fiorucci, but also Americanino (Gecofin), Jesus (MCT), Italiana Manifatture (Pooh), Carrera, Rifle, Riorda, Genius Group (Goldie),

In those years Ellesse, Colmar and Belfe, already present on the market, were joined by Tacchini's Sandy'S and the line of sportswear produced by Fila. Sapporo's victories at the Olympics, followed by the avalanche of Italian skiers and the successes of Panatta in tennis have taken the Italian style of sportswear around the world, establishing a precise image for it of functional qualities and elegance of line and colour.

Between 1974 and 1977 the share of the

export market in clothing held by sportswear rose from 3.7% to 5.2%.[9]

This characteristic of Italian prêt-à-porter – inventiveness matched by particular qualities of production and a high degree of technical innovation – is demonstrated by another sector as well: leather clothing.

Between 1960 and 1970, dozens of companies specializing in the production of leather garments established a reputation for themselves, especially in Veneto and Tuscany: Sicons, Breco's, La Matta, Vagrant, Casa Veneta, Ruffo, Lesy and Enrico Mandelli. Using hides treated to make them resemble the costliest of fabrics, they turn out light, brightly coloured collections that are a perfect complement to collections made from more conventional materials.

The main innovation has been the production of trousers and blazers, and for women skirts, waistcoats and dresses as well, in very lightweight leather, dyed in all sorts of colours and intended for spring and summer use too.

In 1975 the value of the Italian export trade in leather garments was 77 thousand dollars, as opposed to 60 thousand and 31 thousand for those of France and Great Britain respectively. By 1977 exports had doubled in Italy, reaching a total of 139 thousand dollars, while they had fallen to 52 thousand in France and remained unchanged in Britain.

By 1983 Italian exports had gone up to 210 thousand dollars, three times the level in Germany, four times that of France and ten times that of Great Britain.[10]

Milan, City of Fashion

Over the course of fifteen years Italy's output of clothing and knitwear has grown more than 350%. Exports have increased 1000% in real terms and the incidence of foreign demand on the volume of business had risen from 7.3% to 36%. In 1984, for example, Italy exported 1100 billion lire of clothing to Germany, as compared with France's 1234 billion and the United Kingdom's 121 billion. Exports totalling 37 billion went to the United States, as opposed to 180 billion from France, 47 billion from Germany and 117 billion from the United Kingdom.

Italian women's wear is to be found even in more distant countries: sales in Japan have reached 79 billion, in contrast to 28 billion lire of imports from France and 7 billion from Germany. Italy exported 5.6 billion lire's worth of clothing to Australia as opposed to France's 4.5 billion.

Although the primary foreign market remains Germany, absorbing 30% of exports, and the French continue to want Italian fashion products, to a greater extent than they are willing to admit, accounting for 16% of Italian exports, the American market has been expanding since 1981, at an annual rate of 40%. America is now the third largest foreign buyer of Italian clothing, with 13% of the total.

One of the factors that has contributed to these successes has been the concentration in Milan of the most prestigious promotional initiatives specifically concerned with luxury women's fashion, with Modit for the prêt-à-porter manufacturers and Milano Collezioni for the stylists' fashion shows.

The choice of Milan as the venue for Modit and Milano Collezioni by the Industriali dell' Abbigliamento e della Maglieria (Clothing and Knitwear Manufacturers) was made on the basis of a whole range of structural factors, including those of services and communications.

According to the 1981 Census, northern Italy (Liguria, Lombardia, Veneto and Emilia Romagna) was responsible for 78% of total exports of Italian clothing and knitwear. Lombardy, in particular, is the leading region for the production of prêt-à-porter, with 22% of the total number of manufacturers and employees, and second only to Veneto (30%) in terms of the level of exports (25.6%).

Its central location combined with the city's superior services, infrastructures and transport facilities, along with its nearness to the richest export markets of northern Europe, have made Milan a fundamental point of reference in commercial and functional terms. Since the end of the sixties agents and representatives have been coming to Milan, twice a year, to present their sample collections of men's, women's and children's wear to Italian dealers under the label of Milanovendemoda. In 1966 the marketing organization for luxury prêt-à-porter, such as Ferrante, Tositti and Monti, was set up in Milan, attracting foreign buyers to the Lombard capital. On the other hand, all of the main activities connected to the most recent developments in fashion are concentrated in Milan: communications and image: from the development of private television networks to advertising agencies, to the most important editorial groups for the fashion press. 1978 was a settling-in period for Modit, with 45 firms attending in March and 75 in October, and the event was held at Pavilion 29 of the Milan Fiera. The following year, 1979, turned out to be decisive: 200 firms were present at Modit and the stylists decided to show their collections at the Centro Sfilate Collezioni alla Fiera. In March 1979 the first band of top-rate stylists to appear at the Centro Sfilate was made up of Mario Valentino, Walter Albini, Enrica Massei, Claudio La Viola, Ken Scott and Laura Biagiotti.

By October all the stylists who were involved in creating the international myth of the "Italian look" were present, along with a number of very important foreigners. On show were the collections of Versace, Fendi, Basile, Missoni, Caumont, La Viola, Ken Scott, Biagiotti, Complice, Armani, Krizia, Ferré, Albini, Massei, Genny, Sanlorenzo, Callaghan, Geoffrey Been and Miyake.

Modit and Milano Collezioni are innovative in terms of specialization and dimension.

Milano Collezioni, in particular, is the first combined initiative in the field of stylism. It has an exclusive image, but at the same time is contained in a single, especially designed, large structure. It is equipped with an organization and services which improve and make conditions pleasant for buyers and the press.

The shows take place in four rooms, three of which have 1,200 seats and one with 700 seats. These spaces have permanent lighting and music systems.

Statistics relative to Modit reveal the impact that these new initiatives have had. In an eight year period, while the number of participants at the events has not increased, the buyers have grown from 5,000 to 22,000. Journalists are reported to have gone from 100 to 600, of which 250 are from foreign countries.

1. *Abbigliamento '85. Relazione del Presidente all'Assemblea Generale sui problemi del settore e sull'attività dell'Associazione*, A.I.I.A., Milan, May 1986,
2. *L'industria italiana dell'abbigliamento. Evoluzione strutturale nel decennio 1971-1981*, A.I.I.A., Milan 1984.
3. *Le sfide dell'industria italiana dell'abbigliamento*, A.I.I.A., Venice, November 1984.
4. *Guida all'abbigliamento italiano*, A.I.I.A., Milan 1961.
5. *Quarant'anni di abbigliamento*, A.I.I.A., Milan 1985.
6. B. Saviantoni, *La distribuzione T.A. in Italia*, production-distribution report, Eni, December 12, 1976; Commercial distribution in the T.A., ISDI, Milan 1980.
7. *Due interventi delle Partecipazioni Statali*, F. Coltorti, G. Mussati, Milan 1976.
8. Report on the Zegna Convention of the International Apparel Federation Berlin, June 1986 (A.I.I.A.).
9. *L'abbigliamento sportivo in Italia*, A.I.I.A., Milan 1984.
10. *L'industria italiana dell'abbigliamento in pelle: strutture e prospettive*, A.I.I.A., Milan 1986.

CLOTHING MANUFACTURERS IN THE SIXTIES: BETWEEN CRISIS AND INNOVATION

Elisabetta Pagani, Rosanna Pavoni

In the 1961 edition of the *Guida della Confezione*,[1] the president of the Italian Association of Clothing Manufacturers (A.I.I.A.), Giulio Goehring, while emphasizing that only 30% of the total consumption of articles of clothing was satisfied by the ready-to-wear industry as a result of the continuing success enjoyed by cottage industries and the workshops of individual tailors and dressmakers, predicted a doubling of output over the course of the next three or four years, followed by a phase of rethinking and therefore stagnation.

Some ten years after these remarks were made, the Guido Ruggeri firm closed its doors, after having been the leading manufacturer of women's wear throughout the decade and having made a decisive contribution to consolidating the grip of ready-to-wear clothing on the market. An attempt to identify the causes of this "model" collapse will allow us to throw some light on the motivations for a very widespread crisis: a crisis that overwhelmed some of the most prestigious manufacturers towards the end of the sixties, wiping out the certainties on which the ready-to-wear industry had based its growth.

Let us go back to Goehring's words: with prophetic vision, the president of the A.I.I.A. had foreseen the onset of a phase of rethinking which, if understood, would have prevented the stagnation of production leading to the definitive closure of companies. This rethinking was clearly called for, from the middle of the decade under examination, by the evident changes in the demands of women, who were increasingly influenced in their choice of an article of clothing by the tenets of fashion, rather than by the traditional factors of price, quality and cut. It was on these latter that Ruggeri and the other major clothing manufacturers had concentrated in their bid to compete with their artisan rivals.[2]

Yet the suggestion that it was time for a period of reflection was ignored. On the contrary, the fear of stagnation was kept at bay by expanding sales without any attempt to renew production at the same time. This choice, which came into conflict with a fashion that demanded variety and diversification, had the inevitable consequence of saturating even the sector of the market – a constantly shrinking one – that was content with a well-made jacket or coat at a reasonable price even if already out of fashion.

In a report on the Italian market compiled in

Coat in beige woollen whipcord, lining, collar and cuffs in long-haired rabbit fur. Designed by Jole Veneziani for Marzotto. Amica, no. 41, 1964.

1971 by those in charge of planning and marketing at Ruggeri,[3] faced with the spread of what was described as "the latest confused and bogus fashion" (remember that 1970 was the year of the maxi and of folk styles) that was subverting "... any possible logic of industrial planning and in the end even the capacity for management of the retail distributors themselves," three kinds of action were indicated as effective ways of containing the crisis in production: a) the establishment of sales outlets by the company itself; b) the strengthening of the internal commercial structure and better training of those responsible for sales and assistance to customers; c) the consolidation of consumer support by means of a more intense publicity and promotional campaign.

One is perplexed by the absence of any mention of the problem underlying a drop in production that had resulted in the company having a smaller share of the market than in 1965. This drop was certainly not exclusively due to the inadequacy or inefficiency of the sales network. Rather it was to be blamed on a product that no longer responded to the "creativity" of choice of the market, a market that no longer took into consideration the fact that the quality of manufacturing guaranteed a garment "better made than by the tailor."[4]

Of course, the battle against the habit, still widespread during the sixties, of turning to the dressmaker in order to add to one's wardrobe had been a tough one. It had probably contributed, in the majority of cases, to stunting the growth of an independent personality in the ready-to-wear business.[5] Revealing of this is the slogan that recurs in the promotional leaflets distributed by Cori (Gruppo Finanziario Tessile) through its own sales points for the 1965 Spring-Summer collection.

A series of little suits embellished with refined accessories, such as would fit into the categories of "elegant morning-daytime wear" and "elegant afternoon wear,"[6] was accompanied by the reassuring and encouraging refrain: "Cori offers you the pleasure of choosing in front of the mirror the model that does the most for you, that pleases you the most, that convinces you the most." Again there was no reference to "fashion" as a value to be taken into consideration in the choice; instead, there was a constant reminder as to the wearability of the garment, no longer the exclusive prerogative of clothes made by hand.

Another attempt to gain ground on made-to-

COUPE
D'OR
DU
BON
GOUT
FRANÇAIS

una scelta sicura per la vostra eleganza

Cori vi offre il piacere di scegliere davanti allo specchio il modello che più vi dona, che più vi piace, che più vi convince.

NEI MIGLIORI NEGOZI DI ABBIGLIAMENTO PER SIGNORA TROVERETE QUESTO O ALTRI MODELLI CORI E CORI-BIKI. MODELLI CORI A PREZZO PREFISSATO.   CORI-LADY PER LE TAGLIE FORTI.

Suit in pearl grey figured wool, accompanied by hat in the same material. Cori, Spring-Summer 1965.

Illustrative leaflet, Gruppo Finanziario Tessile archives.

measure clothing was represented by the research carried out in those years with the aim of introducing order into the still approximate area of sizes. The intention was to be able to dress the largest possible number of customers, with the minimum of adaptation.

In a feature devoted to the great dressmakers that appeared in *Il Corriere della Sera* in 1965,[7] Mila Schön was asked whether she thought that the ready-to-wear industry was in a position to build on its success. She replied

the ready-to-wear manufacturers were concentrating on this new clientele, in the awareness that it was in a position to finally burn the bridges with the tradition of garments sewn by dressmakers in imitation of the models of haute couture. Hence the young woman was sought after, courted and flattered; she was dazzled by the novelty of a different style, deliberately conceived and realized for her and for her needs.[9]

But in essence, apart from the declarations of

the rash of editorials in which "youthful," "new" and "fun" had become watchwords was made by the magazine *Amica*, under the editorship of Antonio Alberti. In April 1965, the journal began to include a section known as "The club of the very young," a space reserved for suggestions, news and the presentation of new products for a readership of under eighteen. Moreover, in October 1964 the magazine had started to publish "The wardrobes of Amica,"[10] a series of features that gave a lot of

La giacca di moda

Suit in nut-brown tweed, designed by Germana Marucelli for Italian Style - Marzotto. Amica, no. 40, 1965.

Coat in light blue Shetland wool by André, with ring-shaped collar in beaver, in Amica, no. 45, 1966.

that the future belonged to prêt-à-porter, as long as it took its cue from the American manufacturers by increasing the number of sizes available so as to "offer the maximum guarantee of a perfection that was really ready to wear."[8]

From the same year dates the anthropometric study carried out by the Gruppo Finanziario Tessile, with the aim of identifying the physical characteristics of a new and constantly growing segment of the market, the "very young." All

intent that crammed the editorials of the more important women's magazines at the end of the sixties, nothing changed in the style of or approach to ready-to-wear clothing made by the leading manufacturers in the sector.

In the end, it was left largely up to the fashion reporter, especially over the years 1964-66, to serve as a mediator between a production that tended to diversify as little as possible and a youthful market in search of a specific aspect of its own. A decisive contribution to

space at each change of season to ready-to-wear clothes, along with (and this was a new element) the addresses of retailers and the relevant "controlled prices." In this connection, the editorial by Marta Schiavi, "The big names in Ready-to-wear Fashion," published in issue no. 3 of 1965, is significant as a clear attempt to make the models presented credible with a clientele that had become more demanding.[11]

In reality, when one tried to match the actual garment with the editorial description, one ran into problems. This could be traced back to a stylistic policy that was undoubtedly conscious of taste and fashions, but which tended to "tame" the new ideas rather than to swallow them whole. In other words, there was a tendency to use them as reference points (vaguely hinted at in the actual line of the garment, fully emphasized in the editorials), which served to attest to their up-to-date nature and their compliance with the dictates of fashion, something which was otherwise very difficult to detect in

rather, its imitation) is preserved, "reminding" the buyer of the haute couture original to which the ready-made product makes reference.[12]

This stylistic compromise comes down once again to the lack of any attempt on the part of the ready-to-wear industry to produce original designs for clothing with a style of its own and not just one based on the mythical models of traditional tailoring; designs that could be realized in harmony with the techniques and requirements of mass production. It was at this

panies with their greater flexibility of production were able to cope with such a development without running the risk of accumulating too high levels of unsold stock.[13] The idea was to make plans by mutual consent and to standardize the season's range of colours and fashion trends.

Even in the autumn of 1965 the features devoted to the "Wardrobes" had given preference to a number of basic colours. But the garment which provides the best example of the accord

Red jacket; on the left: double-breasted just below the waist, Cori model; medium length, Marzotto; close-fitting cut, Max Mara. Amica, no. 11, 1967.

Coat in cotton whipcord and dress with the same "slashed" print in white with yellow and blue lines in silk twill. Designed by Biki for Cori. Amica, no. 12, 1967.

the clothes produced.

Paradoxically, it could be said that the garment was "dressed up" with a presentation that it was not entitled to, but which made it more desirable, in the same way as it was "decorated" with fake stitching to simulate non-existent cuts, cuts that would be too expensive in mass-produced clothing because of the waste of fabric involved. Hence they are stripped of the "function" of "construction" of the garment, while their role of being a sign of quality (or

stage, when there was a risk that an essentially monotonous output would bury even the few attempts at originality, that an agreement was reached between the five major clothes manufacturers, Gruppo Finanziario Tessile, Hettermarks, Marzotto, Max Mara and Ruggeri. The agreement, made in the mid-sixties, had the backing of the magazine *Amica*, which gave space to an attempt to create a common front against the threat of an excessive diversification of fashion trends. Only the small com-

at work is the *red jacket*, published in issue no. 11 of *Amica* in 1967. The theme of the sports jacket, without substantial differences from traditional jackets, was interpreted by Cori, Marzotto and Max Mara, all of whom adopted red as the colour and produced variations of the "sailor's jacket" that had met with a great deal of success some years earlier. Hence the jacket was proposed, once again, as an "ageless youthful style," suitable for "town and country... for the woman out shopping or at the office... for

Coat in green wool, treated with Zepel for resistance to stains, by Germana Marucelli for Marzotto. Amica, no. 41, 1968.

the student at school or over the weekend"; different accessories were provided for it, so that both the "young lady" and the "sporty" or "trendy" girl each had three possible sets of combinations.

Thus the red jacket represents an example of standardized production, in which the tops conformed to the traditional line with shaped shoulders and a close-fitting cut, and the skirts were essentially straight but with lengths that varied from a few centimetres above the knee to a few centimetres below. The red jacket was also the significant product of a fashion in which the innovations applied to the necks which, where not rounded, had lapels of the kind usually to be found on men's jackets, and in which stitching was used to counterfeit a non-existent cut or to draw attention to a real one, in explicit reference to the tenets of haute couture.[14]

This stylistic reference to haute couture remained a constant feature in the output of almost all the ready-to-wear manufacturers throughout the sixties. It was a dependence that would lead to two separate negative consequences. On the one hand, it got in the way of the search for and creation of a style of its own for ready-to-wear clothing, fearful of stepping out of the ranks of an established and codified elegance.[15] On the other, the decision to align ready-to-wear garments with the creations of haute couture in order to stem the tide of "casual" wear that was flooding the market, turned out to be a mistake because high fashion itself, by the end of the sixties, was no longer in a position to exert a decisive influence over the taste and therefore the choices of women.

Even in 1966, when Giulia Borghese wrote "... new patterns, new ideas, new myths will begin their descent from the high fashion made for the few, to arrive in the space of a month or two in more down-to-earth fashion, the one made for everybody, where they glitter and then die out,"[16] one could already detect the warning signs of the crisis that was gradually to overtake high fashion,[17] and the passivity of an uncreating ready-to-wear industry, condemned to wait for "new ideas" to come down from Mount Olympus in order to be able to copy them on a mass scale.

This unproductive relationship reached its climax with the *High Fashion-Industry Accord*, initialled in 1971 by textile manufacturers, ready-to-wear manufacturers, haute couturiers and designers of boutique fashion. The agreement, set up to define common trends in fashion some fourteen months in advance of the time when the collections came onto the market, was intended to answer to two different requirements: one of image (on the part of the aforementioned industrialists) and the other economic (on the part of the creators of high fashion who were facing a grave financial crisis).

The latter were in fact guaranteed a subsidy drawn from the fund set up for the purpose by

White suit in gabardine by Ruggeri. Amica, no. 13, 1969.

Tartan coat with large cream and brown checks and flared skirt; the fabric of the skirt is the negative of that of the coat. Sportmax. Amica, no. 43, 1969.

Coat in twilled tweed, in the colours
off-white, hazel, brown and russet.
Manufactured by Ruggeri. Balduzzi
collection.

Suit in tartan matelassé cotton,
manufactured by Max Mara. Max Mara
archives.

Large black jacket by Ruggeri with lining in
synthetic fabric. Balduzzi collection.

Ministry of Commerce, the Ministry of Industry, the ready-to-wear manufacturers and the textile manufacturers (roughly Lit. 500,000,000 in 1971), on condition that at least 40% of the models included in the couturiers' collections were in keeping with the tendencies (line-colour-fabric) agreed with the manufacturers. This subsidy increased in proportion to the number of garments "in line" with the dictates drawn up by the signatories to the accord.[18] The idea was to calm down the market, by introducing uniformity into consumer demand; to "make a fashion last longer, restore reliability to the market and protect distributors against the risk of unsold stocks,"[19] by offering, as a guarantee of the up-to-date elegance of industrially produced clothes, correspondence with the fashion shows of haute couture.

The failure of the accord marked, in a sense, a watershed between a decade when ready-to-wear clothing had made great strides on the market but was hampered by an unsuitable approach, and the beginning of a phase of radical change. The seventies were a time of innovative ferment to which prestigious companies like Rosier, Hettermarks, Ruggeri and many others were unable to react with an adequate rethinking and reorganization of their own systems of production. It was the inevitable, however undesired, fate of an industry more concerned with containing and taming stimulation from outside than with coming up with its own and original answers. It was not yet ready to invest in the redefinition of its own style and image.

Max Mara: The Reason for Success

The limits on the ready-to-wear industry during the sixties, whose causes and effects we have been examining, did not however apply indiscriminately to the whole output of ready-to-wear clothing.

On the contrary, a number of companies emerged strengthened from the "crisis of growth" that the majority were unable to cope with.

One of these was Max Mara. The reasons for the firm's success can be reduced to two essential factors (the same ones, in fact, that constituted insurmountable obstacles for many other manufacturers). These were liberation from the stylistic dictates of high fashion and expansion and diversification of the lines produced, making it possible to satisfy different segments of the market.

High fashion was quick to lose its guiding role for Max Mara, or rather for its owner Achille Maramotti, even though in the early sixties he had utilized the "toiles" (i.e. the basic designs) of the great French couturiers as a basis for his own collections. In 1965 he presented a breakthrough collection that was called Pop, in confirmation of the fact that it was a first step towards a complete detachment from the canons of couture. The models, created by Lison Bonfils, a member of the editorial staff of *Elle*, for the 1965-66 winter season, were a

Coat in green twilled wool, manufactured by Ruggeri. Amica, no. 40, 1968.

Grey wool suit designed by Lison Bonfils for Max Mara (Pop line), Winter 1965-66. Max Mara archives.

"Fru-Fru" unlined jacket by Ruggeri for Autumn 1971, in brick red plaid wool with bands of coloured stripes. Hood of double-thickness fabric attached to neck. Balduzzi collection.

positive and timely response to the demands of the new "junior" clientele. Particularly interesting, because of the way it underlines the lucid awareness of these new requirements, is the editorial printed by Max Mara for the presentation of the Pop collection. It returns to and appropriates the major themes that had been debated in those years by all the ready-to-wear manufacturers, but this time there was a genuine link between them and the clothes that the company was producing.

port, took place through a process of collaboration with some of the most highly esteemed fashion designers on an international level.

Already the decision to seek the assistance of stylists not on the company staff had set Max Mara on a different plane to other ready-to-wear manufacturers during the sixties. But it was above all the idea of alternating such different designers as Emanuelle Khan, Karl Lagerfeld, Nanni Strada and Colette Demaye that made the case of Max Mara exemplary of a

style conceived and desired for the company's trade-mark itself.

Maramotti first began to seek the collaboration of stylists from outside after he had finally dropped the idea of working from the patterns of French haute couture. But the designers whom he selected to create the new collections were still French.[21] For two years, from 1966 to 1967, his designer was Emanuelle Khan, a pioneer along with stylists like Christiane Bailly of that avante-garde fashion that had shifted

Design by Karl Lagerfeld for the jacket in the adjacent photograph, black felt pen on paper mounted on board, 24.8 × 32.2 cm. Sample of blue cloth.

Large cloth jacket, unlined. Hood attached to neck. Max Mara, Winter 1968-69. Max Mara Archives.

Hence the idea of diversifying the lines and giving them a specific style of their own, no longer drawn exclusively from classic and traditional fashion, gained ground with Maramotti before it began to affect the output of rival companies, although it was not until 1969 and the creation of Sportmax[20] that one could speak of a trade-mark independent of that of the company itself. This evolution, from the first shrewd intuition to the development of a true programme that gained ever increasing sup-

successful stylistic policy built on the contributions of many, but always aimed at consolidating the "fashion image" of the company.

In other words the practice adopted by Maramotti of having each stylist design an average of four collections meant that the ideas of the individual designers did not have the time to establish themselves as permanent characteristics of the trade-mark. On the contrary, the ideas were used because they were in line (and for as long as they remained so) with the

from the "rive droite" to the "rive gauche." From 1967 onwards Colette Demaye was also working for Max Mara but, as we have seen, the Pop collection of 1965 had already been designed by the French woman Lison Bonfils.

In 1965 Graziella Fontana also worked for Maramotti, introducing the novelty of fur borders on the jackets and coats of the Max Mara collection. For two seasons in 1968, Jacques Delahaye collaborated on the Max Mara line: this collection continued to have a more classic-

Two designs for suit with blouse; black and sepia Indian ink on board, 22 × 29.2 cm; to left suit and accessories; to right blouse and skirt; bottom right suit seen from behind. Samples of ecru and light brown study wool. Anonymous stylist for Max Mara, 1962.

Design for coat; felt pen on paper, 20.3 × 30.5 cm; top right detail of cuts on back. Three samples of "casentino" slashed woollen cloth in the colours light blue, pink and green. Designed by Graziella Fontana for Max Mara, Winter 1966.

Design for suit made up of jacket and trousers; felt pen on paper, 21 × 30.7 cm. Sample of cream-coloured "casentino" woollen cloth. Designed by Emanuelle Khahn for Max Mara (Pop line), Winter 1966-67.

al accent than the Pop one, designed for the winter of 1968 by Colette Demaye.

1968 also saw the beginning of the collaboration with Guy Paulin and the one with Karl Lagerfeld, which was to last for two seasons. During the period in which Lagerfeld was designing for Max Mara, Sportmax was set up, in 1969. It would be characterized as the line of "total look" and of coordinates, as a complement to that of Max Mara, which continued to concentrate on the production of jackets and coats.

The first Sportmax was greeted with enthusiasm it that is was made up of garments that could be "combined" with one another. According to the editorial presenting the collection that was published in *Amica*, this was in fact a small revolution in the field of fashion, extremely useful to those who wished to solve the problem of the "outfit for every occasion" with just a few elements. "This collection known as Sportmax is created by Max Mara and, as the name implies, is marked by a sporty and youthful style ... What is it made up of? Of coats, jackets, trousers, skirts, blouses, pullovers, all easy to coordinate with one another..."[22] The first "trial run" was followed in 1970 by an entire collection of coordinates designed by Nanni Strada, who continued to work for Sportmax for a number of years.

With this proven formula based on short-term collaborations and diversified lines, Maramotti was able to handle the "post-crisis" period of the early seventies with success, alternating stylists like Castelbajac, Soprani, Lattuada and Beretta and gradually expanding the number of associated firms.

1. G. Goehring, "L'industria della confezione in Italia," in *Guida della Confezione Italiana*, published by the Associazione Italiana Industriali dell'Abbigliamento, Milan 1961, pp. 13 et seq.
2. This reversal of trend was definitively confirmed by an inquiry carried out by the Ente Italiano Moda (Italian Fashion Board) over the period September-October 1968 and covering 302 retailers throughout the country. It revealed that buyers under the age of twenty-four were particularly sensitive to the influences of fashion, while with increasing age it was the traditional factors (range, quality, price) that took on predominant weight. Ente Italiano Moda (ed. by), "Relazioni tra produttori, distributori, consumatori dei prodotti di moda," in *Quaderni*, no. 3, 1971.
3. *Il mercato italiano*, ed. by UNI.MA.C. s.p.a., Milan, duplicated page 11, January 1972.
4. In a desperate attempt to adapt to a less codified style, Ruggeri proposed in 1971 a formula that had already been launched by Max Mara two years earlier: "Sectionals."
5. In the booklet *Quarant'anni di abbigliamento*, printed on behalf of the Associazione Italiana degli Industriali dell'Abbigliamento in 1985, it is revealed that the share of the market held by ready-to-wear clothing in 1955 was 22%; by 1965 it was 56%. Yet in 1965 the magazine *Amica*, which stood out in those years for its support and encouragement of the ready-to-wear industry, published the results of a poll held in collaboration with the Italian Cotton Board to elect the "Dressmaker of Italy." The report disclosing the outcome of the poll was entitled "The fashion of the dressmaker of Italy" (no. 28/1965), and reproduced the hundred models selected, along with the names and addresses of the dressmakers who had produced them.
6. This type of classification was in common use both among professionals and in the editorials of fashion magazines in order to denote precise and unmistakable models to be worn

strictly on particular occasions.

7. Brunetta (ed.), "Parlano le grandi sarte," in *Il Corriere della Sera*, 13/11/1965.

8. The thorny problem of an inadequate range of sizes was to last for a long time. Attention was drawn to it again in Pamphlet no. 3/1971 published by the Ente Italiano Moda, *Relazioni, distributori, consumatori dei prodotti di moda*, which lamented the absence of any standardization of sizes.

9. The new clientele to which the manufacturers hoped to turn covered the range of girls and young women up to the age of twenty. In the research cited by the Gruppo Finanziario Tessile, these two specific groups had been identified within the range: that of "girls" between the ages of 9 and 15 and that of "young ladies" over the age of 15.

10. An example: Cori proposed three different lines, "Cori-Biki" (designed by the haute couturier Biki), "Cori" (created by the firm's own designer, as is revealed in the report that appeared in issue no. 40/1964 of *Amica*) and "Cori-Tris" (models at more moderate prices). However none of these was aimed at any specific age group.

11. The ready-to-wear manufacturers whose names appeared in the report were: Rosier, Max Mara, Andrè, Hella, Cori, Apem, Hettermarks, Comber, Belfe, Lux Sport, Marzotto, Monti, Confit, Stylbert, Ruggeri, Mirum, Merving, Aba, Vestebene, Abital, Bassi and Vogue Italiana.

12. In an interview with P. Fallaci entitled "Extraordinary encounter with Cinzia Ruggeri" (*Annabella* no. 19, 1985, pp. 35-36), Ruggeri had the following to say about her work in her father's company: "Another problem: the cut. Certain carrés were expensive precisely because of the cut, so I thought that by utilizing the nylon thread in a particular way I would give the impression of a cut that in reality was not there because there was a seam."

13. Cf. A. Ciabattoni, *Il sistema moda*, Turin 1976, p. 53, note 10.

14. However the invention of diversifying to some extent could be detected among the major ready-to-wear manufacturers, although the garments they produced had essentially similar characteristics. Cori and Marzotto attempted to raise the quality of production with garments with a predominantly elegant appearance and that were well-made. Ruggeri on the other hand flanked its traditional output with a number of models that experimented with original combinations, such as the coat of white synthetic fur with red loop fastenings that can be seen in issue no. 40/1966 of *Amica*. Max Mara tended to stand out for its line of sporty garments.

15. It is interesting to note how in 1967 "style" was still a term applied "illegitimately" to mass-produced ready-to-wear clothing. With regard to the success achieved by the clothing industry, cf. Giulio Goehring's preface to the 1967 edition of the *Guida della Confezione*.

16. G. Borghese, "Al grande magazzino tutti i temi di attualità," in *Il Corriere della Sera*, 19/3/1966.

17. Let us not forget that as early as 1955 among the exhibitors at the first International Clothing Market and Show (SAMIA) in Turin, could be found the mark "Veneziani-Sport."

18. The delegation of creators of High Fashion at the negotiating table was made up of Mila Shön, Ognibene Zendman, Sarli and Veneziani; the five manufacturing companies were Gruppo Finanziario Tessile, Hettermarks, Lebole, Max Mara and UNI.MA.C.

19. The text of the accord that we have quoted from is appended to the collection of six duplicated pamphlets compiled by UNI.MA.C. (Ruggeri) in January 1972, entitled respectively: *The company; The staff; The Italian market; The foreign market; Analysis of the current productive and economic-financial structure; Prospects and goals*.

20. Increasing the number of trade-marks and diversifying them has remained a constant goal for Max Mara up to the present day: in 1976 Vanity was set up with three new brands: Sherry, Albinea and I Blues. The following year saw the establishment of the Manifattura del Nord that, with the brand Penny Black, catered to the demand for a youthful style at moderate prices. Alongside it were created two new companies, Maxima and Marina Rinaldi, to cater to the market for outsize clothes.

21. On the subject of the large numbers of French stylists working for Italian companies from the middle to the end of the sixties, cf. I. Vercelloni-F. Lucchini, *Milanofashion*, Condé Nast, 1979, pp. 110 et seq.

22. R. Rimini (ed.), "La moda componibile," in *Amica* no. 43, 1969, p. 83.

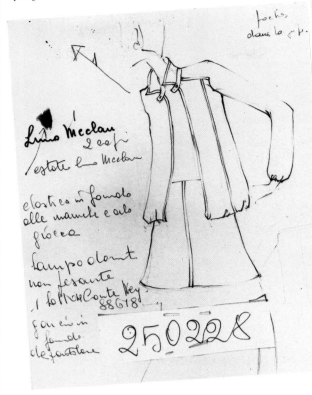

Jacques Delahaye, design for suit; pencil on paper, 21 × 27 cm. Fabric sample (light brown) at top left. Max Mara, Spring-Summer 1968.

Jacques Delahaye, design for suit made up of long jacket and trousers; pencil on paper, 21 × 27 cm. Detail of bottom of trouser leg at right Max Mara, Spring-Summer 1968.

Design for coat with hood; black felt pen and pastels on board, 26.8 × 37.3 cm; detail of back at top right. Two samples of camelhair wool. Designed by Colette Demay for Max Mara (Pop line), Winter 1968.

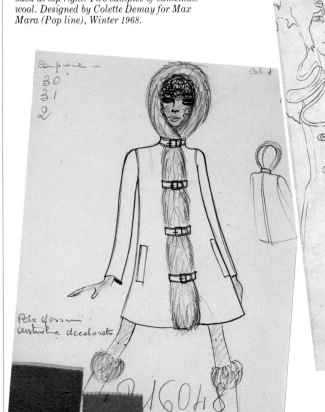

Design for coat; photocopy to which a detail has been added in pencil and coloured with felt pens, 22.6 × 34.9 cm. Sample of red Harris tweed. Designed by Nanni Strada for Max Mara (Sportmax), Winter 1970.

Clothing Manufacturers

Alessio Bassi

The firm Alessio Bassi was founded in 1954 in Milan, at no. 16 Via Filargo, and ceased activity in 1976. Its output centred on ready-to-wear clothing for women and girls, distributed to Italian clothes stores under the trade-mark Alessio Bassi. The firm participated in a number of fairs, including that of the SAMIA. The firm, wholly owned by Alessio Bassi, was regarded as one of the most important in the sector during the period 1954-1967. (*A.B.*)

Apem Spa

Apem was founded in 1950 and had its head office near Milan, at Vimodrone (Strada Statale Padana Superiore Km 11). The firm manufactured women's clothing and shirts, distributed under the trade-mark Apem to department stores and specialized retailers. Apem had two factories, employing 1000 workers in 1960 and 600 in 1970. The company belonged to the Gruppo Rinascente until 1970, when it was sold to the clothing manufacturers Romano. Under the new style of Apem-Romano it continued to operate until 1973-74, the year in which the company was closed down. (*A.B.*)

Basile Spa

Basile Spa was founded in 1951, with head offices at no. 28, Via Lancetti in Milan. Originally devoted to men's wear, its production was expanded to include women's wear, sportswear and leather clothing in 1970. Apart from the registered trade-mark Basile, the company also produces and distributes the lines created by Luciano Soprani, serving boutiques and specialized shops in Italy, France, Germany, the United Kingdom and the United States. Basile Spa participates in initiatives such as Milano Collezioni. During the fifties and sixties the company was controlled by Remo Basile, but is at present owned the Monti family. The number of workers employed by the company, which has registered stock of 3000 million lire, has risen from 40 in 1969 to 171 in 1980; its turnover in 1984 was 32,000 million lire. (*A.B.*)

Cidat Spa

Founded in 1965, Cidat's head office is at no. 35, Corso Vigevano in Turin. Cidat produces and distributes women's clothing designed by Valentino and Ungaro, serving boutiques in Italy, the EEC, the United States and other countries. The joint-stock company belongs to the Gruppo Finanziario Tessile owned by the Rivetti family, and has a registered stock of 700 million lire and 300 employees. Its turnover has risen from 54,000 million lire in 1983 to 75,000 million in 1984. (*A.B.*)

Conber Spa

The company was set up in Vicenza, at no. 6, Via Cottone, and ceased to operate in 1976. Conber manufactured women's clothing: skirts, suits, coats and overcoats. Under the registered trade-mark Confezioni Beriche, its products were distributed to specialized shops and boutiques in Italy, France and Belgium. The company took part in initiatives like the SAMIA Conber Spa, controlled by the Rossi family of Schio, employed 247 workers in 1973. (*A.B.*)

Confit Spa

Founded in 1957, Confit's head office is at no. 62, Viale Ramazzini in Reggio Emilia. Its production centres on women's clothing, from coats and jackets to light clothing and coordinates. These garments are distributed retail under the registered trade-marks Confit, Mytho and Selezione. Confit sells on the Italian, Swiss, French, German and Belgian markets. Set up as a limited partnership, it became a joint-stock company in 1973, with a registered stock of 1,000 million lire. In 1973 the company employed 350 people, while in 1985 it had 118 employees at the factory in Reggio Emilia and 81 at the one at Carpineti (R.E.). (*A.B.*)

Daina Srl

Daina Srl was founded in 1958 and its premises are located at no. 8, Riviera Matteotti in Mira (Venice). The firm produces women's outer garments, distributed under the registered trade-marks Daina Venezia and Martina Boutique, serving specialized retailers in Italy, Switzerland, Germany, Holland, Spain and Japan. Among the initiatives in which Daina Srl takes part are Modit and Mode Woche. The company has two factories in Mira and its turnover in 1984 was 8,000 million lire. (*A.B.*)

Fiorucci Spa

Fiorucci Spa was founded in 1974 and its head office is located at no. 15, Via XXV Aprile in San Donato Milanese (Milan). The company produces and distributes clothing and other articles, from stockings to accessories and gadgets, under its own registered trade-marks Fiorucci and Wrangler (the latter only for Italy and Switzerland). As well as its own stores, Fiorucci supplies specialized retailers, shops selling casual wear and clothing for young people in Italy, the EEC and the United States. The company participates in Pitti Bimbo and Milanovendemoda. 45% of the joint-stock company is controlled by the financial trust of Aki A. Nui, who is currently managing director of Fiorucci, while the remaining 55% is divided equally between Benetton and Elio Fiorucci. The company, which employed 212 workers in 1985, had a turnover of 67,000 million lire in 1984. (*A.B.*)

Fias-Lo Presti, Turba & C.

Fias-Lo Presti, Turba & C. was the outcome of the reorganization of two previously existing companies. In 1918 Umberto Turba set up a company in Milan, with premises at no. 1, Via Sirtori, with over 600 employees. In 1919 it was taken over by Lo Presti, Turba & Cuzzi Sas, to be definitively transformed into Fias-Lo Presti, Turba & C. Spa in 1924. The company's output, centring on women's clothing, included furs, underwear and children's clothes. Distribution, under the registered trade-mark Fias, was entrusted to textile retailers with direct sales through various sub-agencies throughout the country. Abroad, agents of Fias handled the markets in London, Berlin, New York, Cairo, Baghdad, Vancouver and the Bermudas.

Turba was the first major company in the sector of women's ready-to-wear clothing to emerge in Italy. In 1919 it already had a factory covering 5,600 m^2 and a significant output of mass-produced clothing. By 1926 the company had 870 employees and a turnover of around 28 million lire. In 1919 it added a department of patterns for dressmakers, given the name "Modelia." The company's factory became a casualty of the war in 1943 and it moved to Como-Camerlata, where it shared premises with the Fisac company. Returning to Milan, the company remained active until 1966. Out of its closure in 1966 emerged the firm Chantal, with premises at no. 60, Via M. Loria in Milan and owned by Luigi Turba, son of the founder of Fias. Chantal still produces clothing for women and expectant mothers. (*A.B.*)

Genny Spa

The company was founded in 1961 in Ancona, at no. 18, Via Pesaro. Its output consists of women's clothing, sportswear and leather clothing, and is distributed to boutiques in Italy, the EEC and the United States. Its various registered trade-marks Genny, Byblos, Complice, Claude Montana and Malisy also make use of different stylists. Thus the Genny lines are designed by Gianni Versace, those of Complice by Claude Montana and those of Byblos by Keith Varthy. The company participates in Milano Confezioni among other events. The joint-stock company is controlled, as are Byblos and Reporter, by the Girombelli family. The number of workers employed by Genny Spa rose from 80 in 1964 to the current level of about 500. In 1984 the turnover of the Girombelli Group was 129,000 million lire, of which Genny accounted for 74,000 million, Byblos 35,000 and the F.G. 20,000. (*A.B.*)

Gruppo Finanziario Tessile

Founded in 1927, the company's head office is at no. 6, Corso Emilia in Turin. Its vast output includes men's and women's clothing and sportswear. Distribution is by retail, supplying specialized shops, boutiques and department stores in the United States. The Gruppo Finanziario Tessile has registered a number of trade-marks, including Facis, Giorgio Armani, Mani, Valentino Uomo, Miss V by Valentino, Mix & Match, Profilo, Sidi, Louis Feraud, Ungaro Parallel, Cori Lady, Solo Donna, Tris and Tris Lady. The group also takes part in events like Pitti Uomo. As well as Italy, the company's markets include the EEC, the United States and Canada, with exports accounting for 37% of its turnover in 1984. Owned by the Rivetti family since 1952, the company is one of Italy's three largest manufacturers of women's clothing. The group employs 5,500 workers and has 11 factories in Italy and one in Mexico. Consolidated sales in 1984 amounted to 710,000 million lire in 1984, of which women's clothing alone accounted for 124,000, to which must be added the 75,000 million lire turnover of the affiliated company Cidat. (*A.B.*)

Hettemarks Italiana Spa

Hettemarks Italiana was founded in 1959, with premises in the vicinity of Bari (Strada Provinciale Aeroporto, 22), and ceased its activity in August 1977. Its production centred on women's clothing, from coats and jackets to dresses, skirts and trousers. Under the registered trade-marks Hettemarks, Mammi, Sprint, Linea 4 and Harrison's, the company's products were distributed to retailers in Italy, Germany, Sweden and other countries. Among other events, Hettemarks participated in the SAMIA. At the end of the seventies the joint-stock company, controlled by the Hettemarks family of Sweden, was one of the five largest manufacturers of women's clothing in Italy. (*A.B.*)

Juvenilia Spa

The firm Juvenilia was founded in 1949 and has its head office at no. 22, Via Bainsizza in Turin. Its output covers outer garments for women and children and casual wear. Distribution, under the registered trade-marks Juvenilia, Ilia and Les Rimes, is to specialized retailers in Italy, the United Kingdom, Sweden, Kuwait and, irregularly, Australia. The joint-stock company, controlled by the Borello family, possesses two factories, one in Turin and one in Savignano (Cuneo), and had a turnover of 15,000 million lire in 1984. (*A.B.*)

Maska Spa

Maska was founded in 1967 and has its head office in Scandiano (Reggio Emilia), in Via Contarella. Its production is centred on women's clothing: coats and jackets, light clothing and coordinates. Several trade-marks have been registered: Maska, Mabba, Giallo, Cerruti and Femme. The company also produced and distributed La Cordée clothing from 1976 to 1984. It supplies specialized shops and boutiques in Italy, the EEC and the United States. Among other initiatives, Maska takes part in the Modit. The company was a partnership up until 1974, and then was transformed into a joint-stock company controlled by the Crotti and Violi companies, with a registered stock of 3,050 million lire. Maska, which employed 295 workers in 1985, has seen its turnover rise from 22,500 million lire in 1983 to 29,000 million in 1984. (A.B.)

Max Mara Spa

Founded in 1951, its head office is located at no. 66, Via Fratelli Cervi in Reggio Emilia. The company's output, which exceeds 3.5 million garments a year, covers the whole range of women's clothing. The company's registered trade-marks are Max Mara, Sportmax, Marina Rinaldi, Penny Black, I Blues and Pianoforte. Its products are distributed to women's clothing stores and boutiques in Italy, the EEC, the United States and other countries, with exports accounting for 30% of total sales. The lines produced by the Maramotti group have been designed by stylists like Emanuelle Khan. Jacques Delaye, Karl Lagerfeld, Castelbajac and Anne Marie Beretta. Fairs attended by the firm include Milano Collezioni.

The firm was established as a limited-liability company, but was transformed into a joint-stock company in 1980. With a registered stock that currently exceeds 16,000 million lire, it is owned by the Maramotti family. Along with the other companies controlled by the Maramotti group, Max Mara is one of the three largest Italian manufacturers and also one of the biggest in Europe. In fact the group, to which the Max Mara and Maxima stores also belong, had a turnover of 230,000 million lire in 1984, of which Max Mara Spa accounted for 98,000 million and Marina Rinaldi 37,000. (A.B.)

Mila Schön Srl

Mila Schön was founded in 1965 and has a head office at no. 2, Via Montenapoleone in Milan. At first the company's output was confined to women's clothing, with a prêt-à-porter division set up in 1974, but production of men's clothing commenced in 1978. The clothes are distributed retail under the trade-mark Mila Schön, mainly to boutiques in Italy and the EEC and department stores in the United States. Mila Schön participates in events like Milano Collezioni, Pitti Uomo and Uomo Moda in New York. The limited liability company, controlled by the Schön family, has a factory at no. 20, Via E. Mattei in Sedriano (Milan), and employed 90 people in 1985. Its turnover in 1984 was 16,000 million lire, of which 55% came from exports. (A.B.)

Mimmina Spa

The firm was set up in 1963 with offices at no. 52, Via Roma in Badia Al Pino (Arezzo). Mimmina manufactures women's clothing which is distributed to specialist retailers under the trade-marks Mimmina, Incontro, Gian Dol and Lady M. Its markets are in Italy, Europe, the United States and Canada. Mimmina Spa attends the Modit, among other events. The joint-stock company, with a registered stock of 600 million lire, employed 271 workers in 1983 and had a turnover of 21,000 million lire in 1984. (A.B.)

Mirum Spa

The firm was established in 1958, with head offices at no. 54, Corso Garibaldi in Ancona, while its factory was located on the outskirts of the city (Strada Statale 16 - Baracolla industrial zone).

The firm closed down in April 1983. Its production comprised coats and jackets, women's dresses and raincoats for men and women, which were distributed under the trade-marks Robus, Discobolo, Mirum, Damina, Mirette, Mirabelle and Mirlady. These lines were supplied to ready-to-wear clothing stores and distributors specializing in women's clothing in Italy, Austria, Germany, the United Kingdom, Belgium, Canada and Japan. Mirum took part in initiatives like the SAMIA.

It was a joint-stock company controlled by the Bulgaro family, with a registered stock of 470 million lire in 1978. The company employed 150 people in 1964 and 135 in 1981-82. (A.B.)

Rosier Spa

The firm was founded in 1953, with offices in Piazzale Accursio in Milan, and closed its doors in 1977. It manufactured women's clothing, including coats and jackets, light clothing and sportswear.

Under the trade-marks Rosier, New Rose, Pauletto and Way, the company supplied wholesalers and retailers in Italy, the EEC, the United States, the Middle East and Japan. Rosier took part in events like the SAMIA.

Set up in the form of a partnership, it was transformed into a limited company by the merger of Rosier, Tessitura di Agrate, Morina, Mizar, Nebula and Immobiliare Accursio. In 1970 the company was one of the largest manufacturers of women's clothing in Italy, employing over 2000 workers and utilizing five factories (in Milan, Agrate Brianza, Solbiate Inferiore, Presezzo and Caprino Bergamasco). Its turnover in 1975 was 10,000 million lire. (A.B.)

Salvatore Ferragamo Spa

The company was founded in 1945 and has its office at no. 2, Via Tornabuoni in Florence. Its comprises women's clothing, footwear for men and women and accessories; all are distributed under the company's trade-mark, Ferragamo.

The company, which owns 12 shops in Italy and 4 abroad, has a huge market that includes the EEC, the United States, Japan and another 20 foreign countries. Ferragamo takes part in Milano Collezioni.

In 1985 it had 300 employees and a factory at Osmannoro (Florence). Its turnover was 100,000 million lire in 1984 and 130,000 in 1985, rising to 160,000 if the sales from shops abroad are including. Clothing and leather articles account for 25% of sales, footwear 65% and accessories the remaining 10%. (A.B.)

Selene Srl

Founded in 1959, the firm's head office is at no. 86, Via della Repubblica in Cavriago (Reggio Emilia). Selene manufactures women's clothing and, up until 1983, children's clothing as well. Its products are distributed to specialist shops and boutiques under the registered trade-marks Selene, Amuleti, Mariella Burani and Scatola Magica. As well as the Italian market, it serves those of Switzerland, Austria, France, Germany, Holland, Belgium, the United States and Japan. Selene is present at the Modit and at the Milan showroom at no. 3, Via Montenapoleone.

Established as a partnership it became a limited company in 1970, with current registered stock of 1,500 million lire. The turnover of the company, which employed 206 workers in 1985, has risen from 16,000 million lire in 1982 to 24,000 million in 1983 and 28,000 in 1984, with exports accounting for 20-25%. (A.B.)

Unimac Spa

The firm was founded in 1963, with a head office at no. 50, Via C. Battisti in Vimodrone (Milan), and ceased operations in July 1975. Unimac manufactured women's clothing, from coats to suits, that were distributed under the trade-mark Guido Ruggeri to wholesalers, read-to-wear clothing stores and shops specializing in women's clothing. Its markets were in Italy, Germany and other countries.

Unimac took part in events like the SAMIA. The limited company, controlled by the Ruggeri family, had a registered stock of 1,400 million lire. (A.B.)

Vestebene del Gruppo Tessile Miroglio

The company was founded in 1955 and has its head office at no. 11, Via Santa Barbara in Alba (Cuneo). Vestebene produces women's clothing: coats and jackets, light clothing and coordinates.

The company has registered a number of trade-marks, including Vestebene, Alba Confezioni, Vè Bè, VB, Lilian's Star and All Day. Its products are distributed to wholesalers and retailers in Italy, Switzerland, Austria, France, Germany, Belgium and other North European countries. Until 1981 a limited company, Vestebene is today a division of the Gruppo Tessile owned by the Miroglio company. Together with its sister companies, Vestebene is the largest Italian and European manufacturer of women's clothing.

The number of people employed by the company rose from 1,615 in 1978 to 2,700 in 1985, including the affiliated companies Langa Confezioni, Grande Confezioni and three others based abroad. The Vestebene division has seven factories in Italy and four abroad. Their total output is 8.5 million garments, including 1.5 million coats and jackets. 3.5 million of these are exported. In 1984 the total sales of the Vestebene division amounted to 256,000 million lire, and of the entire Gruppo Tessile Miroglio, 436,000. Exports earned 73,000 million for Vestebene and 187,000 for the group as a whole. For the two years 1985-86, the clothing division plans an investment of over 30,000 million lire. The group also controls four factories located abroad, one in Greece, one in Egypt and two in Tunisia. (A.B.)

ANTI-FASHION
MILANESE EXAMPLES

Alessandra Gnecchi Ruscone

The sixties were a period of great revolution in modes of behaviour throughout the western world. From the United States to Holland the younger generations suddenly turned their backs on existing models and sought new forms that broke with the past. It was a mass phenomenon that contaminated every sector of daily life: from relations between the sexes to the attitude to work and the use of time. The chief vehicle of this contagion was English and then American rock music, embodied by groups and singers whose popularity broke through every barrier of politics or language. The image presented by these figures carried as strong a message of rejection of traditional values as did the words and music of their songs. And since the majority of these singers were men, it was men's clothing that was the first to undergo traumatic changes.

Hair, which had already created a scandal when it began to cover the ears and the forehead, grew longer and longer. The ankle-boots, striped jumpers and tight-fitting trousers of the early days, derived from American casual wear, gave way to an unbridled freedom in the combination of colours, materials and styles. Charismatic figures like Mick Jagger or Brian Jones, the legendary guitarist of the Rolling Stones who was considered the most elegant man in the rock world, flaunted lace frill, velvets, lamé, furs, tights, mousquetaire boots, accompanied by necklaces, earrings and outrageous make-up. Not since the 18th century had man presented such a gaudy and sexually provocative image of himself, invading the territory of women and outclassing them at the start. In order to keep up, women were obliged to play the same game: highly accentuated make-up, long and black-combed hair, tight trousers, very close-fitting jumpers and T-shirts, boots that covered the knee, fishnet stockings and finally the revolutionary mini-skirt which barely covered the groin.

This new style of dress, spread first into the contiguous sectors of entertainment and art and then to the majority of the younger generation. The dominant feature of this "anti-fashion," as it was quickly baptized, was that it lay outside any canon or rule, leaving everyone free to dress in the manner he or she found most comfortable and amusing.

At the beginning of the sixties, the style of dress in Italy was even more sober and uniform than in other countries, and the advent of the new fashion came as a very sharp break.

Nuccia Fattori, owner of the boutique Cose, wearing a dress of her own design, in two pieces of lurex, 1966. Fattori archives.

Hence it was very difficult for young people to find a response to their growing demand for different clothes. While traditional channels totally ignored the phenomenon, regarding it as marginal and short-lived, a few enterprising individuals took the initiative of bringing the new style of dress onto the market. Their activity was often almost amateur in its approach, and backed up by limited resources. Many of them vanished after a short time and even those who survived were restricted to a local clientele. Only Fiorucci managed to establish himself on a first national and then international level.

The skill of these pioneers lay largely in their ability to pick up on innovations and trends that manifested themselves abroad and bringing them out at the right moment in Italy. Alongside this, almost all of them carried out their own creative activity, usually with small-scale artisan workshops, but always along the lines of the various fashions as they were imported from abroad.

It would be difficult and rather pointless to try and reconstruct an overall view of an activity that was extremely fragmented in Italy. If one has to make a choice, Milan would seem to be the most significant city, in that it was the first to be influenced by the new trends and to develop them in subsequent years. Even within Milan itself, the scope has been further reduced to cover only those boutiques and stores that showed more ability than others in developing a distinct image of their own, and were able to make themselves into a point of reference for fashion among young people over the span of almost a decade. A common element for all these stores was the fact that they catered to a younger clientele than that of traditional boutiques, keeping their prices lower and paying particular attention to their image, from the name of the boutique itself to its graphics, interior decoration and shop windows.

"Cose"

The first boutique with a difference to appear in Milan was "Cose." It opened in 1963 at Via della Spiga, no. 8. This was a back street that contained only one other boutique, selling French prêt-à-porter.[1] "Cose" was opened on the initiative of Nuccia Fattori, urged on by her friends who were desperately seeking a new way of dressing. In its first year the boutique only sold its own production of women's clothes, made by Nuccia Fattori and Ja Bellotti and taking their inspiration from models to be found in the French magazine *Elle*. They were largely items of knitwear, together with a few dresses. The shop was an immediate success and within a short time built up a clientele made up of the wives of young professionals like Crepax, Gregotti, Tadini and Adami, who were to remain faithful to "Cose" in the future. By the end of the first year, demand had already exceeded the production capacity of the boutique, which was obliged to turn to small artisan workshops in order to cope. For instance the famous Sherlock

the first in Italy to import clothes by Emanuelle Khan, Paco Rabanne, Sonia Rykiel, Daniel Hechter, Karl Lagerfeld's Chloé, Foale & Tuffin, Biba, Ossie Clark, Zandra Rhodes and, later on, Kenzo and Norma Kamali. The quest for foreign products was extended to the world of markets, boutiques and department stores in the search for curiosities, novelties and ideas. As far as Italy was concerned, Nuccia Fattori kept up a constant collaboration with Walter Albini, but had little to do with other stylists: a few items of clothing by Silvano Malta, E.

various stages of fashion in the intervening period: folk, tie & dye, lurex, op, pop, etc. However the predominant sector remained that of knitwear and the most famous item of clothing sold by the shop was perhaps the long and very close-fitting black dress with long sleeves and a large red heart embroidered in the pubic region. The production retained its artisan character and was made from month to month on the basis of demand. As well as being sold by the shop in Via della Spiga, it was distributed by other Italian boutiques that bought it directly and by a

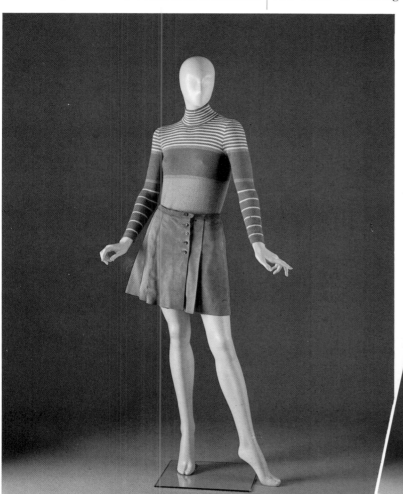

Cose, skirt in pink suede (owner: Patrizia Ascari) and mini-pullover in satin-knit wool with horizontal stripes (owner: Fabrizia Baldissera), 1966-70.

Cose, dress in satin-knit blue wool with appliqués, 1974-80. Owner: Nuccia Fattori.

Holmes model of jacket, based on the English sports jacket for men with four buttons, with two strips applied in front and behind and belt with buckle, in a winter version in tweed and a summer one in raw linen, was made by a tailoring firm in Bologna that produced no more than thirty a month. Hence "Cose" began to make purchases abroad at the same time, first in Paris and London, then in the East and the United States. Nuccia Fattori was considered to have a remarkable nose for searching out emerging talents, and her boutique was one of

Khan's collection of mini-skirts for Missoni and, at the end of the seventies, Cinzia Ruggeri.

The boutique had a highly personal image, linked to that of its proprietor. It sold a wide range of clothing, from the extremes of avant-garde and eccentricity to a very simple and practical style that was easy to wear.

Clothing produced under the "Cose" label always remained an important part of the boutique's turnover, although it decreased over the course of the years until it accounted for no more than 20% in 1980, passing through all the

number of stores in England. Nuccia Fattori did not take part in fashion shows or promotional events, with the exception of a number of show cum parties held in the sixties in a garage and in a night-club in Corso Vittorio Emanuele.

Particular care was taken over the impact produced by the shop itself, both by a continual renewal of the window displays and with an unusually innovative lay-out of the interior: all the clothes were on display and could be chosen by the customer without the aid of the sales staff. There was a large entresol reached by a

Pelliccia non-pelliccia per una giacca, per una tunica

Gulp, mini-coat in bright red synthetic fur, with leather pendant for the zip fastener and raglan sleeves. Vogue, *December 1966 (photo Aldin).*

painted metal staircase with rubber-covered treads, a cylindrical changing-room made of metal, granite counters, one wall of unplastered brick and another of concrete. The dominant colours were yellow, black and red.

Still more advanced was the conception of another shop that Nuccia Fattori opened in Milan during the sixties. "Altre Cose" was made entirely out of metal and perspex. The clothes were contained inside transparent cylinders hanging from the ceiling that were lowered when a button was pushed on a control panel on the counter. The boutique was only open at night, and linked to the Bang-Bang discotheque underneath by an elevator, another transparent cylinder in which only one passenger could enter at a time, and in a semi-reclining position. "Altre Cose" had to close after a short time because of licensing problems.

In 1977 Nuccia Fattori formed a partnership with the manager of the "Cose" shop, E. Merlini, and attempted to get the production organized on a better footing. In 1984 the boutique was taken over by Procomi Srl, which carried on its activity under the same name.

"Gulp"

The other Milanese boutique that quickly became a point of reference for the young in the sixties was "Gulp," at no. 14 Via Santo Spirito. It was opened by Gabriella Barassi, a member of the staff of "Cose." The boutique was inaugurated in May 1966 with fittings and decoration produced in collaboration with Amalia Dal Ponte. The shop had no partitions and all the clothes were displayed on a stand in the middle or in white boxes lining the walls. The counters were of the industrial kind and the changing rooms had no doors. The ceiling had lamps hanging from protuberances. One wall was painted with yellow, red and brown waves. At the back stood a bar and a juke-box.

The men's wear department was in the basement, with plaster reliefs of the torsos of men and women, shirts and jeans. The merchandise was almost all produced by the boutique, manufactured from month to month in this case too, by a small artisan tailor's workshop.

Some of "Gulp's" creations made news, such as the scandal caused by the mini-dresses worn by some photographic models to a première at La Scala in 1966, the clothes in lurex and embroidered with mirrors of the same year, the phosphorescent ones, the "musical" dress covered with thousands of tiny bells linked together with ribbons. In 1969 a sensation was caused by the boutique's nude-look with clothes made out of transparent cloth, lace, knitwear full of holes with plunging necklines, exposed navels and backs and extremely clinging tunics.

For just this reason, "Gulp's" style was very popular in the world of entertainment: the boutique's clients, whose pictures were frequently in the weekly magazines, included people like Caterina Caselli (who had "Gulp" make her a very short wedding dress in a rosy yellow),

DI SERA SENTIRSI GITANE

In questa pagina: stile gitana versione mini. L'abito in leggero cotone nero a fiori rossi è mosso da tre volants a partire dai fianchi. Un volant solo in fondo alle maniche semilunghe. Di Gulp. Notare: la cintura a catena con feticcio posata dove comincia il primo volant.
Nella pagina accanto: stile gitana versione maxi. Blusa di organdis bianco trasparente e una gonna ampia che arriva a metà polpaccio, in shantung Rhonel nero a fiorellini gialli. Vita stretta-stretta dalla cintura-corsetto su cui scorrono tante catene e orlo decorato da ghirlanda bianca di macramé. Di Tiktiner. Sui piedi cerchietti dorati. Tutti i sandali in questa e nelle pagine precedenti sono di Marina Tecchio per Fiorucci.

Gulp, gypsy-style dress, mini version, in cotton with red flowers. Vogue, *June 1968*

Stretch bermudas in polyamide with flowers by Croc'Madame for Fiorucci, cotton blouse with Mexican embroidery by Fiorucci. Vogue, July-August 1968 (photo Baeger).

Ornella Vanoni, Mina and Carla Fracci.

As well as clothes "Gulp" sold a range of accessories. These included the luminous brooches made for the inauguration in matching colours to be worn with the lurex mini-dresses, stockings of all kinds, belts made out of plastic discs, velvet, coloured feathers and metal with stylized butterflies, elephants and other animals, hippystyle necklaces, handbags covered with mirrors, sunglasses and so on.

The majority of the clothes manufactured by "Gulp" were the work of Gabriella herself, with the sporadic collaboration of Ja Bellotti, Amalia Dal Ponte and others. They were distributed not only through the shop in Via Santo Spirito but also through a second boutique opened in Forte dei Marmi in 1967 and for a few years through "Gog-ma-gog" in Rome.

Fiorucci

Elio Fiorucci opened a boutique at Galleria Passarella no. 1, on the corner of Corso Vittorio Emanuele, in 1967. He had begun his career by working in his father's shoe shop and had opened one of his own in Via Torino in 1962. The imaginative footwear that he started to produce to sell in the shop aroused interest among fashionable young people. The coloured galoshes he brought out in that same year of 1962, for instance, became famous, as did his boots in every shade, including gold and silver, his plastic sandals with daisies stuck on them, clogs, rope-sandals, multi-coloured corded velvet moccasins and, with the arrival of the mini-skirt, his mid-calf length boots.

The shop in Galleria Passarella was on three floors and was decorated by Amalia Dal Ponte in a highly modern style, utilizing among other things shelving made out of slender steel frames with the actual shelves made of white plexiglass, quartz iodine lamps and enamelled tractor seats instead of the traditional stools. Salesgirls wore Fiorucci's most showy clothes and rock music was played constantly at full volume. For the inauguration a "fashion show" was staged in the shop window, with models wearing mini-skirts or very tight flared trousers. The crowd that collected was so large that the traffic police had to intervene.

The shop sold shoes, accessories, t-shirts, sweaters, trousers for men and women, mini-skirts and hot pants. Almost all of these were foreign-made at the outset, imported from every part of the world: first from London (Carnaby Street, Portobello Road, Kensington Market), and then from Paris, the United States, the Far East and Central and South America. The clothes were designed by Ossie Clark, Zandra Rhodes, Biba, Anne d'Alban, Ellis Pollock and E. Khan, among others. Fiorucci's own output was limited to shoes, boots and sandals, along with accessories such as western-style leather saddlebags, pop bags and belts, some with starn-shapes cut out of them and others with appliqué landscapes and butterflies. After 1969 a sporadic output of

The musical group Equipe 84, 1967.

Fiorucci, tennis shoes with wedge. Red cotton uppers with white plastic appliqués. Now in the Fiorucci archives.

Sample used as a basis for a line produced by Fiorucci, 1972-73.

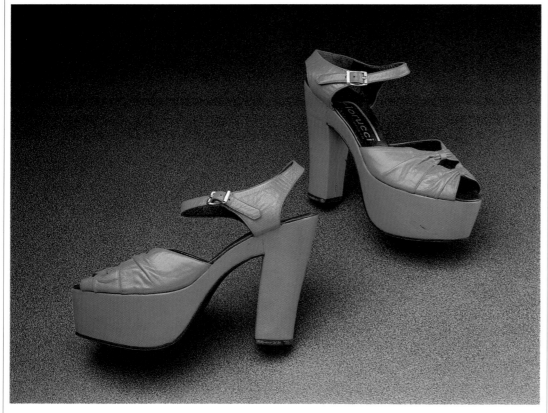

Fiorucci, sandals in red-painted leather with very high heels and elevated soles, 1970. Owner: Cristina Rossi.

clothes was added, such as miniskirts made out of pieces of different coloured cloth, square-fronted painter's smocks in single colours, tartan or flower-patterns, clinging t-shirts in every colour with printed Provençal florets and flared jeans with embroidered poppies. The shop turned out a continuous stream of new products. His speed in picking up on the demands of the public and responding to them is one of the reasons for the success of Elio Fiorucci, who claimed that a new fashion had to reach the market within fifteen days in order to be effective.[3] In this way Fiorucci overthrew the old commercial criteria, which regularly assigned the store a passive role as a mediator between producer and consumer.

Fiorucci's clientele was much larger than that of ordinary boutiques. Prices were very low, within the reach of the mass of young people who constituted the really big market that had opened up for the new fashion. The quality of fabrics and manufacturing was often not very high, but the particularly low prices made a new attitude towards buying clothes possible, one which envisaged very short periods of use and continual replacements. At the same time the heterogeneous supply of items on sale left buyers free to choose from among a wider range of alternatives than was customary, and to establish an image of their own, independently of the dictates of the current fashion.

Fiorucci was not himself a stylist, by his own admission. His activity developed gradually, from the mere purchase of clothes from others to an output that was largely copied and, eventually, the establishment of his own hallmark recognizable throughout the world. His ability lay in reinterpreting and reproposing already existing articles without prejudice as to materials or colours. Typical of these were the traditional military combat suit produced in shocking pink or the overalls made out of paper.

His success was enormous right from the start; in 1972 the first company, Fiorucci S.r.l., was set up, achieving a turnover of one billion lire in its first year of activity. In 1974 Fiorucci S.p.A. was founded in partnership with La Standa, which made it possible for Fiorucci to expand his distribution system all over Italy and abroad. In 1974 a second shop was opened in Milan too, in Via Torino.[4] It was huge, covering 1500 square metres, and set up in such a way as to house the widest variety of articles and activities. The decoration, entrusted to Franco Marabelli, was in the industrial style, illuminated by a skylight and with a fountain in the middle surrounded by plants. The shop was born out of the idea of establishing a genuine meeting-point in a street that was already much frequented by young people.

With respect to the expanding and world-wide activity of the Fiorucci Company, the two stores in Milan played a role of image creation, with frequent changes in the window displays and decoration. Distribution in Italy became increasingly widespread: by 1977 there were over 600 outlets; a new head office was opened at Corsico, with warehouses at Buccinasco. At the same time distribution abroad was on the increase, and within a few years Fiorucci stores could be found in every country in Europe, in the United States, South America, Japan and Australia, with a variety of commercial set-ups. Two stores were opened in London in 1974. In 1975 Fiorucci Inc. was established in the United States, distributing to major department stores and, in the same year, opening a shop on 59th Street in New York. In 1976 another was

Taiwan and Hong Kong (coats and jackets, shirts), in Korea (bags, footwear), in China (knitwear) and in India (T-shirts). The production of jeans was very important, accounting for half the total turnover in 1975 (300,000 pairs sold in 100 days).[7]

There was a very large number of models, and they were constantly changing to keep up with evolutions in fashion: from the "Buffalo" with 32-centimetre-wide bell-bottoms that covered the whole shoe, to the "Montreal" with 26-centimetre bottoms, the "Panama" with patch

usual and sometimes extravagant ways: handkerchiefs printed with the designs of orange wrappers, potato sacks sold as shopping bags.

This style succeeded in impresssing on the public an image – whether that of a pair of Victorian angels or of American fifties-style pin-ups – capable of embracing highly diverse products that were not in themselves immediately recognizable.[8] Particular attention was devoted to active promotion, with inaugurations abroad that involved personalities like Andy Warhol, fashion shows like the one held at

Fiorucci, mini-skirt in green woollen cloth (owner: V. Crepax), 1971, cotton jersey (owner: D. Travaglio), 1972, and overcoat in black wool (owner: A. Zanuso), 1967-70.

Fiorucci, headscarf bag in synthetic fibre, 1969-75. Now in the Fiorucci archives.

opened in Boston as well as one in Los Angeles.

Fiorucci's output grew in step with the increase in size of the company: over the space of ten years some 10,000 articles were designed for men, women and children, not counting the knitwear sector.[6] While design remained the responsibility of a team of people working within the company, manufacturing was largely carried out outside it, mostly by small firms and specialized workshops scattered throughout Italy. For some years after 1976, a certain amount of production was done abroad, especially in

pockets in front and behind and the "Bogotà." Apart from the classic denim, fabrics included corduroy in a variety of colours, cloth and cotton. Using the same fabrics, Fiorucci produced dungarees, shorts with a bib and overalls. These were accompanied by pinafores, in "pre-maman" style, skirts, coats, jackets and cloaks, made not only out of fabrics but also out of synthetic materials, plastic and the like.

As well as actual garments, Fiorucci continued to turn out its own accessories, often reinterpreting objects of everyday use in un-

Studio 54 in New York or the festival at Paris's Beaubourg. Milan saw the walls of the shop in Galleria Passarella decorated by Keith Haring in a live performance.

"Equipe '84"

Yet another case is that of the "Equipe '84" chain of stores. These emerged out of a company, the "Equipe 84 Saloon," that was set up on the initiative of Bruno Manturini and Pierre Farri, agent of Equipe 84, the most famous of beat groups in the sixties.[9] The idea was to

Fiorucci, Buffalo model jeans, 1974,
Panama, 1975, Montreal, 1975 and Bogotà,
1975. Now in the Fiorucci archives.

utilize the image of the music group to distribute clothes, 80% of which were produced by a clothing manufacturer at Trecate (Novara) owned by one of the major shareholders in the company, Signor Ferruta. Hence in 1966 the "Drogheria Solferino – Equipe 84 Bazaar"[10] opened in Milan, to be joined between 1968 and 1974 by another five shops in Milan and, thirty-eight throughout Italy, on the franchising system. The music group took part in the inaugurations, guaranteeing immediate attention from those organs of the press read by the public that the boutiques hoped to attract. The production, mainly of men's wear, had an avant-garde image connected to the transgressions of style typical of Equipe 84: shirts made out of dishcloth material, lace, transparent fabric, damask satin, Nehru jackets, ponchos, high boots, leather jackets, knapsacks and hippy necklaces. But the major part of the output, behind this facade, was in reality made up of much more conventional garments, although they were characterized by a style that was very much up-to-date.

As in the other cases that we have examined, the décor of the shops played a very important role as far as image was concerned. The Drogheria Solferino had mining trolleys painted in different colours that ran around an old-fashioned cash-desk at the centre of the shop. Concealed beneath the brightly coloured and striped carpet were switches that regulated the lights and music when trodden on. The walls were decorated with pieces of furniture inserted in relief; bits of a bedroom, drawers, cupboard doors. It is interesting that "Equipe 84" tended to use premises that had previously been occupied by quite different sorts of activity for its stores: a grocery in Milan, a confectioner's in Vigevano, a butcher's somewhere else. The characteristic features of the original premises were often retained. This was combined with an open-minded and amusing use of salvage materials such as mirrors, barber's chairs, doorways and even laboratories in the case of the shop in Viareggio. Franco Marabelli, responsible for the decorations until he went to work for Fiorucci, came up with his designs in a spirit of experimentation and fun. The accord with the music group lasted until 1974, large-scale production until 1976. Thereafter distribution on behalf of third parties prevailed and the image of the shop gradually changed.

Other Centres of "Anti-Fashion"

Other vehicles for "anti-fashion" to which young people with limited financial resources could turn were the numerous department stores that proliferated in Milan during the sixties. They sold jeans, pullovers and imported or American-style sports jackets, in the most popular colours and materials. Sales structures were kept to a minimum, often using basements or premises previously used as stores or warehouses. They were usually run by families or with a minimal staff; purchase was on a self-service basis, changing-rooms improvised and

Fiorucci, baseball shoe in cotton, synthetic material and plastic, gold with black trim, 1969-75, and sandal with gold-painted leather wedge, 1977. Now in the Fiorucci archives.

the available space exploited to the maximum. All this made it possible to reduce costs to levels that had previously been considered unthinkable, thereby helping the new style of dress to spread to broader and broader sections of the younger generations.

The open-air markets (the Fiera di Sinigaglia) and secondhand clothing and military surplus stores marked yet another step in the direction of an increasingly economic and "casual" way of dressing. Towards the end of the sixties, the

where practicality was far more significant than aesthetics: fabrics were not very attractive and often heavy; garments were almost always two or three sizes too big for their wearer and were worn by men or women. This was the true "anti-fashion," which did away with the criteria on which people have always based their choice of clothing. When this extreme phase was over, it left behind it a number of changes in the attitude of the younger generations towards clothing. A myriad of small shops sold clothes

1. "Adriana" at Via della Spiga, no. 22.
2. The name "Gulp" is taken from the interjection commonly used in comic-strips.
3. Elio Fiorucci in an interview, *Playboy*, February 1975.
4. The shop in Via Torino remained open until 1979.
5. In Brompton Road, Kensington, and in Bond Street, two strategic points for shopping in London.
6. The paper patterns for all the creations produced after 1974 are preserved at the San Donato offices of Fiorucci.
7. Elio Fiorucci in an interview, *Il Giorno*, July 17, 1975.
8. A few examples of bags and posters have gone on exhibition in a number of museums. The Victoria and Albert Museum of Canada has printed a postcard that reproduces one of Fiorucci's bags depicting a stylized television set.

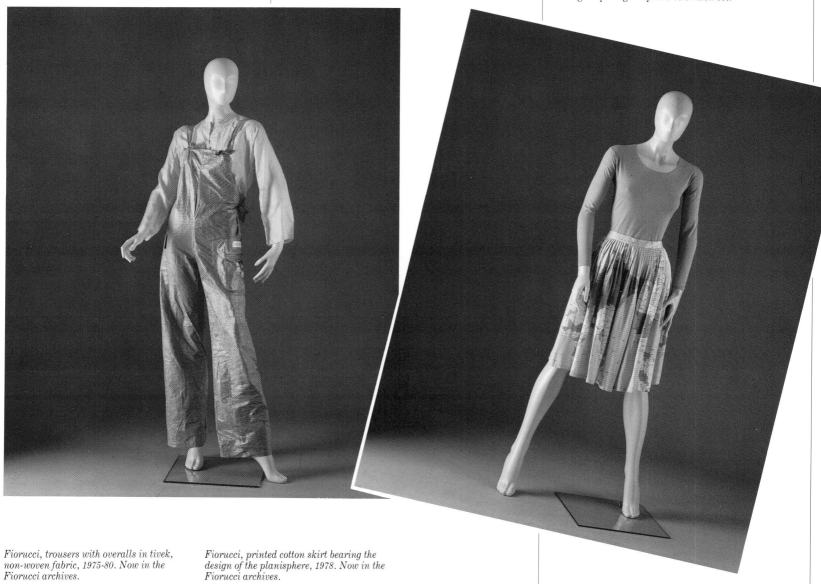

Fiorucci, trousers with overalls in tivek, non-woven fabric, 1975-80. Now in the Fiorucci archives.

Fiorucci, printed cotton skirt bearing the design of the planisphere, 1978. Now in the Fiorucci archives.

climate of politicization led to the freakish clothes which had caused such an upset only a few years earlier being regarded as frivolous and exhibitionistic, and the very young showed a growing tendency to dress in plain and practical clothes. Hence there was a gradual return to uniformity, to the uniform that showed at a glance that its wearer belonged to a homogeneous group. Young people drew on the imported stocks of discarded or obsolete military clothing. In general it was a style of dress

used by the "average American," especially jackets and coats, and this superabundant and comfortable style was diametrically opposed to the clinging and "sewn-on" forms characteristic of Italian clothing. It was out of just this new conception of forms and proportion that emerged during the eighties what came to be known throughout the world as "Italian Style." An important role in its final evolution was played by the few entrepreneurs who were the first to recognize the signs of a changing market.

9. Achieving success with Italian versions of celebrated songs by the Rolling Stones and other English groups and then with the songs of Lucio Battisti, they were famous for their extravagant look, similar to that of their Anglo-Saxon colleagues but with indigenous connotations, such as the "zampogna" or bagpipe-look.
10. At no. 1, Via Solferino.

Evening mini-dress in yellow silk crêpe-de-chine, with long, narrow sleeves of yellow voile and dyed ostrich feathers at the cuffs and neckline (circa 1963-68).

Model of close-fitting line, with a V-shaped neckline in front. Label: "Cose in via della Spiga," sewn inside the left hip. State of preservation: good. Measurements: shoulders 37 cm; waist 36 cm; hips 45 cm; length 85 cm. Owner: Luciana Crepax. *(A.G.R.)*

Ensemble made up of satiny large-knit maxi-dress and long satiny fine-knit waistcoat in a contrasting colour (1966-70). The closefitting dress has a round neckline and long narrow sleeves; both dress and waistcoat have whipstitching and borders in a contrasting colour. Label: "Ferange. Disegno di Nuccia Fattori," glued to inside of neckline at back. State of preservation: fair. Measurements of dress: shoulders 56 cm; waist 35 cm; hips 42 cm; maximum length 136 cm. Measurements of waistcoat: shoulders 47 cm; maximum length 127 cm. Owner: Nuccia Fattori. *(A.G.R.)*

Fiorucci

Jeans in cotton with embroidery in coloured cotton yarn depicting a meadow with poppies and butterflies (1968). The garment, one of the earliest produced by Fiorucci, has a very low waist with a slightly raised band and a vent in the rear. Label indicating the size "46" on the left hip. State of preservation: excellent. Measurements: waist 40 cm; hips 40 cm; maximum length 107 cm. Owner: Ottavia Bassetti. *(A.G.R.)*

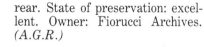

Hot pants in chamois-leather patchwork (1969-72), decorated with large flowers of coloured leather. Visible seams of cross-stitching made out of grey leather. Measurements: waist 30 cm; length 40 cm. Worn with a black T-shirt of cotton knit with short sleeves and V-shaped neckline, bearing the words "Andy Warhol's Interview" and "Fiorucci" in grey (1981).

The garment was produced on the occasion of Andy Warhol's participation in a festival organized by Fiorucci in New York in 1981. Label: "N. Camp. 2141. Data E.M. 5/4/81" glued onto inside of neck at rear. State of preservation: excellent. Owner: Fiorucci Archives. *(A.G.R.)*

Denim skirt with wool, satin, satin jersey and strass appliqués (1976). Model of straight cut, covering the knees; two slit pockets in front and two patch pockets behind; slit on left side. Label: "Fiorucci" on inside at back. Measurements: waist 34 cm; hips 43 cm; length 78 cm; length of slit 27 cm. It is worn with a satin top with appliqués of the same material in the shape of rockets and stars (1969-72). The garment is made out of a trapezium of fabric gathered at the neck by a satin lace that is tied at the rear. Label: "Style 041 Size. Exclusive of trim rn 20561." State of preservation: excellent. Measurements: longest side of the trapezium 42 cm; shortest side 27 cm; width 43 cm. Owner: Fiorucci Archives. *(A.G.R.)*

Gulp

Evening mini-dress in smooth purl yarn made up of 40% kid mohair, 40% virgin wool and 20% silver lurex. Slightly flared, without shoulder-straps and held up by three triangular pieces of perforated mirror at the front of the neckline and fastened by a chain that passes around the neck. The model was presented in 1966 at the fashion show staged in a boxing ring by the boutique Gulp. Label: "È di Gabriella Gulp. V. S. Spirito 14. Milano. Tel. 794903" glued onto inside of neck at back. State of preservation: excellent. Measurements: dress formed out of a trapezium, shortest side 34 cm, longest side 51 cm, width 62 cm. Owner: Gabriella Barassi. *(A.G.R.)*

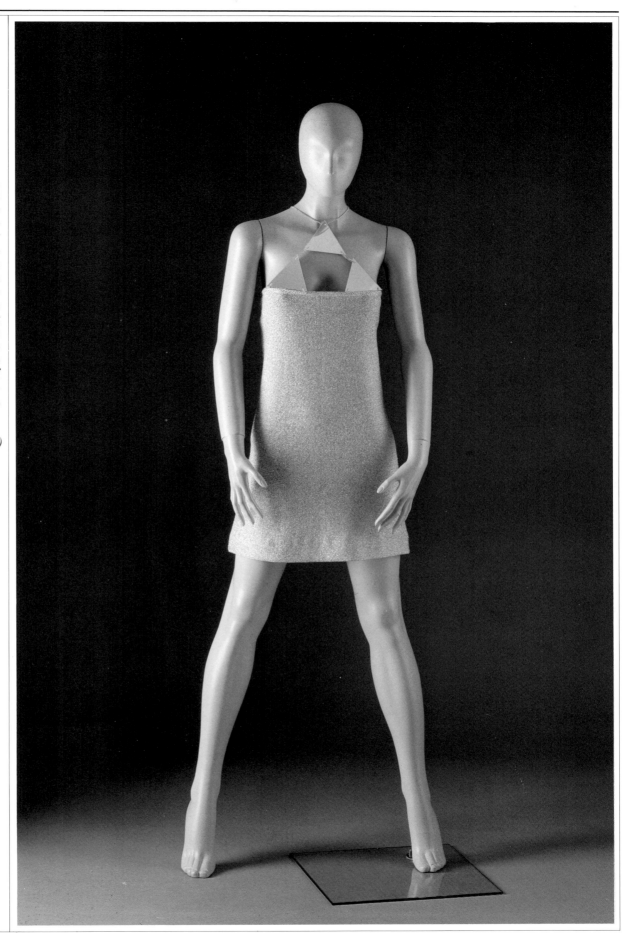

Evening mini-dress in black silk velvet embroidered with flowers (1967-70). Model with low-cut round neck, central pleat starting from the waist, long slightly gathered sleeves and high cuffs; a high black satin belt at the waist with silver buckle. Zip fastener at mid-back. Label: "Gulp. al 16 di V. S. Spirito. Milano" and "42" sewn to inside of neck at back. State of preservation: excellent. Measurements: shoulders 33 cm; waist 30 cm; hips 40 cm; maximum length 88 cm; maximum width 96 cm. Owner: Luciana Crepax. *(A.G.R.)*

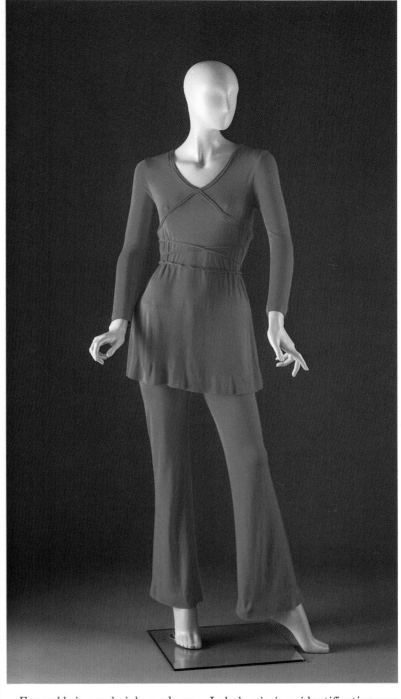

Evening mini-dress in two shades of pink and green, smooth purl yarn made up of 40% kid mohair, 40% virgin wool and 20% coloured lurex (1966). The dress, slightly flared in shape, is supported by shoulder straps fastened with metal clasps. The same model, with minimal variations, was made by Missoni during the same period. Label: "È di Gabriella Gulp. V. S. Spirito 14. Milano. Tel. 791903" glued to inside of neck at back. State of preservation: excellent. Measurements: waist 38 cm; hips 42 cm; width at shoulder 5 cm; length shoulder 15 cm; maximum length 87 cm. *(A.G.R.)*

Ensemble in coral pink, made up of bush-shirt and trousers, in synthetic jersey. The bush-shirt is long, with long and narrow sleeves and a V-neck in front; a raised trim applied to the neckline continues below the bust, from where commence two laces which, wound several times around the body, gather the bush-shirt; zip fastener at mid-back. Long slightly flared trousers, with elastic at the waist. The outfit presumably dates from 1970, the date when similar garments appeared in the magazines. Label: missing, identification was based on information supplied by the owner and on recognition by Gabriella of Gulp. State of preservation: good. Measurements of bush-shirt: shoulders 35 cm; maximum length 78 cm. Measurements of trousers: maximum length 94 cm. Total maximum length 141 cm. Owner: Luisa Gnecchi Ruscone. *(A.G.R.)*

STYLISM
IN WOMEN'S FASHION

Enrica Morini, Nicoletta Bocca

Transformation of a Model of Production:
The Sixties

The case of Max Mara is emblematic of one fact: the simple solution to a crisis of identity lies in the utilization of a stylist, in other words a personality who puts into effect an ideational process capable of transforming a product or, more precisely, capable of changing the relationship between product and market. But the solution is only apparently a simple one. In point of fact, something was invented over the course of the sixties that did not previously exist and that was to totally transform the productive sector of the clothing trade.

Up until that time there had been essentially two channels for the production of fashion and clothing in Italy: haute couture and the garment industry, based on a traditional and engrained division of society and the market.

Haute couture, in which the knowledge of highly skilled craftsmen is placed at the service of an object that tends to stray into the realms of art, was directed at a small élite destined, by its social role,[1] to *make fashion*. Its influence spread to all strata of society through a network of dressmakers – and stores selling fabrics and clothing accessories – that drew on the original source through fashion sketches and the specialized magazines.

The garment industry, on the other hand, was not concerned with making fashion: its logic was the strictly industrial one of the production of goods, and therefore of the factory and of standardized manufacturing. Hence the product tended to be fairly immutable, or at least subject, in its changes, to the criteria of rationalization and optimization of the manufacturing process. This type of clothing was aimed at a medium to low level of the market, unaffected by the influence of fashion, almost as if it was still concerned with satisfying those physiological demands which Maslow places at the first stage of human necessities.[2]

A third channel did exist, more akin to the first than to the second in its prices and exclusiveness. This was the luxury boutique. A special channel that had its origins in the distribution of refined accessories, of high quality and produced by wellknown names, that were intended to accompany articles of high fashion and were largely aimed at an international market.[3] Here too what counted was the high level of craftsmanship, but with a difference from that of haute couture: the object was not a "one-off piece" created for the client, but could

Faye Dunaway wearing a Krizia outfit, in Life, *January 12, 1968.*

be reproduced and so have a market.

It was on the basis of this logic that the first articles of clothing were produced to be distributed through the same system and to accompany accessories that were so successful as to become marks of high fashion in themselves. Roberta di Camerino took this road: the printed *tromp l'oeil* that had been characteristic first of her bags and then of her headscarves and umbrellas was turned into clothing. With everything done by hand, lengths of jersey fabric were printed one at a time to ensure highly accurate reproduction of the colours and then used to make up extremely simple and linear garments, without any hint of fashion in their cut.[4] The distribution network was made up of exclusive or quality boutiques that sold every line of Roberta di Camerino products, so that the article of clothing took its place as a complement to and completion of other fashion articles that had already risen to the level of status symbols.

All this worked up until the sixties. But this decade was to see a change that, at first imperceptibly and then in literally riotous fashion, was to affect the entire social sphere.

Patterns of living that derived from the class divisions of the capitalist system, or whose roots extended as deep as the old peasant world, were thrown into crisis and brought down one after the other.[5] While in industrial society the object, the product, had served as the focus of desires and of meanings, in the new model, which was based on services and not on things, the object as such tended to be neglected in favour of the psychological need and the identification of the individual, and identification for which the object could become instrument, fetish or variable mask.

A typical example was cited by Toffler:[6] in 1959 Mattel Inc. launched a new type of doll on the market: Barbie. Within the space of ten years over twelve million of these dolls had been sold throughout the world, a figure which by itself gives some idea of what is meant by the concept of mass society. But at the end of the seventies Mattel announced the appearance of a new improved Barbie. However the novelty lay not in this, but in the promotion that the company came up with at the time of the doll's launch: "for the first time, every girl who wishes to purchase a new Barbie will be given a discount against return of the old one."

At first sight this might be seen as the solution to a simple problem of increased production. But closer examination reveals it to have totally revolutionary aspects: in the first place the introduction of a new product that is designed to fulfill a desire, a demand that does not belong to the realm of necessity, but to that of individual fantasy. The target is a child who already has a doll, and what is more the same type of doll, to whom an improvement is offered: a realistic appearance which can facilitate play or bring about a more immediate sense of identification. In the second place a

problem of supplying primary necessities, which always come down to the same thing, and was able to give free rein to psychological factors and take up the cry of "up with fantasy."

This kind of model was addressed to a particular section of society, which was used as an unconscious and unwitting *prophet*: the young. An easily identifiable social stratum, continually forgotten by industrial society, far better educated than it had ever been in the past and

fashion, mainly in Britain and France, aimed *exclusively* at the young. An alternative market to the traditional ones had been born, but it had no structures as yet.[7]

And above all, while the garment industry sought an unlikely salvation by establishing ties with haute couture or by the pretence of a privileged market for products devoid of character, the clash between the self-determination of social behaviour and the 19th-century rules of the industrial system grew increasingly fierce

Gianni Berengo Gardin, the Pirovano boutique on Via Montenapoleone in Milan (1970), in L'occhio di Milano. 48 fotografi 1945/1977, *exhibition catalogue, Milan, n.d.*

new *philosophy* is taken for granted: that of the surpassing and cancellation of the past and of memory. The desire is in the present and must be satisfied in the present; yesterday is the past to be thrown away, tomorrow will be a present with *new* needs and *new* desires to be satisfied. And the way to identify them in real time is to transform them into images, it matters not whether they are mythical or fetishistic ones. Yet all this was possible because the western world of the sixties had overcome the

with a culture instilled in the schools – and therefore decidedly more homogeneous than the kind of knowledge derived from experience – and by definition open to the new because it is less burdened with memories of the past.

The Time of Fashion

The world of fashion suddenly found itself confronted by a youth culture that clashed with the adult world, especially in its choice of image and responded by creating a boutique-based

and implacable. The familiarity of the class struggle was replaced by the centrality of movements created and led by a diversity of groups; groups that were asserting their independence and uniting for uncommon purposes: young people, women, hippies, peace in Vietnam, India, drugs, etc.[8]

The traditionally recognizable character of dress was overthrown: no longer could it be divided into that of the élite, the 2nd division and the need to cover oneself, to which categor-

Fashion boutique designed by Silvano Malta for Marina Lante delle Rovere, in Il genio antipatico, *Mondadori, Milan 1984.*

ies had been added that of the young. The consequence of this *addition* had been to throw all the patterns into confusion.

But the fashion system was not capable of supplying the new individuals in society or the groups with which they identified with the articles of clothing for these costumes; it was not in a position to *control* the patterns of change and therefore to respond to needs and desires in time. Especially if one takes into account the fact that this *time* had been enormously reduced.

There had been a sudden shift from a time which used as a category the useful value of the article (different time and use for haute couture and for the garment trade) to a present time based on psychological, cultural and aesthetic factors and therefore on image.[9]

Neither the manufacturers – shackled to factories that were too large to permit rapid changes – nor haute couture – inevitably tied to traditional social models – were able to respond to this need. Instead it was the market that responded: stores were set up at a frantic speed to sell not only French and British prêt-à-porter, but second-hand clothes and folk dress imported from its country of origin: the response to an incredible demand which had not been foreseen by manufacturers was a supply that inevitably underlined the logic of fancy dress.

It was against this background that the Italian production system took a qualitative leap forwards: in parallel with a garment industry that was going under or hanging on desperately in the hope of a last-minute reprieve and a haute couture that was looking on helplessly as its own influence went into drastic decline, something new was on the move. A few boutiques started to produce items especially designed to be sold under their own trademark, and at the same time small companies were set up or adapted to specialize in the production of prêt-à-porter.

The Stylist

At this point the figure of the stylist puts in its appearance. His function was fixed from the start: it was not to be confused with that of the couturier of high fashion or with that of the director of a company manufacturing garments. He did not create clothing for a client, but had to decide who were going to be his clients, in other words the market at which he was aiming. He did not run the company, but had to be familiar with its limits and its production capacities, if only so as to be able to suggest how to get over them. He had to make use of manufactured materials and accessories, but at the same time he must be able to intervene with specific requests so as not to go on turning out the same old stuff as the rest of the industry.

What was introduced with this figure was a new *point of view* that permitted a shift to a planned production in which the conception was matched both by the level of manufacturing and by the level of distribution.

The beginning was not an easy one, in part because, as always happens, all the models of production were present side by side – and with a relative importance that was a measure of the past and not of the future – and above all because this new kind of professional creator was not easy to find.

But if the industrial designer, notwithstanding the utopias of the twenties and thirties, was required to modify the form of objects in order

France. Even at the beginning of the sixties there were French stylists like Jean Baptiste Caumont working in Italy. The latter had recognized the great readiness for change inherent in the Italian production system and was putting out products under his own name and manufactured by a Venetian company, AMICA, which had accepted this arrangement in order to expand its own market.[11] Over the course of the decade, the inability of the French production system to allow a stren-

sional contract; a group of manufacturers, who are responsible for making the various components (ranging from fabrics to accessories) that make up the items of clothing; a distribution system, at the beginning based on individual contacts and sales backed up by events like the SAMIA or the fashion shows held in Palazzo Pitti and only later passing on to a more specific and efficient kind of organization; a market, whose values came to play an increasingly central role in the process of design, in that it now

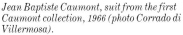

Jean Baptiste Caumont, suit from the first Caumont collection, 1966 (photo Corrado di Villermosa).

Laura Biagiotti, model from the 1973 Spring-Summer collection, drawing by Angelo Tarlazzi, in Harper's Bazaar Italia, *January-February 1973.*

to adapt them to new uses and thereby make industrial products more acceptable, the stylist had an entirely different task ahead of him: he had to devise an intellectual technology that would make it possible to hold together a system which embraced the stages of invention, decision, production and consumption.[10] A sort of ring that must not be broken.

Once the objective had been identified, however, its attainment could not be held up by a problem of resources. And the answer was

ghtening of the system of distribution through boutiques, which risked undermining the power of haute couture, encouraged French stylists like Karl Lagerfeld, Emanuelle Khahn, Christine Bailly and Graziella Fontana to come and work within the Italian system. The only true Italian stylist was Walter Albini, but even he had a Parisian apprenticeship behind him. So a system began to take shape involving a designer and creator, who proposes a line of models to a company to which he is bound by profes-

became the true objective to be attained through diversified solutions permitting a range of choice. Thus Italian fashion was born out of the union between stylists and a special kind of manufacturer – people like Mariuccia Mandelli (Krizia), Papini, Missoni, Maramotti (Max Mara) and Zanini (Lux), or like Billy Ballo and Cose, but also including Etro, Falconetto or all those who produced exclusive fabrics designed by stylists for their models.

But the new problem was that of getting at

the market in a systematic way, and above all taking into account the fact that the target was not an undifferentiated customer, but the one whose needs and psychological and cultural characteristics had been identified and selected at the moment the product was designed. This problem was solved at the outset in those cases where the buyer was a boutique with its own well-defined clientele, but was left completely open in others.

In those years Italy saw the birth of a varie-

of an organizational and cultural nature. Each "name" could parade with sixteen models and, what with the monotony of Italian production, instead of holding a championship of collections (which would have had the undoubted result of failing to show any difference between the manufacturers) the preference was for putting together a small ad hoc collection, as individual as possible. However this often had no connection with what was actually being produced. It was not, therefore, a particularly useful oc-

image of fashion.

Yet it was bound to be here, in or around this event, that the new figure began to assert itself and above all to demonstrate its function. In 1968 Albini was represented at Pitti by five collections for five different companies and, although they shared an unmistakable hallmark, it was evident that they were founded on five different basic ideas.[13] A situation that up until then had perhaps only been guessed at now began to reveal itself clearly: the creative

Jean Baptiste Caumont, two outfits from the 1973-74 Autumn-Winter collection.

Walter Albini, evening dress by Misterfox, 1973-74 Autumn-Winter collection, in Harper's Bazaar Italia, December 1973 (photo Bob Krieger).

ty of events set up for the presentation of prêt-à-porter (which included ready-made clothing produced both by the couturiers and by the garment industry) but the fashion show held twice a year at Palazzo Pitti remained the most important.

By now Florence was really behind the times. Apart from the formalism that accompanied the shows,[12] totally antediluvian when compared with the life styles that society was raising to the level of fashion, the problem was

casion for presenting the new, but one that tended, on the contrary, to favour the well-known and established names that in themselves constituted a guarantee with respect to what was not on show.

It was an outmoded event for another reason too: at a time when new social types were coming into the limelight, with new aesthetic requisites and new psychological needs, embracing a multitude of new highly diversified and fragmented markets, Pitti offered a uniform

process demanded of the stylist did not coincide with the work that had to be carried out by the company director or entrepreneur. The work of the former involved co-ordination of the chain and probably for just this reason he had to remain detached from all the stages specifically concerned with production or marketing. This need for the stylist to remain autonomous became all the more unequivocal when he was required to create a highly distinctive image, to introduce into the fashion product that culture which would coincide with a section of society, in such a way as to induce a need. This was all the more true since the linguistic elements necessary to the creation of an image no longer pertained to industrial production, but to the realm of the mass media. Entertainment, the visual arts, music, graphics and above all photography,[14] which mass society was recasting to suit its new needs, had to become the instruments of fashion too.

Palazzo Pitti, however, did not allow any of

The first thing to go was the *designated place*, and this was perfectly in keeping with a culture that had turned away from all the traditional locations.

In the same way hotels, cafés, clubs, restaurants and circuses began to be used as more or less neutral back-drops for fashion "events" in which the completeness of the fashion image was accompanied by a spectacular aspect intended to stay in the memory for the duration of a season and to become a mark

The Choice of Image

In 1971 *Vogue* published a small inquiry, interviewing around twenty fashion designers to whom five questions had been put.[16] When asked to outline the woman of that year, the couturiers of high fashion, both Italian and French, responded with a series of adjectives that were at bottom fairly common: different from what one sees in the streets, seductive, youthful; modern, even if classical, new. The designers of prêt-à-porter, on the other hand,

Cadette, outfit from the 1973-74 Autumn-Winter collection in Harper's Bazaar Italia, *October 1973 (photo Bob Krieger).*

this. Consequently, after a few attempts at an internal split, a breach was inevitable. On April 6 and 7, 1972, Albini, Cadette and Ken Scott staged a show in Milan. There is no doubt that Milan had become the centre of production for the new fashion and that it was therefore more convenient all round to take the buyers to the place where the showrooms were located, but it should not be forgotten that the shows were completely different from those held in Florence.

of recognition for the ultimate user of the clothing. This mark could be of various kinds: from Albini's camelias to Cinzia Ruggeri's avant-garde "happening," from the parties for singing journalists staged by Lux to the organizational accident transformed into spectacle so as to become a distinguishing feature.[15]

But the great innovation lay in the personification of differences. Each parade became a proposal, a choice of image and of style that was addressed to its *own* public.

almost always came up with a cultural reference, an image with which to identify, no matter if it were mythical or fetishistic. Along with Clocchiatti, who put forward the category of freedom, and Ossie Clark who spoke of individualism, Caumont evoked Wally Simpson, Krizia a kitsch-girl, a mockery of Marilyn Monroe, Lagerfeld the Hollywood style of the American dream, brought to life through the images of Donna Jordan and Jane Forth, and lastly Biba, the London boutique, which went back with almost academic precision to the style of 1938-1939.

And even this indicated the break-down of a pattern: fashion was no longer an imposition, but the proposal of solutions between which it was possible to make a choice, even if the choices had already been foreseen and canalized.

Haute couture neither knew how nor was able to make this leap.

Yet there was a cultural link between the seemed to mark the new generations, asked himself in amazement "for who knows what perfidious instinct for the unearthing of the ridiculous and the necrophilic, are young women... dressing up in the rags[17] that had made their grandmothers irresistible."

It is no coincidence that Marmori compared the appearance of people's clothing to an activity that looked as if it ought to be based on other factors: that of the exhibitions. In those days an exhibition entitled "Illustrators of "Years around 1925," and above all another exhibition on the "Fashions of the Crazy Years 1919-1929" staged at the Musée de la Mode et du Costume in 1970 had aroused the interest of all those who could provide pieces to go on show, flushed out of their hiding places in the trunks of mothers and grandmothers.

But it was the combination of old lace and modern mannequins that seemed to set off the kitsch game of revival: the same girls who until a day before had been dressing up as guerrillas

Walter Albini, drawing of the outfit in the following photo, 1971 (Luciano Papini collection).

Walter Albini, suit by Misterfox for Vogue Italia, *in* Vogue Italia, *May 1971 (photo Alfa Castaldi).*

proposals of the stylists: the revival. The past, rejected as a temporal category, became a land of conquest, an infinite theatre from which myths could be plundered. And the phenomenon was a far more profound one than can be conveyed in these brief notes.

L'Espresso of January 21, 1973, contained a colour supplement with the title "The Art of Dressing Badly." In it the same Giancarlo Marmori who three years earlier had commented on the growing desire for dressing-up which Fashions and Manners in 1925" had opened at the Galerie du Luxembourg. It was the last in a series that had started off with H. Guimard and then had moved on, first to Burne-Jones and the pre-Raphaelites, and then to Tamara de Lempicka, covering a whole range of refinements from the end of the 19th century up to the thirties. But the phenomenon was a much broader one, even as far as Paris alone was concerned: in 1966 the city's Musée des Arts Figuratives had held an exhibition on the or Berbers threw themselves into this new game. But in this one there were rules that fashion too could follow or impose, and the Italian stylists of those years concentrated almost exclusively on the twenties and thirties, neither preceding nor aping the cultural events and popular fads.[18] It was all absolutely simultaneous, as if these professional image-makers had really performed the miracle of an accord between production and society.

Partly as a result of their cultural back-

Gianpaolo Barbieri, portrait of Walter Albini.

Walter Albini, "flag" show at the Società del Giardino, 1972 Spring-Summer collection.

ground, Albini and Caumont became almost the symbol of this revival. But it changed its nature in their hands: gone was the playful aspect of dressing up in rags, replaced by the creation of atmosphere, style, the slightly ironic reanimation of a lost age, but one that was reassuring because familiar. And at bottom it also took on the aspect of the cultivated game of identification with a cosmopolitan, but élitist and refined society, a way of creating a bond of imagery between all those who thought they could escape standardization by making a cultural choice. The result, obviously, was the opposite of what was intended, but the illusion was to some extent a psychological deliverance.

The Case of Albini

When Albini returned from Paris in 1962, he found work in that sort of crucible of Italian fashion, *Krizia*, but the demand for professionals of his kind was growing and by 1964 he had already begun his collaborations and consultations with newly-formed companies and boutiques, or with ones that were undergoing total reorganisation.

Albini offered, apart from that French allure that was so in fashion in those years, an impeccable system of design. His drawings[19] were neither illustrative sketches nor technical drawings, but something which blended the qualities of both techniques. They have that capacity to assemble a total look in which the details become elements of atmosphere – with an obvious reference to the great fashion illustrators of the twenties and thirties[20] – but with all the elements necessary for the manufacture of the garment clearly indicated. And all this always in a single drawing, as if the sheet of paper itself was the visual expression of a total co-ordination of all the parts involved in the production of that item, with that image, for that clientele. By 1967/1968 Albini was already famous, at least among those in the field who were engaged in discovering and proposing something new. In October 1967, *Vogue Italia* picked him out from the young and successful designers of Italian fashion and devoted an editorial of six pages to the models he had created for Krizia, Cadette and Billy Ballo. In the lengthy captions to these illustrations he was described as a stylist who had chosen prêt-à-porter for reasons that lay outside the specific language of fashion, "because it goes out to meet life, because it is for all women and helps them not to renounce – a beautiful trip for a dress, for example."[21]

The perspective had changed. Albini did not feel he had to impose a fashion; he proposed a style, many styles for all women, in a sort of creative generosity bursting with experimentation and enthusiasm. It was during these years that he encountered Luciano Papini, another *new* personality in search of a place in the fashion market. A few years earlier, in fact, Papini had set up a small clothing company and had been selling – almost door to door – to a

Walter Albini, evening model from the
fashion show at Caffè Florian, 1973-74
Autumn-Winter collection, in Vogue Italia,
October 1973 (photo Barry Lategan).

distribution network that was practically non-existent, but which rapidly took shape as if by magic.[22] The fact that he was not part of the industrial establishment permitted him a remarkable degree of flexibility and above all the chance to look for a role of his own outside the already established ones, free from the presumption of being able to go it alone.

The realization came to him at a Billy Ballo fashion show in which Albini's clothes were presented in a totally unusual manner: in a

were replaced by an indiscriminate mixture of mini- and maxi-skirts and by a completely different approach to dress. The clientele that Papini had laboriously built up was "horrified," but it was quickly replaced by the network of specialized boutiques that was being established during that period; boutiques run by people aged between 25 and 30 – little older than their customers – and for this reason more capable of grasping and complying with the desires of the new markets.

tled on was for the artist to remain freelance, a choice in which Papini assumed the function of the agent who sorted and checked the offers and drew up the contracts, standing firm on the model: payments had to be proportionate to the professional service, but not linked to profits. On the one hand this guaranteed the stylist a recompense independent of the commercial success of the collection and on a time-scale more in keeping with the kind of service he offered, but on the other it did not lay the foundations for

Antonio Lopez, advertising campaign for Missoni, 1983-84 Autumn-Winter collection, in Donna, *September 1983.*

Antonio Lopez and Silvano Malta, collage design for the 1974-75 Autumn-Winter collection by Silvano Malta for PIMS.

hotel room – into which the audience was packed and jammed together, as if to underline the difference and the lack of connection with the formality of the Sala Bianca in Palazzo Pitti – with barefoot and dishevelled models made up in absurd ways. Over the next few days Papini tracked Albini down and managed to make an agreement with him to produce a collection for his line, "Mireika." The result of the show held at the SAMIA was to transform its image overnight: rigid garments full of darts and tucks

The collaboration between entrepreneur and stylist was a fruitful one. But for this very reason the problem arose of defining and rationalizing the relationship between one part that played a stable, fixed and recognizable role and another that was characterized as changeable, elusive and unfettered. The problem was how to give a status to an intellectual profession that, in its generosity, ran the risk of inflating itself and even throwing itself into disrepute in potentially negative relations. The solution set-

any continuity in his image. All the more so since the contracts almost always excluded any mention of the designer's name on the label.[23]

Yet the continuity of the *Albini style* had to be bound up with the line produced by Papini, a line which was destined to go through a rapid and tumultuous process of evolution. It was not long, in fact, before the Ente Moda invited Papini to take part in the Florence fashion show. This was his official entry into the world of prêt-à-porter and for the occasion he decided on the creation of a new image, in keeping with the new status. The collection, given the name "Misterfox" which had been suggested for it by Anna Piaggi, went on show at the Palazzo Pitti in the spring of 1969, with the regulation sixteen outfits. Eight of them were black and entitled the "widows" and the other eight flesh-coloured and referred to as the "brides." On top of all this came a cultured reference: the twenties.

The show was an enormous success, both on the spot and subsequently in the press, but the certainty of the outcome all came afterwards. Until a few days before Albini and Anna Piaggi – and therefore two people with the most reliable points of view for predicting the reactions of the public – had expressed doubts about the acceptability of a proposal of this kind which, while it took up the stimuli of an international cultural choice, transformed them into something that, apart from putting the skills of the industry (fabrics, cut, embroidering, etc.) to the test, had the characteristics of the cultivated look, refined, rarefied and rich in irony and atmosphere. A model of identity that fell outside the canons of the cult of youth and that was aimed at a new section of the market, one that was assumed to be more open to the tricks of elegance than to the game of dressing-up.

It was in the light of the collection's success that the outdatedness of Palazzo Pitti was revealed in full: out of the whole collection, which comprised some sixty items of clothing, almost the only ones to be sold were the sixteen that went on show. And in a totally abnormal manner: Misterfox received orders to the tune of 948 million lire. They managed to deliver 50 million's worth. But quite apart from this, which was in any case a factor of no small concern: the manufacturers of new fashions found themselves increasingly constrained in a structure that obliged them to create an image for all the others who were unable to get out of the impasse between garment industry and haute couture.

Papini and Albini began to look for alternative solutions. It was Massimini that came up with the answer: the future of fashion lay outside the limitations of Palazzo Pitti and above all the problems and interests that came to a head in that location. The future could only be Milan, combined with a totally new technique of presentation that still had to be worked out.

But there were many difficulties that had to be overcome. The first were of an organizational character, ranging from the involvement of specialized sections of the public – and in particular that of the fashion reporters – to making the best use of locations that lacked any tradition and consequently the appropriate facilities as well. The second were of a structural nature: it was not possible to keep a hold on the market with a single line of garments. It was absolutely necessary to present a complete collection – and Misterfox was only capable of producing dresses – and to be able to count on an efficient

Aldo Fallai, advertising campaign for Armani, 1982-83 Autumn-Winter collection (model Angela Wilde).

Basile, evening dress from the 1979-80
Autumn-Winter collection worn by Lauren
Hutton (photo Irving Penn).

distribution system. Out of this developed the contact with Ferrante, Tositti and Monti who, under the acronym FTM, had devised a new pattern of distribution in Italy and who were also backing it up by the transformation, support and even take-over of those companies that were essential to the production of fashion.

In April 1970 an interminable fashion parade was held at the Circolo del Giardino, involving 177 outfits. This was a revolution in itself, but more importantly the agreement with FTM had led to the collaboration of five firms with different specialities in the manufacture of Albini's collection:[24] Misterfox for the dresses and especially the evening wear, Basile for jackets and trousers, Callaghan for jersey, Escargots for knitwear and Diamant's – soon to be replaced by Sportfox – for blouses.[25] Along with these, FTM took care of distribution.[26]

In this way the roles took on clearer shape and the differences emerged between stages of production and those concerned with coordination and linkage. And the figure of the stylist began to acquire value as an image to be added to that of the collection. Since he was offering concrete models for identification and proposing life styles identifiable as his own cultural choice, he himself became a personality to put forward as a choice.[27] The labels on the clothing in the three collections produced by these five companies confirmed this by stating that the garment was by *Walter Albini for…*, followed by the name of the manufacturer. Towards the end of 1972 the alliance broke up, probably in a fairly tempestuous manner. Albini and Papini found themselves alone again and facing a set of problems they thought had been solved. Hence they concentrated on the only real resource available to them: the skill of the stylist and his name.

On April 27, 1973, a company was set up in front of a notary public under the name Albini s.r.l., with Albini and Papini as the sole partners. The aim of the company was "the creation and distribution of high fashion garments, articles of clothing and various allied wares under the regularly filed trade-mark W.A."[28] and would confirm them on the road they had already taken. On December 18 of the previous year, in fact, Albini had held a fashion show at Blokes Hotel in London, with the backing of Brown's, in which the collection of clothes bore exclusively his name. The initiative arose out of yet another innovative decision, that of transforming Misterfox into a second line to be marketed alongside a main line, the WA, of very high quality – and prices that would be described as astronomical. The latter was intended above all to establish the image of the Italian designer definitively and to open up the doors for him onto that international market which was by this time looking at Italy with interest.

The show in London, however, was a rather strange one. In the first place it had been very restrained and only skirts and dresses had been presented – the jackets and coats were replaced by blouses. Secondly it had been held at a

Cinzia Ruggeri, drawings for the advertising campaign of the 1985 Spring-Summer collection, in Donna, *March 1985.*

Armani's androgynous image, in Donna, March 1984 (photo Fabrizio Ferri, model Isabella Rossellini).

Giorgio Armani, cover-story, in Time, April 5, 1982 (photo Bob Krieger).

Advertising mural for the Emporio Armani, 1986 Spring-Summer season (from a photo by Aldo Fallai; photo Vedovello).

decidedly late date with respect to the time required for manufacture of the clothing and finally the garments did not bear the label WA, but still that of *Walter Albini for*, even if the name of the company was missing.[29] This leads one to think that it was a solution adopted to get over the earthquake that must have followed the split with FTM, and that the initiative was deliberately staged outside the normal channels in order to emphasize the aspects of promotion and image. Yet it was a resounding success and

never have bought ready-made clothing before. A style that was based on an incredibly high level of professionalism, but it also involved the personal charm that Albini seemed to place at the service of the building and perfecting of a charismatic image, until he himself, and his life style, became the basis on which his output was judged.

It is no coincidence that stylistic perfection became more and more the characteristic feature of his models, which not only were minutely

this highly expensive publicity campaign, while the possibility of earning "royalties," i.e. an income from the trade-mark itself, did not yet exist.

The company so recently set up with Papini founded as a result of a clash between the partners over strategic decisions and Albini went it alone in a venture that, failing to evoke a response from his market, marked the end of his upward climb.

In the autumn of 1974 he put a collection of

Romeo Gigli, skirt from the 1986 Spring-Summer collection in Elle *(American edition), February 1986 (photo Oliviero Toscani).*

the following year, in May, "everybody who counts" had their eyes on Albini's show at the Caffè Florian in Venice, closed for a day with the permission of the Ministry of the Interior. By this time all the elements of the myth were present[30] and Albini's name was beginning to be heard outside the confines of the fashion world. The secret? "In one word: Style. Elegant, exciting, inimitable: Style." A style built on prê-à-porter, but capable of getting it into the most exclusive stores, to be sold to people who would

studied in all their details, including accessories, but which were only sold as complete outfits, that is, with all the items and accessories with which they were presented at the fashion parade or in the design. It was the apotheosis of the total image, of the life style transformed into a finished work of art. Here too the press took the hint and began to compare Albini to the Great Gatsby.

But probably the time was not right yet, the proceeds from Misterfox were insufficient for

haute couture on show in Rome, perhaps in an attempt to give a final touch to his image of stylistic perfection.

But, in spite of the beauty of the clothes and the cultural depth of his "Homage to Chanel," the high fashion market closed its doors on him and he was left with no alternative but to recommence his collaboration with clothing companies. But these had none of the productive skills and flexibility of the ones he had worked with before.[31] *E.M.*

*Byblos, model from the 1986 Spring-Summer
collection, designer Keith Varthy (photo
Pamela Hanson).*

From the Anonymity of the Stylist to the Anonymity of the Industry

After a further defection from Palazzo Pitti, other fashion houses began to hold their shows in hotels, restaurants and private clubs in Milan in October 1974.

Many more names were present than in 1972, especially those of Krizia and Missoni, two names that really counted and that were sufficient to tip the balance and definitively shift the centre of interest of Milan. It was not just

acceptance of the shortcomings of French glamour,[33] but also derived from feelings of guilt with regard to Palazzo Pitti, abandoned with the promise that they did not wish to play more than a small part in the overall game.

1974 was a decisive year, above all because the crisis in the sector that had emerged in 1973-74 as a consequence of the rise in oil prices presented a serious threat and cried out for a solution. This drove many middle-sized and large companies to the realization that the

was a solid one and if the person who served as an intermediary between the stylist and the company knew what he was doing.[35] With one eye to the trail-blazing example of Cadette[36] and the other to the FTM group, and following the example of a relationship between manufacturer and stylist that did not involve too many risks, nor much glory either, a company based in Ancona that had been producing a line of mostly formal clothing since 1961 set off down the same road. This was Genny, a firm owned

Basile, model from the 1974-75 Autumn-Winter collection, designer Muriel Grateau, worn by Eva Malestrom, in Harper's Bazaar Italia, December 1974 (photo Bob Krieger).

Lino Lopinto, folk quilt, in Harper's Bazaar Italia, July-August 1976 (photo Bob Krieger).

that they were bigger companies than the small-scale manufacturers who had moved their shows in 1972, but also that they were well-known names in the history of fashion. The Missonis, for instance, had won the Neiman Marcus award in 1973.[32]

Perhaps there was not yet a conscious awareness of the possibility of a new image, but it appears in any case that the idea of Milan with a fashion of its own linked to industriousness and efficiency had its origins not only in an

transition from the philosophy of production to that of the product carried by its image was a fundamental one. The change was already in the air but only the small companies had had the flexibility and perhaps the foolhardiness to take the risk. A convincing example had been provided by the FTM group which, finding itself in a situation where the risk of stylism was the only course available,[34] had shown how it was possible to survive the loss of the stylist if the choice of market and image to be pursued

by the Signori Girombelli. It was destined to launch the career of the stylist Gianni Versace and to become one of the most visible companies in the panorama of fashion presented by magazines in the sector during the second half of the seventies.

Monti, who was working for Callaghan, had with him the young Versace as a replacement for Albini, in his first experience of working with a company. He "shared" him with Genny, which was in need of a stylist.

capelli corti, trucco deciso, abito maschile

UN NUOVO TIPO DI DONNA UN TIPO ARMANI

Capita, a volte, che una top-model abbia la fortuna e l'intelligenza di avere la faccia giusta per la moda del momento. È quel che è successo a Leslie Winer, newyorkese diciannovenne, protagonista di questo servizio. Ha deciso di tagliarsi i capelli perché «suonavo il basso elettrico in un complesso rock e tutti i ragazzi del gruppo erano pettinati così». Per il taglio si è rivolta a Jean Louis David, e da allora è richiestissima. Le piace vestirsi da maschio: sa che così può far paura a molti uomini ma la cosa non la preoccupa perché, dice, «mi piace un solo tipo d'uomo: quello, appunto, a cui non faccio paura».

Soprattutto le sono piaciuti questi vestiti d'Armani: ne hanno valorizzato il tipo, tirato fuori la personalità. «La donna '81 - dice Giorgio Armani - ormai libera dagli schemi, da un lato quello di dover assumere un atteggiamento, anche estetico, poco frivolo, 'impegnato', per farsi prendere sul serio, e dall'altro quello più tradizionale della donna-oggetto, è ora più libera di vestirsi come vuole, usando i vestiti come si usa qualsiasi mezzo di comunicazione, come espressione di se stessa, non più intralciata da regole inflessibili: sia poi questa un'espressione di comodità, di modernità, di sessualità».

In effetti questo tipo di donna corrisponde in pieno a una tipologia che sta avendo successo in molti campi: nell'estetica (tutte le top-model hanno ora i capelli cortissimi), nello spettacolo (le più applaudite show-girl sono dei tipi facilmente assimilabili a quello fotografato qui), nell'attuale concetto di femminilità (abiti e atteggiamenti maschili per le donne fanno ormai parte del nostro bagaglio culturale e hanno sostituito nella moda il concetto di pin-up rilanciata qualche anno fa).

speciale il lancio del mese

Queste giacche pantaloni camicie della nuova collezione di Armani sembrano ricalcare il modello classico maschile, ma ne hanno in realtà solo l'immagine, perché sono pieni di dettagli nuovi, anche femminili, molto interessanti come costruzione e come linea. «I particolari più importanti - spiega ancora Armani - sono le spalle arrotondate da un taglio a kimono alto, lo sfondo piega laterale nei pantaloni, le camicie col collo. La linea è essenziale ma morbida, in un gioco continuo di contrapposizioni».

G.B. e N.G.

Giacca in pesante lana tweed (Rivertex) gigante con maniche a kimono, pantaloni di covercoat (Housaumaan) con sfondo piega laterale. T-shirt di seta. Scarpe Lario per Armani.

Oliviero Toscani, the new Giorgio Armani woman, in Donna, *July-August 1980 (model Leslie Winner).*

The somewhat paternalistic attitude with which Monti still speaks today of this sharing was also a sign that a relationship between stylist and manufacturer such as the one that had been established by Albini only a few seasons previously was still far from being accepted. Both stylists and industrialists were afraid of such a relationship and it took another two or three years for the former to realize that their bargaining power and the moment were favourable for a policy based on personal image, and for the latter to see that, backed up by a careful policy of second lines, it was possible to take a risk whose consequences were still fresh in everyone's memory. Perhaps what was needed was the example of Giorgio Armani and the relationship he developed with the Gruppo Finanziario Tessile, although its particular form was to remain a unique case. Still around the middle of the seventies the GFT, in the person of Marco Rivetti the director of the women's wear sector, was on the lookout for someone who could modernize the structure of jacket and coats in the company's lines like Cori or Tris lady. The GFT did not want a stylist who would design a complete line with a consistent style and image of its own, but only someone with technical know-how in the field of cutting who would be able to transfer it to the company's existing system of manufacture. Inevitably Rivetti came to Giorgio Armani, whose experience in the manufacture of men's wear at Cerruti's Hitman made him without a doubt the best qualified man on the market, having always devoted his attention to heavy garments and to jackets in particular. What Rivetti wanted was a consultancy that would have no effect on the company's structure or its philosophy of production. Armani however, who had only left Cerruti a few years earlier at the urging of his friend and partner Sergio Galeotti, wanted something more. To go back to a relationship with which they were already familiar made no sense and Galeotti, who rather than a specific training[37] had an incredible nose for business, realized that there was no point in losing the opportunity by agreeing to a relationship of mere consultation. Instead he saw the possibility of doing something new with the backing of the large company. At Rivetti's request, Galeotti came up with a counterproposal: manufacture the Giorgio Armani line. After long months of discussion an accord was reached in 1977.

Naturally there were advantages for the GFT in the set-up, as it provided an indirect source of knowledge previously unavailable to the company: "A worker who had worked on one of Armani's jackets," recalls Rivetti, "instinctively made use of similar devices when making a Cori jacket later on. As time went by a variety of machines were added to the traditional structures of the large factory and it was learned how to make use of the basic ideas of the stylistic collections in the company's own lines."

Gianni Versace, evening dress for the
Complice Spring-Summer collection, in
Harper's Bazaar Italia, *May 1975 (photo Bob
Krieger, model Veruschka).*

*Gianni Versace, "Oriental" trousers from the
1981 Spring-Summer collection (photo
Richard Avedon).*

A lot of water had passed under the bridge since Caumont's contract with AMICA. As well as being a sign of interest on the part of major companies, the one between the GFT and Armani was also a more flexible kind of relationship that allowed for a degree of autonomy on both sides that bordered on the hazardous, with a very clear division of responsibilities. Unwilling to be entrepreneurs themselves, Armani and Galeotti felt that their stylistic studio[38] should be concerned with design,

and the help of good advisers. Things had also come a long way since the time when it was the aspiration of fashion designers to own their own factories, as had been the case with Ken Scott, the Missonis or Mariuccia Mandelli.

The crisis of the seventies undoubtedly played a determinant role in dissuading stylists from attempting to set up their own businesses, but a contributing factor was the fact that by this time the profession of stylist was a very precise one which could no longer be muddled

cussions: the key figure in this was the "products man," a figure capable of guaranteeing continuity of both product and image, avoiding those sudden seasonal shifts in fashion by which the industry was plagued, especially up until 1983. On the other hand the stylist, who grew more and more emancipated, leaving behind the company ties out of which he had emerged to move from the status of a mere designer of clothes under the orders of a boss who decided what should be made or copied, to

Gianpaolo Barbieri, the military look in the Complice advertising campaign, stylist Gianni Versace, 1978-79 Autumn-Winter collection.

image and also the relation with clients who came to make purchases during the fashion shows. Of course they also continued to work as consultants independently of the Group, not just for the manufacture of perfumes and scarves under license, but also for other lines of clothing at a medium and high level.[39] Three years after the breakdown of the relationship with Albini, the example of Armani indicated that a reliance on the name of the stylist could function if it was backed up by iron discipline

with that of the entrepreneur as it had been in the sixties.[40]

The case of the Girombelli group and that of Giorgio Armani, for all their distinctive features,[41] were the two models on which the relationship between stylist, industry and image was constructed at the end of the seventies. On one hand the company that relied primarily on its own lines aimed at a medium to high level of the market and on the possibility of changing stylists without disastrous reper-

that of an equal, with a division of roles within the company, eventually reaching a situation where his personal image overshadowed that of the company. Over the space of a decade the tables had been turned, going from the anonymity of the stylist to the anonymity of the industry. Apart from the extreme case, there was in any case the completely normal fact that people did not know how and where the products of Ferré, Versace, Moschino and many others were manufactured. Of course in a complex and highly dynamic situation each model tended to assume characteristics that were typical of the other, and so the companies that relied on their own lines ended up also producing prêt-à-porter designed by their stylists, allowing themselves to slip into the background. This was what happened with Basile and Soprani or with the Girombelli group that manufactured Montana's clothes while the latter has in turn been the designer of the Complice line since 1980. Alongside the lines sold

tion) decided to intervene on behalf of the Milan collections, with the aim of setting up other levels of production alongside the fashion shows that might be able to benefit from an eventual reflection of prestige. Beppe Modenese was given the task of carrying out this mediation between the needs of industry and those of the stylists. After a fruitless attempt to collaborate with those bodies already involved in staging the events,[42] he came to a direct agreement with those entrepreneurs like

how to turn what looked like a weakness into a strength and set his sights on the image of Milan as a link between fashion and industry, an image that would be decisive to the new way of seeing the profession in relation to design, at the beginning of the eighties. With the birth of *Milano Collezioni* the industry officially admitted that stylism was by now the dominant force in the sector. At the same time it launched a policy of synergism among industrial products of wider distribution that was materialized in

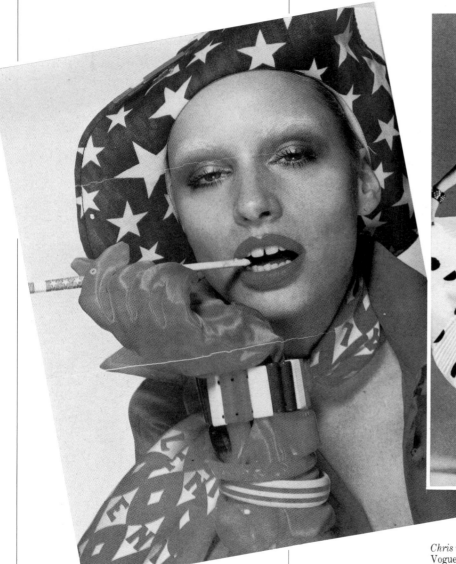

Chris von Wagenheim, Donna Jordan, in Vogue Italia, *May 1971.*

Luciano Soprani, Harlequin and Pierrot outfits from the 1982-83 Autumn-Winter collection (photo Francesco Scavullo).

under their own names, the stylists continued to design for the big name company lines, as with Soprani who designs for Basile or Versace who has maintained his links with Genny.

In 1978, by which time almost all the most important name brands were already in existence and the Milanese fashion world had settled into a fairly stable pattern, another significant development helped to strengthen prêt-à-porter: the Associazione Industriali dell'Abbigliamento (Clothing Manufacturers' Associa-

Monti, the Missonis or Mariuccia Mandelli who were open to the idea, since they had a better understanding than others of the function of such an operation.

The site chosen to bring all the shows together was that of the Fiera. As Ciampini recalls: "For those who were used to commuting between the Palace, the Permanente and the Manzoni, the idea of coming to the Fiera, associated in their minds with machine tools, was not a pleasant one."[43] But Modenese knew

the policy of differentiation between first and second lines and one of whose consequences would be that of contributing to the diaspora of some of the names that emerged out of Milano Collezioni between 1983 and 1985.

The relationship between primary and secondary lines is one of those that look as if they form a loop, but turn out instead to be an ever open and increasing spiral: the more industry saw that the image helped sales, the more weight it gave to it; the more weight it had, the more the line corresponding to this image had to be designed for and aimed at a higher level of the market; the more this happened, the smaller the market reached. The solution to this problem was to come up with a secondary line aimed at a wider market but on which the image of the primary line and its desirability would rub off. In order to avoid any possibility of confusion between the two lines, the first one had to differentiate itself still further and become even more elitist.

Armani entered on that spiral which would lead him within a short time to feel the need to create a line that would be distributed more widely and through a special system of sales outlets. This is the Emporio Armani line sold in shops that handle his clothes exclusively, in which all the merchandise is displayed as if in a sort of self-service market where everyone is invited to create his own combinations and his own Armani image. The idea works because the type of clothing proposed by Armani is de-

consequent loss of the symbolic value of the first line. The prices of the latter began to increase and its market to shrink still further.

In 1982, after the collection inspired by the film *Kagemusha*, Armani decided not to hold any more fashion shows. The extremely interesting collection which was a great success with the press and the buyers left the clientele he had built up highly perplexed and created a backlog of unsold goods. Armani was forced to rethink his relationship with industry and his

Helmut Newton, advertising campaign for the Gianni Versace, 1978-79 Autumn-Winter collection.

Following this circular pattern a number of stylists would end up by moving away from the Fiera, where the aseptic quality and uniformity of the setting did not permit sufficient individualization.[44]

Let us look at the case of Giorgio Armani again. Between 1978 and 1982 his personal fame grew, culminating in the cover story dedicated to him by *Time*, but also in breakdown in his relationship with the GFT and the creation of a different one with the same group. Thus

signed on the basis of a philosophy of interchangeability that falls outside the traditional canons of ritualized dress, but it also works because unlike many other secondary lines, the name, and therefore the image, of Armani is fully in evidence, with his symbolic crest, an initialled eaglet, a source of profits as well as of an infinite number of imitations.

However the ease with which the secondary line can be identified seemed to run the risk of confusing different levels of the market, with a

image, deciding to return to his origins as an industrial designer, a reality that could itself have the force of an image. In order to defend this image from the distribution of the Emporio on such a vast scale, he was obliged to turn to a highly restricted market. This had inevitable repercussions on his relations with the GFT. In 1983 the group drew up a new contract with the Giorgio Armani SpA: manufacturing of the top line, which would change its label by adding the address Via Borgonuovo 21 to the name, would be entrusted to a number of small companies with which Armani had been working for some time and which had no problem in producing a limited number of garments. It would be stretching things to go on calling them prêt-à-porter, even if the system of cutting and mechanisms of design remained the same. The group would take care of the manufacture and distribution of a secondary line given the name Giorgio Armani in the United States and Mani in Europe, where it comprised

the brand would be now. In terms of creativity and personal fame, this is a kind of suicide, but for the large industry it would mean a lower but more continuous flow of business."

An example of this process is provided by someone who had opened up the way for the idea of mass-produced designer clothing. In 1980 Giuliana Camerino began to dismantle her company Camerino Spa in order to create another, known as Camerino Band Diffusion, that would take care of management and distri-

handle the design of fabrics themselves, eschewing any cooperation with the cloth manufacturers' own designers. A stylist like Romeo Gigli, for whom the fabric represents a significant stage in the design process, due in part to a simplicity of cut that enhances it, handles the design of colours, fabric and printing for 60% of the materials he purchases. Correggiari even works with the yarn itself, while at a conference held at London's Victoria and Albert Museum in October 1985 Gianni Versace put it

635

KRIZIA
"FAMIGLIA HORROR"

KRIZIA
I VOLANTS SENZA LEZIOSAGGINI

Ingigantiti e sovrapposti, i volants di Krizia diventano molto più di un dettaglio: hanno la funzione di trasformare completamente i volumi dei tradizionali capi invernali – il cappotto, il blouson, l'abito – e di dare movimento anche ai tessuti pesanti. In vendita nelle boutiques Krizia di Milano e Roma, e da Raspini a Firenze. Orecchini Pellini Bijoux, cappelli Krizia, scarpe Andrea Pfister per Krizia, Poltrone Dalila da Cassina.

Mariuccia Mandelli, drawing of pleated jumpsuit by Krizia 1981-82 Autumn-Winter collection.

Mariuccia Mandelli, flounces from the Krizia, 1982-83 Autumn-Winter collection, in Donna, *July-August 1982 (photo Oliviero Toscani).*

women's wear exclusively. Armani's case is an example of the kind of situation in which almost all stylists now found themselves. Faced by this rapid trend towards a very up-scale and limited production, a kind of production that seemed to be turning into ready-to-wear high fashion, many industrialists like Rivetti find themselves perplexed: "I have worked on the name of Giorgio Armani in such a way that they are now close to turning it into a brand in America. The moment for making the shift to

bution of the Roberta di Camerino brand and work in partnership with the giant Japanese company Mitsubishi.

A vital link in the chain that has given birth to Italian fashion and to stylism has been the one connected with the manufacture and printing of fabrics. From the beginning of stylism to the present day the relationship between cloth manufacturers and stylists has evolved a long way from its origins in mutual collaboration. In fact today it appears that many stylistic studios

like this: "A good design starts out from the material. So I advise you to use your own fabrics."[45]

Gimno Etro on the other hand has handed the responsibility for dealing with stylists on to his son, and opened a clothing store in Via Bigli. There he sells highly classical garments made out of his own fabrics, in a sort of reversal of roles between stylist and cloth manufacturer.

In reality there has been no reversal of roles.

Genny, overcoat from the 1985-86 Autumn-Winter collection, designer Gianni Versace, in Donna, *September 1985 (photo Giovanni Gastel).*

In general the stylist asks for no more than modifications of the fabrics proposed to him by the manufacturers, and it is only at the printing stage that the intervention of the stylist becomes a predominant factor.

In the new view of fashion as a branch of design the fabric, as the material out of which the article of clothing is made, takes on a particular value. It is the object of a great deal of technological research, and it is this which determines the high cost of a product whose in-

dency that burst onto the scene between 1975 and 1977 was the fashion for outsize shirts and blouses. In the spring of 1975 this fashion, imported directly from Paris, had been a response to the exhibition on the Impressionists held at the Grand Palais in 1974. It was an influence openly acknowledged by all those who drew inspiration from it, making Victorine Meurand, the model who had posed for Manet's painting *La femme au perroquet*, the new reference for women's fashion.[47]

An important aspect of this fashion, which asserted itself over the course of 1975 in such a way as to leave no room for doubts, rendering episodes like W. Albini's high fashion show "Homage to Chanel" definitely anachronistic, was the feeling that *prêt-à-porter* was at last facing up to its humble, so to speak, roots in everyday life, in what ought to be its real market. The elements of folk styles to be found in fashion from 1975 to 1978 had nothing to do with those of the early seventies, which were

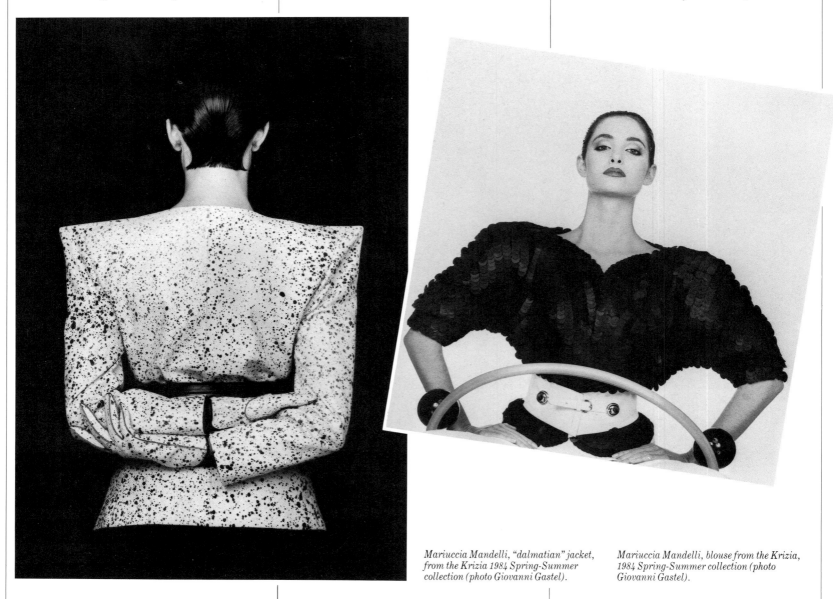

Mariuccia Mandelli, "dalmatian" jacket, from the Krizia 1984 Spring-Summer collection (photo Giovanni Gastel).

Mariuccia Mandelli, blouse from the Krizia, 1984 Spring-Summer collection (photo Giovanni Gastel).

dustrial methods of manufacture would not otherwise justify such exorbitant prices.[46]

Looking at the Street

By the beginning of 1974 the vogue for revivals, whose main protagonists had been Camount and Albini but which had extended its influence to many other designers, was already showing signs of flagging. The short-lived go-between that would serve as link between the dominant classical style and the new folk ten-

The least that could happen to the classical style was the loss of much of that tendency to take itself seriously which had been eliminated by the fashion for revivals. In December 1974 *Harper's Bazaar* published a feature by Bob Krieger mocking the classic garment to be worn on special occasions. The statuesque Eva Malestrom was immortalized in elegant costumes while in the act of adding a sauce to the pasta on which she had flung herself as soon as she got back from a first night at La Scala.

still tied to haute couture, the attraction lying in their spectacular colours, unheard-of materials and innovative forms of decoration. What counted now were the aspects of naturalness and nostalgia. It was a battle, rather than a rejection, which turned into direct political protest in all the major cities of Italy.

Prêt-à-porter had to cope with elements of clothing and cuts that were completely new to it, with the use of cheap and untreated materials and with unrestrained forms that made no attempt to imitate couture, not having the means. Extremely interesting in this connection are the studies carried out by Gianfranco Ferré during this period. Ferré went to India on behalf of the firm Sangiorgio to study oriental styles of dress and to adapt them so that they would be easy to reproduce industrially. More than ever before the stylist was operating as a link between the demands of the market, its desires, and a suitable supply, without any pretence of being a guide. This humble attitude

garments taken from the collection for men were sold at the new shop opened in Paris by Cerruti in 1967. His jacket achieved the definitive mark of the status symbol when it was worn to the Oscar award presentation ceremony by Diane Keaton, a protagonist of engaged cinema with links to feminism.

His clientele was a fairly peculiar one, in that it was made up of women who had not until then shown any interest in fashion, who had never "dressed up" and who still conveyed this

tween ancient and modern, that meeting-point with which our civilization is obsessed, poised as it is on the threshold of the many changes which the growth of the service industry seems to have set in motion.

The revival of the past and of folk styles is linked to futuristic elements and technical inventions, with mediation kept to a minimum, almost evoking that future shock which inspired the title of Toffler's book on the changes in contemporary society.

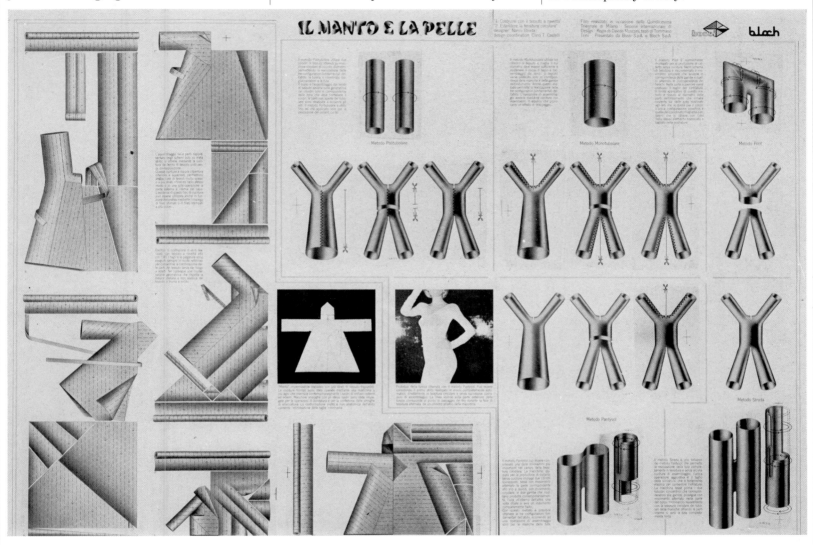

Nanni Strada, the "Cloak and Leather" project presented at the Milan Triennale in 1974 and winner of the Compasso d'oro award.

emerged just at the time when the stylist was beginning to feel in a stronger position and to have a clearer sense of his identity. Armani's realization of the importance of and desire for a new way of dressing for women that would get away from the ritual character of the division not only of roles but also of the different parts of the day connected with them, was one that was forced on him.[48] He says himself that it was women who gave him the idea by wearing items from his lines of men's wear, as when

impression of casualness by wearing destructured apparel, deriving from the tradition of men's sportswear of Anglo-Saxon origin.

Gianni Versace on the other hand is a representative of the other, complementary direction, attracting a market already accustomed to following fashion with novel and up-dated proposals. Overshadowed at the start by the legacy of Albini when working for Callaghan, he rose within a few seasons to the position of being the perfect interpreter of the junction be-

From Design to High Fashion

With the assassination of Aldo Moro in May 1978 Italy entered the so-called "years of lead," a period which was to produce a social reaction in what came to be known as the withdrawal. In effect this was a desire to cancel the past, to disassociate oneself from it in the hope that along with it would disappear an unpleasant part of the present.

The military style that dominated the 1977-78 autumn-winter season was the transitional

Gianni Versace, evening dress from the 1986-87 Autumn-Winter collection (photo Richard Avedon).

Richard Avedon, publicity campaign for the Gianni Versace 1983 Spring-Summer collection.

stage between the *repêchage* of fashions among the young, such as that of the military surplus stores of Livorno and Naples and the call to order of the return to the classical that was to mark the 1979 seasons and which was already manifest in the return, alongside the military style, of tight and clinging suits.

In the 1979 spring-summer collections the return to formalism was evident in the clothes lifted from the forties and fifties and in a nod in the direction of the sexy woman, with slits and see-through garments. Armani's collection was dominated by chiffon blouses, opening like petals in front to expose bare skin. But the tendency was also visible in Versace's collection which deliberately took its inspiration from the figure of the starlet, in the elaborate drapery of W. Albini's clothes which left shoulders and legs exposed to view, in the suit designed by Venturi for Erreuno with a bra top and in the super forties style produced by Moschino for Cadette, including black stockings with seams.

In the quest for a style suited to its new identity, Italian ready-to-wear discovered the linear and geometric forms that were to be a distinctive mark of the first half of the eighties. *Vogue* said it in its "Viewpoint" feature in the January 1980 issue and confirmed it in an editorial published in the same issue which likened fashion to art in the sense of constructivism, Fontana and Op-Art. But it was put most clearly in the editorial of the first issue of the revived magazine *Donna*[49]: "Having exploited the upsurge of spontaneous fashion which gave the stylists themselves their starting-point, fashion is now back in their hands. Once again it is a matter of study and research, it is evolution and no longer improvisation. Professionalism is being rewarded and the most successful clothes are the ones conceived and constructed as pieces of design."

This new rapport between fashion and design found confirmation in a wider setting, forming the backbone of many studies of fashion design and finding an outlet in exhibitions like the one staged in May 1982 at the Massachusetts Institute of Technology under the title "Intimate Architecture: Clothing and Contemporary Design" and the one held at the Pac in Milan in 1983.

The discovery that fashion is a branch of design derived from the new relationship with industry, a relationship that made stylists aware of their role in providing an external contribution of aesthetic value to the mechanism of production. It encouraged them to move away from a segregated professional environment with a reputation for frivolity.

It is a discovery that may have important consequences, both as a possible model for a professional identity different from that of the couturier, and as a way of increasing individuality, something that the policy of cultivating an image makes more important with every passing day.

In the meantime a new kind of research into

Herb Ritts, Ferré advertising campaign, 1985 Spring-Summer collection (model Linda Spiering).

modes of dressing had emerged in France: the new Japanese style that goes back to the costumes of popular tradition in order to make use of their refined materials with a plain appearance, their simplicity of form that recreates itself on the body and above all the proposal of a new type of femininity. After an apocalyptic début[50] the latter has revealed itself to be more natural, more intimate and more concerned with individuality than with beauty.

The Japanese fashion of Yohji Yamamoto,

fluence that has not changed the course of fashion but which fitted into it in perfect harmony by smoothing the way for an increase in flexibility and looseness.

To pick out the tendencies would be impossible and equally pointless. One might speak of a new elegance that does away with the citations and excesses of 1983, of a return of men's fashion in 1985 and a modification of sartorial elegance in 1986, but one is left with the feeling that it is impossible to impose a uniform ten-

vidualization on the part of each stylist, making his own style different from everyone else's and preserving it from changes.[52]

The image of the designer as having ties to the needs of mass production and being aware of having a social role to play, left part of the terrain acquired between 1979 and 1983 to that of the couturier, a reference that turned out to be a deeply-rooted one.[53]

Alongside the prevailing attitude that fashion should be neglected in favour of a style, the

MADE IN JAPAN

Bruce Weber, Rosemary McGrotha symbolizing the eighties woman's ideal of natural beauty, in Vogue Italia, *March 1981.*

Yohji Yamamoto, oversize blazer, in Donna, *May 1983 (photo Fabrizio Ferri).*

Comme des Garçons and Issey Myiake has fallen on fertile ground: the desire for greater simplicity was already widespread in Europe too. Whether the new suppleness of style in 1983 was connected with the slump in sales due to the excesses of image in previous seasons, or the result of a natural process of ebb and flow, or derived from the influence of this Japanese fashion, it is difficult to say. What is certain is that by 1984 the influence of Japan would be acknowledged by many Italian stylists,[51] an in-

dency on the situation, let alone an overall picture.

What is evident is that the new elegant simplicity that took root in the spring of 1983 is nothing but the endpoint of the process whereby the figure of the stylist became more and more substantial, eventually taking the place of the couturier in the guise of the designer. An endpoint that is also the starting-point for a new kind of high fashion that has emerged out of an industrial policy of encouraging indi-

recognition of an eclectic situation in which there can be no absolute creation and in which the sole possibility seems to be a conscious acceptance that what can be done is to recover the already invented took on new meaning. This is what Moschino is doing when he stresses that the style should declare itself as such, without seeking to be fashion or invention. A way of handling clothing that is at the same time an invitation to reflection on the profession and the identity of the stylist.   *N.B.*

*Gian Marco Venturi, model from the 1984
Spring-Summer collection (photo Fabrizio
Ferri).*

Giorgio Armani, evening model from the 1985-86 Autumn-Winter collection, in Donna, *October 1985 (photo Fabrizio Ferri).*

* The authors wish to specify that this article is the result of a joint effort which was subsequently divided for clarity.

1. T. Veblen, *The Theory of the Leisure Class*, London 1899.
2. A.H. Maslow, *Motivazione e personalità*, Rome 1973.
3. Examples of this are Gucci, Ferragamo and Roberta di Camerino in Italy and Hermès in France,
4. It was often the boutiques themselves, to which the lengths of material were supplied, that made up the garment to the client's measurements.
5. Later on they would be revived, but as part of a political or cultural choice that was in some cases an attempt to resist indiscriminate and degrading standardization and in others had an élitist and mythological foundation.
6. A. Toffler, *Future Shock*, Milan 1972 (2nd ed.), pp. 57, 58.
7. Apart from the places in London and Paris which at once became part of the mythology of the young, all those interviewed during the research for this article were in agreement that stores where one could buy "fashion" did not then exist in Italy. Only a few recently opened boutiques, such as Cose, Gulp or Billy Ballo, were importing English and French clothes and a scanty number of Italian producers, like Krizia and later on Missoni, fitted in to this trend.
8. Cf. D. De Masi (editor), *L'avvento post-industriale*, Milan 1986 (3rd ed.), p. 23.
9. It was the time of pop art, i.e. of the apotheosis of the object which passed rapidly from its status as fetish to that of refuse. A use-and-throw-away time which would even affect symbolic objects like the wedding dress. Versions of the latter made out of paper were on offer, which could be used "to make splendid curtains for the kitchen after the ceremony."
10. Cf. Domenico De Masi, *op. cit.*
11. Other stylists who did not come from France, such as Ken Scott and Miguel Cruz, were working in Italy over the same period. The former had his own label which was best known for its use of fabrics that he designed himself – produced by *Falconetto* and printed in large, brightly-coloured designs derived from wallpaper patterns. The latter worked as a freelance.
12. An example of this: in the spring of 1970, Papini was denied entrance to the parade of the Misterfox collection, of which he was the manufacturer, because he had left his invitation in the hotel and above all because he was not wearing a tie. He got in at the cost of an argument.
13. The collections were for: Trell, Krizia Maglia, Montedoro, Billy Ballo and Princess Luciana. Cf. I. Vercelloni, F. Lucchini, *Milano fashion*, Milan 1975, pp. 110, 111.
14. It is no coincidence that the hero of *Blow Up*, the film in which Antonioni portrayed the London of the sixties, was a photographer specializing in fashion photography and social reportages based on David Bailey.
15. In the parade for the presentation of his Summer 1971 collection at the Società al Giardino in Milan, Albini's models appeared on the runway bare-chested. This was a last resort device to cope with the fact that the truck transporting the blouses made by Sportfox had overturned in an accident on the motorway. Over the next few months there was much talk of the return of the topless and even *Panorama* used that image to illustrate a feature on the new fashion. Cf. M. De Cesco, "Fino all'ultima vertebra," in *Panorama*, November 11, 1971.
16. Those interviewed were: Mila Schön, Yves Saint-Laurent, Irene Galitzine, Rocco Barocco, Federico Forquet, André Laug, Walter Albini, Pino Lancetti, Jean Baptiste Caumont, Carosa, Sonia Rykiel, Ossie Clark, Enzo Clocchiatti, Dorothée Bis, Krizia, Mr. Freedom, Biba, Karl Lagerfeld and Zandra Rhodes. Cf. *Vogue Italia*, January 1971.
17. And they were rags, but rags which had found a market ready to search them out and put them on sale. "In Paris," observed Marmori, "this mercantile fever is at its height. Rags from "Reine," "Lili" and "Bidule 60" are on sale at the flea market at the Porte de Clignancourt. In the quarters of La Nouffe, Saint-Germain-des-Prés and, above all, Les Halles, "Boutique 6," "Maude" and "Berangère" are doing the same thing. A similar phenomenon is to be found in London, not so much in Portobello Road and Petticoat Lane, as at "Biba" in Kensington High Street, the "Flea Market" in Carnaby Street and "Essences" in the King's Road. Cf. Marmori, "L'arte di vestirsi male," in *L'Espresso. Supplemento colore*, January 21, 1973, pp. 7-8.
18. In connection with this synchroneity, it is worth remem-

bering that the film *The Damned* was made in 1969 and *The Great Gatsby* and *Death in Venice* date from the following year.

19. Since we were not permitted access to the CSAC, it has not been possible to examine Albini's original drawings, donated to the archives in Parma run by Arturo Carlo Quintavalle. Hence we take the opportunity to thank Sig. Paolo Rinaldi, a colleague of the late stylist and executor of the donation, who did his utmost to supply us at least with the photographic proofs of this material, and Sig. Romano Sudati who provided us with the drawings of his later period along with those kept by the firm Basile and Luciano Papini.

20. It was certainly no coincidence that Albini had bought the

The enterprise was made difficult by the lack of sales points, but Papini discovered an opening in the milliner's shops. He often left clothes on deposit and it became common not only for the clothes to be sold more easily than the hats, but even for the milliner's shops to be turned into boutiques.

23. The draft contract with *Cole of California* for the summer '71 collection explicitly stated: "The present agreement excludes any written reference to the Walter Albini trademark in: labelling of the garments, letterheads, advertising material, etc., etc., except by express authorization from Sig. Albini himself." Document in the possession of Sig. Luciano Papini.

24. Many newspapers would announce this event in the titles

26. In *Interest* of June 14-15, 1971, the figures relating to the sales performance of the so-called "Walter Albini line" were published with evident satisfaction.

27. Specialist magazines, newspapers and even books exaggerated this trend by putting forward a picture of the fashion designer that turned out like a carbon-copy of the lives of the artists. Obscure beginnings, restless wanderings of the world in search of experience, encounters with myths, the difficulties and finally, as in all good fairy tales, the recognition of his genius. But, of course, this kind of *cursus honorum* is like the laurel wreath on the hero's head; it does not explain the facts and can wither from one moment to the next.

28. Document in the personal archives of Sig. Luciano Papini.

Bill King, advertising campaign for the
Enrico Coveri, 1986 Spring-Summer collection.

entire collection of historic magazines put on sale by the Noberasco couturiers in Paris.

21. Albini brought up this concept again in an interview he gave to Mirella Appiotti that was published in *La Stampa* on May 14, 1971.

22. Papini's beginnings are exemplary too. While still an employee, he realized at a certain point that his wife, with a small workshop producing knitwear, was making much more money than he was. This simple realization drove him to try his hand. So he opened a small clothing workshop where, like everyone else, he made garments by copying French models. Obviously he had no distribution network, and so he went round Italy, again like everybody else, looking for clients.

of their fashion feature, such as *La gazzetta del mezzogiorno* of May 22 with its "Cinque cavalli da corsa per il giovane stilista 'à-la-page'" or the *Women's Wear Daily* of June 7 with the article "Putting it together."

25. Obviously the selection of these firms was not made at random. Callaghan, Basile and Escargots were in FTM's sphere of influence, although in different ways. Basile, in fact, already belonged to the group, while Escargots, a Friulan company specializing in knitwear, had been acquired for the occasion. In the same way, Papini had added Sportfox to Misterfox to get round the inconveniences that resulted from the presence of a foreign company in the group, the Swiss firm of Diamant's.

29. Cf. garment p. 107

30. And Albini, with great perspicacity, added that of Venice, but selecting the more international, elegant and exclusive aspect of the city, as Visconti had already done in *Death in Venice*.

31. WA was revived at the end of the seventies by a new company set up with Mario Ferrari. Once again the partnership was with an entrepreneur and distributor, and had a company as its basis. But in this case too – as if the story had to repeat itself – everything fell through after two seasons and for motives that, in all likelihood, had nothing to do with the quality of the product, but rather with disagreements over the image.

Fabrizio Ferri, Brigitte Nielson.

32. The award created by Neiman Marcus, owner of the department store of the same name in Dallas, is considered a mark of great prestige. Italian fashion designers to have won it include Mirsa in 1953, Pucci in 1954, Roberta di Camerino in 1956, the Missonis in 1973 and Giorgio Armani in 1979.

33. Silvia Giacomoni, *L'Italia della moda*, Milan 1984, p. 95.

34. Ferrante, Tositti and Monti started out by acquiring Basile, a firm manufacturing garments for Hitman, at the moment when it had declared bankruptcy, together with Callaghan, which han been concentrating manly on the underwear sector, supplying the army as well, a sector that was also in dire straits. It was a situation in which little or nothing was to be lost by taking the route of stylism on which the whole operation was founded.

35. Their long experience in the sector of distribution had imbued the members of the FTM group with an expert knowledge of the Italian market. This put them in a position to clearly identify areas of the market and the type of product to offer them, a skill that they were among the first to apply to the ready-to-wear business.

36. Cadette, founded by Enzo Clocchiati in the mid-sixties, based its activity from the outset on collaboration with stylists, while maintaining a highly individual image. In 1976 it came under new management but was soon taken over by its present owners, the Fantonis. Stylists who have worked with Cadette include Walter Albini, Nanni Strada, Karl Lagerfeld, Giorgio Correggiari, Franco Moschino and Quirino Conti. The story of the beginnings of Cadette has been reconstructed by I. Vercelloni and F. Lucchini, but Clocchiati's role in laying the foundations of the company's policy is worthy of further investigation. But Clocchiati's death and the departure of his companion and partner Christine Tidmarsh makes this a difficult undertaking.

37. Before entering into partnership with Armani, Sergio Galeotti had worked in an architectural studio in Pietrasanta and then moved to Milan where he joined the Belgioioso, Peressutti and Rogers studio. Galeotti met a premature death in the summer of 1985.

38. The idea of a stylistic studio free from involvement in the production phase emerged in the early 1970s and was put into practice in 1973. Armani then resumed his relations with those firms that had sought his collaboration while he was working with Cerruti and before designed the Montedoro, Gibò, Tendresse and Courlande lines before launching the Armani line.

39. See the case of Erreuno for instance.

40. This was the case with Mariuccia Mandelli. The problem was that there were no prêt-à-porter structures in which to insert oneself and anyone who wished to do this kind of work either had to pass through High Fashion or to become the stylist for a manufacturer. The only other alternative was to produce one's own clothing and attempt to distribute it by going from door to door, as M. Mandelli herself recalls.

41. One particularly interesting aspect of the relationship between companies and stylists was the extreme variety of solutions adopted to manage it. It would have been useful to examine the case of Gianni Versace and the investment trust formed by Dott. Luti and the stylist's brother, Santo Versace as well, but space does not allow it. Hence we refer the reader to S. Giacomoni, *op. cit.*, p. 75, ch. "Come si amministrano."

42. Having contacted Mario Goracci, Beppe Modenese took him to the Fiera to show him the future Centro Sfilate. Goracci withdrew in horror, saying: "For the love of God, fashion is the realm of elegance and should have a worthy setting."

43. S. Giacomoni, op. cit., p. 110.

44. This happened with Giorgio Armani and Mariuccia Mandelli, but also with those stylists who, not having much industrial influence, were sacrificed at the least favourable time. The case of Cinzia Ruggeri and Enrica Massei is typical.

45. In *Gianni Versace at the Victoria and Albert Museum*, Milan 1985, p. 8.

46. On the subject of the use of technological processes in the manufacture of fabrics designed by stylists see the article by Nicoletta Gasperini in *Donna*, no. 40, February 1984, pp. 132, 133.

47. In an article by Silvana Bernasconi in the December 1974 issue of *Vogue*, a very exact parallel is drawn between the Paris collections and the exhibition at the Grand Palais.

Gianfranco Ferré, evening model from the High Fashion collection presented in Rome on July 22, 1986 (photo Maria Cristina Vimercati).

Come Michèle Morgan nel "Porto delle nebbie": trench di gabardine e basco di traverso. Scarpe da Luisa Via Roma, Firenze.

Per chi si sente hippy, vestito a cuori e fiori ed un poncho sulle spalle. Bijoux Moschino, sandali Linea Lidia per Moschino.

Sopra il vestito un blazer, sotto, una camicia con cravatta: e sei subito yuppie. Accessori Moschino.

Un vestito per gonna, uno per top, uno per turbante, più una giacca-cashmere: voilà Carmen Miranda. Accessori Moschino.

Cowboy di città: abito jeans, gilet di camoscio e immancabile cappellaccio. Scarpe Linea Lidia per Moschino.

Moda on the road, stile autostoppista: jeans sotto la seta, impermeabile sotto il braccio. Occhiali Persol, sandali Moschino.

Stile punk: giubbotto vissuto in jeans, cinture peace and love e manciate di catene. Stivaletti Andrea Carrano.

Graffiti graffianti: quasi un omaggio all'artista e stilista americano Stephen Sprouse. Bracciali e scarpe Moschino.

La più nuova versione di Carmen: fiori di seta, blouson di pelle, scialle di pizzo. Olé.

Ricordando Abbe Lane: grandi cuori sull'arancio e una camicia multicolor. Cappello di Moschino.

Franco Moschino, many looks for one model, in Donna, *April 1985.*

48. Cf. Arturo Carlo Quintavalle, "Il peccato di Giorgio Armani" in *Armani*, Milan, FMR 19, pp. 20, 21.

49. The monthly magazine *Donna*, founded by Flavio Lucchini and Gisella Borioli, appeared in March 1980. Until then the two founders had been working for the Condé Nast group (Lucchini had been the editor of *Uomo Vogue*).

50. In the first shows the models appeared with a make-up that used spots of cosmetics, smears of enamel and dishevelled hairdos in order to create the impression that they were not made-up, but rather the survivors of some disaster. It was immediately baptized the post-atomic look.

51. In this connection see the statement made by Armani to Donatella Sartorio and published in *Donna*, February 1984: "The Japanese stylists have brought me only one message, but an important one, that is a greater sense of freedom."

52. Cf. *Donna* no. 58, October 1985, which devoted its editorial to the personality of the stylist as a master of the philosophy of life, along with a long article entitled "Io e il mio stile," in which each stylist spoke about his uniqueness and recurrent features.

53. Under pressure from the president of the Chamber of High Fashion Loris Abate, in July 1986 a number of Milanese stylists presented their collections of evening wear at the Roman fashion shows and Gianfranco Ferré showed a complete collection of High Fashion.

Sergio Caminata, advertising campaign for the 1985-86 Autumn-Winter collection by Franco Moschino.

Silk-screen in 6 colours on flesh-coloured paper, 47.7 × 33.2 cm. Illustration accompanying the press release for the first Misterfox fashion show at Palazzo Pitti for the 1970-71 Autumn-Winter season. The two garments depicted had been selected as a symbol of the collection: the black of the widows, the pinkish beige of the brides. The publicity photographs of the two models, made out of Châtillon muslin jersey by Etro and accompanied by jewellery designed by Albini and shoes by Italo Colombo, were published in the July-August 1970 issue of *Vogue Italia*. (*E.M.*)

Trouser suit in wool jersey in narrow camel-coloured and brown stripes, lined with nylon jersey. Short jacket with revers collar and padded shoulders; it is double-breasted and ends in two points to create the effect of a waistcoat. The back terminates in a point and is shaped with cuts underlined by stitching. Very wide trousers flared at the bottom. Measurements of jacket: shoulders 37 cm, sleeves 57 cm, length in front 51 cm; trousers: waist 33 cm, length 109 cm. Label in jacket: "WALTER ALBINI per BASILE." State of preservation: good. Owner: Fiore Crespi, Treviso.

1971-72 Autumn-Winter collection designed by Albini and manufactured by five firms, each with a different specialization. The ensemble as photographed is a re-proposal of the style of the late thirties, especially in the cut of the jacket. (Cf. J. Robinson, *The Golden Age of Style*, London 1976, p. 123). The outfit was completed by a cashmere pullover made by Escargots (cf. show release, 2nd entrance, no. 307). (*E.M.*)

Summer suit for the daytime made up of jacket, mini-skirt and body-stocking. Cotton in a blue and white Prince of Wales pattern printed with groups of three flags in the colours yellow, green, beige, red and blue, manufactured by Etro. The body-stocking is made out of blue synthetic jersey. Measurements of jacket: shoulders 37 cm, bust 45 cm, waist 40 cm, length at front 67 cm; skirt: waist 34 cm, length 55 cm; bodystocking: length 70 cm. Label in jacket: "WALTER ALBINI per MISTERFOX" and the size "44." State of preservation: good. Owner: Luciano Papini.

The outfit belongs to the 1972 Spring-Summer collection, which was based on two subjects: the fruits of the Mediterranean and maritime themes. The flags in particular almost became the symbol of the show. The models are a return to the close-fitting line and reduced proportions typical of the early seventies, which derived in turn from a style of the forties. The stylist's line of research can be detected primarily in the selection of fabrics and prints. These became the principal referent on which to base accessories and coordinates and hence to create a total "look." The working drawing is kept at the CSAC of Parma. Along with the drawings of the clothes there are a number of "atmosphere" drawings showing pin-ups wearing them and dancing with sailors. (*E.M.*)

104

Short evening gown. The black fabric is entirely covered with sequins that form a pattern of coloured rhombs (yellow, orange, blue, red, green, purple) on a black ground. The edges are marked with hand appliqués of strass and cannelées. Measurements: shoulders 36 cm; waist 33 cm; length 109 cm. Label: missing. State of preservation: good. Drawing: CSAC, Parma. Owner: Marisa Curti, Milan.

The gown was manufactured by Misterfox for the 1972-73 Autumn-Winter collection. The very simple line was evidently chosen in order to draw attention to the Harlequin embroidery, emphasized by the patterns of light created by the sequins applied at the bottom, producing a slightly rusticated effect. Apart from the fascination that this costume has always exercised on fashion designers, the constant research carried out by Albini into the styles of the twenties and thirties may justify a reference to Schiaparelli and the collection that he devoted to Harlequin and the Italian commedia dell'arte (cf. *Inventive Paris Clothes 1900-1939*, a photographic essay by Irving Penn, with text by Diana Vreeland, New York 1977, p. 83; *Hommage à Elsa Schiaparelli*, Exhibition staged at the Pavillon des Arts, Paris 1984, p. 49). *(E.M.)*

105

"*Chemisier*" *evening gown* in black lace with satin lining in the same colour and collar and cuffs in white satin. Black chamois leather belt with pearl-encrusted buckle. The chemisier is mounted on a slip with shoulder straps that support the arm-holes. The skirt, made out of two flared pieces of cloth, is cut in such a way as to be bordered by the scalloped edge of the lace, which is in a highly complicated floreal pattern. Measurements: shoulders 38 cm, bust 40 cm, waist 32 cm, sleeves 83 cm, length 146 cm. Label: missing. State of preservation: fair. Drawing: CSAC, Parma. Owner: Marisa Curti, Milan.

The dress, made by Misterfox, comes from the 1972-73 Autumn-Winter collection. The reference, extremely precise in line, material and the choice of accessories – such as pearl buttons – is to Coco Chanel. The myth of the French fashion designer is one that has had an influence on the whole range of Albini's output, to the point where he decided to dedicate to her his sole collection of high fashion for the 1975 Spring-Summer season. The inspiration for the dress in the photograph comes from the Chanel style of the thirties (cf. a photograph of Coco Chanel taken by Cecil Beaton in 1935 and published in E. Charles Roux, *Chanel and Her World*, London 1981, p. 219). (*E.M.*)

Long evening gown for the summer with blouse. The blouse is in purple chiffon with a gradually lightening shade; the gown is in white chiffon printed with patterns of wisteria flowers and embroidered with iridescent white sequins. Measurements of gown: bust 45 cm, hips 45 cm, total length 149 cm; blouse: shoulders 43 cm, bust 49 cm. Label: inside each garment "WALTER ALBINI PER" and the size "42." State of preservation: good. Drawing: CSAC, Parma. Owner: Marisa Curti, Milan.

"Nuit de Chine" model presented at the show held on December 18, 1972, at the Blokes Hotel in London, the first in which Albini appeared with his own brand. The reference to the twenties, so congenial to this stylist, is emphasized by the choice of materials and by the low-waisted cut. (*E.M.*)

Evening blouse in black silk crêpe georgette by Terragni with appliqués of glass tubules in the same colour and white strass. The highly simple shape is matched by rich embroidery: on a base of black glass tubules, attached in vertical lines, are inserted three horizontal bands in which the pieces of white strass repeat the motif W/A, the trade-mark of the stylist. Measurements: bust 43 cm, sleeves 48 cm, height of embroidered band 11 cm. State of preservation: very mediocre. Owner: Marisa Curti, Milan.

The blouse comes from the 1973-74 Autumn-Winter collection that was shown at the Caffè Florian in Venice. The evening wear in this collection, especially the embroidered garments of which the one in the photograph is an example, took the inspiration for their shapes, decorative patterns and materials from the twenties. The trade-mark, based on Albini's initials superimposed in an art déco graphic style, was adopted the year that this collection came out. (*E.M.*)

Evening gown with jacket. The gown is in black silk crêpe, the jacket in black satin with printed motifs and geometrical patterns in pink, purple, green, black and fuchsia. The jacket, which conveys the impression of a cloak reminiscent of the oriental-style ones in vogue at the beginning of the century, has a back in the shape of a broad inverted triangle with a rhomboid pattern printed in the middle. Measurements of gown: shoulders 42 cm, hips 52 cm, sleeves 66 cm, total length 166 cm; jacket: shoulders 72 cm, length 91 cm. Both garments carry the label "W/A." State of preservation: ex-cellent. Owner: Fiore Crespi, Treviso.

The outfit belongs to the 1975 Spring-Summer collection of High Fashion that was shown in Rome. Much of the collection was dedicated to Chanel, but these garments were probably influenced by the cloaks which Mariano Fortuny designed on the oriental pattern. However Albini's reference is only a stylistic one. The fabrics he used are in fact industrially produced, although the satin print used for the jacket was probably designed for the purpose. (*E.M.*)

Summer wedding dress composed of a top in turquoise cotton knit and a skirt made out of three layers of polyamide cotton gauze, in the colours sunshine yellow, brick red and turquoise. Measurements of top: length 37 cm; skirt: waist 37 cm, length 105 cm. Label: missing. State of preservation: good. Owner: Marisa Curti, Milan.

The ensemble comes from the Trell collection for the 1977 Spring-Summer season. It takes its inspiration from the clothing worn by Indian women from which the stylist has borrowed both materials and forms. (*E.M.*)

Giuliana Camerino

Dress in wool jersey printed in black, light grey, dark grey and brick red. Measurements: total length 156 cm, zip 42 cm, shoulders 39 cm, waist 38 cm, hips 44 cm. Label: missing. State of preservation: fair. Owner: Roberta di Camerino Archives, Venice, where the preparatory design can also be found.

The dress belongs to the collection for the Roberta di Camerino brand for the season. The model, given the name Gatsby, takes the inspiration for its print from the clothing styles of the twenties. It illustrates the solution adopted by Giuliana Camerino in order to produce garments of simple cut, quick to manufacture and easy to wear, thereby maintaining a more personalized character in comparison to mass-produced clothing of the period. The garment belongs to the trompe l'oeil period in which different items of the wardrobe were printed onto jersey cloth, as an ironic comment on the traditional costume and its limits of practically. For this design Camerino won the Compasso d'oro in the retrospective awards of 1979. (*N.B.*)

Dress in jersey printed in twelve shades of green, red, purple, blue and black. Measurements: total length 158 cm, waist 44 cm. Label: "Roberta di Camerino/Made in Italy." State of preservation: excellent. Owner: Roberta di Camerino Archives, Venice, where the preparatory design is also kept.

The model represents a stage in Giuliana Camerino's development of trompe d'oeil, an evolution that is discussed by Vittorio Sgarbi in his preface to the catalogue of the exhibition of designs held in Venice in February-April 1985. The garment's drapery is formed by the apparent interlacing of strips of pleated fabric that recall Mariano Fortuny's "delphos." The design of the print was produced in 1968, while the dress is a later model. The models were in fact made out pieces of fabrics printed several times in order to allow the dye to dry without spreading into the subsequent print. Bibliography: V. Sgarbi, *Roberta di Camerino, i disegni: 1955-1975*, Venice 1985, pp. 7-14. (*N.B.*)

Summer dress with bolero jacket and turban in dark brown crêpe de chine printed in ochre and cornflower blue squares, overlaid with ornamental patterns, taken from geometrical abstractionism, in green, beige, cornflower blue and ochre. Measurements of jacket: waist 37 cm, total length 116 cm; bolero jacket: shoulders 36 cm, length 36 cm. Label: missing. State of preservation: good. Owner: Fiore Crespi, Treviso. From the 1971 Spring-Summer collection. The details of the neckline and above all the design of the fabric recall the fashion of the early forties and the figurative culture of the two preceding decades. (*E.M.*)

Summer evening gown in blue crêpe de chine printed with large red and yellow polka dots outlined in white. Measurements: waist 35 cm, hips 45 cm, length 171 cm. Label: missing. State of preservation: good. Owner: Fiore Crespi, Treviso.

Biarritz collection shown at Mare Moda Capri for the summer of 1973. The very name of the collection is an explicit reference to a refined and elegant cultural climate of which this seaside resort was one of the symbols in the twenties and thirties. (*E.M.*)

Winter suit composed of 7/8 jacket and skirt in mélange woollen cloth in tones of grey, produced by the Cini & C. weaving mill. Collar and cuffs in grey Arctic fox. Measurements of wrap: shoulders 39 cm, length 98 cm; skirt: waist 33 cm, length 67 cm. Label: missing. State of preservation: excellent. Owner: Fiore Crespi, Treviso.

1973-74 Autumn-Winter collection. *Vogue Italia* devoted its editorial "Il punto di vista di Vogue" in the October 1973 issue to Caumont's style. In its analysis of a version of this model, the article drew attention to the details that help to create a look described as "classic." (*E.M.*)

"Chemisier" dress in white silk crêpe. Measurements: bust 42 cm, waist 35 cm, length 100 cm. Label: "Boutique Caumont S.p.A. Made in Italy" and the size "40". State of preservation: good. Owner: Cristina Brigidini, Milan. The dress, which probably dates from 1974, is inspired by women's tennis costumes of the forties, adapted to a quite different use (cf. photograph by H. Landshoff in *Harper's Bazaar*, July 1942 and published in *La moda*, part two, Milan 1983. (*E.M.*)

115

Evening gown with overcoat, scarf and turban in pearl grey crêpe de chine with grey Arctic fox trimming. Measurements of gown: bust 47 cm, waist 35 cm, length 148 cm; overcoat: shoulders 40 cm, length 105 cm; scarf: length 236 cm, width 37 cm. Label: missing. State of preservation: excellent. Owner: Fiore Crespi, Treviso.

The model, probably dating from 1975, revives the thirties style in an almost literal manner, even with regard to the colour and the choice of materials, especially the fox. (*E.M.*)

Silvano Malta

Short evening gown in black silk taffeta with appliqués of glass beads and strass. Measurements: shoulders 43 cm, total length 110 cm. Label: missing. State of preservation: good. Owner: Elisabetta Catalano, Rome.

The gown comes from the 1979-80 Autumn-Winter collection designed for Lux-International. With its relatively simple materials and cut it evokes an image of seduction that combines the traditional form of the alluring dress, typical of American glamour in the fifties, with a decorative feature that is linked to the old-fashioned symbolism of feminine charm. This is partly the result of Malta's training in the theatrical costumiers of Rome, from which she has derived a form of irony based on the possibility of manipulating dramatic and symbolic elements. Bibliography: *Vogue Italia*, December 1979 (collared version). (*N.B.*)

SILVANO MALTA

Ken Scott

Outfit composed of polyamide jersey dress printed in black and various shades of orange and silk georgette overgarment in the same colours, but with a different decorative pattern and trimmed with ostrich feathers. Meaurements of dress: total length at mid-back 144 cm, shoulders 36 cm; overgarment: total length at mid-back 150 cm, shoulders 40 cm. Label: "Ken Scott/Hand printed in Italy." State of preservation: good. Owner: Ken Scott Archives, Milan, where the preparatory design can also be found.

The garment belongs to the "Circus" collection shown in Rome in July 1968 in the setting of a circus tent. As well as from clowns and other traditional circus figures, the models take their inspiration from wild animals, representations of which are printed on the fabric. This is a recurrent theme in Scott's work. The extreme liveliness of the prints reflects Scott's international background, including the influence of Anglo-Saxon decorative arts and the hippy movement. Bibliography: *Queen*, December 1968. (*N.B.*)

Evening gown in silk jersey printed in different shades of yellow, red, light blue, green, lilac, white and black, and embroidered with spangles in the same colour as the print underneath. Lined in black silk crêpe georgette, it is accompanied by three ostrich feather boas predominantly in black but with some green, yellow, blue and fuchsia plumes. Measurements: total length 151 cm, shoulders 34 cm, waist 36 cm. Label: "Ken Scott." State of preservation: good. Owner: Ken Scott Archives, Milan, where the preparatory design is also to be found.

The model comes from the collection shown in 1969, and is an example of the use of printed flower patterns, a distinctive mark of Ken Scott's output of clothes, which are characterized by the combination of very intense, almost psychedelic colours with large flowers or leaves that leave no empty spaces in the design of the fabric. This sort of design for a long and straight evening gown, in which the material is the outstanding feature, has recently reappeared in Milanese prêt-à-porter (see the Ferré and Armani 1984-85 Autumn-Winter collections), although with different proportions and patterns. (*N.B.*)

Giorgio Armani

Evening outfit made up of jacket in mole grey silk satin and black silk velvet and trousers in black silk and sequins. The culottes-trousers, which reach to below the knee, have a three-dimensional shape based on a series of asymmetrical pleats that intersect and are sewn in the form of a fan both in front and behind, a structure that is typical of Japanese historical costumes. Measurements of jacket: length at back 66 cm, waist 40 cm, shoulders 45 cm; trousers: waist 32 cm, length at side 56.5 cm. Label: "Giorgio Armani Made in Italy." State of preservation: good. Owner: Fashion Institute of Technology, New York.

The model comes from the 1981-82 Autumn-Winter collection, given the same "Kagemusha" since it took its inspiration from the historic dress of Japanese samurai as represented in A. Kurosawa's film. In this collection Armani came up with designs that go beyond his interest in men's sports clothes of Anglo-Saxon origin. It also marked the beginning of a crisis that led to his absence from the fashion shows from the 1982-83 Autumn-Winter season to the 1983-84 Autumn-Winter season. He devoted this period to reflection on the relationship between creativity, saleability and style that is still a mark of Armani's work. It is worth noting how the forms, fabrics and decorations drawn for Japanese culture and used in the daytime garments have all been grafted onto the structure of the suit, composed of jacket, blouse and skirt, in this case transformed into "culottes." In keeping with his interest in everyday and working clothing, Armani did not turn to the ceremonial costume of the samurai but concentrated on transforming their combat armour into evening dress. Bibliography: *Donna*, September 1981, p. 186; *I dogi della moda, travestimento o realtà*, Venice 1984, pp. 12, 13. (*N.B.*)

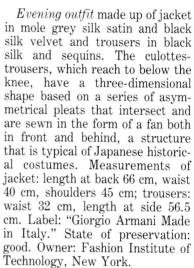

Daytime outfit made up of jacket in mixed cotton and silk Jacquard knit with a motif of palms in light blue and mud brown and wrap skirt in the same material and pattern, but in the colours light blue and knaki so as to produce a negative-positive effect. The shirt that originally formed part of the outfit is missing. Measurements of skirt: maximum length at mid-back 74 cm; jacket: shoulders 44 cm including the pads, total length at mid-back 74 cm, waist 45 cm. Label: "Giorgio Armani Made in Italy." State of preservation: good. Owner: Giorgio Armani Archives, Milan.

The model comes from the 1978 Spring-Summer collection and in it can be found the origins of several themes that have become constant features in Armani's work. For example, the use of an exotic kind of fabric in a blazer, a typical item of the western wardrobe. This element can be found again in his 1986 Spring-Summer collection. Even the skirt takes from the sarong only the concept of a slit combined with the freedom of gesture with which it is closed, a trompe l'oeil closure in that the real fastening is of the wallet kind with two press studs. (*N.B.*)

Daytime outfit made up of sports jacket in brown and pink leather and trousers in brown leather. Measurement of sports jacket: shoulders 65 cm, total length at mid-back 69 cm; trousers: total length 83 cm. Label: "Giorgio Armani Made in Italy." State of preservation: good. Owner of trousers: Rosanna Armani, Milan; jacket: Tania Giannesin, Valdagno (Vicenza).

The model comes from the "gaucho" collection for the 1982-83 Autumn-Winter season. The name derives from the use of a number of forms from the traditional working dress of Argentinian cowboys and the use of leather typical of the zone. After his experience with the 1981-82 Autumn-Winter collection, based on Japanese influences, Armani no longer dwelled on the citation of ethnic themes. What primarily interested him in Argentinian dress was the naturalness of its use of leather. Hence he coupled with the trousers an item of clothing that has had a similarly consistent pattern of use in western tradition: the blouson or windcheater, with its ties to the tradition of sportswear and its utilization for heavy work by people such as truck drivers and policemen. (*N.B.*)

Daytime outfit composed of jacket in grey linen by Solbiati and silk crêpe skirt made out of yarn dyed beige and black, resulting in a nonuniform grey. The silk crêpe is given a pleated effect by means of thin strips of elastic that run inside it horizontally. Measurements of jacket: shoulders 50 cm, waist 50 cm; skirt: waist 36 cm, total length 91 cm. Label: "Giorgio Armani Via Borgonuovo 21 Milano." State of preservation: excellent. Owner: Giorgio Armani Archives, Milan, where the preparatory design is also to be found.

The outfit comes from the 1984 Spring-Summer collection and is an example of one of Armani's numerous experiments with the structure of the jacket and especially of the traditional blazer. The model makes explicit Armani's idea of the shirt-jacket, that is aimed at showing the extent to which the jacket has become a part of contemporary women's wear, to the point where it has assumed the softness and informality typical of the blouse. The union between the traditional structure of the men's blazer in the upper part and that of the blouse, whose edges are knotted in feminine fashion on the hip in the lower part, draws one's attention to the ambiguous sexual character of Armani's style. Through the "wrinkled" appearance of the crimped fabric Armani emphasizes the typically Anglo-Saxon concept of elegance as "already lived in." Bibliography: *Vogue*, French edition, February 1984, p. 391. (*N.B.*)

Daytime outfit made up of jacket in wool by Etro, blouse in yarn-dyed black and white cotton crêpe and trousers in grisaille. Measurement of jacket: shoulders 47 cm; waist 47 cm; total length at midback 72 cm; blouse: shoulders 50 cm, total length 76 cm; trousers: waist 38 cm, total length 104 cm. Label: "Giorgio Armani Made in Italy." State of preservation: good. Jacket and trousers owned by Rosanna Armani, Milan; blouse owned by Edgarda Ferri, Milan. Preparatory design in the Giorgio Armani Archives, Milan.

The model comes from the 1984 Spring-Summer collection, whose success marked a surge of interest in men's wear, reflected in much of Milanese fashion the following season. It is interesting how Armani uses trompe l'oeil as a technical, and therefore "artificial" device to simulate the naturalistic effect of movement and gesture: the way in which collar and lapel are mounted flat in order to obtain the same effect as could be had naturally by turning the collar up and putting the hands in the pockets. The use of non-colour in this model is also characteristic of Armani, who intends the combination of greys and neutral colours to set off the face, which becomes the focus of attention in terms of colour as well. This allows the clothing to play a secondary role to the expression and personality of its wearer. (N.B.)

123

Daytime outfit made up of woollen jacket in large black and grey squares, satin-weave woollen blouse patterned and yarn-dyed in vertical grey and black lines and grey trousers. Measurements of jacket: shoulders 51 cm with shoulder-padding, waist 46 cm, total length 74 cm; blouse: shoulders 50 cm, waist 56 cm, total length 85 cm; trousers: waist 35 cm, total length 106 cm. Label: "Emporio Armani" in the trousers; "Giorgio Armani Made in Italy" in the shirt; "Giorgio Armani, Via Borgonuovo 21 Milano" in the jacket. State of preservation: good. Owner Silvana Armani. Preparatory designs in the Giorgio Armani Archives, Milan.

According to information supplied by Silvana Armani, the outfit is made up of garments that belong to different lines. The jacket comes from the 1984-85 Autumn-Winter collection, where it was shown in combination with some other garment, as was the blouse from the same season (although the label appears to be that of preceding ones). The trousers come from the Emporio Armani line. Such a combination is made possible by the fact that Armani's work has been more concerned with an evolution of clothing as collective behaviour than with creativity bound up with the internal evolution of fashion in the sense of "couture." In the mid-seventies Armani came out with a modified version of men's wear, responding to a demand spontaneously manifested by women, who utilized it not only as a symbol of a break with their traditional role, but also for its practical nature and the freedom of movement it offered, a factor that had become indispensable. Armani's ability to pick up on this widespread demand has permitted the creation of a style that could be offered to different levels of the market, without any loss of quality. (*N.B.*)

Evening outfit made up of black crêpe de chine blouse printed with white crescents and lined with chiffon and long skirt in tulle lace embroidered with flower patterns in gold thread and orange strass, lined with tulle and supported by a double layer of rigid tulle. Measurements of blouse: shoulders with padding 54 cm, waist 46 cm, total length 62 cm; skirt: waist 33 cm, hips 53 cm, total length 100 cm. Label: "Giorgio Armani Via Borgonuovo 21 Milano." State of preservation: excellent. Preparatory design in the Giorgio Armani Archives. The skirt is preserved in the Giorgio Armani Archives, while the blouse, a one-off piece that never went into production, is the property of the singer and actress Milva Biolcati.

The model comes from the 1985-86 Autumn-Winter collection in which Armani produced proposals for evening dress that are consistent with the forms and fabrics of his daytime wear and yet capable of playing the role of ceremonial dress. The basque of sewn pleats eliminates the volume of the upper part of the skirt, thereby avoiding the risk of an anachronistic revival. Rather it seems to suggest, alongside the influence of the ballroom gowns in the film *The Leopard*, a kinship with the sort of flared skirt worn by Brigitte Bardot at the end of the fifties. When taking elements from the past, Armani never concentrates his attention on haute couture, but on clothing worn over a much wider range of social strata. Bibliography: *Vogue* (American edition), August 1985, p. 344 (skirt only) (*N.B.*)

125

Daytime outfit composed of jacket in pink shantung made out of a mixture of silk and cotton, blouse in mixed silk and linen and Bermuda shorts in hound's tooth check wool. Measurements of jacket: shoulders 52 cm, waist 47 cm, length at mid-back 77 cm; blouse: length at mid-back 70 cm; trousers: waist 34 cm, width of leg 34 cm, total length 55 cm. Label: "Giorgio Armani Via Borgonuovo 21 Milano." State of preservation: good. Owner: Giorgio Armani Archives, Milan, where the preparatory design is also preserved.

The model comes from the 1986 Spring-Summer collection and represents another version of Armani's treatment of the jacket with the lightness of the shirt. Characteristic of Armani is his capacity to make use of the most widespread tradition of dressing in order to conjure up collective memories, including elements of the world of childhood, as in this model where the shape of the Bermuda shorts is reminiscent of the trousers worn by young boys in the thirties and forties. Consequent on this approach, which results in a feminine image suffused with tenderness, is the choice of a non-traditional erogenous zone, such as the neck and in particular the nape, the areas most evocative of the fragility of the female body and brought out by very low collars and broad shoulders. Bibliography: *Vogue*, January 1986, cover; *Donna*, April 1986; *Elle*, (American edition), March 1986, p. 151. (*N.B.*)

Daytime outfit made up of Jacquard-knit woollen jacket with flower patterns, blouse and trousers in wool crepon. The fabric is held in pleats by very thin internal pieces of elastic that run horizontally. The model is completed by a cap in the same fabric as blouse and trousers. Measurements of jacket: shoulders 49 cm, waist 45 cm, length at mid-back 67 cm; "niki" blouse: shoulders 50 cm, total length 70 cm; trousers: waist 30 cm, total length 112 cm. Label: "Giorgio Armani, Via Borgonuovo 21." State of preservation: excellent. At the moment of writing the model still forms part of the sample sales collection for the 1986-87 season. The preparatory design is in the Giorgio Armani Archives.

The model belongs to the 1986-87 Autumn-Winter collection, whose theme, visible in this outfit too, is an attempt to probe the roots of the contemporary classic wardrobe in its links with sportswear, taking the suit as an emblematic representative. (*N.B.*)

Laura Biagiotti

Evening outfit in silk taffeta printed with roses. Measurements: shoulders 40.5 cm, waist 35 cm, length of trousers 110 cm, total length 155 cm. Label: "LAURA BIAGIOTTI PRÊT À PORTER MADE IN ITALY," size 42. State of preservation: excellent. Owner: Laura Biagiotti Archives, Rome.

The model comes from the 1981-82 Autumn-Winter collection (the date was provided by the Biagiotti Archives; outfits of the same design and fabric appeared in the advertising section of *Donna*, October 1982, and *Casa Vogue*, insert, October 1982.

The stylist often resorts to silk taffeta, of rather stiff weft, to obtain particular effects of fullness and volume, and to the technique of ribbing to liven up the surface of the cloth. The print takes its inspiration from the flower-patterned fabrics used for furnishings in the late 18th century. (*M.L.R.*)

Summer dress in white, grey and black cotton. In the shape of a trapezium, it is made out of two crosscut semi-circular pieces of cloth, each of which is formed out of four alternately white and grey rhombs. Appliqué black stripes mark out a large tartan pattern on the dress. Measurements: width at bottom 187 cm, maximum length 110 cm. Label: "Laura Biagiotti made in Italy," with indications as to washing, material and the size 38. State of preservation: excellent. Private collection.

The model comes from the 1986 Spring-Summer collection. It is a typical example of the "Bambola" line that Laura Biagiotti has been producing since 1974: the models, for daytime and evening wear, are linked by their shape, which is reminiscent of the trapezoidal cut that dominated the collection that Yves Saint Laurent designed for Christian Dior in 1958. (*M.L.R.*)

Overalls made out of a fabric composed of 50% natural fibre and 50% synthetic fibre, rendered thermostatic by means of a special processing technique. Blue on the outside, the inside is lined with a white fabric with groups of vertical yarn-dyed blue lines. The fabric is quilted to form a regular decorative pattern. Seen in plan, the overalls, with a system of zips, assume the shape of a rectangle from which two smaller rectangles emerge to form the sleeves. As well as a means of doing up the garment, the zips serve to let out the overalls, allowing them to be used for other purposes than an item of clothing. Measurements: total length 212 cm. Label: missing. State of preservation: mediocre. Owner: Giorgio Correggiari Archives, Milan.

The overalls were designed for a SNIA fashion show held at Palazzo Grassi in Venice in March 1976 that was intended to publicize new synthetic fibres. Eight Italian and French stylists took part in the show, in which the presentation of a design for overalls was obligatory. The model demonstrates Correggiari's interest, dating from the mid-seventies, in designing clothing in relation to the setting in which it will be worn and to its industrial method of production. This places him in that stylistic trend with close ties to the philosophy of design, concerned with the durability of the product and the rationality of manufacturing processes. (*N.B.*)

One-piece garment in yellow wool treated so as to make it react in different ways to thermic stimuli. The garment can be worn in a variety of ways as it is constructed on a modular basis. Seen in plan, it is made up of a single piece of fabric with different material qualities creating three craped strips and two smoother areas. Measurements: total length 291 cm. Label: missing. State of preservation: excellent. Owner: Giorgio Correggiari Archives, Milan. There is no preparatory design as agreement over the final form of the module was reached in the factory in consultation with technicians.

The garment comes from the 1986-87 Autumn-Winter collection and is the result of a long process of research into yarns carried out by Correggiari in Japan. Made out of natural fibre, the yarn has been treated to make it react to the thermic processes to which it is subjected during weaving. As well as this stretchable yarn, Correggiari has studied and produced thermostatic fabrics, chameleon-like fabrics that change colour with variations in temperature, yarns made out of paper and ceramic materials and a number of other techniques, treating the fabric as the primary element from which the form of the garment should be derived. Bibliography: *Donna*, April 1986, p. 146. (*N.B.*)

Summer trousers and blouse in cotton piqué on a sky-blue ground decorated with stylized flowers and touches of dark blue, cornflower-blue, white, black, green and yellow, cotton printed on sky-blue ground with large daisies in white, green and yellow spots, and cotton printed on a white ground with daisies in patches of red, sky-blue and green. Measurements of shirt: shoulders 47 cm, length 92 cm; trousers: waist 34 cm, total length 101 cm. Label: "ENRICO COVERI MADE IN ITALY," size 42. The designs are kept in the Enrico Coveri Archives, Florence.

The model comes from the 1986 Spring-Summer collection. Fabrics printed in large patterns appeared in the stylist's first collections, at the end of the seventies, both those of his own line and the clothes he designed for Touche. The design, with large fields of colour, generally take their inspiration from the plant and animal world or from the figurative and folk traditions of the great civilizations of the Americas. In both cases the patterns are redesigned and geometrically simplified in the print, which is also used in the winter collections. The quest for interchangeability is characteristic: the ensemble can be combined with other pieces of knitwear and cotton decorated with the same pattern. *(M.L.R.)*

Summer evening dress. Made with black and white spangles applied by hand to black cotton knit, hand embroidered in two pieces to form vertical abstract white patterns on a black ground. The dress has a straight line, with shaped arm-holes and round neckline. Measurements: length 115 cm, shoulders 70 cm, width at bottom 46 cm. Label: "ENRICO COVERI" at back of neck. State of preservation: perfect. Private collection. The designs are to be found in the Enrico Coveri Archives, Florence.

The dress comes from the 1986 Spring-Summer collection of evening wear, known since 1985 as *Paillettes*. Dresses completely covered with *paillettes* or spangles are a classic design of Coveri's. They have been appearing in his collections since the first one, shown in Paris in 1978, in various forms and colours, but generally with a close-fitting, "mermaid-like" line. Appliqué spangles are regarded by the stylist as a creative element that should not be reserved exclusively for elegant occasions, but that can be used for casual wear as well, as an ornament for ordinary T-shirts for instance. (*M.L.R.*)

133

Daytime outfit made up of "pea jacket" in ivory woollen cloth with a "Bemberg" artificial silk lining in the same colour, crêpe de chine blouse printed in groups of light brown vertical lines and worked with diagonal lines to give a honeycomb effect, and divided skirt in soft brown leather finished with stitching. Measurements of pea jacket: total length at mid-back 71 cm; blouse: length at mid-back 67 cm; divided skirt: waist 34 cm, total length 70 cm. Label: "Gianfranco Ferré made in Italy." State of preservation: good. The preparatory design is at the CSAC in Parma. The pea jacket is the property of Sig.ra Giulia Re, Milan; and blouse and skirt are now in the Gianfranco Ferré Archives, Milan.

The model comes from the 1981 Spring-Summer collection, whose source of inspiration was the Muslim culture of the Mediterranean basin and of Marocco in particular. This was the first season in which Ferré openly used themes from ethnic cultures in his top line, although he had been using their cutting methods for some time. The model demonstrates how his modifications of cultural traditions were based not only on those of costume but also on those of architecture and decoration. An example of this is the decorative pattern of the fabric of the blouse, which derives from the geometric motifs of traditional Muslim decoration, based on the prohibition against using figurative representations in sacred places. Another example is the shape of the neckline which imitates a form widely used in architectural constructions. The divided skirt is perhaps the most obvious derivation from North African culture: sarouel trousers transformed into a skirt by eliminating the lower part and made out of a single material. Bibliography: *Vogue*, December 1980, pp. 196, 197. *Vogue*, March 1981, pp. 368, 369. (*N.B.*, *M.C.V.*)

Evening outfit made up of cape in black silk duchess wound together with silk taffeta dyed in the weft in the colours sky-blue, pink, red, yellow, orange and gold, bodice in red silk taffeta and trousers in black silk duchess. Measurements of cape: length at mid-back 93 cm; bodice: waist 38 cm. Label: "Gianfranco Ferré made in Italy." Preserved in the Gianfranco Ferré Archives, Milan. Preparatory design: CSAC in Parma and Gianfranco Ferré Archives, Milan.

The outfit comes from the 1981-82 Autumn-Winter collection inspired by Japanese culture. It represents the balance between citation and modification in the lifting of elements from Oriental cultures reached by Ferré in this season. The bodice is a citation of the enlarged *obi*, while the cape, a garment that does not belong to that culture, provides an example of the modification of certain decorative features, such as the use of elliptical lines. Another citation is to be found in the slashes of colour in the lining, reminiscent of the free brush-strokes of the Japanese painting technique connected with Zen, while the trousers are a modification of typical volumetric features of that tradition. The references to Japanese costume, architecture and decoration are not due solely to the influence of A. Kurosawa's film *Kagemusha*, but are an inevitable salute to their similarities, to the lucidity of design they have in common with Ferré's approach to clothing, which in this collection marks the beginning of a method of building up three-dimensional shapes on the basis of solids of geometrical origin. Bibliography: *Vogue*, December 1981, p. 126; *Vanity Fashion*, suppl. No. 6 *Vanity*, p. 47 (trousers only). (*N.B.*, *M.C.V.*)

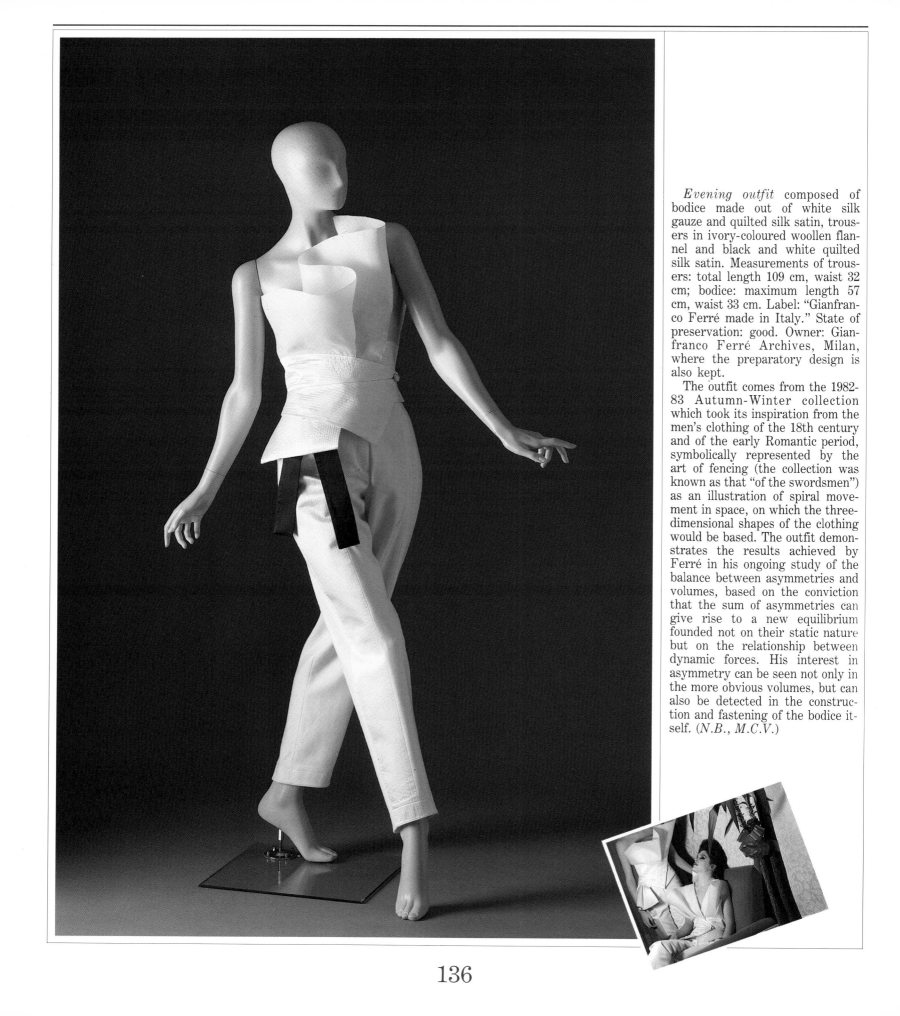

Evening outfit composed of bodice made out of white silk gauze and quilted silk satin, trousers in ivory-coloured woollen flannel and black and white quilted silk satin. Measurements of trousers: total length 109 cm, waist 32 cm; bodice: maximum length 57 cm, waist 33 cm. Label: "Gianfranco Ferré made in Italy." State of preservation: good. Owner: Gianfranco Ferré Archives, Milan, where the preparatory design is also kept.

The outfit comes from the 1982-83 Autumn-Winter collection which took its inspiration from the men's clothing of the 18th century and of the early Romantic period, symbolically represented by the art of fencing (the collection was known as that "of the swordsmen") as an illustration of spiral movement in space, on which the three-dimensional shapes of the clothing would be based. The outfit demonstrates the results achieved by Ferré in his ongoing study of the balance between asymmetries and volumes, based on the conviction that the sum of asymmetries can give rise to a new equilibrium founded not on their static nature but on the relationship between dynamic forces. His interest in asymmetry can be seen not only in the more obvious volumes, but can also be detected in the construction and fastening of the bodice itself. (*N.B., M.C.V.*)

Daytime outfit composed of jacket, trousers and blouse. The jacket is made out of grisaille and basket-weave silk, the trousers of grisaille and the blouse of crêpe de chine. The jacket has an adjusted kimono collar and very wide raglan sleeves. In front a sort of waistcoat creates the effect of a double jacket. The back of the blouse is made out of a rectangle and the front out of two overlapping right-angled triangles. Label: "Gianfranco Ferré Made in Italy." Measurements of jacket: length at mid-back 61 cm, shoulders 55 cm; Measurement of trousers: waist 33 cm, total length 106 cm; blouse: length at mid-back 65 cm. State of preservation: good. Owner: Gianfranco Ferré Archives, Milan, along with the preparatory design.

The model comes from the 1983 Spring-Summer collection. After having gone to the extremes of geometrical construction in the previous season, he returned to a design of great fluidity, transferring the geometric forms into the cut and making them invisible in the garment when worn. The new volume is based on the cut and the abundance of the fabric, built up in this model around the supporting point of the shoulders. As well as this static function, the latter has the dynamic one of emphasizing the gait of the wearer and transmitting it to the whole of the model. The total lack of buttons expresses in the detail, always highly important, the underlying concept of the whole collection. The double texture proofing is the new interpretation that transforms the functional element into decorative element. The use of double texture proofing would be fully developed in the following collection, bringing together apparently contrasting fabrics in order to alter the use of a model and to embellish the garment. Bibliography: *Donna*, March 1983, cover and p. 391; *Vogue Italia*. (N.B., M.C.V.)

137

Evening outfit composed of jacket made out of Taroni wool-silk with a satin effect on the inside and a faille one on the outside, trousers in enlarged black and grey hound's tooth check wool and satin and silk chiffon singlet embroidered with golden glass tubules and trimmed with silk knit. Seen in plan, the jacket is a slightly shaped semi-circle, supported by the padded shoulder. Measurements of jacket: length at mid-back 60 cm, approximate width at bust 116 cm; singlet: length 32 cm, width 50 cm; trousers: total length 113 cm, waist 34 cm. Label: "Gianfranco Ferré Made in Italy." State of preservation: good. Owner: Gianfranco Ferré Archives, Milan, except for the singlet which is the property of Rita Airaghi, Milan. Preparatory design also in the Gianfranco Ferré Archives.

The model comes from the 1983-84 Autumn-Winter collection. The geometric theme developed is that of the semi-circle. This season also saw, a year before the boom in "androgynous" fashion, Ferré working on the tradition of men's clothing in order to graft it onto that of women, combining uses, fabrics and forms that traditionally belonged to opposite sexes. Notable in the fabrics is the combination of dull and shiny materials, which Ferré uses to solve the problem of the luminosity created by the presence of cold and dull colours throughout the collection. (*N.B., M.C.V.*)

Daytime outfit composed of jacket in rust-coloured iridescent shantung silk made by Derseta, lined with "Bemberg" artificial silk in the same colour, and mustard-coloured suede skirt lined with "Bemberg" and orange shantung. The jacket, with a blazer-style neckline and buttoning, is in reality constructed in such a way as to obtain, once the bow at the back is tied, the effect of two points in front. The long skirt, reaching to just above the ankles, has a high waist and a V-shaped cut at the centre of the basque in the front, allowing it to be turned downwards. Measurements of jacket: length (with tails) 99 cm, shoulders 52 cm; skirt: total length 110 cm, waist 36 cm, hips 49 cm. Label: "Gianfranco Ferré Made in Italy." State of preservation: excellent. Garments and preparatory designs preserved in the Gianfranco Ferré Archives, Milan.

The model comes from the 1985 Spring-Summer collection and exemplifies Ferré's return to volumes constructed out of rigid materials after a long period in which they had almost vanished from his output. This new kind of volume brings together all his previous lines of research: from the experiments with fluid volume, it takes the transformation from the geometry of the design in plan to the softness of the final proportions (in this case it is the bow that emerges out of two parallelepiped) and, from studies predating the 1983 Spring-Summer season, the creation of semi-rigid volumes that are developed in space. His familiarity with Oriental cultures is decisive in the use and selection of colours that become a means of expressing the concepts of equilibrium or energy. Bibliography: *Vogue Italia*, January 1985, pp. 162, 166, 167. (*N.B., M.C.V.*)

Evening outfit composed of a black woollen jersey in knitted fabric with appliqué cuffs and collar of white organza, embroidered with silver and gold glass tubules, gold thread, strass and barbottiglia, and trousers in grey flannel cord and satin. Measurements of trousers: total length 114 cm. Label: "Gianfranco Ferré Made in Italy." Clothes and preparatory designs are preserved in the Gianfranco Ferré Archives.

The outfit belongs to the 1985-86 Autumn-Winter collection and represents that solution defined by Ferré as "evening uniform," produced by the combination of simple garments similar to those worn during the day, and therefore thoroughly familiar in terms of movement and gesture. These interchangeable garments are "decorated" by a jewel that becomes a constituent part of the clothing. In this model can be found both the embroidered jewel indissoluble from the garment itself and the jewel detached from it, such as the horseshoe collar that derives from the baroque volute, symbol of the centrality of "ornament." It is a quite new concept of "ornament": the close-packed, dense and asymmetric embroidery goes beyond the mere function of embellishment to become a new way of indicating its use and expressing its volume with density and luminosity, in contrast to the opacity of other materials. (*N.B.*, *M.C.V.*)

Dress in soft red leather with "Bemberg" artificial silk lining in the same colour. The apron-like garment has a bib at the front supported by two shoulder straps converging in the middle of the back, leaving the back almost bare. Measurements: total length 100 cm, hips 43 cm, waist 35 cm; belt: length 130 cm. Label: "Gianfranco Ferré Made in Italy." State of preservation: good. Garment and preparatory design preserved in the Gianfranco Ferré Archives.

The model, designed for the 1986 Spring-Summer collection, takes its inspiration from an Oriental culture that has now been assimilated to a Western type of gesture and awareness of the body, and demonstrates the importance of the accessory, intended by Ferré to form a constituent part of the garment. When he reorganized the construction of the volume so as to shift the geometric design into the cut in the 1983 Spring-Summer season, the element that inherited the function of giving visible expression to the geometry was in fact the belt. The latter is given a structural role, that both brings out the point around which Ferré decided to construct the volume of the garment and emphasizes movement, introducing a dynamic thrust into the spatial equilibrium of the model. (*N.B.*)

141

Daytime outfit composed of a 9/10-length coat and "pea jacket" in coral pink mixed Alpaca wool made by Agnona, skirt in red woollen cloth and polo-necked jumper in red ribbed wool knit. Measurements of coat: shoulders 58 cm, total length 110 cm; pea jacket: length at mid-back 77 cm, shoulders 59 cm; skirt: 33 cm, hips 47 cm, total length 60 cm. Label: "Gianfranco Ferré Made in Italy." State of preservation: excellent. At the moment of writing the model is still part of the production sample collection used for press reports. The preparatory designs are in the Gianfranco Ferré Archives, Milan.

The model is from the 1986-87 Autumn-Winter collection and is an example of Ferré's effort to expand the concept of "uniform" for the evening to daytime wear as well, creating a garment in which naturalness and practicality, traditional features of sportswear, are applied instead to canonical elements of women's clothing. The short and close-fitting skirt is not intended to be "sexy" but complementary to a strong and swift silhouette where the black stockings, worn like a pair of overalls, are not supposed to draw attention to the legs, but to free their movements. The tight waist of the jacket and the receding basque do not derive from a traditional sartorial cut of the fifties, but from a simple industrial cut combined with the feminine gesture of tying the belt at the waist. Hence for Ferré the concept of glamour seems to be liberated through the awareness that feminility is above all attitude and gesture. (*N.B.*, *M.C.V.*)

Romeo Gigli

Outfit made up of blouse in black and green Jacquard silk organza, bodice in cotton jersey and trousers in black silk grosgrain. The original bodice and trousers have been replaced by similar models. Measurements: maximum length 112 cm. Label: missing. State of preservation: good. At present the garments form part of the production sample collection used for seasonal photographic features. The preparatory design is in the Romeo Gigli Archives, Milan.

The model, part of the 1986 Spring-Summer collection, is a fine example of two cardinal points in Gigli's work: research into fabric and study of the silhouette. In this case the use of a rigid material both contrasts with and balances the use of a soft material such as jersey. What interests him in the organza is not its rigidity but its sense of lightness and evanescence, which is in keeping with the final image of the model. The silhouette is determined by the initial geometric cut and not by contrivances of tailoring. One decisive element on which the forms are based is that of gesture, here emphasized by the cut of the very long sleeves that fold back on themselves almost to form armguards. This draws attention to the hand as the key point of any gesture. As for the various aspects which have been brought to light by the work of Japanese stylists, Gigli's cultural roots are decidedly European, as is indicated by certain silhouettes linked to the proportions of the Empire style or the design of the neckline which swathes the shoulders in the same way as the dresses of the 1850s. Bibliography: *Vanity*, May-June 1986, p. 66; *Vogue* (English edition), June 1986, p. 169; *Marie Claire Bis*, Spring-Summer, 1986, p. 137; *Vogue* (English edition), March 1986, p. 226; *Vogue* (English edition), February 1986, p. 139. (*N.B.*)

143

Evening outfit made up of a shirt-jacket in polyester lamé and viscose, with black and gold Jacquard designs representing the heads of wild animals, trousers in black cotton faille and viscose and "pagoda-like" collaret in gold-laminated and hot-stamped leather. Measurements of jacket: shoulders 45 cm, waist 44 cm, length 71 cm; trousers: waist 37 cm, length 84 cm; collaret: width 59 cm, length 23 cm. Label: "Krizia/Made in Italy." State of preservation: excellent. Owner: Krizia Archives.

The model, which comes from the 1981-82 Autumn-Winter collection, takes its inspiration from the costumes of the Peking Opera-House and tends to recreate an aesthetic atmosphere that derives largely from allusions, such as the colour gold, the shape of the collaret, the leopard's paws or the crutch of the trousers. But it is from the very contrast between the elements of composition and the overall image that the fantastic impression created by this model derives, with the linguistic structure of a familiar item of Western clothing used to evoke the fabulous appearance of the world of the Celestial Empire. (*E.M.*)

Evening overalls in pleated black silk taffeta trimmed in rustcoloured silk-satin over a lining in the form of overalls made out of the same material. There is a concealed belt. Measurements: waist 33 cm, length 150 cm. Label: "Krizia/Made in Italy." State of preservation: good. Owner: Krizia Archives.

In this model, which comes from the 1981-82 Autumn-Winter collection, the silk and the plissé are used to create an effect of rigidity in the large fans which camouflage the body, turning the figure into a sort of totem. But the curved lines are transformed into unpredictable waves as soon as the body moves, creating forms and graphic effects which are in perpetual transformation. (*E.M.*)

Coat in brown woollen cloth with belt. The ankle-length coat, of straight cut, has kimono sleeves. Two high flounces border the neckline and extend along the upper seam of the sleeves as far as the cuff. Other flounces run diagonally along the sleeves to join the first ones at the cuff. Measurements: waist 60 cm, height of flounces 19 cm, length 132 cm. Label: "Krizia/Made in Italy," on the inside. State of preservation: good, although the original belt is missing. Owner: Mariuccia Mandelli's private archive.

In this model, which comes from the 1982-83 Autumn-Winter collection, two contrasting constructions and types of proportion are used. The straight lines of the lower part of the garment are matched by a greatly expanded upper part. The importance of the bust is further emphasized by the effect of volume that is created by the movement of the flounces. The flounce is almost a synonym for frivolous dress and always made out of materials that point up this concept (laces, silks, etc.). Here, made out of a "heavy" material, it serves to create a volume that enfolds and conceals the body, and is independent of it. (*E.M.*)

Evening suit made up of jacket and trousers in lined black acetate velvet and viscose. The straight-cut jacket has a V-neck inserted in a large piece of art deco-style embroidery, with appliqué glass beads, metal studs and pieces of black plexiglas, marking out two wide arcs on the shoulders. Measurements of jacket: shoulders 53 cm, length 71 cm; trousers: waist 34 cm, length 114 cm. Label: "Krizia/Made in Italy." State of preservation: excellent. Owner: Krizia Archives.

The model, belonging to the 1983-84 Autumn-Winter collection, displays the curving shape and accentuated shoulders typical of Mariuccia Mandelli's designs. Its interest lies in the heavy embroidery that, while it introduces an element of art deco style, is in no way an attempt to recreate the atmosphere of the thirties. The almost literal citation does not in fact refer to a detail of couture, but to a work of architecture: the top of the Chrysler skyscraper in New York. The result, deliberately "kitsch" in its extrapolation of a detail and its insertion in a context that modifies its functions and meaning, is revealing of the ironic manner in which the European world perceives its relations with the United States, but without going so far as to openly ridicule the idea of "dressing up as a skyscraper." (*E.M.*)

Evening suit composed of a short jacket covered with black and slate-grey opaque spangles attached to a viscose base, trousers in white viscose and white rubber belt. The two front flaps of the jacket are cut into three-quarter circles, shaped to form the hip and the half sleeve, producing kimono sleeves and waist-hugging hips with an accentuated basque. The two superimposed front flaps form a semi-circle, with a V-neck. Measurements of jacket: waist 40 cm, length 55 cm. (The original trousers are missing). Label: "Krizia/Made in Italy." State of preservation: excellent. Owner: Mariuccia Mandelli's private archives.

The model comes from the 1984 Spring-Summer collection and forms part of a line of research into materials that Mariuccia Mandelli has been conducting for some time. Here the subject of study is the spangles used as a primary element, creating the effect of the scaly carapace of some fantastic animal. The result is not the image of an animal, a recurrent theme in this stylist's work, but the magical impression of possessing the skin of an animal "that does not exist." (*E.M.*)

148

Evening gown in synthetic crêpe embroidered with grey, green, red, purple and blue spangles, glass beads in three shades of green and three of brown and dark green and red glass tubules. The dress is entirely covered in grey spangles, surrounding large purple hibiscus flowers that form a background to an enormous serpent with its coils wrapped around the body and its head resting on the right shoulder. The forked tongue is made out of two long strings of red glass tubules that hang from the animal's mouth. Measurements: bust 42 cm, hips 47 cm, total length 135 cm. Label: "Krizia/ Made in Italy." State of preservation: excellent. Owner: Krizia Archives along with the design.

The dress comes from the 1984 Spring-Summer collection and testifies to Mariuccia Mandelli's interest in embroidery as a mode of expression. Apart from her love for animal subjects, the choice of the serpent and the way in which the image is handled can only be interpreted as a symbol of "femininity." In contrast to Western iconography the relationship is settled: the serpent rests its head on the woman's shoulder and offers its tongue for her to play with. In this case too, the combination of references, allusions and ambiguities is an example of that taste for bizarre and ironic fancy-dress that appears in many of this stylist's designs. (*E.M.*)

149

Daytime outfit made up of kid jacket printed so as to resemble the skin of a dalmatian and trousers in black wool gabardine. Measurements of jacket: shoulders 53 cm, waist 45 cm, length 71 cm; trousers: waist 33 cm, hips 53 cm, length impossible to determine. State of preservation: good. Owner: Krizia Archives.

The model illustrated, which comes from the 1984 Spring-Summer collection, is an example of two of this stylist's lines of research: materials and the line of the shoulders. These are emphasized by the padding and constructed and underlined by the stitching until they take on a morphology of their own, becoming the "form" around which the jacket is constructed. As far as the material is concerned, the kid, a hide commonly used for garments of this kind, mimics a different material: the skin of a dalmatian dog. There is something childish about this choice: the desire to turn the Disney fable on its head, making it reassuring by removing every aspect of cruelty and thus of the nightmare. (*E.M.*)

Outfit composed of a large unlined jacket in red moufflon wool and skirt in grey tweed with thin red and mustard lines that intersect at right angles. The shoulders are cut in the shape of a ring, extending to form two semioval wings. Measurements of jacket: shoulders 56 cm, length 88 cm; skirt: waist 34 cm, hips 46 cm, length 70 cm. Label: "Krizia/Made in Italy." State of preservation: excellent.

The model comes from the 1985-86 collection and demonstrates the stylist's interests in the use of curved lines as a basic element of composition in the design of clothing. The oval, in its essence as a two-dimensional geometric figure, forms the basis for the cut of the fabric and survives in the finished garment as a graphic element, constructing "unfamiliar" geometries around the body. (*E.M.*)

151

Daytime outfit made up of a waistcoat in mud-coloured gabardine wool, white crêpe de chine blouse and white viscose trousers. Measurements of jacket: shoulders 43 cm, waist 38 cm; blouse: shoulders 42 cm, bust 53 cm; trousers: waist 33 cm, hips 53 cm, length 115 cm. Label: "Krizia/Made in Italy." State of preservation: excellent. Owner: Krizia Archives.

The model is based on the triangle, the "perfect" geometric figure around which the whole of the 1986 Spring-Summer collection was built. The waistcoat in particular reveals this pattern of composition in all its details, whether empty or full. As always, it is a two-dimensional and flat triangle, emphasized not only by graphic details such as the white line that borders the V-neck of the blouse, but also by effects that create a contrast, like the inverted pleats at the back to produce volume or the decidedly rounded shoulders. (*E.M.*)

Enrica Massei

One-piece dress with curled collar in purplish-grey pleated mixed cotton and synthetic fabric. Measurements of dress: total length 103 cm; collar: height 28 cm. Label: "Enrica Massei Made in Italy." State of preservation: good. Owner: Enrica Massei Archives, Rome, along with the preparatory design.

The dress comes from the 1982-83 Autumn-Winter collection and testifies to the study of materials carried out by Massei. The pleating is the outcome of research into yarn leading to a fabric that is able to hold the pleat horizontally as well, where traditional plissé tends to give, and at the same time eliminates the need for hand processing. The patented fabric is mechanically folded and cut afterwards. Massei's approach to her work is similar to that of the industrial designer, finding the limits set by industrial manufacturing a stimulus in the search for solutions that combine the requirements of design, productivity and aesthetics. (N.B.)

Coat in red and black woollen cloth with red perspex buttons. It is constructed out of a black semicircle and a red rectangle that, hanging down in front and behind, takes on the appearance of a square. Measurements: length of semicircle 103 cm in front and 105 cm behind; length of square in front 58 cm. Label: "Enrica Massei, Made in Italy." State of preservation: good. Owner: Enrica Massei, Milan. The preparatory design is in the Enrica Massei Archives, Milan.

The model comes from the 1983-84 Autumn-Winter collection having taken its inspiration from the use made of colour and geometry by the Russian constructivists. Ever since the beginning of her career, when she was working for Sanlorenzo, Massei has concentrated on the study of colour, making it the dominant feature of her collections. In its application to clothing, she has used it both in its pure form and as a combination of cold and warm colour ranges. In this case the colour is closely correlated to the form, as sharp and precise as the coupling of red and black, and draws attention to the structure created by large geometric figures. Massei, who was trained as an artist, has always shown a great deal of interest in particular contemporary movements in painting or artists, such as De Stijl, the Bauhaus, the work of Sonia Delaunay or that of Burri, as well as the constructivists. Bibliography: *Donna*, October 1983, p. 328. (*N.B.*)

154

Franco Moschino

Outfit made up of two skirts, one in figured black silk organza and the other in red crêpe de chine, polo-neck jumper in black ribbed wool and trench-coat in black wool crêpe with buttons made out of five pearls mounted in a floral pattern. The model is completed by a double ruff in red crêpe de chine. The flared skirts with their attached flounces and frills are worn one on top of the other and have strings along the sides that allow them to be shortened. Measurements of skirts: waist 34 cm, total length 91 cm; trench-coat: total length 142 cm; ruff: 5 × 43 × 9 cm. State of preservation: excellent. Owner red skirt: Marilisa Leuzzi, Milan; black skirt: Simona Passalacqua, Milan; ruff: Moschino; trench-coat and polo-neck jumper form part of the sample collection for the 1986 Spring-Summer season.

The model designed by Moschino for the Cadette 1982-83 Autumn-Winter collection exemplifies the basic concept underlying the stylist's work: assembling traditional garments that have entered into common use in different cultures in a new way. In this case the model is based on the contrast derived from the combination of two classic items of apparel that belong to different cultures and traditions of dress, if not directly opposing ones: Spanish tradition with the flamenco dancer's skirt and that of English sportswear with the trench-coat, almost in a citation of the work done by Lagerfeld on Chanel. Traditional Spanish dress, a constant reference in Moschino's work since he began his collaboration with Juan Salvado, has always interested him because of its equilibrium between vulgar opulence that borders on kitsch and almost classic and assertive elegance in the garment when worn. (*N.B.*)

Daytime outfit made up of "Prince of Wales" tweed jacket printed in spots of colour and one-piece dress in printed crêpe de chine produced by Bini and simulating tiger and leopard skin. Measurements of dress: maximum length of skirt 85 cm, waist 37 cm; jacket: length at mid-back 51 cm, shoulders 45 cm. Label: "Franco Moschino," a heart and "Milano." State of preservation: dress: good; jacket: excellent. Owner dress: Franco Moschino Archives; jacket: collection of the press office.

The outfit combines two articles from two different collections: the dress is one of the best-selling models from the 1985 Spring-Summer collection while the jacket comes from the 1986-87 Autumn-Winter collection. Coordination of the two pieces was suggested by Moschino himself and does not conflict with his philosophy of going back to the "already invented." Once again the combination is of two garments from different cultures and traditions of dress. The dress is a modification of the pin-up dress in vogue in America during the fifties, made out of a fabric whose printed pattern underlines the impression of sexiness. The jacket, printed with drips in the style of Jackson Pollock, is an element of the classic Chanel *tailleur*. The constant reference to Chanel is an act of homage to her creations. An ironic reference to Chanel's homeland is the wine-waiter's *bijou* depicting a corkscrew. American culture offers examples of the kind of eclecticism that Moschino is working on, along with other European designers like Gaultier, and which can now be found in the whole of contemporary culture with the advent of the post-modern. The dress was worn by Rochelle Redfield in E. Montesano's 1985 film *A me mi piace*. Bibliography: *Donna*, April 1985, pp. 311-315; *Vogue Italia*, January 1985, p. 193. (*N.B.*)

Two-piece evening costume made up of bodice in elasticized green lycra and skirt in crêpe de chine, printed in the colours white, red, green and black, and black velvet. The floor-length skirt with a printed design in the shape of a cow gets its fullness from the pleated fabric and the double support of the petticoat. Measurements of bodice: maximum length in front 37 cm; skirt: total length 129 cm, waist 32 cm. Label: Never attached as the garments were used solely for show. State of preservation: fair, the underskirt is completely ruined. Owner: Franco Moschino Archives, Milan.

The model was shown as part of the 1985-86 Autumn-Winter collection. The model Pat Cleveland wore a mini-skirt and a pair of moon boots. The model never went into production as it had been realized exclusively for the fashion show staged by the theatrical costumers Casa d'Arte Fiore in Milan. However the printed design of a cow whose dappling represents a mirror image of the planisphere was used for blouses that did go into production. The model is based on the form of the 19th-century evening gown as represented in oleographs from the fifties and Disney cartoon films. The ingenuousness of this fairy-tale princess' dress is underlined by the decorative design with which it is printed. Unusual or ironic prints are a common feature in Moschino's collections for they permit innovative effects that do not interfere with the traditional formal structures of the clothing. Another element of which Moschino makes use is the Italian tricolour, inspired by the political and allegorical prints of the early 20th century, and is intended as an ironic comment on the exaggerated publicity given to the "Made in Italy" trade-mark. Bibliography: *La Gola*, April 1985, for the print and application of the cow; *Vanity*, July 1985, p. 54. (*N.B.*).

Winter outfit composed of blouse in greyish-blue crêpe de chine, trousers in brown woollen cloth and large jacket in synthentic white fur sewn in horizontal strips. Measurements of blouse: shoulders 44 cm, bust 60 cm; trousers: length 107 cm, waist 35 cm; jacket: length 80 cm, shoulder 50 cm. Label: "CINZIA RUGGERI". State of preservation: excellent. Owner: Cinzia Ruggeri Archives, Milan.

The model comes from the collection designed by Cinzia Ruggeri for Bloom for the 1981-82 Autumn-Winter season, a collection in which appliqués are extensively used but not purely for purposes of embellishment. Usually endowed with moving parts, such as chain-stitches, they are intended to discharge the inner feelings of the wearer with simple gestures of the hands, replacing other more mechanical ones such as playing with the small chain worn round the neck. The appliqués help to give a new appearance to clothes that are traditional from the stylistic point of view. The use of synthetic fur is linked to entreaties made by ecologists in the early eighties and is something which the stylist has stuck to in more recent collections as well, such as that of the 1985 Spring-Summer season. (*E.M.*)

"Ziggurat" two-piece evening dress and blouse in transparent green synthetic material with feather appliqués. Measurements: total length 150 cm, bust 46 cm, waist 46 cm. Label: missing. State of preservation: excellent.

The model, called "Ziggurat" in reference to the stepped towers of the temples built by the ancient civilizations of Mesopotamia, was shown at the Fiera in Milan as part of the Cinzia Ruggeri 1984-85 Autumn-Winter collection. It presents a characteristic feature of the stylist's work, the treatment of the actual structure of the garment as a volume independent of its wearer's body, extending in space to create a three-dimensional form that overcomes the traditional limits imposed by the view from in front and behind. The stepped pattern, seen by the stylist as a symbol for becoming and movement, is a recurrent one in both her clothing designs and her artistic activity. (*M.L.R.*)

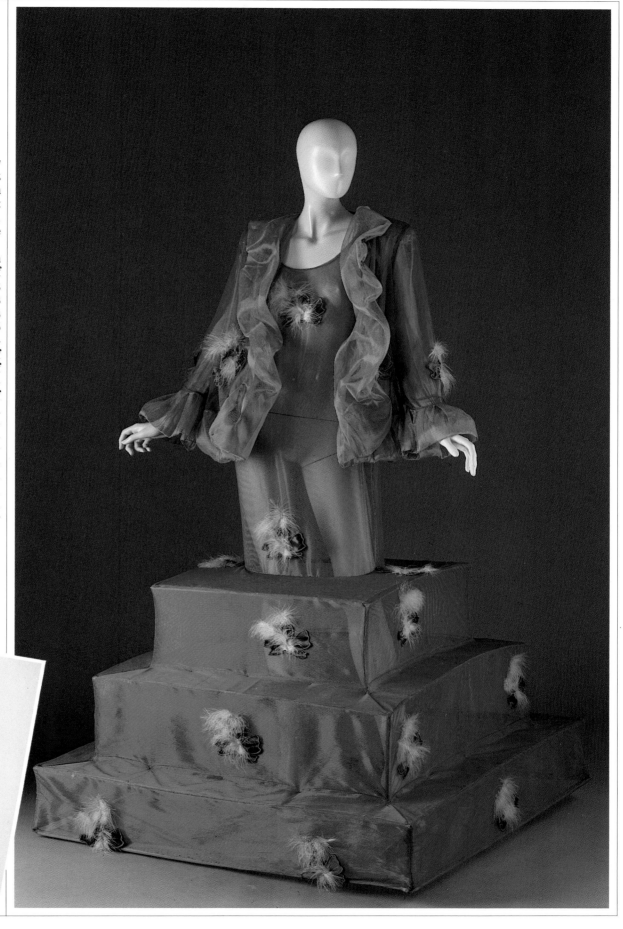

Winter outfit made up of jacket in variegated grey and ecru woollen cloth with appliqués of marmot fur and inserts of black leather, bloomers in corduroy with alternating light blue and beige ribs on a black ground and appliqués of black leather and blouse in silk woven in a pattern of small diamond-shapes, producing an effect of areas of shininess and dullness, on which are printed two large wild ducks in natural colour. Measurements of jacket: shoulders 94 cm, sleeves 74 cm, length 82 cm; trousers: waist 38 cm, length 60 cm; blouse: shoulders 53.5 cm, bust 58 cm. Label: "LUCIANO SOPRANI. Made in Italy." State of preservation: good. Owner: Luciano Soprani Archives, Milan.

The model comes from the 1981-82 Autumn-Winter collection, the first one to carry the stylist's name. It was characterized by references to military uniforms and sports or hunting outfits from the thirties, visualized through the images of the Duke of Windsor and Coco Chanel and made out of a combination of plain fabrics with soft ones and with fur, used as an unprocessed material. (*E.M.*)

Daytime outfit made up of sports jacket in beige-gold silk with white stripes, blouse in white linen and organza and trousers in iron-grey shantung silk. Measurements of sports jacket: maximum width 156 cm, length 53 cm; waistcoat: 33 cm, length 50 cm; blouse: bust 53 cm, width at shoulders 80 cm; trousers: waist 34 cm, length 110 cm. Label: "LUCIANO SOPRANI. Made in Italy." State of perservation: excellent. Owner: Luciano Soprani Archives, Milan.

From the 1984 Spring-Summer collection, this "ambiguous" model made up of apparent superimpositions is a fairly clear example of the way in which Soprani plays on details and "classic" effects in his work. Bibliography: *Linea Italiana*, April 1984, cover. (*E.M.*).

161

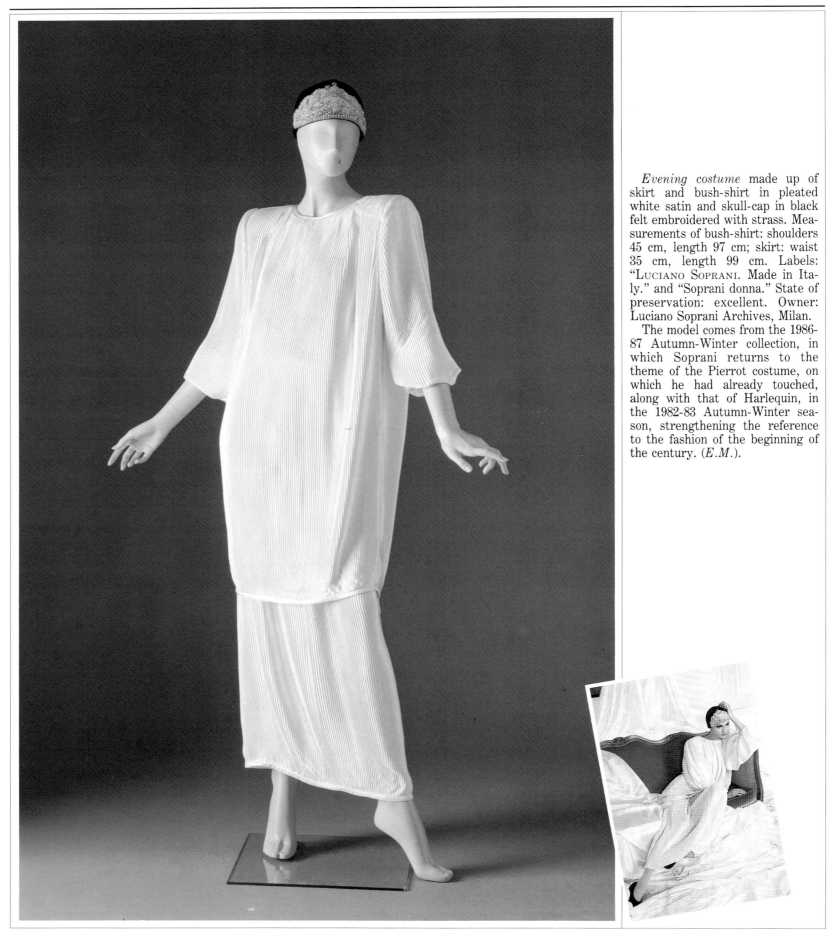

Evening costume made up of skirt and bush-shirt in pleated white satin and skull-cap in black felt embroidered with strass. Measurements of bush-shirt: shoulders 45 cm, length 97 cm; skirt: waist 35 cm, length 99 cm. Labels: "LUCIANO SOPRANI. Made in Italy." and "Soprani donna." State of preservation: excellent. Owner: Luciano Soprani Archives, Milan.

The model comes from the 1986-87 Autumn-Winter collection, in which Soprani returns to the theme of the Pierrot costume, on which he had already touched, along with that of Harlequin, in the 1982-83 Autumn-Winter season, strengthening the reference to the fashion of the beginning of the century. (*E.M.*).

Nanni Strada

One-piece dress in Solbiati linen yarn dyed in green and black. Measurements: total length 121 cm, shoulders 57 cm. Label: "Nanni Strada." State of conservation: excellent. The dress is one of the models on sale at his shop cum show room in Milan. The preparatory design is in the Nanni Strada Archives, Milan.

The pleating of the dress is achieved by twisting it up and keeping it like that for some time, a manual process that, because of the characteristics of the fibre, cannot be replaced by technical devices of the industrial type. The dress belongs to the line of "Travel Clothes" designed by Nanni Strada for the 1986 Spring-Summer season and is an attempt to turn to advantage something that has always created a problem for the traveller, creasing and wrinkling. This concept of establishing a relationship between the design of an object and analysis of the environment in which it will be used is typical of the culture of industrial design which has exercised a strong influence on Nanni Strada right from the start of his career. This "twisting" technique, whose results are reminiscent of the delphos of Mariano Fortuny, was taken from Indian culture. It is a testimony to the studies of ethnic costume carried out by Nanni Strada at the beginning of the seventies with a view to combining design for mass production and artisan skill. Bibliography: *Donna*, April 1986, p. 148. (*N.B.*)

One-piece dress in black wool gabardine manufactured by Tesil-strona with detached collar in white piqué. Measurements: total length at mid-back 123 cm, shoulders 54 cm. Label: "Gian Marco Venturi." State of preservation: good. The preparatory design is in the Gian Marco Venturi Archives, Florence. Owner: Carla Gabetti, Milan.

The dress comes from the 1986 Spring-Summer collection and combines the characteristics of two "uniforms," the school smock and the priest's habit. Venturi has always shown interest in the simple forms of uniforms and has passed, during the course of his career, from study of the more opulent and showy military uniform to that of the "civilian" uniform. Bibliography: *Donna*, February 1986, p. 330. (*N.B.*)

Overalls in wool crape yarn-dyed in brown and grey and jacket made of woollen cloth in grey, mustard and brown checks, lined with patterned brown fabric. Measurements of jacket: width at soldiers 50 cm, total length 55 cm; overalls: total length 155 cm, shoulders 55 cm (with padding); hips and waist 51 cm. State of preservation: excellent. The preparatory designs are in the Gian Marco Venturi Archives, Florence. Owner: at the moment of writing the model forms part of the show room sample collection.

The outfit comes from the 1986-87 Autumn-Winter collection and demonstrates the study of proportions carried out by Venturi. A short and square shape made more evident by the width of the shoulders is in contrast to the overalls, obtaining an effect that breaks up the unity of vision and creates a double image. Overalls are a type of garment frequently utilized by Venturi because of their characteristics of functionality and a cleanness of form that are in keeping with his search for simplicity in design through the use of straight or curved lines, always on a grand scale, the elimination of decoration including all that is not functional in the form, and the choice of colours. (*N.B.*)

Outfit composed of trousers and top in silk georgette printed with flower patterns in blue, amaranthine, red, two shades of green and ivory and jacket in soft red leather with gold stitching. Measurements of trousers: total length 126 cm, waist 31 cm; top: length 144 cm; jacket: total length 75 cm. Label: "Gianni Versace." State of preservation: good. The preparatory designs are kept at the CSAC in Parma. Owner: Gianni Versace Archives, Novara.

The outfit comes from the 1981 Spring-Summer collection which took its inspiration from traditional Oriental forms of dress, emphasized by decorative motifs, both appliqué and printed, that are based on leaves and flowers typical of subtropical vegetation. These can be seen in the print used for this model. The study and use of elements from ethnic traditions have always played an important part in many of Gianni Versace's collections, as well as in the Complice collections of the second half of the seventies, when the stylist concentrated on a renewal of different modes of dress, drawing on ethnic and historical influences in order to make a break with the revival of styles from the twenties or forties which had been a mark of the first half of the decade. The trousers are an almost literal citation of the Indian jodhpurs. Versace is one of the stylists who have most insisted on research into the wide variety of solutions for this garment, achieving decidedly unheard of results in our tradition. Another recurrent feature of his work is the coupling of leather garments with contrasting materials such as silk, especially in evening wear where the contrast between the femininity of one material and the terse aggressivity of the other is a highly stark one. (*N.B.*)

Outfit composed of jacket in rust-coloured ribbed woollen cloth, waistcoat made of light bordeaux sheepskin and divided skirt in mustard-coloured wool and corduroy of the same colour. The sheepskin waistcoat, bordered with leather and braid in the same colour, is worn over the jacket. Seen in plan, the two front flaps of the model overlap to form a high V-neck; when worn they tend to move apart, making for greater fullness at the back. Measurements of jacket: total length 64 cm, shoulders 45 cm, waist 47 cm; waistcoat: total length 66 cm, shoulders 50 cm; trousers: waist 34 cm, total length 89 cm. Label: "Gianni Versace." State of preservation: good. Owner: Gianni Versace Archives, Novara.

The outfit comes from the 1981-82 Autumn-Winter collection, whose theme was the historical male costume, although not so much court dress as the hunting costume or formal dress. These influences are evident in the solution adopted for the cuff of the jacket and in the waistcoat worn over it, references to traditional garments such as the cuff of the riding-coat or the leather jerkin. The divided skirt is another example of the formal research carried out by Versace into the structure of trousers and derives from forms and cuts typical of historical Japanese costume. Versace, in fact, combines costumes from more or less the same era but distant countries, in the conviction that contemporary culture is moving in the direction of a cosmopolitanism that merges different cultural traditions. The choice of colours and fabrics is based on the Italian Renaissance tradition of the use of cloths and velvets, although produced by contemporary techniques. (*N.B.*)

Evening outfit composed of bodice and trousers in bordeaux velvet and taffeta and velvet jacket in the same colour embroidered with strass, silver beads, and red glass tubules. Measurements of jacket: total length at mid-back 60 cm; length of sleeve 76 cm; bodice: maximum height in front 35 cm; trousers: total length 110 cm. Label: "Gianni Versace Made in Italy." State of preservation: good. Owner: Gianni Versace Archives, Novara.

The model comes from the 1982-83 Autumn-Winter collection, which aimed at a considerable simplification of the silhouette and concentrated on the graphic quality of decorative elements, with the exception of those models of evening wear that still showed signs of the opulence of previous seasons. The inspiration for the trousers comes from the Greco-Albanese tradition, already filtered through its revival by Leon Bakst, although the theme of the skirt worn over trousers is one that Versace has returned to many times, with different proportions of length and width taken from different cultural traditions. The jacket is decorated with a type of embroidery that takes its inspiration from the work of the Bugattis in wood. Versace has made extensive use of embroidery, both on leather for evening wear and in casual clothing like that of the 1980-81 Autumn-Winter collection. In recent seasons there has been an evolution in his use of embroidery, with some of the garments in the 1986 Spring-Summer collection entirely covered in glass tubules. (*N.B.*)

Daytime outfit made up of blouse in crêpe de chine printed with geometrical patterns in black, white and beige and plain black crêpe de chine, and skirt in black cotton gabardine. Measurements of blouse: width at base 51 cm, length of seam along hip 23 cm; skirt: waist 36 cm, maximum length 61 cm. Label: "Gianni Versace Made in Italy." Owner: Private collection of Marina Mascazzini, Milan.

The model comes from the 1983 Spring-Summer collection in which Versace grafted onto the distinctness of form achieved in the preceding season a number of indispensable and traditionally seductive features as part of his effort to embellish the clothing and render it more feminine. The "op-art" motif of the print is a recurrent feature in his work, which has always been open to influences from the decorative arts. It draws attention to the sartorial technique required to adapt highly geometrical decorative patterns to feminine forms and draped fabrics. The blouse represents a tendency to be found throughout the collection, to which Versace himself has given the name "means plus means," to combine in the same garment different fabrics and contrasting colours in two or four equal and opposite parts, almost in a revival of the 14th- and 15th-century tradition of parti-coloured costumes. (N.B.)

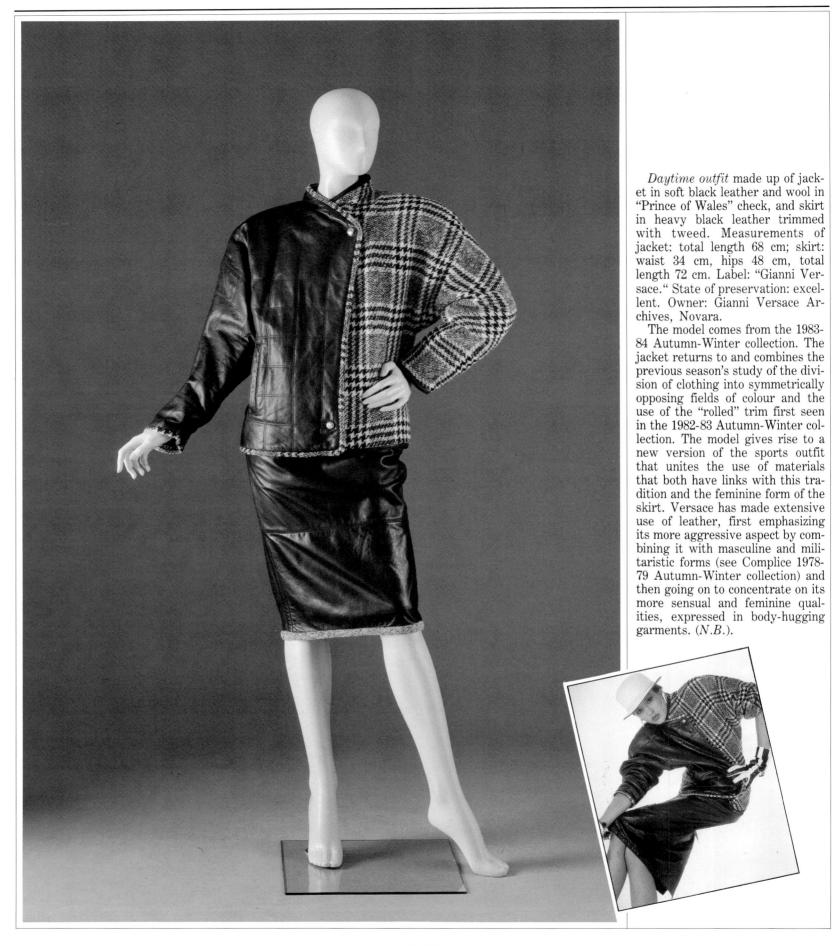

Daytime outfit made up of jacket in soft black leather and wool in "Prince of Wales" check, and skirt in heavy black leather trimmed with tweed. Measurements of jacket: total length 68 cm; skirt: waist 34 cm, hips 48 cm, total length 72 cm. Label: "Gianni Versace." State of preservation: excellent. Owner: Gianni Versace Archives, Novara.

The model comes from the 1983-84 Autumn-Winter collection. The jacket returns to and combines the previous season's study of the division of clothing into symmetrically opposing fields of colour and the use of the "rolled" trim first seen in the 1982-83 Autumn-Winter collection. The model gives rise to a new version of the sports outfit that unites the use of materials that both have links with this tradition and the feminine form of the skirt. Versace has made extensive use of leather, first emphasizing its more aggressive aspect by combining it with masculine and militaristic forms (see Complice 1978-79 Autumn-Winter collection) and then going on to concentrate on its more sensual and feminine qualities, expressed in body-hugging garments. (*N.B.*).

Daytime outfit made up of jacket in raw hemp made by Braghenti with threads of ivory-coloured silk inserted in the weft and trousers in raw linen. Measurements of jacket: total length at mid-back 85 cm: trousers: total length 108 cm, hips 60 cm. State of preservation: good. Owner: Gianni Versace Archives.

The model comes from the 1984 Spring-Summer collection. After a number of seasons based on the compact and clear construction of the garment around the body, the stylist started to go back to freer forms, made more so by new asymmetrical designs. The use of asymmetry at the bottom of garments, combined with drapery, is a recurrent feature that is revealing of his early training as a tailor. It is interesting to note how the influence of Oriental or exotic themes has grown more sober, leading to the use of materials like the unbleached fabrics of popular tradition. The unusual form of the jacket is a reminder of one of this stylist's fundamental characteristics: a creative restlessness and fertility that finds expression in a methodology based on the constant revision of ideas and a continual flow of intuition whose innovative richness is not always as fully developed as it might be. Bibliography: *Moda*, March 1984, p. 195; *Vogue* (French edition), March 1984, pp. 378, 379. (*N.B.*)

Coat in red wool duvetyn with soft leather trimming on the pockets, of "mermaid" shape. The model is worn with a jersey knit dress cut in the same "mermaid" shape as the coat and with a short scarf fixed around the neck. Measurements: total length 132 cm, shoulders 60 cm, waist 40 cm. State of preservation: good. Owner: Gianni Versace Archives, Novara.

The model comes from the 1984-85 Autumn-Winter season when Versace set about adapting men's style of clothing for women. He succeeded in coming up with a completely new kind of "sexy" clothing based on the combination, without modifications, of contrasting forms from the clothing of both sexes. Yet it is a combination that leaves no room for ambiguity. The tailoring technique of the cut is a highly interesting one, producing almost sculptural "effects" with regard to volume and substance. Bibliography: *Vogue*, French edition, August 1984, p. 229. (*N.B.*)

Daytime outfit composed of short silk jacket in silk woven with graphic motifs, tunic of shantung silk figured with similar patterns and printed with stylized flowers, and trousers in shantung silk with the same flower pattern printed in negative. Measurements of jacket: total length at back 61 cm; tunic: total length 93 cm, hips 49 cm, waist 39 cm, shoulders 60 cm; trousers: waist 34 cm, total length 96 cm. Label: "Gianni Versace. Made in Italy." State of preservation: excellent. Owner: Gianni Versace Archives.

The model comes from the 1985 Spring-Summer collection in which Versace abandoned all references to ethnic, historical and folk themes, to concentrate on study of the print and fabric design, on the use of black and white with only small touches of colour and on experimentation with lengths. Versace's decision to bring to a close, with the 1985-86 Autumn-Winter collection, an era marked by frequent historical and ethnic revivals, where past and future were always in a dynamic and unresolved contrast, is hinted at in advance here by the quest for modernity expressed in the decorative theme. Natalia Aspesi, Gianni Versace, "Le graphisme en noir et blanc," in *Vogue*, French edition, no. 654, March 1985, pp. 392, 393; *Donna*, March 1985, p. 531. (*N.B.*)

173

One-piece evening gown in printed metallic mail with black satin trimming along the neckline and cuffs. The mail, made out of a light alloy whose main ingredient is aluminium, is formed out of tiny octagons of metal with points that fold back inwards, acting as hooks that are attached to small metal links making up the connective material. The metal is printed in gold to form geometric patterns of spirals and small squares, with pieces of orange-coloured strass set inside them. Measurements: total length 149 cm, width of neck 30 cm, depth of neck 13 cm. Label: "Gianni Versace Made in Italy." State of preservation: fair. Owner: Gianni Versace Archives. An identical model has been donated to the permanent collection of the Chicago Historical Society.

The model comes from the 1985-86 Autumn-Winter collection, which makes extensive use of decorative themes from the works of the Viennese Secession. This model in particular takes up the motif of the spiral which is recurrent in the paintings of Gustav Klimt. Versace's choice, prompted by the growing interest shown by a variety of cultural groupings in Central European culture and manifested in major exhibitions in Venice, in May 1985, Vienna and Paris, is also connected with some of his earlier researches. The coat of mail, with which he had begun to work during the 1982-83 season, represents a characteristic type of research, centred materials not normally used for clothing. It should be remembered, however, that this material had been used at the beginning of the seventies, although to somewhat less interesting effect, by a number of boutiques, such as Nuccia Fattori's "Cose." These followed in the wake of the metal garments designed by Courreges and Cardin in the mid-sixties. (*N.B.*)

Biographical Notes

Walter Albini

Born in 1941 at Busto Arsizio, died in Milan in 1983, Walter Albini was active from 1962 to 1982, with offices from 1972 to 1974 at no. 2, Via Pietro Cossa, Milan.

His models carried different labels: from 1970 to 1972, "Walter Albini per"; from 1972 to 1974, "W/A" or "WA"; from 1974, but discontinuously: "Walter Albini"; from 1978 to 1979: "WA"; from 1979: "Walter Albini."

Trained at the T. Cremona Art College for Fashion and Costume in Turin, Albini soon began to work as an illustrator for a number of fashion magazines such as *Mamme e bimbi*. Moving to Paris, where he stayed for four years, he continued with this kind of work for Italian magazines and French agencies. Returning to Italy in 1962, he began to work for Gianni Baldini and Krizia, on whose collections of knitwear he collaborated up until 1967. From 1964 onwards the number of such collaborations rapidly piled up, with him designing for Cadette (1964-68), Billy Ballo (until 1970), Callaghan (until 1971), Cole of California, Trell, Montedoro (until 1971), Princess Luciana, Anaspina (in 1969), Glans (1969) and Paola Signorini (in 1970). In these years came his encounter with Luciano Papini, for whom Albini designed first the line Mareika and then that of Misterfox. After two collections shown at Palazzo Pitti and his participation in events like Mare Moda Capri, Palazzo Grassi and Idea Como, his accord with Papini was extended to include the FTM group. Albini coordinated three collections that were shown in Milan and manufactured by five different companies: Misterfox, Basile, Escargots, Callaghan and Diamant's, later replaced by Sportfox.

Walter Albini's top line ("WA") was the object of a partnership accord between Albini and Papini, proprietor of the firm Misterfox (April 27, 1973). Two collections were shown: the first for summer 1973 in London in December 1972 and the second for the 1973-74 Autumn-Winter season in Venice in May 1973, after which the company was wound up. In the autumn of 1974 Albini tried to break into the world of high fashion, showing a collection for the 1975 Spring-Summer season in Rome.

The negative outcome of this experiment compelled Albini to go back to collaborating with manufacturers: Trell, again, until 1978, Lorenbetty in 1976 and Helyett in 1977. Then, for two years, a company was established with Mario Ferrari that revitalized the Walter Albini line, backed up by a manufacturing plant of its own. After three seasons this partnership broke down too and in subsequent years the line was produced by different companies, without any accord of a lasting nature (Lanerossi for three seasons, from 1979 to 1980, and Peprose for two, from 1980 to 1981).

Worth remembering are several collections shown at Pitti Filati with Lane Grawitz and then Hamilton, Arlanda and Maska, ending with Blumarine in 1981. Throughout his career, he maintained a constant collaboration with the manufacturers of textiles, which Albini designed to suit his collections. One particularly strong relationship was with Etro, which supplied him with practically all his printed silks.

Exhibitions and shows: March 21, 1974, exhibition of drawings by Albini held at the showroom at no. 2, Via Pietro Cossa; spring 1976, Studio Marconi, presentation of the men's wear collection for the 1976-77 Autumn-Winter season by means of photographs of Albini taken by 15 famous photographers; January 1977, presentation of the men's wear collection for the Summer 1977 season staged with white masks that reproduced the image of the stylist; 1977, Galleria Eros, Via Solferino, exhibition of phalli disguised as personalities from the world of fashion; 1982, design of the costumes for a show by Luca Ronconi. The costumes never got beyond the drawing-board owing to the illness and subsequent death of Albini.

The majority of Albini's drawings have been donated by Paolo Rinaldi to the CSAC in Parma. However a number of others have been preserved by various companies or in the private collections of the stylist's friends or colleagues. (*E.M.*)

Giuliana Camerino

Giuliana Coen Camerino, born in Venice, began her career in Switzerland with the production of handmade bags. Returning to Venice in 1945, she broadened the range of her activity. In 1947-48 she was discovered by Elsa Robiola, who got some of her work published in *Bellezza*. During the fifties she began to produce the first items of clothing under the trade-mark Roberta di Camerino, taking part in the very first shows at Palazzo Pitti. In the sixties she moved on to prints on jersey with trompe l'oeil effects. These met with a great deal of success and, along with her handbags with inserts of figured velvet, brought her international fame.

In 1965 she acquired an island in the lagoon of Venice, previously the site of the Venetian Republic's powder-magazine, where her collections were shown from 1966 to 1979. Production, however, was transferred from the original establishment at the Zitelle to the industrial centre of Mestre. But in 1980 the Camerino S.p.A. began to be dismantled in order to create Camerino Brand Diffusion, the agency that manages the distribution of products under the brand licensed out to the Japanese company Mitsubishi. At present the range of products produced under the trademark Roberta di Camerino include men's ready-to-wear and classic and casual women's wear, leather goods such as handbags and shoes, accessories like headscarves, stockings and slippers, along with household fabrics and linen, cutlery, fountain pens, etc. The archives on the Isola della Polveriera contain all the proofs of prints for fabrics, some items of clothing and cloth patterns. (*N.B.*).

Jean Baptiste Caumont

Jean Baptiste Caumont worked in Milan on Via Durini, 20 (in two different premises) up until 1984; he then transferred his offices to Corso Venezia, Milan and opened four showrooms in New York as well. The label, "Caumont," reproduces the signature of the stylist in italics. Caumont came into contact with the fashion world at the age of 18 when he worked as a draughtsman for Pierre Balmain for a few months. However his principal activity was as an illustrator for fashion magazines like *Vogue, Fémina, Marie Claire* and *Album du Figaro*.

In 1959 came his first contacts with Italy and collaborations with fashion houses: designing fabrics for Legler from 1959 to 1961, with Apem, the manufacturing company of Rinascente, from 1960 to 1963, and with Rosier from 1963 to 1966.

In 1965 he began his collaboration with a Venetian manufacturing company, AMICA, which led to the creation of the Caumont line the following year. The accord lasted for five years, until 1971 when the Caumont brand shifted to the Gruppo Finanziario Tessile. Throughout this period, the stylist had been showing his collections at Palazzo Pitti, but in 1974 he accepted the proposal to move to Milan.

From 1978 to 1982, having broken the contract with the Turinese group, the line was produced by Mediotessile of Bologna, but with negative results. Hence he established a new accord with the GFT, but on a completely different basis. The Caumont collections were now produced in Mexico by two of the company's subsidiaries (Grinta in Mexico City for clothing manufacture and a firm in Cuernavaca for the fabrics) and aimed at American markets. A second line of prêt-à-porter under the same name was manufactured in New York for the United States and Japan. In 1986 production of clothes and luxury accessories (sportswear, knitwear, shirts, leather goods for men and women) began in Italy too, although still aimed at the American market.

His output of knitwear commenced in 1969 with Clamy's and of men's wear with the line Caesar in 1970. These developments had been envisaged in his agreement with the GFT: in exchange for the production of his brand, Caumont served as a consultant for the creation of the firm Black and White. In the seventies, on top of his constant work with textile manufacturers on the fabrics for his collections, he broadened the range of his collaborations and consultations, always on an anonymous basis, covering every sector of the fashion market including belts, shoes and perfumes. He designed the clothes worn by Ira Furstenberg in the film *I baroni*.

Caumont has kept none of his designs — which he considers of little importance — and hence they are probably scattered amongst the various companies with which he has worked. He does however possess an archive of photographs and press cuttings that documents the whole of his career. (*E.M.*)

Silvano Malta

Born in Genoa, he moved to Rome at a very young age, where he worked from 1965 to 1967 as a costume designer for the cinema and television. In 1968 he began to design collections for the high fashion couturier's Antonelli, taking the place of André Lang. This collaboration, which included the design of a line of ready-to-wear high fashion, lasted until 1975. Over the same period Silvano Malta also worked for the Marina Lante della Rovere boutique between 1970 and 1972; for Pims, whose line of prêt-à-porter he designed until the mid-seventies; for Paola Signorini, a firm that produces light clothing made of jersey, silk organzine and crêpe de chine, for eight years; for Trell in 1972; for Mirella Petteni's Cole of California for six seasons, during which time he took part in numerous shows of Mare Moda Capri and finally for the Milena Mosele knitwear mill. In 1977 he started to design Lux sport and Lux international for the line L. The same years saw the beginning of his collaboration with Giancarlo Ripà, for whom he designed both furs and clothing to accompany them. He also designed furs, though exclusively for the American market, for the Coopchik.

Since 1982 he has had a contract with the Japanese firm Renown, which produces and distributes a line of prêt-à-porter under his name in Japan. As far as knitwear is concerned, he has worked with Malo Tricot and the Scottish firm Ballantines. Yet his relations with foreign companies have not got in the way of collaborations with Italian firms, both those with which he had worked in the seventies and new ones like Lips, for which he has been designing collections since 1983. He grants concessions for the use of his brand-name or establishes contracts of temporary collaboration. For this reason he works out of his own home or from the offices of various companies. He has kept a file of press cuttings that document his career from the Roman period up to the present, but has retained no photographic documentation or specimens of the clothes. (*N.B.*)

Ken Scott

Born at Fort Wayne, in Indiana, USA, he began at the age of 18 to attend the Parsons School, an art school for interior decorators, illustrators, graphic artists and fashion designers, but soon moved to a school of painting and engraving. In 1946 he moved permanently to Europe and began to work in Italy in the midfifties, designing fabrics for Falconetto, a company that he had been running in partnership with Fiorazzo since 1956. At the first show held at Palazzo Pitti the Falconetto Boutique presented garments manufactured by the Steiner sisters. In those years Ken Scott opened a boutique in Milan's Via del Gesù with four or five workers and in 1963 began to show under his own name, shifting his office to Via Bagutta where he opened a small factory. In subsequent years he also showed in the United States, the Italian boutique's true market, and from 1966 in Rome alongside the collections of haute couture. From these years date his collections using the same prints for men and women, the gypsy one with prints depicting foodstuffs like fruit, vegetables and spaghetti and the sports one held at the Palazzetto dello Sport in Rome. In 1967 he moved his offices again, opening the Ken Scott Emporium in an old factory in Milan's Via Corridoni and then, from 1969 to 1975, in a restaurant. In 1970 he opened a boutique in Via Montenapoleone and then in Via Manzoni, while the factory was shifted to Via Cadolini. Currently, Ken Scott has sold the factory, in which he works only on the artistic side.

Since 1965 a collection of leather goods has been produced under the name Ken Scott, followed by a line of linens produced by Zucchi, of headscarves by Ratti, a perfume, stockings, cutlery, etc.

Ken Scott's archives, in Via Cadolini in Milan, contain almost complete documentation of printing proofs with the relative colour variations for different designs and a selection of his most representative items of clothing. (N.B.)

Giorgio Armani

Born in Piacenza in the July of 1934, Giorgio Armani began his career in 1965. His first offices were located in Corso Venezia where he remained until 1977. He then moved to Via Durini, no. 24, where his administrative offices are still to be found today, although the seat of his stylistic activity was shifted to Via Borgonuovo, no. 21, in 1983. The Giorgio Armani firm has been a joint-stock company since 1975, while during the three years previous to this date Armani had worked as a freelance professional with contracts of consultation. Since the 1984 Spring-Summer season the company's label has been "Giorgio Armani Via Borgonuovo 21, Milano," with the old label "Giorgio Armani Made in Italy" being transferred to a second line produced by the GFT and distributed solely in America.

Armani left his native city in order to come to Milan and continue his studies at the Faculty of Medicine. Leaving university after only a short time, he worked as a window dresser and later as an assistant to the buyers at La Rinascente. During this period he came into contact with Nino Cerruti who, in 1965, hired him as a stylist for his company. Armani stayed with Cerruti for seven years, laying the foundations for his future career as a freelance designer. At the same time he produced garments for Sicon's of Vicenza,

though without any contract as he was tied to Cerruti's company. In 1973 he left the latter and in partnership with Sergio Galeotti opened a stylistic studio, designing between 1973 and 1975 collections for the lines Courlande, Tendresse, Gibò, Sicon's, Montedoro and Soldano. This brought him into contact with the world of women's wear, holding shows first at Palazzo Pitti and later (only a few houses) at the Carminati restaurant in Piazza del Duomo in Milan. In 1975 he and Galeotti established the Giorgio Armani S.p.A. and in the same year he showed his first Giorgio Armani collection of women's wear for the 1976 Spring-Summer season.

The 1983-84 Autumn-Winter collection was presented with the aid of a videotape at the new premises of his shop at no. 9, Via Sant' Andrea. The Spring-Summer collection for the same year was shown at the new offices in Via Borgonuovo. From this season onwards Armani has continued to perfect his own style in the study of fabrics and forms of men's wear, mellowing it in a variety of details. Alongside his own top line, Armani has designed collections of leather clothing for Mario Valentino up until to 1983 and the line Erreuno since 1982.

He has also designed collections for his licensees: shirts for Bagutta, knitwear for ICAP until 1983, ties for G.M., a line for Sicon's, coats and jackets for Hilton and raincoats for Allegri up until 1983. At the same time he has been producing the Mani lines since 1982, Giorgio Armani men's and women's wear lines distributed exclusively in America since 1983, the Emporio Armani line since 1982, Giorgio Armani children's wear and Giorgio Armani underwear since 1985. On top of all these come licenses for Valextra leather goods, Overdrive headscarves, Tiffany umbrellas, Lario shoes and the Helena Rubinstein line of perfumes.

Armani has designed costumes for the singer Martin in Stravinsky's opera *Die Erwartung* in 1980 and for Louis Falco's ballet *Heco*, again in 1980. Armani's clothes have been used in the films *American Gigolò*, *Streets of Fire* in 1984, Dario Argento's *Phenomena*, *Thief* in 1983, *Speriamo che sia femmina*, *La sposa americana* and *Il mistero della pietraverde*.

The Armani archives consist of a collection of press cuttings from 1973 to the present, a photographic archive of fashion shows and advertisements (somewhat incomplete for the first 5 seasons) and a small archive of clothes. The press archive is located at no. 24, Via Durini. There is another archive, of drawings, at no. 21, Via Borgonuovo, but up until the 1983 Spring-Summer season all his designs were donated to the CSAC in Parma. (N.B.)

Laura Biagiotti

Laura Biagiotti was born in Rome in 1943. Her mother, Delia, opened a dressmaker's at no. 3, Via Salaria at the end of the forties.

After attending classical school and entering university to study archaeology, she decided to break off her studies and join her mother's business. In 1965 Biagiotti Export was set up alongside the dressmaking firm, in collaboration with Gianni Cigna. The aim was to export and produce the creations of haute couturiers like Capucci, Schubert, Heinz Riva, Litrico and Barocco, not only copying their prêt-à-porter but also producing models to designs supplied by the couturiers themselves, who also helped to select the fabrics.

In 1972 she showed her first collection under the brandname Laura Biagiotti at the Circolo della Stampa in Florence. It comprised about 50 garments and was distributed by Biagiotti Export. In April 1974 she showed her 1974-75 Autumn-Winter collection in New York, during an exhibition devoted to Italian fashion. Her 1978 Spring-Summer collection was shown at the Museum of Decorative Arts in Vienna. In the meantime, having moved to Milan where she made contact with other stylists like Albini, she opened a showroom in Via Montenapoleone. These premises were used to show her collection until 1978, when she began to present them at the Modit, in the Fiera.

In the spring of 1980 she moved to Via Borgospesso. Since 1982 Laura Biagiotti's head office has been in the Castello di Marco Simone (which she had restored between 1978 and 1982) at Guidonia, with branch offices in Milan and Florence.

In 1981 she entered into an agreement with Lebole Euroconf and Lanerossi of the Eni group for the creation of the line Portrait by Laura Biagiotti, a collection made entirely from quality materials such as silk, linen, cotton and wool. Again with Lebole, she created the line Laurapiù in 1984, intended to fill the stylistic gap for women who wear clothes larger than size 48. She also served as a consultant for Alcantara, a new fabric produced by the company of the same name from the Eni group.

Important in the activity of the stylist, right from her first collection, has been the use of cashmere in knitwear, with new methods of production and a vast range of colours. Since 1985 she has been designing the lines Laura Biagiotti cashmere and Macpherson's Diffusione, for men and women. The collection jeans Laura Biagiotti came out in the spring of 1986.

The stylist also has a series of licences. For clothing: Linea Junior by Intergriffe, Knitted underwear for Bellia, Bathing costumes by Marson. For accessories: Stockings by Levante, Ties by Seta & Seta, Shoes by Colette, Headscarves by Isa, Yarns by Mario Boselli, leather goods by Copel, Spectacles by Oxsol, Pens and lighters by Oto and Perfumes and Cosmetics by Ellen Beatrix. For furnishings: Household linen by Eliolona, Furniture by Corsini and Ceramics by Tagina. Specimens of clothing and press cuttings

are preserved in the archives of the main office. (M.L.R.)

Giorgio Correggiari

Giorgio Correggiari, born at Pieve di Cento (Bologna) on September 5, 1943, began his career in 1968. He has had an office at no. 5, Via Goito since 1980. Prior to this date he worked out of the offices of the companies for which he was serving as a consultant.

After studying political science, he spent some time working as an apprentice in textile companies in England, France and Germany. Back in Italy, he opened the boutique Pam pam at Riccione in 1968. The following year he opened premises in Milan as well, with the assistance of his brother Lamberto. In 1972 he made contact with the New Delhi firm Fancy, a company producing fabrics and ready-made clothing that was responsible for the design of the models. Leaving the boutique in his brother's charge, Giorgio Correggiari spent a year in India, returning to Italy in 1974, when he began his collaboration with the Gruppo Zanella, designing the U.F.O. line of jeans (items from this collection are on show at New York's Museum of Modern Art). Between 1974 and 1976 the boutique continued its activity, but on a more commercial level, while Correggiari concentrated his attention on the line he designed for Daniel Hetcher in 1975, the one of men's wear for Herno, collections of leather goods for Igi of Perugia, the Reporter line of men's wear based in Ancona and the Cleo e Pat line of knitwear. In March 1976 he presented a set of work overalls at the Snia show. Around 1977 he designed the Cadette collection and in the same period signed a contract with a Japanese company. He also began to design the Giorgio Correggiari line of women's wear, produced in 1980 and 1981 by Lanerossi. In the field of textile research he served as a consultant to the International Wool Secretary. He also advised Cantoni on printed velvets in 1979, the International Institute of Cotton in Brussels, the Lana Gatto wool mill and the Tessitura e Filature di Tollegno. He produced a line of sports wear for Star Point and from 1980 to 1985 designed the Mito one, manufactured in Spain by the Induyco company. From 1983 to 1985 he designed the Zegna Baruffa. On the design of furs he worked with Pilligrini from 1970 to 1973, with Trifurs in 1976, with Bencini until 1985 and in the last year with Divi. In 1983 he designed a line of leather clothing for Robrik and the Goccia line of jackets and raincoats for young people for Coral. At present his line of women's prêt-à-porter is made in Japan by the firm World & Co., with which Correggiari has been conducting advanced research into yarns for years.

The archive of press cuttings is complete and in order from the beginnings to the present day; numerous garments have also been preserved. (N.B.)

Enrico Coveri

Enrico Coveri was born in Florence on February 26, 1952. His father is a bicycle manufacturer and he picked up an entrepreneurial kind of creativity from his family.

Abandoning his studies of surveying, he attended a course in set-design at the Accademia di Belle Arti in Florence. After working for the "Lord Brummel" boutique, with branches in Pistoia and Prato, he got in touch with an industrialist from Biella and designed part of his collection of women's knitwear. The following year he designed the Aquarius collection of young men's wear for Lux Sport of Parma (previously designed by K. Lagerfeld and M. Grateau). He went on to work as a stylistic consultant for the women's knitwear produced by Ilaria and the leather clothing made by Tiko's. During these years his designs were shown at Palazzo Pitti under the trade-marks of various companies. In 1975 he convinced three manufacturers, headed by Touche, to combine for a fashion show held at the Hotel Diana in Milan. His first 1977 Spring-Summer collection under the Touche brand was shown during the week devoted to Milano Collezioni.

March 1978 saw the first show of a collection under the name Enrico Coveri at the Espace Cardin in Paris, the city where the stylist now shows all his collections. In January 1979 he created the Enrico Coveri Uomo line of men's wear, presented at Pitti Uomo.

His collaboration with Touche came to an end in 1985, after 17 collections: consultancies and affiliated brands gave way to the single trademark Enrico Coveri, an organization comprising forty-three manufacturers and that was transformed in 1982 from a Limited Liability Company to a Joint-Stock Company. Its registered office is in Milan and head office in Florence. A branch was set up in Paris, in Faubourg St. Honoré, in 1984, under the name Enrico Coveri France. Currently the organization has a series of exclusive boutiques in Italy, in several major European capitals, in Japan and in the United States, flanked by some 3500 outlets throughout the world.

1985 saw the birth of the You Young line of young women's wear, which was joined by You Young Uomo in 1986. Enrico Coveri has designed other lines of clothing as well: the Sportswear collection (1982), Enrico Coveri sport (1985), Linea Abbigliamento Sky (1985), a complete collection of furs (1985) and, for men only, the Contemporary line of casual clothing (1986), Chemises pour Homme (1986) and Enrico Coveri Intimo Uomo. For young children he designed two Baby collections (1983) and for children up to the age of fourteen, Bambino (1982).

Accessories include Paillettes perfumes for women (1982) and Enrico Coveri pour Homme perfumes for men (1983), a line of leather goods, footwear under the brand Enrico Coveri Chaussures (1985, formerly Primigi

by Enrico Coveri) and a collection of silk fabrics for retail sale (1985). In the field of design the stylist has given his name to a line of bathroom accessories and linen (1983) and a line of ceramics for bathroom and kitchen (1983).

Enrico Coveri has designed the sets and costumes for: *Concerto per Fellini* by Katina Ranieri and Riz Ortolani (1984); *I sonetti di Michelangelo* by Piera degli Esposti (1985) and *Aiuto! Sono una donna di successo* by Ombretta Colli and Giorgio Gaber (1986). (*M.L.R.*)

Gianfranco Ferré

Gianfranco Ferré, born at Legnano on August 15, 1944, began his career in 1969. His first premises were in Via San Damiano and, since 1981, at no. 19/A, Via Spiga, both in Milan. Gianfranco Ferré Srl uses the label "Gianfranco Ferré, Made in Italy" in black on white.

After an education at a secondary school specializing in scientific studies, he went on to graduate in architecture at the Politecnico di Milano. During the last stages of his studies, in 1969, he came into contact with Fiorucci, for whom he designed a number of pieces of jewellery. He collaborated with Albini on iconographic research for the accessories for lines designed by the latter. He continued to work and design alongside Albini until his Wallis Simpson collection for the 1972-73 season. At the same time Fiorucci had introduced him to Silvani who was producing a line of knitwear under the name Loren's. For her he designed a line of jerseys making use of Northern European colours, inspired by a journey he had made to Finland. This was followed by a collection of knitwear that utilized inserts of lurex and marabout, shown at the Teatro dell'Arte. In 1972 he began a collaboration with San Giorgio, manufacturers of the Courlande line which specialized in jackets and coats and at the same time the simpler line Ketch which comprised simple garments that could be worn with the first line. After four seasons the proprietor died and San Giorgio discontinued the experiment.

He designed the Courlande collections from the 1976 Spring-Summer season until the Autumn-Winter one of 1978-79. In the meantime he met Mattioli in 1974, going on to design his Baila line from the 1975-76 Autumn-Winter collection up to the present day. The first seven seasons of the Baila line represented Ferré's main activity during those years.

Contemporaneously he designed three collections for Les Grenouilles, which were shown at Mare Moda Capri from 1974 to 1976, a set of overalls for the Snia Viscose show in March 1976 and, again for Snia, three seasonal collections of linen and clothing for the home, the Trifurs line of furs from the 1978-79 Autumn-Winter season to that of 1980-81 and the Blu 4 line of casual wear that was intended to match the Ketch and Courlande

lines. With the 1979 Spring-Summer season, Ferré began to design the line that carries his name.

Alongside this top line, Ferré designed for the companies that produced his prêt-à-porter: Nadini for beach wear, Redaelli for men's jackets and coats, Marvel for beachwear, underwear and the Resort line and Boulevard for shirts. Other lines designed by him include Mondrian since 1982, Oaks since 1978 (which produced a line of jeans for men, women and children for him in 1985), the Golden Regiment which manufactures cashmere knitwear and a collection of fabrics. To these were added the Night collection in 1985, shown only in America, and a collection of haute couture in 1986. Ferré has also lent his name to headscarves, ties, sun-glasses, luggage, watches, a line of perfumes and interchangeable upholstery for an armchair produced by B&B Italia.

He designed the costumes for the theatrical entertainment Tamara de Lempicka which was first performed in Los Angeles in 1984. The complete and systematic archives are full of material from the Ferré lines of women's and men's wear while a number of drawings and photographs from other lines are also present. There is a substantial collection of the most important items of clothing designed by Ferré. (*N.B.*)

Romeo Gigli

Romeo Gigli was born at Castel Bolognese, near Faenza, on December 12, 1949. He attended the faculty of architecture for a number of years. During the seventies, he was asked to design clothes for several boutiques in Bologna. In 1976 he designed his first complete collection for Quickstep, a line produced by Luciano Papini. The clothes he came up with for this collection had extremely clean shapes, with the attention concentrated on their fabrics, colours and deliberately destructured appearance. In 1977 he designed the first of four seasonal collections for one of Sebic's lines, in 1978 knitwear for Timmi. In 1978 he had designed, in New York, a collection for Dimitri based entirely on classic canons of men's wear. After several years of consultation for various companies, 1981 saw the birth of the Romeo Gigli line with the Spring-Summer collection for the following year. This line is characterized by the simplicity of its forms and his careful study of the silhouette and fabrics, to the point of being an example of that minimalist philosophy which had not previously had an effect on the Italian clothing industry. For some years Gigli has also been designing a line marketed in the United States. (*N.B.*)

Mariuccia Mandelli

Mariuccia Mandelli was born in Bergamo. After a teaching career, she decided to work in the fashion world. With a friend she rented premises in Via Mario Pagano in Milan and began to cut and sew skirts, to which other

items of clothing were subsequently added, which Mandelli sold directly to stores in various cities. In 1954 she founded Krizia Confezioni and, in 1957, presented a collection to the public for the first time, at the SAMIA in Turin. The collection comprised a series of clothes in fabric printed with giant representations of fruit. In 1964 her show at Palazzo Pitti, with clothes entirely in black and white, won her the "Critica della moda" prize. In the meantime the Milan offices of Krizia were transferred first to Via Duse and then, in the seventies, to Via Agnello. In 1966 she founded Krizia Maglia, followed in 1969 by Krizia Baby.

On Capri in 1971 she won the "Tiberio d'oro" prize for her collection, a collection that included extremely short shorts, later given the name "hot-pants," in contrast with the dominant fashion for mini- and maxi-skirts. In 1980 her second line Krizia Poi came out, followed by the knitwear division Poi by Krizia. Numerous lines of accessories are produced under license from Krizia: handbags, sun-glasses, furs, hats, ties, pottery, yarns and two perfumes for women, K di Krizia and, since 1986, Teatro alla Scala.

The head office of Krizia, formerly in Palazzo Acerbi in Corso di Porta Romana, is now in Via Manin. Here has been created, to the design of the architect Piero Pinto, the Spazio Krizia, which can be adapted through movable walls and platforms for the staging of fashion shows and cultural events.

Mariuccia Mandelli is a partner in the publishing company specializing in texts by women writers, "La tartaruga," and sponsors the Piccolo Teatro in Milan. (*M.L.R.*)

Enrica Massei

Born in Turin, Enrica Massei is the daughter of the owners of the Sanlorenzo dressmaker's. After attending art school, she left for Paris to gain experience in the field of high fashion, where she worked for some years at the Promostyl, a stylistic agency providing consultancy services to large companies. On her return to Italy she began work in the family business. At the same time she collaborated with both Hettemarks and Vestebene, designing the Giovanetta collection for the latter. In 1978 the Enrica Massei line was launched.

At present, along with licenses for the production of sun-glasses, shoes, handkerchieves, handbags and bedsheets, she designs a second line with eight sales outlets in Japan under the name I colori di Enrica Massei.

In her studio at no. 11, Via Brera in Milan is located an archive that contains drawings, photographs and press cuttings, while actual garments are kept in Rome. The label in use is Enrica Massei Made in Italy. (*N.B.*)

Franco Moschino

Born in Milan, Franco Moschino began his career in 1972, with premises at no. 14, Via

Santo Spirito, which were transferred to no. 14, Via Cappuccini in 1983. In the same year he set up a limited liability company. His label, black on white, has a red heart set between the name Franco Moschino and that of Milano.

From 1967 to 1969 he attended evening classes at the Accademia di Brera. When his studies were finished he began to work as an illustrator for *Gap*, *Linea Italiana* and *Harper's Bazaar*. In 1972 Monto introduced him to Versace, for whom he designed a series of fabrics that were printed by Genny. His collaboration with Versace lasted until 1977. Along with Mauro Foroni, he took part in the 1976 Mare Moda Capri, presenting modular structures made out of coloured cellophane that could be attached together to form long or short dresses decorated with appliqués. In 1977 he started to collaborate with the firm Dejac, a medium-sized manufacturer of prêt-à-porter based in Paris. 1977 also saw the beginning of his relationship with Nordic Furs, for whom he designed the Hamilton line. After two season Cadette was acquired by the Fantoni who hired Moschino as a stylist. In 1978 a collection of sailing clothes was presented in order to keep the brand on the market. In the 1979 Spring-Summer season the firm began to present regular collections designed by Moschino; the collaboration lasted up until the 1983-84 winter season. With the 1981-82 Autumn-Winter collection Moschino's image began to prevail over that of Lagerfeld's Cadette in a very gradual transition. At the 1983-84 show, a wide variety of themes were presented, as in all his subsequent collections. These included the use of a print similar to that of the Hawaiian shirt, but in a winter version printed on wool. With the 1984 Spring-Summer season his relationship with Cadette came to an end and he began to produce the Moschino collection of women's wear. This was joined by a line of men's wear.

Alongside more important collections, Moschino has designed Barbara Bram's collections from 1977 to around 1979, the Davidoff line of shirts which was later expanded into a more complete line, from 1975 to 1979, the highly classic Ascam line of prêt-à-porter from 1977 to 1979, Lory of Florence for two seasons in 1977, Paola Signorini for two seasons, Max Mara's line Albinea, later renamed Pianoforte, from 1978 to 1980, the Via della Spiga line exclusively for the Japanese market from 1981 to 1984, Helyett for three seasons from the summer of 1983, a line for the Matti furrier's from the 1980-81 Autumn-Winter season up to the present, the patterned knitwear of Blumarine since the 1985-86 Autumn-Winter season, the Armonia line of swimwear from 1980 to the present and Alberto Aspesi's line of light ready-to-wear clothing since 1982. He has had a number of other relationships of collaboration or consultancy of minor import-

ance. He has granted licenses for a line of jeans flanked by jeans for children and teenagers, as well as for handbags, belts, suitcases and other leather goods produced by Redwall and stockings, headscarves, hats, gloves and jewellery produced by Sharra Pagano.

The archives in Via Cappuccini include a complete collection of press cuttings from 1977 onwards, a photographic archive and a number of the most significant items of clothing from the Moschino collections. His designs carried out for Cadette have been donated to the CSAC in Parma (*N.B.*)

Cinzia Ruggeri

Cinzia Ruggeri was born in Milan, where her father Guido Ruggeri was owner of the company with the same name. Initially she devoted herself to artistic studies, attending a course in Applied Arts at the Accademia di Brera.

She spent a year and a half working in the atelier of Carven in Paris. Back in Italy, she went to work for the company belonging to her father (who had in the meantime formed an association with Cori, Hettemarks, Max Mara and Marzotto that was known as "the Group of Five" to produce a line in a coordinated manner) where she was in charge of the design department. She assembled a group of young stylists, sought through advertisements in English and French journals.

In 1974 she began to work as a stylist for the firm Bumblebee, which produced a line of women's blouses known as Bloom and a line of men's wear called Punch, designed by Stefano Ottina.

In 1977 she left the company to create a line of her own, Bloom S.p.A., which shared offices with Punch at no. 6, Via Gandino. The first show, for the 1978 Spring-Summer season, was held at the Circolo della Stampa in Milan. The next two were staged at the Circolo del Giardino and the Hotel Diana.

In February 1979 Bloom moved to its present premises in Via Crocefisso, breaking its links with Punch. From 1980 on the stylist's collections were shown at the Modit in the Fiera, until 1984, the year in which her clothes for the 1985 Spring-Summer season were presented in the former church of San Carpoforo, with light installations designed by Brian Eno. In 1982 Bloom was joined by the brand Cinzia Ruggeri and in 1986 by the Cinzia Ruggeri line of men's wear.

Cinzia Ruggeri is also a designer and does work in the field of interior decoration. In 1984 she designed the look and publicity of the music group Matia Bazaar. She has designed costumes for numerous stage performances and ballets, and for the dancer Valeria Magli in particular.

The artistic events and exhibitions in which she has taken part include: the 1981 Venice Biennale; the exhibition "Italian revolution" at the Museum of Contemporary Art, La Jolla, California; "Performance adinamica," Deposito Figure, Pesaro, 1983; "La casa onir-

ica, Le case della Triennale," Milan Triennale, 1983, Paris 1983; "Per un vestire organico," Palazzo Fortuny, Venice 1983; "T-Show," Studio Marconi, Milan 1984; "La neo Merce, il design dell'intenzione e dell'estasi artificiale," Milan Triennale, 1985; "Vestiti al video," Galleria Locus Solus, Genoa 1986; "Dopo Gondrand," Il luogo di Corrado Levi, Milan 1986.

The stylist's designs are in the CSAC in Parma. At the office in Via Crocefisso there is an archive of clothes and a collection of press cuttings. (*M.L.R.*)

Luciano Soprani

Lucio Soprani was born at Reggiolo on April 12, 1946. After graduating in agronomy, as was the family tradition, he decided to follow his true passion and started work as a dressdesigner for Max Mara in 1968. This apprenticeship gained him experience in dealing with industrial and technological requirements and led to his designing seven collections in the early seventies. In 1974 he ceased to be directly employed by the company, although he continued to serve as a consultant for another three years. He moved to Milan where he started to work as a stylist for various firms, beginning with Dorian (1974-77).

For the Gruppo Finanziario Tessile he designed Cori (1978-79 Autumn-Winter collection), Solo Donna (since the 1979 Spring-Summer season) and Coriandoli and Corilady (1979-80 Autumn-Winter collections). He has worked for the brand Helyett since the 1978-79 Autumn-Winter season. His 1977 Spring-Summer collection for Pims was a great success for the stylist and the following year he was given responsibility for a second line, Garbo, aimed at a young clientele. His collaboration with the company came to an end at the beginning of the eighties. 1978 saw the beginning of his relationship with Basile, for which he designed the collections of women's wear (1979-80 Autumn-Winter season) and men's wear (1982).

His first show under the brand Luciano Soprani took place at the Fiera for the 1981-82 Autumn-Winter season. The line was produced by Basile and distributed by the FTM until 1986, but is now manufactured by Zama Sport. The Luciano Soprani Uomo collection came out in 1984, which were joined by the second lines Segno women's wear (1985-86 Autumn-Winter season), produced and distributed by Denicler S.p.A., and Segno men's wear (1986-87 Autumn-Winter season), less expensive and aimed at a young clientele. 1986 also saw the launching of after, manufactured and distributed by Maska, with garments in sizes up to 52-54. The stylist also designs a line of furs for Igi & Igi.

Until 1984 Luciano Soprani's offices were in Via Santo Spirito in Milan. They then moved to Via Serbelloni and in October 1986 to the Palazzo Campari in Via Manzoni. The stylist has exclusive boutiques in Milan, Los

Angeles, Dallas and London, with others to be opened shortly in Tokyo and Paris. The lines managed by Soprani include shoes, belts, women's handbags and leather goods. Under license are produced ties and scarves by Tino Cosma and tiles by Quoghi of Modena. In 1986 Soprani designed the theatrical costumes for La Febbre, a play written by Rosso San Secondo and starring Manuela Kustermann. (*M.L.R.*)

Nanni Strada

Born in Milan, Nanni Strada went to live in Argentina at the age of six, immediately after the war. On her return to Italy she attended the State Fashion School, where she was taught cutting by Giuseppe Menghin, who had been Poiret's cutter.

Nanni Strada began her career as a window-dresser and Art Buyer for the fashion agencies of Anna Piaggi, for whom she worked as assistant, and Alfa Castaldi, but she served her apprenticeship at the Celli couturier's — where Alberto Lattuada was the stylist — which combined straightforward tailoring with the production and distribution of models by Dior, Saint Laurent and Ungaro. After the middle of the sixties, she also began to collaborate with Cadette, whose top line was designed by Albini, coming up with garments in jersey with appliqués of tinfoil. In 1968-69 began her collaboration with C. Castelli and Elio Fiorucci's Intrapresa Design. Nanni Strada's first designs for Intrapresa, produced under the name Giovanna Maltese, date from 1969: a collection for De Parisini shown at Palazzo Pitti, a collection of evening clothes for Montedoro and a series of leather and fluorescent perspex sandals for Fiorucci. In 1971 she designed a collection of coats for Max Mara, for the 1971-72 Autumn-Winter season. In the same season she designed a collection of clothes and accessories made out of tubular knitwear produced by Mangili Diffusione, with the participation of Elio Fiorucci, including apparently formless bolts of wool and three-metre-long knitted tights.

In 1974 she was invited to participate in the Triennale with a design on which she had been working for many years: "Clothing and the skin." This consisted in an attempt to produce clothes out of a yarn that can be woven on the tubular machines used to produce stockings. Bloch supported this research and the result was awarded the Compasso d'oro at the retrospective exhibition of 1973. Since 1980 she has largely concentrated on the design of sportswear collections. She designed a series of "sports underwear" overalls that could get over the problem presented by silk's lack of elasticity, by means of a series of construction and sewing devices (cf. "Dal cucchiaio alla città," an exhibition organized by the Milan Triennale in 1983). From the same period date her windcheaters for Dolomite, motorcycling clothes and suits for Yamaha, professional shirts for Ideal Standard and suits of underwear for Abarth.

In 1983 she designed a collection of clothes made out of jersey intended for the Russian market and in 1984 she began to produce designs for the Portuguese market, where she manufactures and distributes through a chain of exclusive stores a complete line of clothing that includes accessories and knitwear as well. In 1986 she started designing a line of "travel clothes."

Nanni Strada has always worked out of the studio of her husband, Trino Castelli, or the offices of various companies. In 1986 she opened the Nanni Strada Design Studio at no. 4, Via del Gesù. This serves both as a design studio and as a sales office. A fairly complete archive of journals, books, drawings and photographs is located on the same premises. (N.B.)

Gian Marco Venturi

Born in Florence on October 4, 1946, Gian Marco Venturi attended the Istituto Tessile Butti in Prato and went on to take a degree in Economics and Business at the University of Florence. In 1974-75 he began to collaborate with a firm, Domitilla, which produced clothes in jersey in the style of Emilio Pucci, designing a collection for the company that was shown at Palazzo Pitti. In 1977 Lebole entrusted its Arelia collection to him, which he designed for three season. At the same time Venturi began his collaboration with

Sander's on leather garments and with Beba, a knitwear firm in Florence, for whom he worked for six seasons from 1976 to 1979. In 1978 he designed the Lux Sport collection for Lux of Parma, replacing Silvano Malta. In 1970 he was hired by Graziella Ronchi to design the Erreuno collections for six seasons, up until 1981. During his last season with Erreuno, the Gian Marco Venturi uomo line of men's wear was born, followed a year later, when he broke off his relationship with the Ronchis, by the Venturi donna line of women's wear, shown for the first time in April 1981 with the Autumn-Winter collection. Manufactured for the first four seasons by linea L, the same company that produces Lux International and Sport, Gian Marco Venturi's collections have been manufactured by the firm Luisa of Calenzano since 1983. From 1975 to 1978 the head office was at no. 18, Lungarno Vespucci in Florence. In 1977 the show room was moved to the Hotel Diana in Milan, and then to Via Spiga, 31 in 1983. Since November 1985 Gian Marco Venturi's firm has been a joint-stock company, but prior to that date Venturi operated as a freelance professional granting franchises under the registered trade-mark "Gian Marco Venturi." The label used is "Gian Marco Venturi Made in Italy," in black on a white ground.

As well as the line of knitwear Marco's Alex-

ander (since 1973), the stylist currently designs the Sfera collections of men's prêt-à-porter for the same company that produces Venturi uomo, the line Avventura for the firm Luisa and the line Bolero for Sander's, manufacturer of the Venturi donna line of knitwear. He has granted franchises for leather goods, accessories and casual wear: the Dainvest line of leather garments, a line of jeans and casual clothing and a line of sportswear that includes jeans, headscarves, leather goods and perfumes for men and women.

His archives are virtually non-existent. His designs have remained the property of their manufacturers and his garments have never been preserved. (N.B.)

Gianni Versace

Gianni Versace, born in Reggio Calabria on December 2, 1946, began his career in 1968. His head office is currently at no. 19/A, Via Spiga and in June 1986 his stylistic studio was transferred to Via Borgospesso, also in Milan. In 1981 the Gianni Versace limited responsibility company was set up to handle his image and creative work, forming part of a holding company that includes Givi moda S.p.A., responsible for distribution. The label is "Gianni Versace Made in Italy."

At the age of eighteen he began work in his

mother's dressmaker's. In 1971 he took over from Albini as the stylist for Callaghan. In 1974 Monti put him in touch with Genny which took him on as stylist, bringing out the line Complice in which invested the major part of his creative energy until the Gianni Versace Donna line of women's wear came out in 1978.

Versace also designed collections for Luisa of Florence around 1973, Glamour by Luisa during the same period, Florentine Flowers in 1973-74, the Zanella group in 1974, Les Copains, De Parisini and Byblos in 1976, the Spazio line of knitwear for the Alma group and the Istante line since 1985. Alongside the main lines Versace franchises his trade-mark for headscarves, accessories, sun-glasses, tiles, furnishing fabrics, a collection of textiles and a line of perfumes.

He designed the costumes for the ballet Josephlegende at La Scala in 1982, for Mahler's ballet *Lieb und Lied* again at La Scala in 1983 and for Donizetti's opera '*Don Pasquale* and Bejart's ballet *Dioniso*, both in 1984.

There is a complete archive of photographs and publicity material. At the Also factory in Novara there is an archive of garments from various collections. Many of his designs have been donated to the CSAC in Parma, although some of them have remained in Gianni Versace's possession. (N.B.)

THE REACTION
OF ROMAN HIGH FASHION

Massimo Mininni

The historical continuity of the high fashion shows and their internal organization of production were under serious threat during the seventies. Questions and discussions arose over the functions and purpose of a sector that, lying outside the area of social affairs, no longer responded to the ideological perspectives that were taking shape.

For a period of about twenty years, Italian haute couture had been expanding its operations on a large scale: from distribution of its products beyond the national borders – to the point of reaching the top rank of the export market – to the involvement of many satellite industries – textiles, footwear and accessories in general. On the occasion of the shows of high fashion in Rome (1978), M. Goracci – in those years general secretary of the National Chamber of High Fashion – gave vent to all his perplexed feelings about a sector that had been in a situation of "grave crisis" for years and predicted its total collapse by 1985. The only alternative was to adapt to the image of the new society.[1]

In fact there was a widespread conviction of the total uselessness of the effort being made by designers and industrialists to actively insert their products on a shrunken national market and an international one in serious decline. The specialist press was of the opinion that producing haute couture was an "anachronism."[2] The couturiers must first get rid of their outmoded view of the atelier as an elegant salon, the temple of a refined clientele, and at the same time put the "Garment" through a concrete evolution consistent with the times.[3] "No more high costs and exclusiveness" which had discouraged the fashion market and driven it away from the capital.[4] While entreaties to the couturiers were couched in these terms, questions were being raised increasingly often about the amount of faith that high fashion still actually inspired. "Do you feel that times have changed to such an extent that fashion has lost all the value and importance that it held previously?" was one of the questions that cropped up most frequently in interviews. The lack of confidence that affected the whole of industrial production during the seventies did not spare haute couture, which lost much of its significance in the national trade balance. The Minister for Industry and Foreign Trade, convinced that the product was not selling, refused to give any concrete aid to those private and voluntaristic initiatives that the sector was still

Rocco Barocco, 1976 Spring-Summer High Fashion collection.

undertaking in a climate of economic self-sufficiency.[5] The bill proposed as far back as 1963 in an attempt to encourage high fashion never got a reading. The Italian political authorities showed total indifference to a problem that elsewhere – in France for example – aroused interest in a wide range of public institutions that were much more sensitive to the whole phenomenon.[6]

In Italy attention was limited to underlining the dramatic figures relating to the decline in production in order to bring out its most negative aspects concerning employment, but there was no thorough investigation of hardships in the sector through serious market analysis and examination of the possibilities for intervention. As if this were not enough, in 1974 a measure came into force that required importers to deposit 50% of the value of the goods imported with the Bank of Italy as a bond bearing no interest. This hit the clothing industry particularly hard, as all its raw materials – silk, wool, cotton, hides – had to be imported.[7]

In a society radically altered by the upheavals of the seventies, even fashion, creative extension and status symbol of everyday affairs, the image and style of a society, underwent a change: the alienated, the poor and the casual became models of dress. Historic *ateliers* closed down their tailoring activities for good: Forquet in 1971; Carosa, De Barentzen and Schuberth in 1972; Antonelli in 1976; Fabiani in 1977. Biki, Fontana, Veneziani and Gattinoni continued to make clothes for a small clientele but no longer took part in the fashion shows. Lancetti, Barocco, Laugh, Mila Schön, Galitzine, Balestra and Valentino went on producing high fashion, though in a lower key, reduced by this time to the promotional role of a name already sufficiently industrialized and engaged in the production of a wide variety of articles.[8]

Only Capucci, who believed deeply in tradition and preferred his creative freedom to commercial success, continued along his own path, giving himself up to his fantastic and fascinating forms. Haute couture ceased to serve as a source of ideas for industry, which now looked instead to the proposals of prêt-à-porter. These in any case appeared much sooner on the runways of Florence and Milan and were the deciding factor as far as lines and colours were concerned.

Although the Roman couturiers did venture into the realm of prêt-à-porter, it was the Milanese market that held on to the top posi-

*Roberto Capucci, 1975-76 Autumn-Winter
collection (photo Lina Tenca).*

*Roberto Capucci, 1980 Spring-Summer High
Fashion collection (photo Fiorenzo Niccoli).*

Roberto Capucci, 1980-81 Autumn-Winter
High Fashion collection (photo Fiorenzo
Niccoli).

*Valentino, 1980 Spring-Summer High
Fashion collection.*

Renato Balestra, 1983 Spring-Summer High Fashion collection.

tion in this field, with its great advantage of an indispensable alliance between the stylists and major industrial groups. Fashion in Milan was born out of the modern conception of mass-production, although it maintained high levels of quality. This was a very different approach from the hand-crafted processes, with their origins in the Renaissance, that underlay sartorial organization in the *ateliers*.

to some extent the measure of true elegance and sacrificing a degree of sobriety and refinement, clothes were designed with a profusion of embroidery, gaudy jewellery and affectations of all kinds. No longer did the search for perfect line lie at the base of any high fashion creation, but the accentuation of those details that made the garment look "richer."

With the eighties came signs of a resurgence.

magazine were all occasions on which the refined disengagement of intellectuals mixed freely with the snobbism of the new tertiary bourgeoisie.

Dinners and cocktail parties formed the new basis for these events, increasing their allure for the new members of the jet set. The long evening dress and the dinner jacket were de rigeur.[10] Thus when the Fendis held a dinner at

Valentino, 1983-84 Autumn-Winter High Fashion collection.

Valentino, 1984 Spring-Summer High Fashion collection.

During those years the National Chamber and the Roman Centre of Haute Couture realized the necessity of setting in motion a new programme of investment and they glimpsed the possibility of opening up a new market in the Middle East. Everyone felt the need to penetrate those countries and started to come out with collections that made an attempt to interpret the taste of the Arab world.[9] Losing

The years of political commitment and idealism seemed to have finally drawn to a close, giving way to a new social attitude: the quest for pure entertainment, the culture of escapism, a new indifference and the theory of new needs now replaced an involvement with politics. "Worldliness" was the protagonist of every event, even cultural ones: the presentation of a book, the inauguration of an exhibition, the launching of a

Palazzo Venezia to celebrate the exhibition devoted to them at the Galleria Nazionale d'Arte Moderna in Rome (September 1985), they invited eminent personalities from the worlds of culture, politics and industry. The event was typical of the now institutionalized marriage between fashion and culture.

Religious rites and official ceremonies acquired a new importance as well, and became a centre of interest for fashionable society. "Grand weddings" celebrated in a new atmosphere of magnificence attracted the attention of newspapers and weeklies, which devoted considerable space to a minute description of the guests and their clothes. At the marriage of Aliai Ricci and Rocco Forte, luxury, holiness and ostentation constituted the principal motivation for the encounter of a refined group of

flected the new turn taken by ways of life and thought."[11]

Even the Roman fashion shows regained the character of great occasions, of festivals staged in original settings that used suggestive works of architecture as a back-drop – Piazza Mignanelli for Valentino and the courtyard of Palazzo Caffarelli for Lancetti. In the front row actresses, the managers of state companies and

wide-ranging project involved the major textile industries as well, and a new period of growth in high fashion was foreseen.[12] The Milanese exponents of prêt-à-porter are now looking at high fashion as a further outlet for their own activities. In the most recent '86-'87 collections for instance, Armani, Ferré, Versace, Krizia and others have come up with designs for evening dresses. Of still greater significance has

Pino Lancetti, 1986 Spring-Summer High Fashion collection (photo G. Chieregato).

Pino Lancetti, 1984-85 Autumn-Winter High Fashion collection (photo G. Chieregato).

invited guests. And this time it was Capucci who was selected to give a sumptuous expression to the personality of the bride, using the wedding dress to convey her desire for distinction.

Femininity for the woman, narcissism for the man: these were rediscoveries to which fashion was only too happy to give its support. In this new society "fashion and dress accurately re-

eminent figures from the professions. And it was to these above that high fashion turned its attention again, inventing fitting models on which to build the image of prestige and success to which most of them aspire.

In undertaking this new course the National Chamber of High Fashion committed itself to a change of image and to becoming the coordinating body of "made in Italy" fashion. This more

been the decision by the same stylists to join the National Chamber of High Fashion (May 1986). For this reason, in term "high" has been dropped from this body's name, pointing to a change in its functions and aims within the sector.[13]

This development emphasizes the new interest in and definitive revival of *haute couture*, although, by definition, it cannot serve as

Rocco Barocco, 1985 Spring-Summer High Fashion collection (photo G. Morabito).

a fulcrum for the stylists. Engaged in a wider range of activities and necessarily tied to methods of working that are directly concerned with the design of ever new and original models, but models that are adaptable to a broader clientele, they cannot hope to aim at the qualities of great craftsmanship, the opulence of fabrics and the attention to detail that remain the exclusive province of the couturiers.

Once again, then, the question arises of the actual development and role of high fashion over the next few years, given that it no longer has even an official designation and, while it continues its *de facto* existence, has renounced any sort of institutional autonomy.

1. M. Goracci, "Moda e occupazione," in *Il Messaggero*, January 17, 1978, p. 13.
2. N. Calandri, "Un'altra moda che non trova ossigeno," in *Il Messaggero*, July 19, 1977, p. 14.
3. P. Soli, "Le collezioni: per chi, perché," in *Il Tempo*, January 20, 1976, p. 9.
4. N. Calandri, "È davvero esclusiva: infatti nessuno la compra," in *Il Messaggero*, July 16, 1978, p. 19.
5. "Alta moda, una prova di coraggio," in *Il Messaggero*, January 23, 1980, p. 17.
6. A. Tondini, "Il grande rilancio dell'alta moda," in *Harper's Bazaar Italia*, July 1977, p. 385.
7. P. Soli, "La moda sotto il torchio," in *Il Tempo*, July 16, 1974, p. 8.
8. P. Soli, "Le collezioni...," cit., p. 9.
9. E. Pirazzoli, "Gli ateliers di alta moda guardano al terzo mondo," in *Il Messaggero*, January 26, 1975, p. 22.
10. G. Bocca, "È gradito l'abito scuro," in *La Repubblica*, December 17, 1978.
11. E. Scalfari, "È sbocciata l'ora dei quarentenni," in *La Repubblica*, December 31, 1978.
12. A. Mulassano, "L'alta moda femminile ha riscoperto la vecchia Europa," in *Il Corriere della Sera*, July 8, 1985, p. 4.
13. "Cambia nome la Camera Nazionale: il prêt-à-porter entra con i suoi big," in *Il Messaggero*, May 12, 1986, p. 13.

*Pino Lancetti, 1984 Spring-Summer High
Fashion collection.*

LEATHER AND FUR

Federica Di Castro

In the Devoto/Oli dictionary of the Italian language (Florence 1971) "pelliccia" or fur is defined as "the product of the skin of the dead animal treated in such a way as to preserve its coat with its characteristics of softness and sheen"; in the same dictionary one finds under the entry "abito" or item of clothing, "style of dress as materialized in a model or in view of particular circumstances," while the entry for accessory runs "whatever is specifically defined on the plain of functionality or importance as complimentary or secondary."

Thus in the history of Italian fashion, the fur coat finds itself in an ambivalent position, depending on whether the stylistic requirements of the moment call for it to be more one or the other. If the garment is considered the basic element of the line, and the accessory the functional or ornamental detail that makes it stand out, the fur, as far as this country is concerned, plays both roles, as an item that signifies the point where elegance crosses the border into the realm of luxury.

The adoption of the fur coat as an item of clothing "in view of particular circumstances" became gradually but incontrovertibly de rigueur among the representatives of aristocratic society and of that upper middle class which filled the gap between monarchy and the recent regime. It was a short-haired fur: karakul, Persian lamb, otter. The classical line of a garment intended to last depersonalized it.

In the photographs of Ghitta Carrell, the celebrated photographer of aristocracy and the Roman upper middle class in those years, it is easy to pick out the recurrent features of their clothing. The subject – from Iolanda of Savoy to the Countess Ciano – is caught in the dignity of an everyday situation, where the fur figures among the other items of clothing: more of a garment than an accessory, with its own function in a life style that demanded constant propriety.

In Milan the two most important furriers were Matti Crivelli (founded in 1847, subsequently to be renamed Matti) and Città di Mosca. They supplied the nobility of Turin, Milan and Genoa, importing the skins from England, where they also learned, through long periods of apprenticeship, methods for making them supple. According to Signora Nelda Matti, the penultimate generation of the family, to which she belongs, was still required to spend years of apprenticeship in London and Paris after the war and over the course of the fifties.

Mario Valentino, redingotes in soft white leather stamped in relief and skirt in black chamois, 1985-86 Autumn-Winter collection (photo Bob Krieger).

It was also in Milan that Jole Veneziani began her rise to the world of haute couture, starting out in fact as a furrier and with French training. But, as has been pointed out elsewhere, Rome was the city where high fashion really took off. The presence of the film industry and of other means of communication (newspapers, reviews, illustrated magazines), together with the city's role as political capital, were decisive factors. The cinema of "white telephones," during the thirties and forties, did not conceal its ambition of rivalling Hollywood.

Alida Valli, Assia Noris, Mariella Lotti, Irasema Dilian and Marisa Denis, to mention just a few names, were all film actresses who indicated to Italian women new modes of carrying themselves as well as new choices of life style. The model of Italian woman that was later to become the dominant one made great strides during the forties. Simplicity, spontaneity and naturalness lie at the root of its charm. Their restrained smiles widened into open ones, the kind of smile immortalized by the Luxardo photographs. This kind of woman wore furs to go out in the morning or to attend sports: the large jacket of local lamb-skin with its warm tints, or even that autarchic fur, the wolf-skin.

The furrier's par excellence in Rome was the Reder establishment in Via Sistina, founded in 1927. Set up by Signor Reder, a Neapolitan of Austrian birth, and his very young French wife, the Reder firm established a reputation on two counts: that of line and that of functionality. What the firm stood for during the thirties, the years in which it made a name for itself, was the idea that "the client should feel at her ease inside a fur"; the fur was to match the image that the woman had of her own femininity and at the same time comply with her requirements for its use. Signorina Reder recalls a number of important public occasions: the wedding of the Infanta of Spain with Prince Torlonia, the last ermine cowl donated to the new pope, Pius XII, by the German College. But she also recalls faithful customers: Margherita Sarfatti, Edda Ciano, Irene Brin.

Reder was located in the same street where cultural innovations were on display at Gasparo Dal Corso and Irene Brin's Obelisco, the first avant-garde gallery to open in Rome after the war. Irene Brin, the editor of *Bellezza*, was as interested in the arts as she was in fashion. The photographer De Antonis, who produced many features in collaboration with Irene Brin, recalls the Obelisco gallery and the Reder establish-

*Matti, beaver-fur in small squares and finn
raccoon, 1981 (photo Babic).*

ment as two poles of the lively image of post-war Rome.

The fur coat, no more than mentioned in the films of neo-realism, played a leading role in the cinema of the fifties. In order to choose their model of fur, women looked not only to the pages of *Bellezza* and later *Novità*, but also to the cinema screens. In the film *Cronaca di un amore*, Lucia Bosé wears furs from the Matti establishment; the same furrier supplied the ones seen in Antonioni's *Le amiche*. The fur is

At the end of the forties and during the early fifties, even furs were influenced by the "new look": small shawl collars, restrained shoulders from which opened the flare. The fur as a rotating cloak that marks out a precise geometry in space. Over the course of the fifties this process was brought to a conclusion, with fur coats getting smaller and following first the "sack" line and later that of the "trapezium." Not renouncing its qualities of thickness combined with form – up until the seventies furs

an investment for its purchaser. Even though it lends itself easily to alterations, the buyer looks at it in terms of "duration." Hence the choice is always a calculated one, even when made in a hurry, but it matches the temperament of the woman who has much more freedom of choice in this matter than when she is selecting a house. She can approach it in the same way as she would a love affair.

Although many of the manufacturing techniques were borrowed from French fashion,

Tivioli, detail of a model presented at the 1985-86 fashion show.

used in these films as a symbol of wealth and luxury, but it is also used to signify power and female authority.

Alongside the minks, otters and sables, the "spotted" furs, leopard and ocelot, were much in vogue. They were extremely costly furs, but at the same time they gave a sporty tone to their wearer. They were "daytime" furs, during a period when items of clothing were defined in terms of the time at which they were supposed to be worn.

were always interlined as well as lined – the fur coat is an object whose changes do not pass unobserved. It delimits feminine space and proclaims its very structure. Thus, with the artisan manufacturing techniques proper to high fashion, it displayed all the characteristics of the design object. In point of fact it was the fur coat that, over the course of the fifties, created a bridge between fashion and architecture, between project and prototype.

There is another point: the fur coat represents

Italian furs were much more independent when it came to line. Over the course of the sixties, furs began to hug the body and the knee was uncovered. Beneath the knee leather was used to cover a woman's body, with the introduction of boots. The fur par excellence of the economic boom was mink in all its versions, along with otter and leopard-skin. The woman dressed in fur would take greater risks than in other styles of dress: the fur coat was a refuge, a token of prosperity and security.

Nelda Matti recounts how it was Anna Magnani, one of her clients, who asked her to leave the fur unattached to the lining fabric. This suggestion was later to be adopted as a common practice. Officially the company belonging to the Fendi sisters was responsible for all possible innovations in the furrier's art. It was here that the relationship between the fashion house and the stylist was established during the sixties, a relationship that granted the maximum of professional autonomy to the stylist, who contributed his own specific skills. The Fendis first used designs by Miguel Cruz, then moved on to those of Chino Bert, finally developing a lasting relationship with Lagerfeld. Out of the Fendi establishment came the idea of matching furs with other items of clothing, the use of inexpensive furs (moleskin or squirrel) treated as if they were costly ones and the handling of the very costly chinchilla or sable in the extremely natural style of the cheaper furs.

In this way the idea gained ground that what really counted was the design; workmanship and the choice of fur were secondary. Furs had to adapt themselves to the model and not the other way around. With this innovation – which in no way compromised the qualities of Fendi products, indeed it strengthened them – the house of haute couture was able to cross the threshold of the seventies without difficulties. With high fashion condemned to silence, furs moved into the limelight. Their forms were adapted to the social changes that marked the course of the seventies. It was a question of line, of the influence of folk styles or historical evocations. In any case, it was a line that spurned the present, acknowledging its existence solely in terms of the technological contributions it had to offer. The furs of animals with exotic names – vairi, kikubiski polecat, stone-marten, summer ermine, lapin weasel, squirrel heads, mole and pekan – were made into gowns, ponchos, gigantic stoles, jackets, overalls, shawls, cloaks and ground-length overcoats. Once again incursions into the world of cinema served to inject a dose of new vitality, drawing on the costumes of other eras.

To some extent the Turinese firm Tivioli was in a similar position to that of the Fendis, defining its intentions over the course of the seventies after an extremely significant presentation (Rome, Grand Hotel, 1971) of brightly coloured furs.[1] Highly advanced as far as technology was concerned, Tivioli, who produced his own designs, cultivated the image of a femme fatale immortalized by the photographs of Gianpaolo Barbieri. Made out of very soft fur with some variations and gradations in length his coats were synonymous with great elegance and sophistication. They were the main item, indicating a line in its intention to define the direction in relation to the user. While Tivioli kept to the realm of high fashion, both Fendi and Matti had begun to show interest in prêt-à-porter.

Fendi with Lagerfeld, Matti with Moschino.

Trussardi, blazer in soft leather, 1986 (photo Giovanni Gastel).

Out of the collaboration between Matti and Moschino emerged a youthful fur, made indiscriminately out of mink, sable or more modest beaver. Line and tradition were united, a skilled "craftsman" interpreted the designs of an ideal stylist. Irony put in its appearance among the furs, playing them down and making their use less dramatic. The traditional image of the 20th-century fur was toned down, just as it moved away from the archetypal one of the hunting trophy. Together they discovered a new

with regard to its use in the manufacture of accessories, shoes, bags and suitcases. Ferragamo for instance – there was an important exhibition of his work at the Palazzo Strozzi in Florence last year[2] – has been an inexhaustible inventor of basic models of footwear and an innovator in the use of materials, and yet has never sacrificed comfort or forgotten that the function of the shoe is to clothe the foot. Gucci has worked with a number of structures, repeating the same models for years and with growing

elegance over the course of the eighties which identifies with a certain political establishment, while his use of leather indicates the persistence of a "material culture," which ignores the caesura between past and present. An example of a line in a continual process of change is provided by the extensive output of Mario Valentino, really exceptional in its versatility, range of products covered and taste for innovation. But among those turning out new products are also to be found Carrano, Albanesi and a

Gherardini, deerskin handbags, 1985-86 Autumn-Winter collection.

Nazareno Gabrielli, "The tweeds" line, 1986.

space, projecting the images into the future by going back over previous history in a playful manner. The idea gained ground of a fur that could be worn by any woman, since she would be able to invest it, this charismatic object, with a multiplicity of meanings.

Leather

An old history of involvement with craftsmanship puts Italy in the top rank as far as the treatment of leather is concerned, as well as

success, or coming out with new ones that are set, timelessly, alongside the former.

The line produced by Nazareno Gabrielli has been extremely consistent and unvarying, but classicism also marks the output of Gherardini, Roberta di Camerino and the Rossetti leather goods factory, or of the up-and-coming Bottega Veneta. The whole range of Trussardi's products (clothes, bags, suitcases) fits into a highly classical line. It should be observed how Trussardi consciously constructed a proposal of "stable"

whole range of fashion designers who use leather alongside fabrics (Coveri, Ferré, Pancaldi). Hence there is a fairly wide dichotomy between continuous innovation and enduring design.

There is one aspect of this division that stands out: while there is a demand for a high rate of change in the design of footwear, bags and luggage show a tendency to stick to successful forms. When one passes on to the field of clothing, the question becomes far more complex, requiring continual alterations in colour

*Mario Valentino, pumps and laced sports
shoe, 1985-86 Autumn-Winter collection
(photo Marco Lanza).*

Bottega Veneta, purse in crocodile skin, plaited kid, softened Russia leather and lizard-skin, 1970s (photo F. Mapelli).

and line along with variable structural relationships. In any case the fashion designer who uses leather finds himself more in the role of an experimenter than those who work in other fields and with other materials: the search for modes of expression has to be concerned with the choice and treatment of the material before tackling the actual designs of the objects for which it will be used. Working in leather, the designer uses the material to convey a dual message: he treats it in the same way as the cloth manufacturer treats fabric, and he uses it to create the model, as part of the process of design. These two processes are contiguous in any case, and overflow into each other.

The profiles of a number of companies reveal familiar precedents in this field as in that of furs, which have allowed the development of expertise with the material and with techniques for its use. All the modern designers acknowledge their debt to this tradition of craftsmanship, to which they assign as much importance as to their own talent.

The firm of Nazareno Gabrielli, founded in Tolentino in 1907, was originally a bookbinder's. Over the course of time it broadened its range of activity and rose to national prominence. In 1929 the firm was commissioned to handle the decoration of those parts of the first royal train, constructed by Fiat for the House of Savoy, that were made out of leather. Returning to the market in 1970, it now puts out a diversity of products, ranging from handbags and luggage to an extensive line of accessories made out of leather, sometimes in combination with other materials (titanium and gold). In recent years the firm has acquired rights to the manufacture of the historic Frau armchair and has set up the Chienti tannery, now the third largest in the EEC.

Maria Grazia Gherardini, whose activities in Florence brought her to international attention (her first successful collection was presented in the Sala Bianca of Palazzo Pitti in 1969), boasts among her ancestors one who was a "casemaker," with a workshop in Via del Fiordaliso (1885). The secret of her succes lies in improved proportions, in the highly balanced approach to relations, in the selection of colours and in a gradual renewal which is not allowed to affect the stability of a number of basic models.

The Bottega Veneta was set up in Vicenza in 1968 and has established a reputation for a number of special methods of leatherworking, such as plaiting and Russian leather (hot pressing). These require constant supervision by craftsmen alongside the use of machinery. The models have a simplicity that allows the special characteristics in the treatment of the leather and its working to be seen to better effect.

The history of the shoe industry has been one of constant innovation. When skirts rose above the knee during the sixties, the shoe took on a new importance in relation to the body. Boots came into vogue and the leather was softened, so as to hug the leg. It was the beginning of an

Mario Valentino, evening blazer in lurex leather, 1986 Spring-Summer collection (photo Bob Krieger).

Mario Valentino, tunic in perforated leather, printed with mosaic pattern, 1986 Spring-Summer collection (photo Bob Krieger).

evolution in the definition of footwear that led to it mimicking the stocking, at times rising above the knee. Female sexuality was expressed in the brief stretch of leg left bare, often very little indeed. Shoes and footwear grew in importance. The stylist became more concerned with proportions than with materials.

Today the stylists of footwear (Fratelli Rossetti, Pollini, Sergio Rossi, Bruno Magli, Diego Della Valle, Tanino Crisci, Osvaldo Martini and Claudio La Viola) are coming up with intelligent innovations in the areas of combinations, colours and materials, and suggesting new relationships of proportion between heel and upper, accentuating or softening the curve of the foot, or swarthing it in soft leather.

"One cannot think in terms of a single version of femininity" is Mario Valentino's motto. Of Neapolitan origin, his company has been in the forefront of the business for thirty-five years. During the fifties he conquered America with his invention of the stiletto heel. Since then his popularity has increased without a let-up. Starting out with footwear, he has expanded his production into a variety of lines, with leather clothing taking the lead. At the beginning of the eighties he presented a series of woven leather "fabrics" out of which he made garments; he has even succeeded in producing leather piqué. On the other hand, like Fendi, he has availed himself of the collaboration of stylists on matters of design. Lagerfeld, while working for Mario Valentino, produced some highly unusual articles. He is a stylist who, in his collaboration with different fashion houses, manages to come up with different ideas that are suited to the particular requirements of the company he is working with. Muriel Grateau, Giorgio Armani, M. France Acquaviva and, most recently, Gianni Versace have all designed items for Valentino. His shoes have been designed by Montana and Lagerfeld. His image has been publicized in the magazines through the work of photographers like Orsi, Gastel, Mapplethorpe and Newton.

Thus the complex machinery of a company that is now top in its field throughout the world is entrusted to a team. Valentino never tires of seeking out new directors, producing amazing results at every new show. Out of a constant collaboration between research and design is born his image, in its turn cunningly interpreted through photography. Newton sets his dramatic black clothes, designed by Versace, against a marine background, amid rocks and wind. This distinctive approach to objects, as conveyed through photography, plays a decisive role in the relationship with the work of Mario Valentino, in the sense that it is part of his identity.

"The liking for contrast in order to invent new proportions should be indicated as a means, a direction."

1. A. Mulassano-A. Castaldi, *I Mass Moda*, Florence 1979.
2. S. Ricci, *Salvatore Ferragamo*, Florence 1985.

Fendi

Coat in natural summer ermine printed with "scale" patterns, 1986-87 collection. Of full cut with drapery pattern that, starting from the collar, marks the attachment of the raglan sleeve; ankle length, shirt collar, silk lining in the same colour, internal buttoning. State of preservation: excellent. Owner: Fendi showroom. (*M.M.*)

Coat in black broad-tail, 1986-87 collection.

Of straight cut, it is entirely hand-made and has raglan sleeves made out of cross-cut pieces of cloth that hang in a teardrop shape. Ankle length, shawl collar, double-breasted fastening with two large buttons made out of the same material, two large patch pockets and silk lining in the same colour. State of preservation: excellent. Owner Fendi showroom. (*M.M.*)

Coat in natural-coloured female pekan, 1986-87 collection.

Flared cut, formed out of vertical strips. Two cuts at mid-shoulder separate a panel at the rear that hangs down to the feet; "conchshaped" sleeves formed out of horizontal strips. The collar emerges from the central vertical section giving fullness to the shoulders; asymmetric length, silk lining in the same colour. State of preservation: excellent. Owner: Fendi showroom. (*M.M.*)

Suit in soft silvered leather. The long jacket with geometric details has exaggerated lapels, cut at waist, large patch pockets closed by a central metal button, single-button fastening and breast pocket on the left. The skirt is straight with silk lining in the same colour.

The silver coating on the leather was obtained by means of a special process of hot pressing, plus lamination. Label: "Mario Valentino" attached at back of neck. State of preservation: excellent. Measurements of jacket: shoulders 45 cm, waist 80 cm; skirt: waist 72 cm, length 70 cm. Owner: Mario Valentino showroom. (*M.M.*)

Suit made up of skirt in corn-flower-blue soft leather and small jacket in the same material with "batik" flower patterns on a corn-flower-blue ground, 1986-87 collection.

The jacket, patterned by a special silk-screen process, has a very tight-waisted line, small lapels, breast pocket on the left side and wide sleeves that grow narrow near the cuff. The "wrap around" skirt is of straight cut with silk lining in the same colour. Label: "Mario Valentino" attached to the back of the neck. State of preservation: excellent. Measurements of jacket: shoulders 45 cm, waist 75 cm; skirt: waist 62 cm, length 68 cm. Owner: Mario Valentino showroom. (*M.M.*)

Coat made up of narrow bands of nut-brown Chinese polecat, 1986-87 collection.

Large barrel-shaped jacket of asymmetric length, with a gathered flounce that accentuates the asymmetry. Round collar and low sleeves. Label: "Matti" attached to inside of left hip. State of preservation: excellent. Total length 130 cm. Owner: Matti showroom. (*M.M.*)

Coat in nut-brown demi-buff mink, 1986-87 collection.

Line based on a "large T" with wide kimono sleeves that, starting from the hips, emphasize the upper part. From hips to ankles, the coat forms a tube that swathes the body. Round collar and internal buttoning. Label: "Matti" attached to inside of left hip. State of preservation: excellent. Total length 130 cm. Owner: Matti showroom. (*M.M.*)

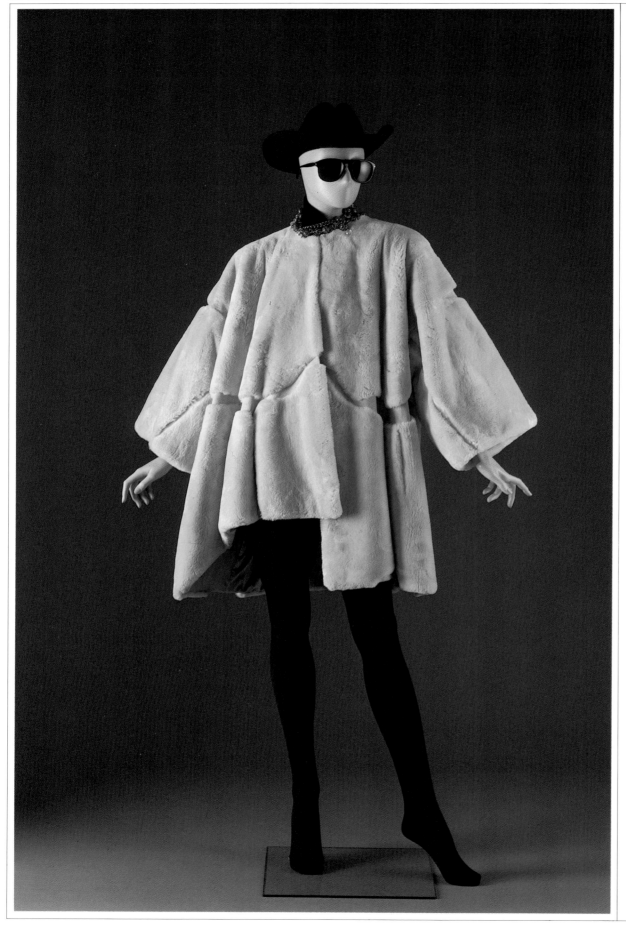

Coat in beige-coloured satiny natural beaver, 1986-87 collection. Large circular coat with kimono sleeves and asymmetrical length in front. An irregular "split" runs across the coat horizontally. Round collar and single button at top. Label: "Matti" attached to inside of left hip. State of preservation: excellent. Length 90 cm. Owner: Matti showroom. (*M.M.*)

Biographical Notes

Fendi

The Fendi house was founded by Adele Casagrande and Edoardo Fendi in 1925 in a small workshop producing bags and furs in Via del Plebiscito in Rome. In 1964 the company moved to Via Borgognona, where its head office is still located. The Fendi house was established on a firm basis over the years through the activity of the five daughters who, after their father's death, joined Adele in the management of the firm. Since 1978, the year when their mother died as well, the firm has been run by the five Fendi sisters and several of their husbands.

Paola Fendi was born in Rome in 1931. She began to work in the family business in 1946, first handling the production and sales of leather goods and then moving on to the fur department. Since then she has been in charge of the purchase of pelts as well as their assembly into garments and all other technical aspects: tanning, dyeing and production methods.

Anna Fendi was born in Rome in 1933 and started work in the company at the age of sixteen, looking after the leather goods department, which she still runs, taking care of planning as well as production. Apart from designing handbags, suitcases and other leather products, Anna is in charge of the design of prêt-à-porter.

Franca Fendi was born in Rome in 1937. After working in various departments, she is now in charge of the press office and public relations.

Alda Fendi was born in Rome in 1940. At the age of eighteen she began to work alongside her sister Anna in the leather goods department. Since 1964 she has been involved with furs, her primary concern being the prototypes for the collections. At present she is in charge of the fur showroom in Via Borgognona.

The Fendi sisters have set out to break the classic rules of the fur trade, introducing new lines, colours and methods of production and eliminating rigidity and conformism from a garment that was previously not considered amenable to changes. They have revived furs that had been forgotten or neglected because they were considered too "lowly," and experimented with new methods of tanning and dyeing and combinations of different furs.

In 1964 Miguel Cruz designed the first collection to make use of eccentric colours. In 1965 Karl Lagerfeld began his collaboration with the Fendis, bringing about a definitive change in the concept of the fur. He created a soft and light garment that was easy to wear, in which artistic creativity and skilled craftsmanship were integrated, developing those ideas of mixtures, inlays, interlacements, quilting, combinations of furs, inserts, lacquering and the use of right and wrong sides that form the basis of the marriage between Fendi and Lagerfeld.

In 1978 the Fendis took their furs to the fashion shows at Palazzo Pitti in Florence, where they had their first encounter with foreign buyers. In the same year they began to produce an industrial line of prêt-à-porter that, in its ideas and quality, closely resembled their High Fashion products.

Since 1974 they have been appearing at the Frankfurt shows. 1977 saw the birth of their line of ready-to-wear clothing, given the name "365," presented the same year at the Milanese shows. Since 1978 Fendi has been selling a collection of shoes, produced by Diego Della Valle, to which were added bathing costumes for the Marson firm, sunglasses with Lozza and stationery with Stassi of Bologna, in production since 1984. In 1985 Fendi lent the firm's name to the uniform of the women's corps of the Roman municipal police and a perfume.

In the same year the Galleria Nazionale d'Arte Moderna in Rome staged an exhibition — "Un percorso di lavoro Fendi – Karl Lagerfeld" — illustrating the stages in the making of furs from the first idea for a collection to the manufacture of the garments of which it is made up.

Throughout these years the Fendis have maintained ties with the world of entertainment, collaborating in the realization of costumes for films by Visconti, Bolognini, Zeffirelli, Fellini, Leone, Wertmuller, Ferreri, Risi and Russell. 1983 saw the advent of the third Fendi generation with "Fendissime," a new, more youthful and economic line of furs and leather goods.

Their products are distributed through boutiques and stores under their own trademark in the major cities of the world. Their markets include Italy, the other major European nations, the United States and Japan. All designs, prototypes and production models are preserved in the firm's archives. (*M.M.*)

Mario Valentino

Mario Valentino was born in Naples in 1927. After getting his school-leaving certificate, he decided to undertake the same career as his father Vincenzo, who in 1908 had opened a leather workshop in Naples's Piazza delle Mura Greche, where he made shoes. It was in a spirit of innovation — since he found his father's collections too classic — that Mario Valentino opened his own shoe factory in Naples in 1952, at no. 38, Via Fontanelle.

His first collection was marked by pink pumps with thin heels which, while respecting the requirements of high quality, represented a new venture in the field of footwear.

In 1954 he was invited to take part in a show of High Fashion held in the rooms of the Grand Hotel. His contribution was a "small folly," a sandal made out of coral. The approval of journalists — Irene Brin and Matt Bally — and the appearance of this shoe on the front page of the French edition of *Vogue* gave Mario Valentino the opportunity to sign a contract with the American company I. Miller, which lasted until 1966. These were the years in which he launched stiletto heels and tapering shoes with metal toe-caps on the American market.

In 1968 he started producing handbags and small leather goods and in 1977 brought out a line of women's prêt-à-porter, a sector entrusted to his wife Bianca. The raw material for the collections was leather, with innovative colours and manufacturing methods that made use of advanced technical procedures without ever losing sight of the aspect of craftsmanship.

Exemplary of such lines of research are the following collections: 1981, models realized out of leather braided in such a way as to produce vertical stripes in various colours; 1983, the leather treated as a fabric, using special tanning processes that rendered it flexible and malleable; 1983-84, pleated and perforated leather; 1986, lurex chamois; 1986-87, the surface treated by a process of "hand-carding" to acquire the appearance of the woollen fabric customarily used to make loden coats, "Mongolian" lamb and vean satin, suede whose lightness and changing colouration gives it similar characteristics similar to those of silk.

In 1979 he brought out his line of men's prêt-à-porter, joined by bathing costumes made by the firm Marson in 1983, umbrellas manufactured by the Ombrellificio Piemme in the same year and headscarves and ties in 1984, distributed by the company Seta e Seta.

His collaborators have included Mauriel Grateau in 1977-78, Marie France Acquaviva in 1978-80, Giorgio Armani from 1980 to 1984 and Gianni Versace since 1984, all for women's prêt-à-porter; Claude Montana since 1982 for men's prêt-à-porter; for shoes, handbags and small leather goods, Karl Lagerfeld from 1965 to 1984 and Claude Montana since 1984.

The products are distributed under his own trade-mark through boutiques and stores in the major cities of the world. His markets are Italy, the other major European nations, Japan, the United States, Australia and the Far East. The designs for all his collections are preserved in his archives in Naples. (*M.M.*)

Matti

The firm Matti-Crivelli was founded in Milan in 1847 by Giovanni Matti, with offices in Via Pietro Verri. In 1943-44 the furrier's moved to Via Manzoni and in 1945 took the name of the partner Barbini as well. When the building was struck by a bomb, the firm moved once again, to Via Matteotti, only to return to Via Manzoni at the end of the war, after liquidation of the partnership. The furrier's was finally moved to no. 14, Via Santo Spirito in 1972. The firm's excellent workmanship and the quality of its furs led to the royal house becoming one of its clients. Until 1973, in fact, Matti's clientele was an exclusive one that demanded made-to-measure products. From 1954 to the present day it has been Nelda, the wife of Costanzo Matti, who has been in charge of this department of the firm. Since about 1964 their son Gianluca has been responsible for the technical side of the trade. Backed up by experience subsequently gained abroad in the treatment and tanning of furs, he has been the proprietor of the company since 1973, along with his wife Mimma. These years saw a renewal of both the firm's production, with the birth of a line of prêt-à-porter, and its style, no longer tied to classical cuts but adapted to fit in with contemporary stylistic research. In order to respond to these new requirements, the firm has availed itself of the collaboration of Franco Moschino since 1979. His skill in the free association of forms and materials — "assembling" different models at different times that take their inspiration from a wide variety of sources — has helped to give a characteristic and completely new appearance to the firm's furs.

Having taken part in the Milan prêt-à-porter shows since 1979, the firm's products have been distributed in the United States, Japan and Germany during the eighties. Sales are made through boutiques and specialized stores. All designs and samples of furs and other materials are preserved in the firm's archives. (*M.M.*)

MEN AND FASHION: CLASSIC TAILORING

*Elisa Coppola, Carla Cavelli Traverso,
Marzia Cataldi Gallo*

Male Elegance in Tailoring

From the end of the war to the early sixties "made-to-measure" clothing was marked by a slow but continuous evolution, a process that brought no important changes but only periodic modification of details. These alterations were mainly concerned with the length of the jacket and overcoat and, to a lesser extent, the width of jacket, collar, trousers and lapels.

As far as changes in taste are concerned, it is important to point out the absence of a truly Italian style up until the mid-fifties. Styles in tailoring were in fact fragmented by the presence of various "schools" of a regional character that were simultaneously at work in the major centres. There was no unifying tendency with the exception of a generic conformity to the classic style of English inspiration.

Yet on the level of international influences and exchanges, a distinction should be made, from the immediate postwar period onwards, between a highly select élite that remained faithful to the great tradition of English tailoring[1] and a new social category, the so-called "nouveaux riches," that showed a preference for the American style. This essentially middle-class group of consumers was also the only one in a position to have new clothes made for it, thereby ensuring the success of the American "bold look," referred to in Italy as the "abito a sacchetto" or "baggy suit." This style entered the country through the influence of the cinema, which offered a new masculine ideal figure, audacious and vigorous in character, that set out to express "the intrepid spirit and self-assurance of the victors in terms of the aesthetics of dress as well."[2]

The "bold look" remained in vogue, with variations to take into account the standard physique of the average Italian man, until the early fifties. This was certainly the crucial moment in the evolutionary process in men's fashion, as a precise trend began to take shape that emerged out of the meeting between different regional tendencies, leading to the definition of a style that could genuinely be described as Italian.

In order to get an overall picture of modes of dress during this period it is worth picking out from among the basic models of the male wardrobe a number of typical styles in made-to-measure tailoring.

Dress of a sporting character comprises the classic combination of a patterned jacket, very often in tweed, and trousers in a solid colour;

Brioni, evening suit with figured silk jacket over black trousers in mohair and wool. The model, worn here with an overcoat, was shown in Florence in 1952 and exhibited at the Fashion Institute of New York in 1985. Rome, Brioni tailoring firm.

this could be completed with a tie or with a wool bow-tie, especially if the waistcoat was replaced by a light pullover, and buckskin shoe. More up-to-date sportswear, from the second half of the fifties onwards, included the club jacket or blazer with gilt buttons; however the typical broad stripes of the original blazer[3] were replaced by more sober patterns and tones, especially in the morning version or in the more formal afternoon one.

Among the innovations in the field of elegant clothing was a kind of evening dress for relatively informal occasions, the jacket and trousers introduced as a style of British and North American derivation,[4] where it was a strict rule that the jacket should be in a darker solid colour than the trousers.

In the sector of evening dress there was a definite bias towards the shawl collar from 1953 onwards. This feature, particularly suited as it was to the single-breasted jacket, made a considerable contribution to the decline of the double-breasted dinner jacket that had been in favour since the thirties. The dinner jacket with shawl collar remained in fashion throughout the fifties and did not make way for the single-breasted jacket with pointed lapels and then the double-breasted one until the early sixties.[5]

With regard to coats and overcoats, tailors showed a decided preference for models that were not too full or bulky. This was partly for functional reasons and partly to differentiate handmade garments for mass-produced ones. The only non-waisted overcoats admitted were the highly classical *chesterfield* and *aquascutum* models.[6]

The rapid increase in the number of motor-car owners led, from the mid-fifties onwards, to a considerable interest being shown in this kind of winter clothing, especially the short coat or car coat. This garment was characterized by its greatly reduced length and its straight cut. Among the numerous models proposed there was a notable preference for styles or details of military derivation. To this brief discussion of the principal types of men's wear in the fifties and sixties should be added a few remarks concerning sartorial "style." The "Italian style" of dress, by this time a synonym for good taste and elegance, showed a clear trend towards simplification. The line was more balanced and comfortable with respect to the past and tended to make the figure more slender. The jacket had more natural shoulders, with heavy padding giving way to thin linings, and a slightly shaped cut, favoured by the use of softer fabrics. Yet alongside these innovations there was no shortage of references to the past, especially where details were concerned. These included the use, in the single-breasted jacket, of a small card-carrying pocket set on the upper right-hand pocket and short slits at the side which, initially received with a certain amount of diffidence, gradually took on a decisive role in the appearance of the modern jacket. In fact their use, at first limited to sports jackets, was resulted in a shift away from the waistcoat, although this trend was criticized by the champions of being "well-dressed." In summer suits were made up of no more than two pieces and it became increasingly common to wear a light mohair pullover on top of the shirt in winter. The most fashionable of these years was the "Borsalino" but especially during summer it became common practice to go bare-headed. The progressive disappearance of this accessory provided a considerable shot in the arm for the ventionality, making it more simple and gradually exerting an influence on the more formal type of garments.

In the design of these casual models a notable source of inspiration was the adoption of styles or particular features taken from military uniforms.

The war over, it was not difficult to update these items of apparel and transfer them into civilian life, in part because they themselves were almost all derived from sporting or work

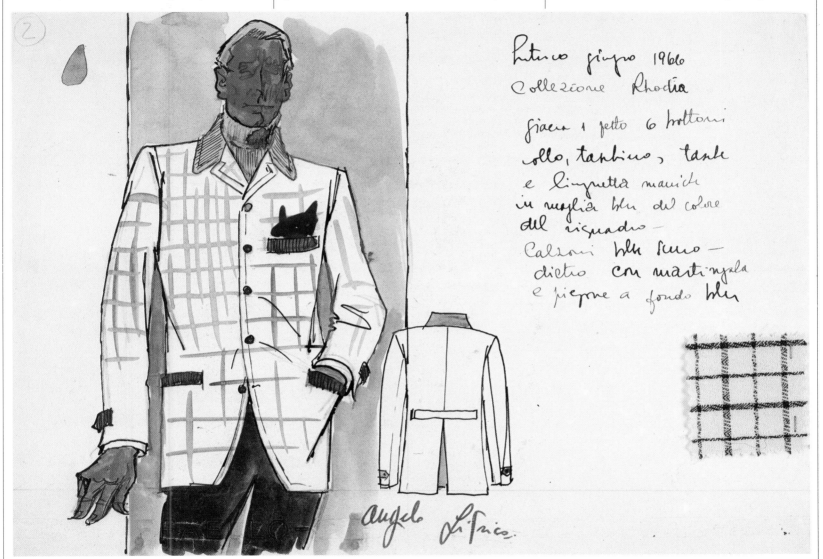

Angelo Litrico, design for jacket made of squares of white terytal, 1962 for Rodhiatoce. Ink and watercolour on paper, 24.5 × 34 cm.

later extended to morning jackets, walking jackets and, more rarely, double-breasted jackets.[7] Quilting grew increasingly popular, from around 1957, in all types of sports jackets; this was another detail lifted from the "belle époque" style of dressing.[8] One of the most interesting developments that took place in the fashion of those years was the process by which certain fundamental elements of men's wear gradually fell into disuse. The tendency towards practical and casual clothing that was a mark of the time umbrella industry.

One constant feature of men's fashion in the fifties and sixties was the tendency to create a less and less rigid silhouette so as to come up with a more practical and unconstrained mode of dress in keeping with changes in society. This demand for practicality received perhaps its greatest impetus from two elements that may be considered characteristic of modern behaviour patterns: leisure and sport. In fact the clothing created for these occasions helped to liberate fashion from a certain con-

clothes.[9] Among the most popular models were the various mountain jackets, later adopted for town use as well, including the duffle coat: a three-quarter length coat known in Italy as a "montgomery" and based in fact on the style of coat with loop fastenings worn by the English general of that name during the war. Then there was the long jacket, without collar or sleeves, derived from the leather jacket worn by British motorized troops.

Another garment with military origins was

Angelo Litrico, design for large double-breasted jackets 1963 Spring-Summer collection. Ink and watercolour on paper, 35.5 × 25 cm. Rome, Angelo Litrico tailoring firm.

the trenchcoat: this raincoat, based on a model in use by the English army ever since the first world war, was revived with great success in 1957.[10] Sports jackets, derived from models used for hunting or golf, and brightly coloured flannel or woollen shirts to be worn without a tie met with increasing favour as well.

From the viewpoint of production it is worth pointing out that in this particular sector of clothing as well the tastes of a highly demanding clientele were catered to by made-to-measure tailoring, especially when sporting or recreational activity required a dignified style of dress, whether on the high seas or in the winter sports resorts.

With the rapid growth of interest in nautical sports sailing apparel aroused a great deal of attention and its designers drew much of their inspiration from the traditional uniforms of the North European merchant marine and navies. To the classic dress of the cruise-liner passenger, made up of navy blue blazer and white trousers, were added short jackets very similar in style to the regulation jackets of the British and American navies, sailor's jackets of Norwegian inspiration and jackets or three-quarter length coats derived from the *parka*, a characteristic garment of very ancient Arctic origin. Already adopted as an item of military apparel during the Korean war,[11] it exercised an influence on styles in winter sportswear as well.

Around the middle of the fifties, alongside the usual clothing of a formal character there was a revival of interest in items of knitwear to be worn during the summer holidays. The return to fashion of these garments was given a considerable boost by the influence of the so-called Capri style, which was very favourably received abroad, especially in America, and had a decisive effect on styles of beachwear.

As far as the more traditional styles of men's wear are concerned, it should be pointed out that made-to-measure tailoring, after reaching a peak in the early sixties, experienced a serious slump as a result of the growth of the ready-to-wear industry and the upsurge of fanciful fashions among the young.

In a world where even the outward differences between social ranks were being eliminated, the figure of the individual "trend-setter" who spent a great deal of his time in laborious consultations and interminable fitting sessions with the tailor went into decline. Elegance came to be seen as a collective phenomenon and interpretation of the prevailing taste was entrusted to a new professional figure, the stylist.

While the decline in traditional sources and attitudes led to the gradual disappearance of small artisan tailoring workshops, it also obliged the couturiers of High Fashion to turn their attention to the changes in taste so as to avoid meeting the same fate, although they took care to maintain the high standard of their work. It was in fact the climate of revival that emerged out of some trends in youthful fashion that provided new opportunities for tailoring.

Among the innovations which sent tremors through the Italian tailoring business was the generous use of colour. Designs emerged with vivid tones, sharp chromatic contrasts and gaudy patterns. This trend did not even spare the more traditional fabrics, such as the Prince of Wales check. But the greatest ferment of ideas came towards the middle of the sixties, with a genuine explosion of fantasy and a consequent proliferation of sartorial styles. It was the moment when the tailor gave in to the temptation to join the

need "was manifested through a return to more traditional and established forms of dress and to a rejection of eccentricity which was perceived as dangerous."[13]

Hence from the first half of the sixties onwards the dominant theme was the classic style. In relation to the history of costume this was no longer a mere return to styles of the past, but a "new," up-dated classic form of dress, revised and promptly taken up and diffused by stylism, while a socially and economically priviliged

and alpaca for the Autumn-Winter season and silk, linen and cotton for the Summer. Colours rarely ventured outside the muted range of shades like iron grey, dark blue and beige. Another sign of the return to the traditional canons of dress was the reappearance, after 1975 of the waistcoat. *E.C.*

Tailoring as a Socio-Economic Phenomenon

The fifties and the beginning of the sixties may be seen as the last golden period of Italian

the Celanese-Brioni Collection...a fashion preview of 1963-64 men's wear thinking

Brioni, casual and town models created in 1963 for the Collection Fiber Company. Indian ink and watercolour on ivory-coloured paper, 29 × 42 cm. Rome, Brioni tailoring firm.

ranks of the innovators.[12]

The climate of uncertainty created by the ideological conflicts of youth culture and the economic recession that was the inevitable result of the oil crisis of 1973 determined a profound change in economic and social structures that was reflected in the realm of fashion as well. In fact after almost a decade of rejection of tradition and consequent proliferation of "free and easy fashions" there were signs of an ever increasing need for stability and security. This

clientele continued to patronize the tailors. By the mid-seventies, after a long interlude following the crisis in the sector, there was a revival of interest in purely artisan styles of clothing. The substantial rise in the prices of ready-to-wear clothing and the return to a classic style gave a new lease of life to the made-to-measure garment.

For the suit with jacket and tie, symbol of the "new" bourgeoisie, high quality fabrics were back in favour: fabrics like cashmere, mohair

tailoring. The economic recovery that came after the destruction and shortages of the second world war had produced a moderate degree of prosperity that was gradually extended to a broader range of social classes and created a whole new host of consumers. The ready-to-wear industry, which, as we shall see, would be the prime cause of the crisis in tailoring, was in its infancy, with only two major manufacturers, Lanerossi and Marzotto. The propensity for risk-taking, entrepreneurship and the ability to

FRAK
1964

Guido Bosi, preparatory design for evening-dress with short waisted jacket, signed and dated 1964. Black felt pen on thin white paper, 28 × 22 cm. Bologna, Guido Bosi.

promote one's own image, all characteristic qualities of the emerging society, entered into the world of tailoring, embodied in men like Litrico, Piattelli, Palazzi, Testa and Brioni in Rome, Nativo and Rettori in Florence, Blasi in Naples, Coccoli in Turin and Caraceni and Tosi in Milan, just to mention a few. These tailors established a reputation for "made in Italy" fashion, setting themselves up in competition with the best upholders of elegant dress of the time, the English and the French.

With a view to publicizing the new tailoring talents on a national and an international level, the Festival of Men's Fashion at Sanremo and the fashion shows at the Accademia dei Sartori in Rome were established in the early fifties. Aimed at the promotion of Italian fashion abroad were the Florentine shows of High Fashion, organized by Giorgini to "open up the prestigious and influential North American market to Italian creativity."[14]

These favourable conditions had kept alive a tailoring industry involving something in the nature of one hundred thousand individual tailors.[15] Most of them were Southern Italians who, following the traditional routes of internal migration, made their way to cities like Milan, Turin, Bologna, Florence, Naples and Rome, as well as to the larger provincial centres, in search of fame and fortune.

This decade saw a modest decline in artisan production as a percentage of garments sold, which was accompanied by an acceleration in the rate at which individual items of clothing were made, due to technical innovations and an increased rationalization of the work process, and a relative increase in the annual output of each tailor. Statistical data published in 1972 by the Italian Fashion Board confirm this tendency: "In the fifties, 16 million adult Italians acquired a suit on average every four years; the tailor made 86% of them. On average each tailor produced 27 men's suits a year, one every two weeks. Ten years later, the adult male population of Italy bought a suit of heavy cloth or a summer suit every two years. 68% of these were made by the tailor. On average each tailor manufactured 66 men's suits a year, more than one a week. Output remaining at this level until the middle of the sixties,[16] when the tailoring industry began to be more seriously affected by the clothing industry, and especially by medium-to-high and luxury prêt-à-porter, whose prices were highly competitive with those asked by the tailors.

The very concept of fashion imposed a priori by a restricted group of tailoring firms that determined and directed the taste of the public, creating models that were then imitated and sold at lower prices, using less expensive materials and with less care taken over the manufacture of the garment, meant a type of clothing that was no longer elitist. Rather it spread spontaneously across a variety of social groups and ended up by giving rise to a multiplicity of demands for different fabrics, fibres, colours and designs, to which the top level of tailoring firms found it difficult to adapt.[17]

The "fashion for rags" adopted by the young protesters of 1968 as a symbol of social criticism and rejection of traditional "bourgeois" dress led to young people abandoning the tailored suit for once and for all.[18] In the meantime the clothing manufacturers had thrown themselves into the gap left between the made-to-measure garment and luxury prêt-à-porter, catering to all levels of the population. Even at the beginning of the

able to turn his valuable skill at cutting to advantage.[21]

By 1969 the number of tailors left was "about 52,200 and they produced an average of 57 men's suits a year; little more than one a week. Over a span of about twenty years (1950-1969) the market tripled in size as a result of increasing income and the impetus provided by mass production, artisan output doubled, rising from 27 to 57 suits, while the number of tailors fell by a third."[22]

enduring fame of its predecessors but rode on the wave of the economic boom.

A very harsh process of selection had gradually reduced the number of tailors, leaving no more than thirty-five thousand of them by the second half of the decade.[23] These artisans no longer found it necessary to emigrate in order to achieve success and build a reputation. They were already earning a good income, even while remaining almost unknown to the general public, thanks to a sufficiently numerous clientele

Activity	Northwest Italy	Northeast and Central Italy	Southern Italy and Islands
Clothing and/or fabric stores	16.1	26.0	19.5
Clothing and/or fabric trade	32.2	8.0	15.6
Other shops	12.9	14.0	14.3
Clerical work	—	2.0	—
Farming	—	16.0	3.9
Employee	19.4	16.0	16.9
Employed tailor	9.7	4.0	3.9
Other activities	9.7	14.0	25.9
Total	100.0	100.0	100.0

Activity	Non-administrative centres	Administrative centres	Large cities
Clothing and/or fabric stores	23.4	8.7	14.3
Clothing and/or fabric trade	14.1	34.8	—
Other shops	14.1	17.4	—
Clerical work	—	—	14.3
Farming	8.6	—	—
Employee	16.4	13.0	42.8
Employed tailor	3.9	8.7	14.3
Other activities	19.5	17.4	14.3
Total	100.0	100.0	100.0

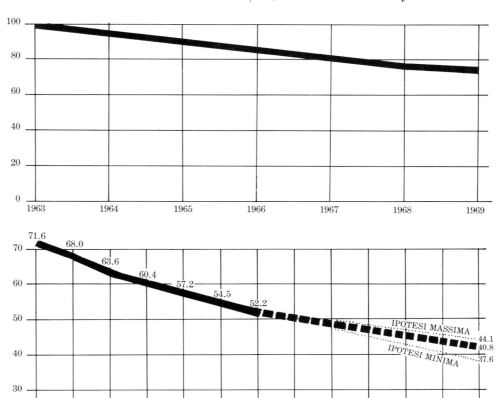

Table indicating extra-sartorial activities carried out by tailors at the beginning of the seventies (from G. Tartara, "Il futuro della sartoria artigiana in Italia," supplement to Informazioni, *bulletin of the Ente Italiano della Moda, May-June 1972, p. 8).*

Tables indicating respectively the numbers of active tailors and new tailors from 1963 to 1969 and an estimate of the number of tailors working in 1975 (from G. Tartara, "Il futuro della sartoria...," op. cit., p. 5).

sixties more than half the garments made in Italy were mass-produced. Within ten or fifteen years the proportion had risen to eighty per cent.[19]

The size of the market for the more competitive kinds of ready-to-wear clothing, thanks to the low price of mass-produced garments, and the high cost of labour[20] obliged the tailor of medium-to-low level quality to give up his unprofitable work as a private individual and get himself a job in the clothing industry, which was

The decline of the tailor as a craftsman producing clothes for the public at large meant an increase in the status and success of those tailors with the greatest technical skills, imagination and business acumen. Thus it was that the new kind of tailor who had emerged at a moment in history not favourable to him was forced to resort to promotional strategies that had hitherto been unthinkable for a member of his profession. The generation that entered the tailoring business during the seventies did not rely on the

that included not only the well-dressed among the Italian middle-classes but also those from abroad: Germans, Japanese, Americans and more recently Arabs too.

In order to give new status and greater reach to the profession, commercialization played an increasingly important role in the tailor's activity.

The tendency, advocated by a number of tailors' associations as early as the end of the sixties[24] and whose origins can be traced back to the same period, encouraged the tailor with a marked degree of commercial flair to replace his customary workshop located on the second floor of some apartment block with a fitting-room annex by a combined workshop and store, a sort of "luxury boutique" where the client had the chance to select the whole of his wardrobe.

Hence many tailors gradually moved on from simply making suits to producing coordinates and accessories.[25] Management of the tailoring firm became increasingly concerned with sales

The Importance of Technique

In my desire to provide an overview of the situation in men's tailoring since the war, I have thought it worth taking a look at the technical aspects that, in a way, are the truly distinctive feature of a tailor-made garment and constitute the fundamental point, apart from style, that differentiates it from both ready-made clothing and from that of the stylist, also made by industrial methods. While remaining artisan activities, tailor's workshops have had to ration-

cutting, the assembly and the fitting.

The taking of measurements is a preliminary operation of decisive importance to the success of the finished product. In fact it is on this stage that the precision of the pattern is based and any mistake at this point inevitably produces defects. Unlike the ready-to-wear industry, which usually makes use of standardized proportional measurements, tailors take their measurements directly from the client's body. The most important of these are the measurements of all the

Litrico, design for sports jacket and trousers with fabric samples, 1966-67 Autumn-Winter collection.

Indian ink and watercolour on paper, 33 × 24 cm. Rome, Angelo Litrico tailoring firm.

and advertising.[26] This change which, especially since the mid-seventies, had affected a large number of tailors to varying degrees, has recently led many of them either to reduce or even to cease their artisan activity altogether, and to replace the made-to-measure garment with semi-mass-produced or ready-to-wear clothing.[27]

In fact the number of tailors has currently fallen to between twenty and twenty-two thousand.[28] *C.C.T.*

alize their working procedures in order to maintain rapid rates of production. This need was felt the middle of the sixties, when the fact that tailors had to remain competitive with ready-to-wear clothing manufacturers became obvious.

To this end various methods have been suggested to synchronize the activity of workers. For example, tables were published that could be used to regulate their activity.[29]

The most important stages in the making of a garment are the taking of measurements, the

circumferences (chest, waist, hips), the lengths of jacket and trousers and the measurements of individual parts. Measurements are taken by means of special methods which are usually thoroughly explained in the cutting manuals. In point of fact this stage is very closely connected with that of cutting, which is done by some tailors on the paper pattern and by others directly on the fabric, according to methods that have either been handed down by family tradition or that are learned from publications for

Ugo Coccoli, preparatory design for "Nehru" jacket, made in 1969. Watercolour on white paper mounted on board, 32.3 × 16.5 cm. Turin, Ugo Coccoli tailoring firm.

Ugo Coccoli, preparatory design for pin-stripe suit made in 1969. Watercolour on white paper mounted on board, 32.3 × 15.2 cm. Turin, Ugo Coccoli tailoring firm.

Mario Donnini and Agostino Caraceni, pin-stripe suit in dark grey worsted with double vertical white stripes, 1974. Genoa, private collection.

tailors such as those by Domenico Caraceni, Domenico Ciracì and Ligas, and from specialized courses like the one in "Men's Fashion" set up in Milan in the fifties or the ones held annually at the Accademia dei Sartori in Rome.[30] Some of the most famous tailors, like Tommy and Giulio Caraceni, completed their training as tailors with Henry Poole in London or Portès in Paris.[31] At these stages in the process, the tailor has the chance to carry out what is perhaps the most important function of made-to-measure tailoring, that of adapting the item of clothing to different builds, and if necessary correcting their defects. He works above all on the concealed parts of the garment right from the earliest stages of its make up. In fact greater care is needed in taking the measurements of a client with a defective body structure and special contrivances can be used, in accordance with the physical defect that needs to be masked, at the cutting stage as well. From this point of view made-to-measure tailoring has an advantage over ready-to-wear clothing manufacturers who, owing to the mass-produced nature of their output, are obliged to ignore a broad range of potential customers.

After the first fitting, the tacking is taken out of the garment in order to correct any defects that have emerged. At this point some tailors take off a paper or cloth pattern which is then stored in the archives. In this way the most reliable tailors are in a position to accept orders by telephone.

Evolution in style has come through modifications that may have involved changes of just a few centimetres in the more classical vein of tailoring, somewhat more in those tailors' workshops with closer links to the different trends in fashion. An example of this can be found in the measurements adopted for jacket lapels by tailors specializing in the so-called "classic line" like Caraceni and Pozzi in Milan or Tommy and Giulio Caraceni in Rome, who have retained a measurement of 8.5 cm unchanged over the years, while a tailor's like Battistoni[32] in Rome, relatively more sensitive to changes in fashion, has changed the size of lapels. In the seventies, for instance, when the jacket became more tightwaisted and close fitting, the size of its lapels was increased to 10-11 centimetres.[33]

The key points are very few in number and, as far as the jacket is concerned, are connected with the handling of internal padding, the lapels and the shoulders. The cut of the trousers depends largely on the presence or absence of darts at the waist, which determine the width at the pelvis. The presence of darts gives a softer and more comfortable line that has been characteristic of the post-war period up until the mid-sixties. The width of the leg has been almost constant with a tendency to narrow at the cuff (20-21 cm). Afterwards the general trend towards a more tightwaisted line led some tailors to produce trousers that were close-fitting at the hips, narrow at the knees and as wide as 28 or 30 cm at the cuff, but this style has been abandoned to return to a more

ARBITER

BIMESTRALE DI MODA ATTUALITA' E CULTURA · ANNO LIV 1981 N. 1 - L. 3.000

SPED. ABB. POST. GRUPPO IV/70

VIA IL PALTÒ, ECCO LE NUOVE GIACCHE.
L'UOMO DI NEVE.
A TEATRO CON SOAVI, DAL SARTO CON STREHLER.

Giorgio Strehler wearing a jacket made by
Bosi, in Arbiter, *no. 1, 1981.*

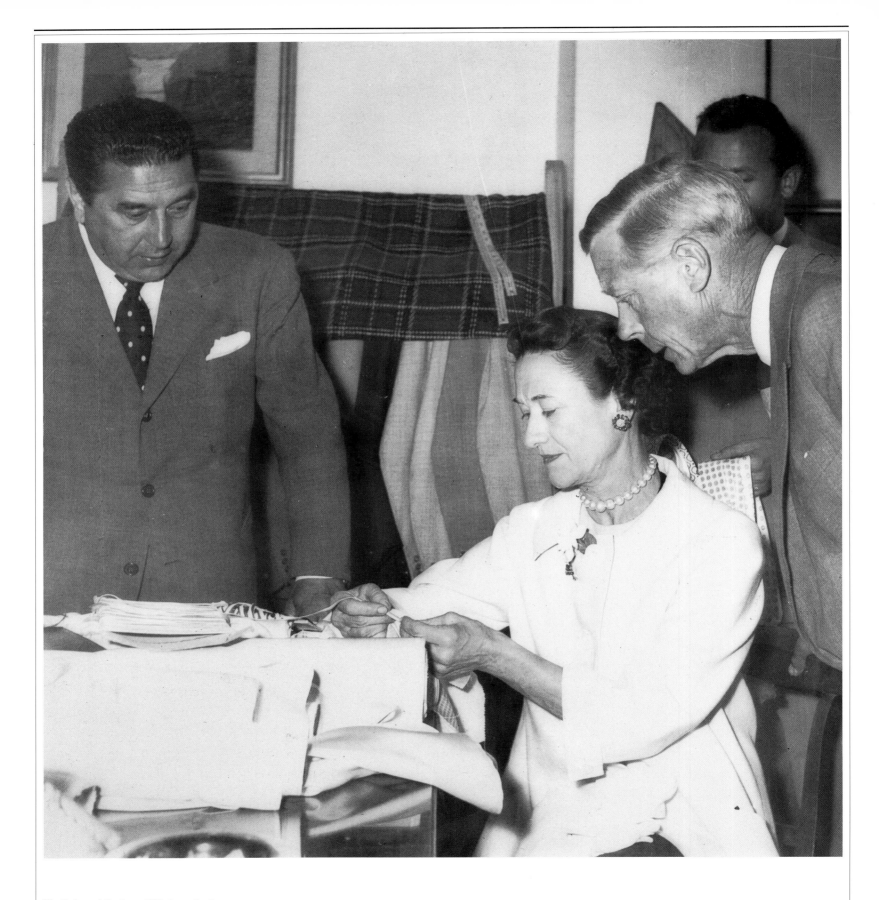

The Duke and Duchess of Windsor selecting
fabrics for shirts with Guglielmo Battistoni,
founder in 1946 of the shirtmaker's and
tailor's of the same name.

"classic" cut with darts at the waist giving about 6 cm of extra girth at the hips and an almost constant width of the leg of roughly 23 or 24 cm.

The technical innovations of the last few decades have lightened clothing and made it more wearable, adapting it to the changing necessities of life and taste.

Changes in custom have led to the disappearance of several details such as the buttonhole behind the left lapel of the jacket which was used to hold a flower, a symbol of refinement that is now only rarely to be seen, or the small grommet in the trousers in which the tongue of the belt buckle was inserted to keep the belt in the correct position.

These trimmings have been retained, even though they have lost their original functions, by a few tailors bent on continuing a tradition of elegance and refinement that has its roots in 19th-century dandyism and that has, perhaps only temporarily, faded away.[34] *M.C.G.*

The Classic Accessories
The Shirt

Since the last war the characteristics of the made-to-measure suit have remained fairly constant, retaining fundamental ties, like a certain type of tailoring, to a style that has shunned the innovations introduced by stylists with an ever increasing frequency since the sixties.

Yet it cannot be said that there have been no reciprocal influences between the two styles. In Rome, for instance, Battistoni has slightly widened and lengthened the points of the collar with respect to classic canons,[35] while in Genoa – a city which is heavily influenced by English and traditionalist taste – Finollo[36] has maintained his model unchanged ever since the shirt factory was opened in 1900: the collar has only been slightly modified so as to be lower and more open or higher and more closed. In this way it can be adapted to the different somatic characteristics of the client (especially where the shape of the face and the line of neck is concerned).

Out of the research carried out in the best-known Italian workshops have emerged a number of constant trends in the use of colours and fabrics: white is the colour most often used for evening wear while coloured (especially light blue) and striped shirts are worn increasingly often during the day, obviously without forgetting the fundamental "rules" by which a pinstripe or check suit has to be combined with a shirt in solid colour.[37] The white collar can be used with a light blue fabric or with a fairly marked stripe.

Many shirtmakers have revealed a certain tendency, especially in recent years, to use Italian fabrics, whereas in the years immediately after the war these were more frequently acquired abroad. In particular, linen and beaten cotton came from France, oxford, poplin and vyella from England, while from Switzerland were imported embroidered fabrics that were used in the sixties to make evening shirts which, in accordance with

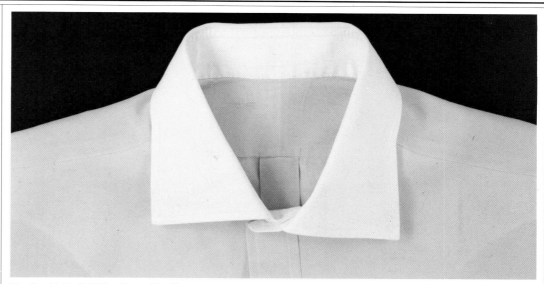

Finollo, shirt in light blue linen with collar in white linen, 1954. Genoa, private collection (photo Studio A.D.V., Genoa).

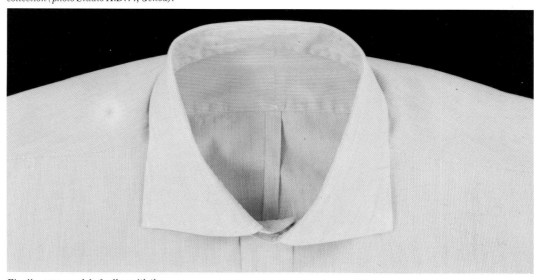

Finollo, 1974, model of collar with the characteristic angle between the rear, and lower, part and the points, designed to *prevent them from "knocking" against the collar-bone (photo Studio A.D.V., Genoa).*

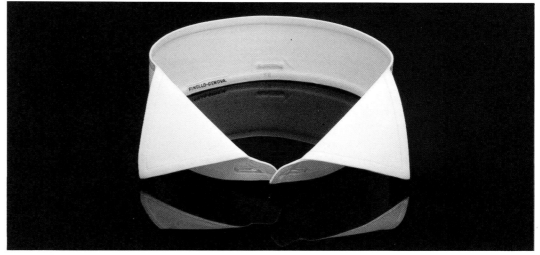

Finollo, raised collar to be worn with ceremonial clothing such as evening dress. E. Finollo collection (photo Studio A.D.V., Genoa).

current taste, were decorated with embroidered vertical lines on the chest. Over the same period fabrics patterned with small geometric motifs in the same colour or in contrast with the background were in vogue. The general bias towards the casual in the fashion of those days led to the disappearance of a number of refined details, such as the tongue used to attach the shirt to the trousers or the strip that passed beneath the crutch.

Even today the collar[38] remains the most important element of the shirt. For the cuffs the model with rounded corners for the daytime and the double one with cuff-links for evening wear are by now accepted. The models for collars are very varied: however the most common are the classic one with more or less open points, the one rounded off to prevent the point from knocking against the collar-bone and the button-down one.

To make their shirts "impeccable" many workshops devote particular attention to the *balzana*, i.e. the part that follows the line of the shoulders at the back. Since the latter are almost always slightly different, the *balzana* is made in two pieces sewn together in the middle, so that the two parts fit perfectly.

The client's initials are usually hand embroidered at chest level, in blue on cotton shirts, in darker shades than that of the shirt itself when made out of silk. The Finollo firm in Genoa inserts them in a coat of arms in which the date is also embroidered. *M.C.G., E.C.*

The Tie

Over the course of the last thirty years the most noticeable changes in the tie have been in its proportions, which have closely followed the evolution of the jacket collar. There was a considerable widening of the tie between the end of the sixties and the start of the following decade, when its widest point was increased to 12 cm. At present its measurements have stabilized around 8-9 cm, which may be described as classic, as can its length that wavers between 130 and 140 cm. The firm E. Marinelli of Naples represents an exception to this, making ties "to measure" in proportion to the build of the client. It is worth pointing out that variations in size have been largely restricted to industrially made ties, while many shops that have preserved an artisan tradition intact have always stuck to the standard size.

Among the main types of decoration that have been in vogue at different times since the war, there was the slightly iridescent tie made out of shiny silk that was very fashionable during the fifties.

In the sixties came the large knit woollen tie and the "figured" silk ones, with small designs in the same colour as the tie itself or embroidered with Art Nouveau-style florets. In more recent years the use of pink and patterned cashmere ties has prevailed.

Alongside these short-lived fashions other classic motifs have retained their popularity and are still among the most widely used today. These include polka dots, geometric patterns and stripes, especially the "regimental" style that, under the influence of English fashion, has been one of the most common ever since the fifties. As far as fabrics are concerned, hand-made ties are almost exclusively made out of English cloth, while nationally produced fabrics are preferred by industrial manufacturers. When made by hand, the tie is cut out of a special piece of cloth, known as a "square," 90 × 70 cm in size, from

Finally the pocket handkerchief deserves a mention, an accessory which the elegant man can add to his dress. Current fashion dictates that it should never match the tie, except in colour at the most. The material most often used for patterned handkerchieves is silk foulard, while the extremely classic white one to be worn with dark suits of a more formal character is made out of beaten or very light linen. The handkerchief to be inserted in the *pochette* should be folded into five points. *M.C.G., E.C.*

technology and the widespread distribution of the industrial product, resulting in a drastic reduction in the number of artisan glovers. The process of making gloves by hand involved a preliminary softening of the hide, necessary in order to be able to stretch it to the dimensions required by the various cuts. Cutting was carried out with the help of the stretcher and the calliper, which gave shape to the glove. Finally came the sewing, which in expensive gloves was done by hand, in "saddle-stitch" for sports

Blue silk tie with hand-embroidered flag. E. Finollo collection, Genoa.

Guido Bosi, regimental cashmere tie in the colours sugar paper, bottle green and beige, 1981. Bologna, Guido Bosi tailoring firm.

which two or at the most four ties can be obtained. The inner part is made out of wool covered with silk or mixed silk, for which can be substituted a "double square."

Another type of neckwear is the bow-tie, made out of silk, satin or velvet and worn on important occasions.

In recent years there has been a revival of this model, with it being worn along with sports clothes as well. The fabric most often used is wool, in a solid colour or with small designs.

The Gloves

From the fifties to the eighties models of gloves have not changed and have maintained the same level of popularity. The only exceptions have been a decline in the use of the skins of protected animals such as deer and gazelle and an alteration in the dimensions of the male hand, probably due to the progressive decline in manual activities.

The manufacturing process, on the contrary, has been modified by the introduction of new

gloves with the leather sewn on the inside and in "piqué" for the elegant evening model, with the two edges superimposed.

Current manufacturing is aimed primarily at the production of functional accessories suited to a wide variety of occasions. For example: driving gloves, whose popularity has increased in step with the progressive rise in the number of cars in circulation (the combination of mesh and leather, both in the "full-finger" and in the "half-finger" version, improves the grip on the

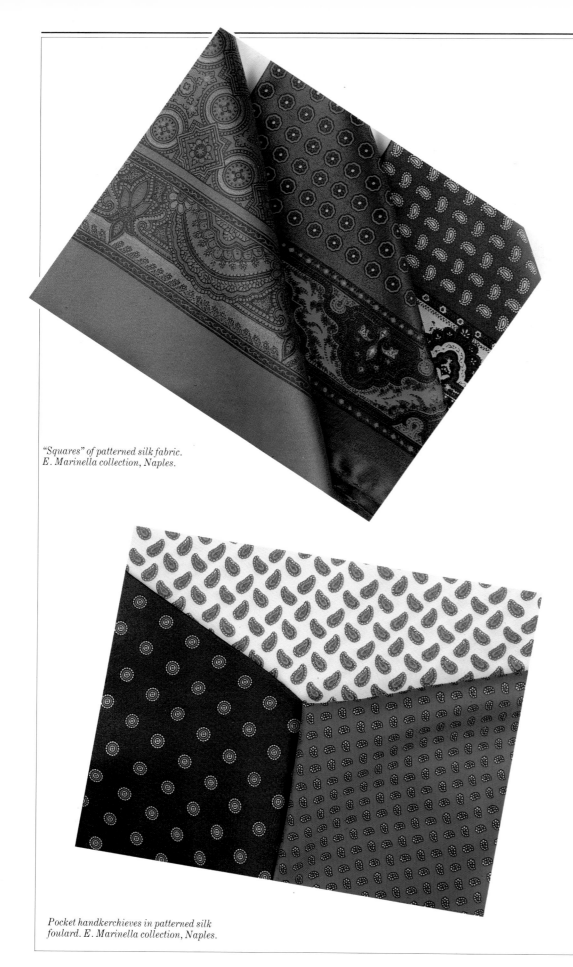

*"Squares" of patterned silk fabric.
E. Marinella collection, Naples.*

*Pocket handkerchieves in patterned silk
foulard. E. Marinella collection, Naples.*

steering wheel), or gloves for golf or riding, which in the first case protect only the left hand, used to maintain a direct hold on the club, and in the second the area where the reins are held, with reinforcements between the index and middle fingers. *C.C.T.*

Footwear

Over the last thirty or thirty-five years there have been few alterations in the shoe, most of them concerning the type of leather adopted and manufacturing processes. The models have remained the same, the "francesina" and the "derby," both with laces.[39] In the sports version part of the vamp and the toe box in particular are decorated with punched or perforated patterns or broguings, while shoes for elegant occasions are smooth and devoid of decoration. The "derby" model is frequently coupled with morning dress.

At the beginning of the fifties the Italian shoe had a number of original features, centering on apt combinations of different materials – impressed calfskin, chamois, smooth calfskin – and costly and exotic hides in matching or contrasting colours, black and grey, brown and beige, burnt brown and ochre, but always with either the light or the dark colour dominating over the other.

Other more casual models, to be worn at all hours of the day and made out of calfskin impressed with fairly indistinct patterns, their classic cut interrupted by punch-marks and perforations, replaced the two-tone models. It was with these that Italian footwear made a name for itself between the mid-fifties and the mid-sixties.

The success of casual styles resulted in a modernization of classic models: shoes with wide soles and rounded toes; loafers with large fringed tongues sometimes with plastic buckles in the same colour as the leather, to which studs and elastic are applied; "francesine" with heavy stitching used in mass-produced shoes to produce the effect of hand-stitching, or with clearly visible perforations running along the edges of the shoes.

Evening wear was still dominated by the slip-on shoe made out of patent leather and grogram, with a blunted and slightly squared-off toe. These models on geometric lines, accentuated by the milling of the heel, were distinctive of footwear in the sixties, arriving at the square sole by the end of the decade.

Over the same period the high boot enjoyed a temporary success, but soon revealed itself not to be very practical and was replaced by the half-boot which reached to the bottom of the calf and was sometimes lined with fur. It remained in fashion up until the middle of the seventies, a period of great popularity for the loafer too. Then fashion began to favour increasingly pointed shapes, with a tendency to be more slender and have lightweight soles and heels. With the shift back to classic styles in the middle of the seventies the shoe regained its lightness and comfortableness. The "francesina" and "derby" models returned, with Windson or straight tacks, in soft leather.

Handmade shoes accentuated this return to the classic by making casual shoes elegant as well, in order to make a clear differentiation between them and the mass-produced versions, which had been gradually gaining ground. The national hide and leather industry gradually abandoned the production of natural materials for handmade shoes, preferring to turn out substitutes for industrial manufacturers. Hence shoemakers had to get their raw material from abroad. Initially it was England that supplied hides and leather. For economic reasons that source was supplanted by Germany for black hides and by France for coloured ones and leather. *C.C.T.*

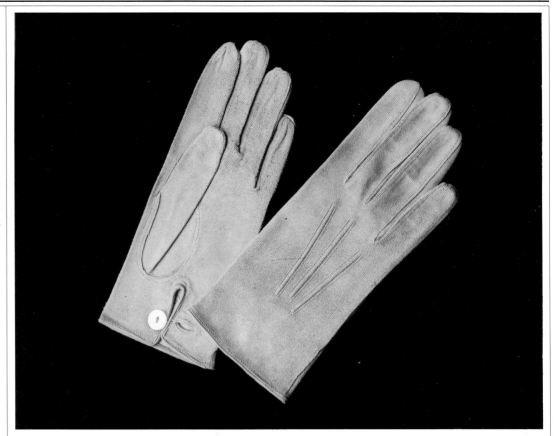

Dress glove in gazelle skin with mother-of-pearl buttons, made in 1958 by Cream of Genoa. Genoa, Cream company.

Sports glove in peccary skin with internal "saddle-stitching," made in 1978 by Cavagna of Turin. Turin, Cavagna company.

1. The main proponents of this kind of dress in Italy are the Caraceni who, active since the early decades of the century, have remained faithful to a classic style of the English type. On the activity, origins and lineage of the Caraceni family, cf. *La Repubblica*, suppl. September 7, 1985.

2. Cf. *Arbiter*, issue XXXV, 1962.

3. Cf. *Arbiter*, issue XXX, 1958. The blazer "is the jacket that those in England or other English-speaking countries who belong or have belonged to a college, a university or a club wear on the occasion of the more important sports competitions (...). The broad stripes of the blazer (...) are in the Colours of the university, college or club."

4. Cf. *Arbiter*, issue XXXVI, 1963.

5. Cf. *Arbiter*, issue XXXVIII, 1965.

6. The "chesterfield" model has a double breast with six buttons and a half-belt that gathers the full width of the coat into loose folds; the "aquascutum" has a flap covering the buttons, round sleeves, patch pockets and straigth lapels.

7. Side slits, common in England since the early 20th century, were only accepted in Italy during those years, taking

"Derby" model shoe in black calfskin, beige calfskin lining and leather sole, made in 1965 by the Albertini company of Milan. Milan, Albertini.

on a classical character over the course of time. Cf. *Arbiter*, issue XXVI, 1953.

8. Cf. *Arbiter*, issue XXVIII, 1955.

9. B. Du Roselle, *La Mode*, Paris 1980, pp. 213-214.

10. It is worth pointing out that in these years the raincoat took on increasing importance and in many cases served as a substitute for the overcoat.

11. Cf. *Arbiter*, issue XXVIII, 1967.

12. Most of the time this aspiration translated into the presentation of a single specimen that becomes the prototype for large-scale runs, usually organized on a production line basis. A number of tailors tried to emulate the activity of stylists by designing lines for industry or even by turning themselves into entrepreneurs.

13. A. Ciabattoni, *Il sistema della moda*, Turin 1976, p. 71.

14. E.V. Massai, "La piccola grande storia della moda italiana," in *Il genio antipatico*, catalogue of the exhibition mounted by P. Soli, Milan 1984, p. 12.

15. It has not been possible to discover the exact number of tailors working in Italy at the beginning of the fifties, in that

the figures tracked down show a fair margin of difference. Hence it was decided to give a median figure: cf. the 1951 statistical survey, "78,000 self-employed tailors and assistants, 66,000 employees," in *Il Maestro Sarto Italiano*, yr. VI/28, 1, January-February 1964, p. 16; "And just think that in the fifties there were about 12,000 men's tailors in Italy," recalled the tailor Antonio Spagnolello, in R. Bosio, "La sartoria cerca nuovi allievi," in *Il Sole 24 Ore*, October 2, 1985.

16. G. Tartara, "Il futuro della sartoria artigiana in Italia," supplement to *Informazioni*, bulletin of the Ente Italiano della Moda, yr. V, 26, May-June 1972, pp. 2-3.

17. A. Ciabattoni, op. cit., pp. 33-34 and note 2.

18. This tendency is confirmed in P. Devril's observations on the fashion of the second half of the sixties; cf. *Vogue 1920-1980. Moda, immagine, costume*, Milan 1980, p. 141.

19. Cf. A. Ciabattoni, op. cit., pp. 34-35 and 168-170, and the articles by N. Liverani in *Nazione Sera*, December 2, 1963, and V. Emiliani, in *Il Giorno*, January 20, 1964.

20. A. Ciabattoni, op. cit., p. 193. In the articles published in *Il Maestro Sarto Italiano*, yr. IX/49, 5, September-October 1967, pp. 4-5 and yr. X/54, 4, July-August 1968, pp. 4-11, the most urgent demands in the sector are discussed.

21. Cf. G. Tartara, op. cit., p. 41 and note 7.

22. G. Tartara, op. cit., pp. 2-5 with its accurate description of the condition in which tailors found themselves.

23. Cf. G. Tartara, op. cit., p. 5.

24. A number of articles that appeared in *Il Maestro Sarto Italiano* in 1968 (yr. X/53, 3, May-June, pp. 5-9 and 56, 6, November-December, pp. 17-18) exhorted the tailor "to come down to street level and set himself up in a shop... A fine shop window, especially when stocked with accessories as well, is often capable of attracting new customers." On the same subject see again G. Tartara, op. cit., pp. 8-9 and the tables on p. 8 that show how even in 1969 there was already a tendency for tailors in the North and in provincial capitals to gradually combine their usual activities with the opportunities presented by the textile market and manufacturing.

25. Information on the realization of coordinates and accessories is supplied in the biographical entries for tailors.

26. At the twenty-sixth World Congress of Tailors in 1975,

André Azioshanoff of the "Office de documentation par le film" showed a series of slides to document and at the same time encourage this new trend in tailoring; cf. *Arbiter*, yr. XLVIII, no. 302, 1975, p. 18.

27. This information has been taken from a sample poll being carried out by the P.B.F. Iniziative Moda di Milano group, the results of which were kindly made available by its director, Mario Pescarini, to whom we would like to express our gratitude.

28. Cf. *Il Maestro Sarto Italiano*, yr. XXVI, 3-4, October-December 1984, p. 7, which also gives the turnover of the tailoring business, amounting to about 2,500 billion lire for the Italian market alone, and *Modavision*, yr. IX, 5-6, September-December 1984, p. 19.

29. Cf. *Il Maestro Sarto Italiano*, 1967, no. 3, year IX-7, p. 10, in which was published a schedule of the "Synchronization of the various phases of work," and idem, 1967, no. 5, year IX-49, pp. 6-7. At the "Incontri moda" held in Sanremo in 1969, master tailors Zenobi and Nazareno Fonticoli (partner of the tailor Brioni) described the organization of an experimental workshop provided with a "zig-zag" machine, a Strobel machine for quilting and a steam-iron and demonstrated the considerable difference that they made to the time required for making a jacket. On the subject, cf. D. Ciracì, "I problemi attuali del sarto artigiano," in *Il Maestro Sarto*, XXIII, 1981-1984, pp. 18 and 25, and *idem*, 1982-2, pp. 4-5.

30. Cf. D. Ciracì, "La scuola di taglio," Rome, and idem, in *Il Maestro Sarto*, XXIII, 1981-1, p. 17. For the Ligas Method, cf. D. Ciracì in *Il Maestro Sarto*, 1967-1968, and following years.

31. D. Pardo, "I maestri dell'aplomb," in *Capital*, no. 6, 1981, p. 110.

32. The Battistoni company began its activity as a tailoring firm in Rome, where it was already manufacturing shirts, in about 1960. Cf. *Carta della moda maschile 1958-59* and E. Della Giovanna, *Ricordi di un amico*, Rome s.d. The personality and the work of the founder are described.

33. There are two kinds of lapels: *pointed* and *indented*. The *pointed lapel* is characteristic of double-breasted jackets and has the peculiarity of possessing a buttonhole on both the left and the right lapel; the *indented lapel* is used mainly for single-breasted jackets and has a single buttonhole on the left. For the Milanese tailor Rovello the point of the double-breasted jacket should be 67 millimetres wide and the collar 6 centimetres; in the single-breasted jacket the "tooth" should be 39 millimetres wide. Cf. F. Novelli, "Est modus in revers," in *Capital*, no. 10, 1984, pp. 353-358.

34. My thanks go to Alberto Gollini for having drawn my attention to these not very obvious details, but ones which have helped to give an impeccable and refined appearance to men's clothing.

35. The Battistoni shirt-factory was set up in Rome in 1946 by the founder Guglielmo, whose sons carry on its activity today, expanding it to include the manufacture of suits and ties. Official suppliers to the House of Savoy and the Royal House of Holland, they have always had contacts with artistic circles, as can be seen from Lucio Fontana's 1953 design for a tie fabric and the model of a collar with shaped points designed in collaboration with the painter Matta.

36. The Finollo shirt-factory was established in Genoa in the early years of the century and built up an international clientele through the quality of its output. These have included the Duke of Windsor and, more recently, the lawyer Agnelli.

37. For a detailed description of colour combinations V. De Buzzacarini, *Fior di camicia*, Milan 1984.

38. On the structure and shape of the collar, cf. ibidem, p. 60.

39. The difference between the "francesina" and "derby" models lies in the lacing. In the first case this is formed out of a single strip, with small "stems" inside the toe-cap, while in the second two lateral flaps come together, forming "stems" superimposed on the toe-cap.

Guido Bosi

Overcoat in pure camel-hair with beige silk lining and horn buttons. The model has a double-breast with six buttons and wide lapels, patch pockets, straight sleeves and whole cuffs. A broad central fold at the back, divided into two pressed lateral pleats; attached at the hips is a half-belt in two pieces. Measurements: length 115 cm; shoulders 47 cm. Label: coat of arms with crown and the inscription LABOR OMNIA VICIT on the left side, "GUIDO BOSI/Bologna - Tel. 263832/Paris - Tel. 5480576/Sig. ..." The coat was shown at the Festival of Men's Fashion in 1959. The preparatory design is kept at the Sartoria Guido Bosi, Bologna. (*C.C.T.*)

Sports outfit in sky-blue mohair and wool. The jacket is of body-hugging line, defined by darts, and is closed by a zip. It has two pockets with flaps, a small collar with rounded lapels and small lateral notches. Worn beneath the jacket is a light, sky-blue wool sweater with a turtle neck. The trousers, that narrow slightly towards the bottom, have lateral zips and a half belt. Measurements of jacket: length 72 cm, shoulders 49 cm; trousers: length 112 cm. Label: "Brioni-Roma, Via Barberini 79. Modello 2000. Luglio 1955." The model was shown in Rome in 1955, on the occasion of the World Convention of Tailors, as a futuristic proposal for the year 2000. In 1985 it was on show in the exhibition "Italy The Genius of Fashion" at the Fashion Institute of Technology in New York. Owner: Sartoria Brioni, Rome. *(E.G.)*

Caraceni

Suit in light blue grisaille of *fil à fil* wool with thin skyblue lines that form large squares of a classic pattern. The single-breasted jacket is reinforced on the chest with horsehair and flax stalks and has lightly padded shoulders. The trousers with double tucks at the waist are fairly wide in the leg (ca. 26 cm) with the width remaining almost constant until it narrows near the turn-up at the bottom. Measurements of jacket: length 82 cm, shoulders 46 cm; trousers: length 110 cm. Label on the inside pocket of the jacket, indicating the name of the tailoring firm of Mario Donnini and Agostino Caraceni, the address, the year 1965 and the name of the client. Owner: private collection in Genoa. *(M.C.G.)*

Dinner jacket in silk fabric with silk lining and lace *cape*. The white jacket is single-breasted with only one button, has pointed lapels and is entirely hand-quilted; the sleeves are closed by three buttons. The black trousers without turn-ups are closed by a zip with an attached loop and a button at the top. The round cape has no collar. Measurements of jacket: length 81 cm; shoulder 46 cm; trousers: length 109 cm; cape: length 128 cm. Label: "tel. 542268/ Coccoli/Torino." The garments were shown by Ugo Coccoli at the January 1978 Men's High Fashion show in Rome. Owner: permanent collection of the Sartoria Ugo Coccoli, Turin. (*C.C.T.*)

Angelo Litrico

Short dinner jacket in black silk velvet woven to form opaque and dark lines; black trousers in smooth silk velvet. 1986-87 Autumn-Winter collection. Youthful evening dress made up of a short jacket with lapels in black silk satin as are the trimmings and the false double-breasted waistcoat; lightly padded shoulders and lining printed with text. The trousers, of fairly broad line, have black silk turn-ups. The model is completed by a white cotton shirt with bands of black and white Jacquard patterns and black silk velvet bowtie. Measurements of jacket: length 72 cm, shoulders 86 cm; trousers: length 113 cm. Label: "Angelo Litrico, Roma." Owner: permanent collection of the Sartoria Angelo Litrico, Rome. *(E.C.)*

Ugo Fulco

Dress shoes in black patent leather and grosgrain, brown lining in English goatskin, leather sole. The shoe has a grosgrain binding with a raised square bow hand-made out of the same material, a projecting tongue and a closed wing tip. It was made in 1968 by Ugo Fulco, a date that is also confirmed by the slightly squared toe. Label: "Calzature/FULCO/V.A. Micca 9 - Torino -." Owner: Ugo Fulco, Turin. (*C.C.T.*)

"Francesina" model shoe in black calfskin, lined with beige English goatskin, leather sole. The shoe has small struts inside the toe box and is tied with laces that pass through five holes. The only decorative feature is the straight tip with brogueings. Made in 1976 by Ugo Fulco in Turin, who has recently wound up his activity. Label: "Calzature/FULCO/V.A. Micca 9 - Torino -." Owner: Ugo Fulco, Turin. (*C.C.T.*)

Guido Bosi

Guido Bosi Monteveglio (Bologna, January 5, 1923, still living) was a pupil of the Bolognese tailor Emilio Musicò, who came originally from Southern Italy. His career, which began in 1954, was marked from the outset by his production of other lines of clothing, primarily that of women's wear which he presented at the Sanremo Festival in 1956. This special interest of his led him to rejuvenate his output of men's clothing by introducing features that had previously been characteristic of women's clothes.

His collections, presented in Rome and in Paris, were founded on colour: his poppy red coat with double faces in blue dates from 1966, while the following year he brought out his corduroy coats (white, light blue, pale green, lobster pink) with closed collars or wide lapels and metal buttons to which the magazine *Arbiter* (no. 266) devoted its cover, and his evening topcoats.

In 1968 came another innovation, men's coats in costly furs – sealskin, otter, broadtail, grey or black lamb – or in much more accessibly priced synthetic fur to cater to a wider range of clientele. This innovative and unconventional style continued throughout the seventies, during which time he came out with patterned jackets embroidered with the paintings of a number of famous abstract artists, an "homage to painting" used as a motif of fashion in order to give space to fantasy. In any case Bosi, who uses his two ateliers in Bologna and Paris for sales, has a clientele that comes mainly from Italian and foreign artistic circles. He himself is intensely interested in painting and is a collector of pictures, jade and art books. (*C.C.T.*)

Brioni

The Brioni house of haute couture was established in 1945 when Gaetano Savini, born in Terni in 1909, in partnership with two other people that later broke up, opened an office in Rome's Via Barberini. The name Brioni was chosen as a homage to the Adriatic island that had been an undisputed centre of elegance for many years. At one time the élite used to go there to play polo and it is from this sport that the "griffe" of the couturier's is derived.

Brioni made his entry into the world of fashion in 1935, with the intention of creating an "Italian style" that would be able to challenge the English hegemony over matters of elegance. An opportunity was offered to him in 1952 when he persuaded Marchese G.B. Giorgini to model a number of items of men's clothing during the Florence fashion shows. Right from this first appearance, Brioni creations were marked by a lissom and slender line, lively colours and new fabrics. In fact one of the "House's" chief innovations was represented by the use of silk. Brioni also gave its "name," from this moment on, to a complete line of accessories to go with each model garment. In July of the same year, the firm was invited to represent Italian tailoring at the "International Dress of Tailors" in Schevening (Holland). Since then Brioni's creations have been present at all major events in Italy and abroad, confirming the trend towards a style that emphasizes line and colour, enlivening the content by means of new details. An almost complete list of the events in which Brioni has taken part can be found in *Men's Fashion Register Brioni*, July 1981.

The growing approval met with by Brioni's models has given the firm an open door onto the most important markets in the world, and has made it necessary to set up a branch to manufacture prêt-à-porter, the "Roman Style" based at Penne (Pescara). This produces ready-to-wear garments by artisan techniques, intended for export. The atelier has also been producing a line of women's clothing for about ten years. (*E.C.*)

Mario Caraceni

The tailoring firm of Mario Caraceni and Mario Pozzi, previously run by Mario Donnini and Agostino Caraceni, has been active in Milan since 1946, with its seat at no. 16, Via Fatebenefratelli. Following the family tradition initiated around the middle of the twenties by the famous Domenico Caraceni, the firm's style is a distinctly classical one. Consequently the garments it produces have remained more or less identical for years, unaffected by the innovations introduced into men's fashion by stylism: the size of lapels is around 10 cm in double-breasted and 8 cm in single-breasted jackets. There has been some variation in the length of vents, which has increased from between 9 and 14 cm after the war to 20 cm in recent years. Trousers, on the other hand, have remained practically unchanged, with a leg width of 25 cm. It is a characteristic of the firm to make the armhole very narrow to prevent the formation of folds on the breast, padded with a minimun of internal reinforcements (horsehair and flax stem).

The highly élitist clientele is made up of well-known personalities from the north of Italy in particular, as well as many foreigners. The firm's archives in which cloth patterns with the measurements of each client are kept facilitate orders, which can even be made by telephone.

Ugo Coccoli

Ugo Coccoli born in Arce (Frosinone) October 23, 1916, got his training as a young man with the Roman firm Farè, which catered to the royal family of Savoy and to Mussolini himself. He was transferred to Turin at the beginning of the forties, and it was there that he set up his own workshop in 1948, establishing a reputation for himself a few years later at the "Festival of Men's Fashion" in Sanremo.

He achieved his greatest success towards the end of the sixties (he began to take part in the Roman shows of "Men's High Fashion" in 1968), when he accentuated the modern and youthful appearance of his extremely classical line, both in its colours and in its close-fitting cut. Preference was shown for stripes and checks, with special attention being paid to colour, as can be seen in the seven complete outfits in bright colors published on the cover of the March 1973 issue of *Herrenjournal International*. Some of the most innovative developments in his output were the terry cloth "poncho" produced in all the colours of the rainbow and presented in Rome in 1968, the dinner jacket and trousers in white and purple and the "Nehru" jacket that were flanked by more traditional designs at the Turin fashion show in 1969.

The seventies were a period of jackets decorated with carrés, darts, inserted unattached half-belts or folding patterns on the back. The bush-jacket with belt and rear half-belt was extremely popular, as the dinner jacket and trousers in different colours, sometimes with the addition of a cloak, still were. His coats, which were double faced as well at the beginning of the decade, (cf. *National Zeitung Basel*, September 15, 1972, fig. 5 and *Arbiter*, a. XLVIII, no. 302, 1975, pp. 70, 71) had trench-coat-type shaped carrés, and his sports jackets, in the same material as the ordinary jackets, had kimono style sleeves and leather borders. The colours continued to be very youthful, and from 1978 onwards were matched with those of Lancia motorcars. (*C.C.T.*)

Angelo Litrico

During the fifties Litrico moved from Catania where he was born to Rome in order to take a job in the Marinelli tailoring firm at no. 51, Via Sicilia. He later took it over and changed its name, and it remains the seat of his own firm up to the present day.

Right from the outset, his models were characterized by the precision of cut and by an audacious use of fabrics, colours and decorations, some of the inspiration for which came from women's fashion. Litrico's imaginative creations can in part be ascribed to the particular period that the capital went through during the sixties, with the presence of numerous American actors and the considerable significance that Rome had acquired as a centre of the entertainment industry. These were decisive factors in the success of an eccentric style with publicity value. Over the same period Litrico was actively involved with the cinema, producing clothes for the "leads" in film like *Frenesia d'estate*, *Sorpasso* and *Congiuntura*.

The sixties also saw the beginning of his involvement with the ready-to-wear industry both in Italy and abroad. In recent years, through an exclusive arrangement with an American multinational, "Litrico" prêt-à-porter and accessories are marketed in every part of the world except Italy where, by contract, the atelier produces only exclusive garments.

Litrico has also moved into the realm of women's clothing, creating a line for Laura Biagiotti in the seventies. It is also worth mentioning that some of Angelo Litrico's creations have been on show at the following exhibitions: "Creators of Italian Fashion 1920-1980," Daimaru Museum, Osaka (1983) and "Italy, The Genius of Fashion," Fashion Institute of Technology, New York (1985). (*E.C.*)

STYLISM
IN MEN'S FASHION

Chiara Giannelli Buss

Stylism and Men's Fashion

In November 1969 the shows of women's wear collections at Palazzo Pitti in Florence were joined by those of twelve houses of men's ready-to-wear fashion: Baratta, Barbaro, Bazzarini, Caraceni, Dotti, Ken Scott, Litrico, Nativo, Pucci (by Zegna), Rosati, Siviglia and Valentini. The first pictures of high-quality ready-to-wear men's clothing produced in Italy published by the press got an immediate positive reaction, for they filled the enormous gap that existed in Europe and America between the exclusive tailored garment, also of Italian origin, whose cost made it inaccessible to all but a small international élite, and the uniformity of mass-produced clothing. Within three years the Pitti Uomo show was launched in Florence. This was held twice a year, a month earlier than the ones devoted to women's ready-to-wear clothing. By the spring of 1978 there were already over 130 exhibitors and the number of buyers from all over the world exceeded 7,000. At that time Pitti Uomo was regarded everywhere as the most influential men's fashion show and it had already taken Italian men's ready to-wear clothing in its totality, from suit to accessory, to the top of the international market. But in September of that very same year, a number of stylists decided to make a break with he lorentine shows, as esigners f women's wear had already done in 1974, and staged their own independent shows in Milan. These were Albini, Armani, Basile, Caumont, Fragile and Versace.

And so a new chapter began in men's fashion as well, that of *stylism*. In fact if quality ready-to-wear fashion had already filled (and continued to fill from the collections shown at Pitti Uomo) the gap between high-class tailoring and mass production towards the middle of the seventies, a new market had sprung up on the one hand, still a small one perhaps but with its own precise requirements, and on the other a number of stylists had demonstrated that they no longer wished to design for industry, but directly for the buyer. They wished to take over responsibility for manufacture by making use of specialized sectors of the industry, and even artisans on occasion, in order to have complete control over the finished product. This freed them from the dictates of mass production which, constrained by the laws of cost of production, tended to tone down, simplify and standardize, when it did not choke at birth, any idea that set out to define a very precise mas-

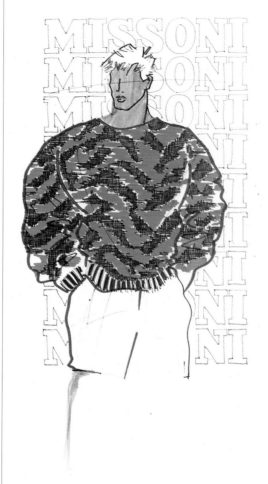

Missoni, design for round-necked pullover, with dropped sleeves, ribbed cuffs and waistband and "wavy" pattern in two colors; the garment was made for the 1982 Spring-Summer collection in Jacquard knit. Light blue, turquoise and black felt pen and black ink on paper, 42 × 32 cm.

culine image, clearly differentiated from all others, that would correspond to a personal style. In fact the stylist is above all a personality, a cross between the designer and the *grand couturier*, even though he frequently neither designs, in the classic sense of drawing fashionplates, nor has things sewn by hand. He creates for quality production, even if still in batches, garments made out of costly materials, manufactured exclusively for him and often completely new, with the experience of hundreds of years of craftsmanship behind them, aesthetically on a par with haute couture, but with much more accent on innovative aspects that, unlike in tailored garments, are the contribution of the stylist himself. In short, the stylist has replaced, in both men's and women's wear, the concept of "made in Italy," hitherto the guarantee of fine materials, excellent workmanship and *good taste*, with that of the "Italian look," the status symbol of a new economic power, conscious of the social implications of fashion and with a decidedly international character. So it is that Europeans, Americans or Japanese, men who especially since the mid-seventies have been torn between the desire for radical change and an equally powerful attachment to the economic gains they have already made, find the solution to their dilemma in the "Italian look": being wealthy and showing it by means of elegant clothing, and at the same time maintaining the proper distance from the traditional values of wealth and elegance.

If the stylist was able to solve the problem of post-1968 man around the middle of the seventies, by the beginning of the eighties his sensitive antennae were perceiving new and more subtle dilemmas looming on the horizon of the "repudiated bourgeois":[1] a great nostalgia for the privileges of dress lost at the time of the French Revolution when "man abandoned his pretensions to beauty and concerned himself solely with the practical."[2] It was in fact "the great renunciation"[3] of colour and decoration (patterned silks and velvets, embroidery, lace, jewellery), in short of the trappings of luxury as a symbol of his social status, reducing him to the "man in black"[4] dressed invariedly in the same sad way up until shortly after the last war. Abandoning the display of refined luxury, he was also obliged to renounce drawing attention to his own physical appearance and power of seduction, replacing it by a new idea of virility displayed through the new style of dress.

*Giorgio Correggiari, designs for the 1980
Spring-Summer collection, in* Gap, *August-
September 1979.*

Luciano Soprani, suit from the 1985-86 Autumn-Winter collection (photo Bob Krieger).

"As far as clothing is concerned, it is certain that modern man is much more rigid and severe than woman, and that the male sense of morality tends to be expressed to a greater extent in his dress. So we should not be surprised if many of the details of the modern man's clothing stand as a symbol of his respect for the principles of duty, renunciation and self-control."[5]

At the same time the man of the eighties demands his right to comfort, that comfort denied by years of traditional fashion and to which the clothing of the sixties had made him accustomed.

To all these more or less conscious desires the more sensitive stylists have come up with a response, at times even in conflict with commercial requirements. Each of these responses is in accordance with the stylist's own homogeneous criteria and at the same time in keeping with what men's clothing is supposed to represent. Out of the many fine stylists who have been active in Italy over the last ten years, only four are represented here by a series of images that covers the evolution of the principal characteristics of their work in an exhaustive manner. This is by no means a selection on a qualitative basis. Rather it has been necessary, for reasons of space, to examine the chronological development of a few stylists and attempt to make an interpretation of their work, something that would have been rendered far more difficult by trying to cover the entire range of a vast output with a single example of the work of each stylist. As for the inclusion of ready-to-wear garments produced by Zegna, this too is an example of a phenomenon, and certainly not a unique one, that is typical of the present situation. Just as in the mid-seventies the stylist filled a gap in the world of men's fashion, manufacturers like Zegna, Marzotto, G.F.T., Hilton and Cerruti, to mention just a few, are responding today to a very recent demand from the kind of man who, with the revival of some of the values of a pre-consumer society, wants guarantees of quality and durability in an up-to-date garment, but not one that is tied to the fashion of a single season, made with care but at reasonable speed, comfortable to wear but less expensive than a tailor-made one. Their response is one that has been made possible by the use of the most advanced technology, a technology that has allowed Zegna to invent the "made-to-measure ready-to-wear." An old established textile company with a reputation for quality, Zegna has ventured to produce a fashion of its own. Relying on computerized systems of manufacturing, it offers a product that is neither mass-produced nor tailor-made, and does not even reveal the influence of a stylist's personality. The customer is able to choose a fabric, select a model for it, request details different from those of the model and then leave his own measurements. These are reduced to one of three basic computerized types and within a few days he is able to pick up a garment manufactured by

Gianni Versace, 1982-83 Autumn-Winter collection.

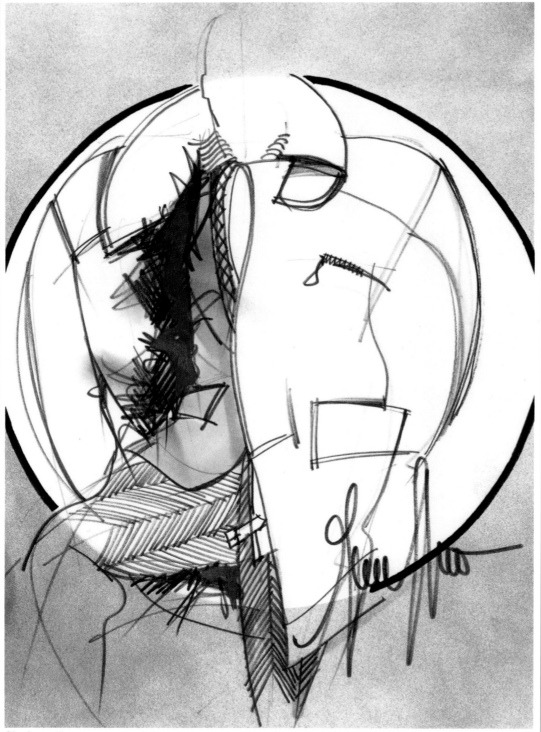

Gianfranco Ferré, preparatory sketch, black pencil and pink and beige gouache on paper, 29.5 × 21 cm; it depicts the salient points of a sport jacket with shirt-style collar above a jacket and trousers with herring-bone pattern; 1985-86 Autumn-Winter collection. Milan, Ferré archives.

the techniques of mass production, but "for him" and made out of high quality materials that he has chosen himself. The article of clothing is backed up by the guarantee of a trademark that is not just the vehicle for an image. Rather it declares that all the materials, from the sorting of the fibre to the spinning and weaving, have been manufactured under the control of the company that actually makes the garment.

This halfway stage between mass production and stylism, the latest addition to the gamut of Italian men's fashion, is a further refinement, thanks to the use of advanced technology, of the system of Creativity-Production-Distribution that forms the basis of the success of the Italian image, and not just for men. For if the creativity, this ability to play with shapes, volumes and colours, has its origins in centuries of involvement with the decorative arts (from multi-coloured marble inlays to the velvet brocades of the Renaissance), the manufacturing, even on the industrial level, is rooted in an ancient tradition of tailoring and in the custom of working with quality materials, and the distribution is based on the organizational skills developed over the last twenty years. These have laid down the methods and times of presentation, diversifying them in accordance with the market. The idea of placing high technology at the service of fashion for the creation of materials and the development of new manufacturing techniques is a confirmation of that protean character[6] that underlies the success of Italian fashion. All this is accompanied by an ability to continually reinvent the image and the technical means of achieving it, so as to satisfy aesthetic and economic demands at practically every level of the market, with an effective range that is both vertical and horizontal.

Thus while the Americans were the first to grasp the desire for colour, the British have been the most sensitive to the faintest nuances of temperament in the new man and the French have been the first to respond to the demand for luxury, Italian stylists have been the only ones to respond to all these desires with multiple solutions, each one aimed at a specific market, in an attempt, which recent sales and export figures show to have been successful.

In fact the intensely innovative English avant-garde tends to create for a small élite, while French stylism, whose extreme refinement is recognized by all, is hampered by a lack of support on the industrial level, both with regard to materials and to manufacturing (the lines of many French designers are in fact produced in Italy or Japan with materials largely manufactured in Italy). As one fashion reporter has rightly pointed out, "the English youth is compiled by the French stylist who influences Milanese stylism, which readapted by the équipes of casual wear is distributed all over the world."[7]

Over the space of ten years the Italian stylist

has invented the new shapes and volumes of comfortable and non-traditional elegance, restored to man the lost privileges of colour, pattern and decoration and the pleasure of costly- or innovative materials so that he too can regain the taste for luxury so long denied him, and finally, given back to him in recent seasons a refined and not too correct version of what 19th-century tailoring knew as "classic" but which was treated with total disdain a mere ten years ago.

interlude of 1968, followed by several years of extravagant interpretations, men, like women, found themselves in the mid-seventies torn between the desire for a radical change in the constrictive forms of traditional fashion and nostalgia for that elegance which only traditional fashion seemed to be able to offer. It was in fact in 1974 that Armani first appeared on the market under his own name, with his "non-structured jacket": comfortable and loose without looking as if it were a size too large and

day, naturally with an evolution in his style but remaining faithful to the basic concept underlying his creation. However two other Italian stylists have interpreted the theme of non-structured clothing in a wholly original manner, with a consistency of aims and research that covers the whole range of their activity. Ever since his first collection of men's wear in 1982, Ferré has concentrated his attention on the volume of the chest, allowing shapes, materials and colours all to play second fiddle to this

Ermenegildo Zegna, detail of summer dress from the 1986 Spring-Summer collection

Shapes and Volumes

The man of the seventies and eighties makes a two-fold demand on fashion. On the one hand he rejects the restrictions of the grey uniform,[8] tight collars and "sewn-on" suits and coats, and demands a comfortable kind of clothing that leaves him ample freedom of movement. On the other he feels nostalgia for the time when he could display his own body, not by means of tight and obsolete jeans, but by means of items of dress that bring out the aesthetic qualities of chest, shoulders, legs and waistline. After the

drawing attention to imposing shoulders and narrow hips without forcing the torso into the constrictive shapes of the traditional jacket. It was a response to the needs of the young man who could once again permit himself to be prosperous and to display the fact through the elegance of his attire, while maintaining the proper distance from the traditional values of wealth and elegance.

Armani was the first to solve the problem of the "repudiated bourgeois," and has continued to refine this principle right up to the present

primary interest. While at the beginning he used materials, colours and decoration (the sleeves) like a sort of graphic construction set, in his more recent collections the volumes of the chest are the culminating point of a style whose principal aim is, in his own words, "comfort as education of the mind."[9] Thus he has combined loose but not voluminous forms, that reveal the underlying structure of the chest without clinging to it, with solid primary colours, plain weave materials made out of modest fibres, creating a "solid"[10] and consistent image for the man who wants a comfort that has been denied him for centuries by Western clothing. While Armani and Ferré have concentrated on producing a comfortable jacket that brings out the chest, Versace seems to be the stylist who has most felt the need for a new interpretation of the trousers in response to the desire for comfort while bringing out parts of the body that have been neglected for two centuries. In his first collection of men's wear for the 1980-81 Autumn-Winter season he presented the "pan-

collection the accent is still on the leg, displayed by a model that wraps, around it in a graphic manner without being tight. But it was in the subsequent collection that Versace fully resolved the problem. While details have changed, since then his trousers have remained basically the same as the model that appeared in the 1984-85 Autumn-Winter collection: waistline set off by a particularly high waistband that gives an impression of slenderness; by contrast chest and thighs are made to ap-

time producing the effect of muscular thighs and calves. His interpretation of the trousers has links with the theme of nostalgia for the pre-French revolution nobleman, a concept that appears to have had a particularly strong influence on Versace. In fact long trousers wiping out any interest in the legs did not become established until 1813-14. Before that time, and throughout the long centuries in which man has worn trousers or breeches, the legs represented an important feature of masculine beau-

Giorgio Armani, sports shoes with uppers in mustard yellow reversed leather, red rubber outersole and leather inner soles; rounded toe and mask with six eyelets. 1986 Spring-Summer collection.

Giorgio Armani, four ties for the 1986 Spring-Summer collection.

talone cavallo" ("horsetrousers"): loose and comfortable above the knee, very tight and decorated with buttons on the calf, to which attention is thus drawn. As is often the case with radical experiments, the trousers did not have much commercial success. And yet the stylist continued along the same course: revealing the beauty of the leg by emphasizing the waistline and at the same time obtaining a highly wearable pair of trousers. In the "muscle" trousers of the 1983-84 Autumn-Winter

pear powerful, no longer displayed tout court as in the '83 model, but hinted at by the extreme fullness of the trousers between the waist and the calf, where the leg narrows considerably and progressively; this adherence allows the leg to be so long that it overhangs the instep. By these means Versace has created a comfortable pair of trousers that are not tight anywhere, even at the waist where it is the height of the waistband that conveys an impression of "tight-waistedness," at the same

ty, emphasized by clothing that in different ways, depending on the period, set out to draw attention to thigh and calf.[10]

Colour

The desire on the part of men to regain the right to be colourful, perhaps the greatest of the many renunciations of the new post-revolutionary man, was felt by Italian designers of men's wear long before the advent of stylism. As far back as 1951, the tailor Brioni included a suit made out of pink shantung in his collection of highly elegant garments that were shown at the Grand Hotel in Florence along with clothing produced by the other great names in tailoring of the time. To a disgusted journalist who asked him what he meant by that suit, Brioni responded that "that horrible suit has already been sold in great numbers."[12] The demand came from very precise areas of the American market, though certainly not that of the young and upcoming executives who wore with self-confidence the pink rather than the light blue, white or canary yellow oxford shirts of the prestigious Brooks Brothers of New York, the status symbol of the most snobbish members of the Wasp establishment. But it is significant that a fashion designer of the calibre of Brioni should have felt this desire to break with one of the most deeply-rooted traditions of 200 years of men's clothing, and should have calmly responded to it, even if only with a one-off and "anomalous" piece. Thirty years later Benetton's pink pullover is no longer restricted to a particular sector of the market, while the raw silk or linen evening jackets in pink or fuchsia presented by Ferré with his customary rigour are in complete harmony with the rest of his Summer 1986 collection of refined men's wear.

The "thin pink line of courage"[13] is certainly not an unbroken one, and there would be almost no connection between Brioni's pragmatic response to a culturally limited demand in 1951 and Ferré's cerebral proposal in 1986, if man's need for colour had not been felt and translated into acceptable terms, indeed ones that were attractive even to the most traditionally minded, by the Missonis in the seventies, in a rapid escalation from casual clothing to the more formal variety for work.

By the end of the seventies the Missonis had already established an international reputation in women's wear. They had been producing under their own name since 1965, introducing into the ranks of elegant clothing items of knitwear and combinations of colours, patterns and textures that were traditionally regarded as discordant, which were baptized as "put-togethers" by the fashion press. What they invented was elegant, expensive and yet understated casual wear. In 1978 they came out with their first collection of men's clothing. For Missoni clothing which already had a style of its own, there was nothing new about it: mixtures of sheep's wool and mohair with a small percentage of synthetic yarn that make the knit soft but not bulky, flowing but not pendulous, the extremely careful handling of the Jacquard knitting-frame, the unconventional combinations of colours and patterns, the comfortable, loose and simple models in forms that have to take second place to the materials. What was new was the idea that a striped pink and green windcheater with a very long scarf could be worn by men, even on informal occasions. It was an experiment; indeed the garment still

Gianfranco Ferré, four belts; from the left: two woollen ones, created for the 1986-87 Autumn-Winter and 1984-85 Autumn-Winter collections respectively, and two summer ones, both from the 1986 Spring-Summer collection. Milan, Ferré archives.

bore the orange label with "Missoni - Made in Italy" written on it in black, the same one as was used for women's clothing, as if the stylists from Sumirago were not yet completely sure that they wanted to produce a line for men. The success of the men's wear collection for the 1978-79 Autumn-Winter season left no room for doubt: the man of the late seventies wanted his coloured plumage back, not so much to be ostentatious and even less to be different, and perhaps only partially because the Missoni garment had become a status symbol, but above all because, and the years to come would confirm it, he was tired of sober shades, of *masculine* patterns and colours, and at least in his free time wished to rediscover the long-lost pleasure of pattern and colour.

Within the space of a mere seven years, the Missonis would be proposing bright colours even for the classic item of apparel of the working man, the suit. Following the signing of an exclusive contract with Marzotto, commencing with the 1985-86 Autumn-Winter collection, the Missonis produced "working" jackets and trousers in their patterns and colours. These were made out of woven fabrics bearing the label "Missoni Uomo." It is interesting to note how in this first collection using fabrics instead of knits, the stylists felt the need to mediate the transition from one kind of material to another with one of their typical artisan experiments. In a suit that was given the name "Tirolo" and which was obviously of folk inspiration, though not so obviously coupled with a shot pattern, they found an ingenious middle course between knit and woven fabric by applying the technique of "cooked" wool to the jacket, thereby creating a contrast with the waistcoat, with identical colours and pattern, but left in its natural knitted state. The same principle was adopted in one of the suits in their most recent 1986 Spring-Summer collection, here used to bring out the contrast between the fabric and the formal appearance: jacket in the classic check of the Anglo-Saxon world, present in all the collections of that season, face to face with masks from Greek drama in the knit of the waistcoat. Described in words, it is a strident contrast, but one that the wise use of colours, shapes and materials renders visually attractive and quite in tune with the recent concept of the young and handsome man who takes care of his appearance while holding a responsible position in society. This has been the key image in the last two years of publicity for men's products, a category to which the photograph taken for the advertising campaign undoubtedly belongs.

And for today's man who demands his right to colour, as a symbol of his equality with women, the Missonis have turned their attention to his feet as well. In the ambit of a style of men's clothing that for two centuries has given precedence to the shoe in terms of innovation and excellence, the Missonis, thanks to an exclusive contract with one of the biggest manufacturers in the sector, have designed socks whose patterns and colours, barely glimpsed between the hem of the trousers and the toe-cap of the shoes, add the last touch to the Missonian concept of the highly coloured "put-together" for men.

Pattern and Decoration

While the Missonis were the first in Italy to satisfy man's desire for a return to decoration in his clothing, in the form of a figured fabric in which the design is secondary to the colours, others, like Armani and Versace though in very different ways, have been the pioneers of the use of figured fabrics in creations in which the design dominates, with colour playing only a marginal role. Armani has always concentrated on small but important details, such as the variation on the "Prince of Wales" pattern. The same principle forms the basis of the designs for ties in his 1986 Spring-Summer collection, in which classic patterns such as the regimental, polka dot and cashmere are reinterpreted with formal and above all tonal variations that make them more "patterned" than their traditional counterparts and many contemporary proposals that chase after novelty at any cost. In the shirts presented for the 1986 summer season we find a version of the classic pattern for shirts, the stripe, which has been evolving from its earliest years towards a textured version that is closer to decoration than to pure pattern. The juxtaposition of two techniques of weaving in the succession of lines and stripes in soft shades of secondary colours replaces the simple line in a highly personal version of pattern perceived as decoration. It may be more significant than the batik designs of flowers and fish to be found on shirts and bermuda shorts in that collection.

Versace's approach to the use of pattern in men's clothing is very different, seeming to move in the opposite direction to Armani. For the 1982-83 Autumn-Winter season Versace proposed silk evening waistcoasts with leafy and flowered shoots hand-embroidered in silk thread. It is the triumph of applied decoration, of traditional craftsmanship, and a symptom, which he was the first to perceive in Italy, of another desire on the part of men in the eighties: a return to more traditional and lavish decoration, "the nostalgia for the courtier."[14] By "courtier" is meant the man who wishes to cover himself with all the glitter of luxury as a symbol of his economic and political power and seductiveness. From 1985 to 1986 other stylists, among them Versace himself, came out with silk evening waistcoats worked in small designs in the same colour as the fabric (Versace, Ferré, Soprani, Coveri), or printed in pinkish white strips and bands with posies of flowers in many colours (Zegna) or in sky-blue stripes on white (Manuel Ritz-Pipò). Thus all the themes of the waistcoat worn beneath the dress-coat at the end of the 18th century were resurrected for a market that had responded only feebly to Versace's "courtier" waistcoat in 1982, but that in 1986 was obviously ready to give free rein to its desire for an item of apparel that even during the darkest century of the man in black, the 19th century, had occasionally permitted itself a dash of colour.

But if the waistcoats of 1982 were only a sample of Versace's interest in patterned fabrics, he has subsequently never ceased to experiment in that field, always starting out from tradition in order to arrive at a totally new solution. Interesting, for instance, are his interpretations of the pin-stripe from 1984 to the present day. For the 1984-85 Autumn-Winter collection he had flannels woven, which he used for both women's and men's wear, in which versions of the pin-stripe were made to resemble the stripe in a pattern of numerous and bold variations of black and grey. These patterns turned up again in the "line and dot" theme that dominated the 1985 Spring-Summer collection and the various striped linen and mixed silk fabrics of the suit, dust-coat and waistcoat for Summer 1986. The logical conclusion of this trend was the "optical" pattern of shirts and ties in which only two colour combinations, black and white and black and beige, and the printing technique, by taking away importance from the elements of colour and three-dimensionality, reduce the decoration to pure line. This increases the force of a design that is already powerful in itself, but still understated when compared with the long brocade coat in multi-coloured silks proposed by Gianmarco Venturi for the 1985-86 Autumn-Winter season. Less loud, and aimed more at the dandy than at Versace's aggressive young man, is the embroidered decoration most recently proposed by Ferré for his evening wear only. These include the black chamois leather slippers with embroidery also in black on the vamp for the 1985-86 Autumn-Winter season and, for the Summer of 1986, the white evening shirts decorated with intersecting spirals embroidered in white thread on front and sleeves as well as the white piqué on the waistcoat fronts. These latter embroideries are a pattern of unbroken curved lines, without any shading or tonal juxtapositions, just the barely hinted-at contrast between the dull background material and the shiny threads used for the decoration. They are intended for the man who feels nostalgia for the refinements of lace and embroidery but wants a very subdued version for the traditionally most elegant moments of his life and will not accept tout court revivals, such as the lace socks proposed by the French for the same season.

Luxury

These last examples of decoration are also a sign of another important trend in men's fashion in recent years, the more or less opulent and flashy display of luxury. Amid the nostalgia for lost privileges the latter has begun to dominate in the last few years, the result of a desire to use one's image to display the marks

Enrico Coveri, 1986-87 Autumn-Winter collection,
in Uomo Vogue, *July-August 1986.*

Valentino, 1986 Spring-Summer collection,
in Linea Capital, *March-April 1986.*

of one's own prosperity and physical appearance by taking care of the body and drawing attention to it with suitable clothing.

Naturally luxury is best expressed through decoration, which has already been discussed, costly materials and complicated details of tailoring. Ever since the first decade of the 19th century, when a masculine style was established that was characterized by the uniformity of dress in every social class, from which colours and decoration were eliminated and whose forms have remained the same until until the last few decades, the bourgeois gentleman has distinguished himself from the rest, amid this apparent democratization, exclusively through the quality of materials and tailoring, the refinement of accessories and the presence in his wardrobe of evening dresses, ceremonial wear and expensive sports clothes. Thus Ferré's embroidered evening wear or his coat lined with muskrat and with a wolfskin collar, whose apparently simple cut is in reality highly laborious and complicated, represent the response to a need for a kind of luxury which, while it is certainly not flashy, is nevertheless evident. It is more the luxury of the dandy than of the bourgeois gentleman, more for the man who is looking for an identity that sets him apart from the crowd but who does not wish to find it in eccentric clothing. What he wants is a heightening of luxury, with a polemic content that does not ask for approval, but if anything the recognition of an established elegance. Valentino has responded to the same type of demand with his riding habits, among which the red fox-hunting jacket is outstanding, and his hound's tooth or Prince of Wales checks with refined collars in black velvet.

Armani's concept of luxury has a quite different tone. It is based on the English pattern of gentleman who since the end of the 18th century had codified luxury into a conservative formality that centred on the maximum of comfort and attention to detail that should not be visible. Typical of this is the expensive coat he has designed for the 1986-87 Autumn-Winter season, made out of 100% camel-hair, a cloth that is usually left in its natural colour so that its value is immediately apparent. Armani, however, has dyed it blue, as if he wished to deny the exceptional nature of the material, and made it into a classic model, but one whose proportions reveal a shift away from the traditional canons of tailoring to obtain that sense of comfort that is typical of Armani's style.

A still understated but highly visible luxury can be found in the Missonis' scarves for the 1986-87 Autumn-Winter season. Here it is not so much the materials that are precious as the Jacquard knit of basically complex designs in more colours that is apparent to the eye. The result is a much broader accessory that provides warmth more through its bulk than through logical and traditional dimensions and, while they do not pass unobserved, does not flaunt its intrinsic qualities of luxury and extra-

Gian Marco Venturi, 1986-87 Autumn-Winter collection, in Fashion, *Spring-Summer 1986.*

vagant use of material and skill. An almost invisible luxury intended for the man who believes that "the ability to spend money is made evident through means that require a fine discrimination on the part of the observer,"[15] can be found in the output of firms like Zegna, where sweaters, overcoats and even casual trousers are made out of the most precious raw materials or the clothes are made out of fabrics that are the outcome of long and costly research in the field of textiles and tailoring.

As we have already seen with his embroidered waistcoat, Versace is catering to quite another sort of man. This can also be seen in his two cardigans in costly wools to be worn one on top of the other and accompanied by silk ties and fur busbies for moments of relaxation, or his sumptuous linen dust-coats to be worn in an imaginary climatic situation. This might be called the luxury of the superfluous, for the man who hankers after that model of masculinity in which the elegance of the whole is combined with the lavish display of materials and decorations as a symbol of power; a power that in this case should perhaps be sought more in the physical sphere than in the economic one. Within the compass of the ostentatious and opulent luxury that will perhaps earn our current era the name suggested by Alberoni of "the golden eighties,"[16] one notes a proliferation in the use of furs. In the same season as Ferré came out with his coat with its complex cut, Cerruti produced a Prince of Wales check coat with a bearskin collar, Piattelli a tweed coat with a large shawl collar of marmot fur and Carlo Palazzi a raincoat lined with Saga mink. This is no longer the understated luxury of the seventies or the "dandy" version of 1985, but the beginning, for men too, of the display of luxury as an unmistakable indication of wealth and, perhaps even more, as a symbol of animal sensuality. For Roberto d'Agostino is certainly right when he observes that "there are no more *innocent clothes*. Everything is related, codified, has connections with something that people know."[17] For a less opulent and bestial luxury, but one where the name of the stylist is no longer sufficient, garments are being proposed in which the decoration has been designed by eminent painters. Trussardi started it in 1985 with a silk dressing gown hand-painted to Guttuso's design, continuing in the 1986 Summer season with cotton shirts printed with large flowers designed by the same artist. For the following winter the Crosa spinning-mill had engaged pinters like Emilio Tadini, Ugo Nespolo, Lucio del Pezzo and Enrico Baj to produce the designs for its men's knitwear.

Materials

One of the main factors behind the success of Italian stylism, in both men's wear and women's wear, is the relationship between stylist and textile manufacturer. Many decades before the advent of stylism, Italian manufacturers had established an international reputation for the quality of their fabrics and their creativity on the aesthetic level. For centuries the areas of Biella and Valdagno for wool and Como for silk, cotton and linen have been supplying fabrics that are among the best on the market. These were distributed through wholesalers and retailers to tailoring firms, private individuals and clothing manufacturers. With the advent of the stylist the cloth manufacturer was obliged to change his whole *modus operandi*, no longer confining himself to the production of a seasonal collection to be distributed or sold directly, as had been happening for some years through coordinated events but also collaborating with the stylist. As the latter aimed to create a total image, he almost always required the fabric to be in harmony with his clothes and therefore wanted it produced exclusively for him, even when it varied only in the tiniest of details from the much larger output intended for the industrial market. Thus the Prince of Wales check was "melted" for Armani and "crumbled" for Ferré, and the hound's tooth check "rounded off" for Valentino.

But the interaction between textile manufacturer and stylist became decisive when the latter began to demand new ways of processing traditional materials and called for experimentation with materials that had never been used before or new techniques during the various phases of manufacture. This is how the stimulating function of the stylist, coupled with the ancient artisan and industrial tradition of the Italian cloth manufacturer, produced the sort of results that have allowed Italian men's fashion to dominate the export market in the last few years. The experimentation has affected different sections of the textile manufacturing process: new techniques applied to traditional fibres or weaves, traditional fabrics put to new uses, mixtures of traditional fibres and new ones, the invention of new fibres or yarns or even the creation of materials that are not woven, out of yarn. Thus, in the field of traditional fibres, silk yarn is "swollen" to make it resemble linen, woollen yarn so combed and twisted that the cloth made out of it is as cool as cotton and has the crease-proof appearance of a synthetic fabric. This last fabric is intended for men nostalgic for the impeccable look of the thirties. For those on the other hand who feel more akin to the Napoleonic hero who believed that it was "necessary to crumple and wrinkle whatever one wears, before putting it on for the first time, for it is never a good idea to appear dressed in new clothes; for this purpose one will keep a servant of the same stature to wear all one's clothes for the first time so that they are thought to be used,[18] the 1986 Summer collections teem with cottons, linens and silks that have been "crumpled and wrinkled," not by servant doubles, but by means of special techniques of weaving or finishing. In the field of yarns much more has been done with those intended for women's clothing, whether for use in fabrics or "designer" ones for home knitting:

Correggiani, Missoni, Versace and countless others, who have created extraordinarily original yarns for women's wear, seem to have limited themselves to traditional ones for men, confining their experiments to casual wear, such as the cooked wool of the Missonis or Correggiari's vests made out of pure cellulose for the 1986 Summer season, to be thrown away after twenty-five washings, or his jerseys made out of ceramic thread. Another area that has been explored much more thoroughly in women's fashion than in men's is that of non-woven materials. Examples from the field of women's clothing are as numerous as they are diversified in the uses to which they are put, covering every moment of the day and the year, from casual wear to swimming costumes and evening wear.[19] But in men's wear significant examples are few and far between and almost exclusively confined to sportswear. Among the first experiments were Versace's 1981-82 sports jacket with rubber "sewn" by laser and his 1982-83 coat of mail and leather for jerkin and crusader jacket. Earlier on alcantara was used for sportswear by many stylists at the beginning of the eighties. Another synthetic material that resembles leather, lorica, was proposed by Trussardi last winter, again for sportswear. This relative scarcity of experimentation with technological innovations seems to be a confirmation of the fact that, while the woman of the eighties appears to be oriented towards the future and new conquests, men seem to be more concerned with winning back privileges of dress that were lost in far-off times, as well as in more recent days, primarily with a view to regaining the symbols of his powers. *C.G.B.*

1. A. Mottola Molfino, in Var. Aut., *Anziehungskräfte. Variété de la Mode: 1786-1986*, exhibition catalogue, Stadtmuseum, Munich, 25.7.1986-6.1.1987.
2. J.C. Flügel, *Psicologia dell'abbigliamento*, ch. 7: "The great male renunciation and its causes."
3. Idem.
4. G. Butazzi, in Var. Aut., *Anziehungskräfte...*, op. cit., pp. 504-508.
5. J.C. Flügel, op. cit., ch. 7.
6. S. Giacomoni, *L'Italia della Moda*, Milan 1984, p. 9.
7. Idem, "London Style," in *La Repubblica*, March 23, 1986.
8. I. Pezzini, "L'ideologia virile: dal borghese all'impiegato," in Var. Aut., *Anzirhungskräfte...*, op. cit.
9. G. Ferré, conversation on January 7, 1986.
10. Idem.
11. G. Butazzi, "Dal cortigiano al borghese," in *Anziehungskräfte...*, op. cit., pp. 216-222.
12. A. Mulassano, *I Mass Moda. Fatti e personaggi dell'Italian Look*, Florence 1979, p. 37.
13. In the novel *The Red Badge of Courage*, a classic work of North American literature written by Stephen Crane in 1895, the subtle line that distinguishes the brave man from the coward is a blood red one, which becomes "pink" when fear prevails over courage.
13. Cf. note 11.
15. T. Veblen, *La teoria della classe agiata*, Turin 1949, p. 150.
16. F. Alberoni, "La vita è bella, siamo nei dorati anni ottanta," in *Il Corriere della Sera*, March 13, 1986.
17. R. D'Agostino, *Look Parade. Gli smodati degli anni '80*, Milan 1986.
18. In "Giornale di mode e aneddoti," January 10, 1804.
19. C. Giannelli Buss, "Il tessuto Status Symbol," in *Anziehungskräfte...*, op. cit., pp. 533-537.

Giorgio Armani

Jacket in twill made of 85% virgin wool and 15% cashmere with "Prince of Wales" design in beige, black and grey with narrow red stripes. Measurements: shoulders 49 cm; circumference of chest 106 cm; waist 90 cm; bottom 96 cm. The jacket, which has no label, is nevertheless traceable, thanks to photographic documentation preserved in the Armani Archives, to the Autumn-Winter collection of 1979-80. Owner: private collection. The trousers in grey vicuña, the cotton shirt and the silk tie, all belonging to the same private owner, came originally from more recent Armani collections. The jacket is classical in its cut, colours and fabric, but has a particular construction that makes it extremely wearable without producing that "painted on" effect typical of haute couture clothing. This is the main characteristic of the "Armani jacket." Variations in the proportions of the design and the matching of colours are already to be found which set the jacket apart from tradition. (*C.G.B.*)

Sketch executed with fine-tipped felt pen and square-tipped brown felt pen on paper, 21 × 29.5 cm. The sketch does not represent specific garments to be made up, but the underlying idea or guiding thread in the design of sports jacket and trousers for the Spring-Summer season of 1986. The garments of this type realized for that collection are all essentially based on the prototype drawn here. The drawing, unsigned, was done by Giorgio Armani in 1985 and is kept in the Armani Archives in Milan. (*C.G.B.*)

Suit made up of jacket, trousers and shirt. Jacket in 100% loose-weave linen fabric, made out of yarn with different sections and twists in various shades of light grey. Hence the effect of a mélange is obtained on a tactile level as well as a chromatic one. Trousers in 100% cotton of a light grey colour. Shirt in mixed-weave 100% cotton fabric: the white stripes are in sateen weave under normal tension whereas the light grey-green interspaces are in plain weave with a "wrinkle" effect. Measurements of jacket: shoulders 55 cm; length at mid-back 80 cm; circumference of chest 108 cm; waist 92 cm; trousers: length 105 cm.

The three garments, designed for the 1986 Spring-Summer collection and worn together at the January show, bear the label "Giorgio Armani - Via Borgonuovo 21 - Milano"; they are preserved in the Armani Archives in Milan. There are very few structural and formal changes in the jacket with respect to that of the 1979-80 Autumn-Winter collection. The linen fabric is the end result of a complex spinning and weaving technique. The shirt apparently belongs to the trend for "wrinkled" fabrics, but the detail of the material's complicated weave sets it apart from the more common versions. (*C.G.B.*)

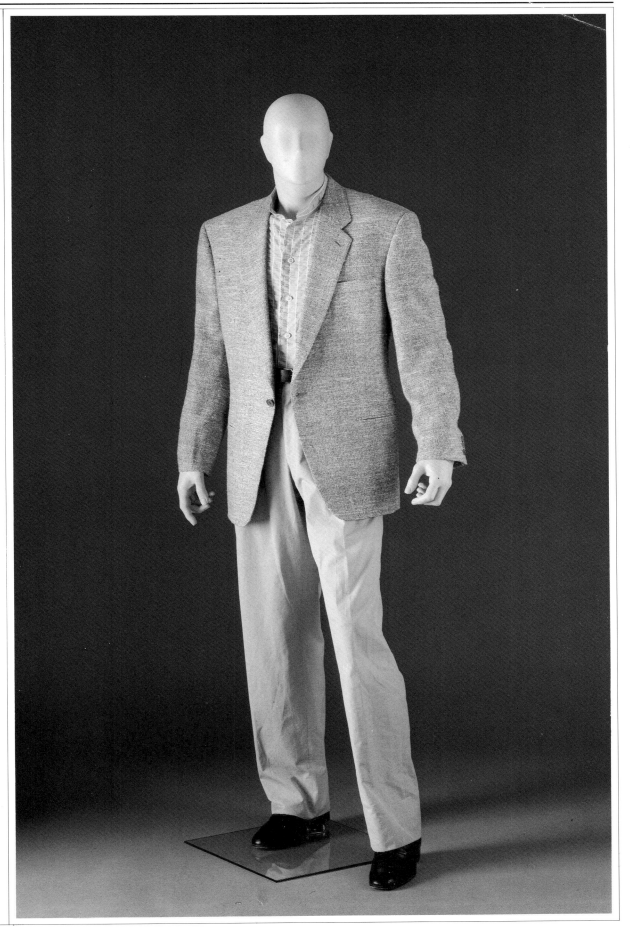

Shirt in 100% dark blue cotton. At the dressing stage the cotton has been subjected to a special treatment that has left it permanently "wrinkled." The shirt was designed for the 1986 Spring-Summer collection and was presented at the January show in combination with a blue suit whose fabric produces a similar, but not identical, effect of "wrinkling," the result of a special weaving technique. Label: "Giorgio Armani - Via Borgonuovo 21 - Milano." Owner: Armani Archives in Milan. (*C.G.B.*)

Suit in very plain wool crêpe with a "crépon" effect, medium grey in colour; versions were produced in dark blue and light grey as well. The same fabric was also used for items in the collection of women's clothing for the same season. Photograph by Aldo Fallai, Florence, taken in December 1985 for the 1986 Spring-Summer advertising campaign. The b/w negative is preserved in the Armani Archives in Milan. (*C.G.B.*)

Suit in 100% virgin wool flannel, in iron-grey with cream-coloured pinstripes, and coat in 100% camel-hair wool, in a shade of dark blue; double-breasted model with six buttons; round sleeve, vent at lower mid-back. Measurements of jacket: shoulders 53 cm; length at mid-back 79 cm; width at chest 108 cm; trousers: length 107 cm; coat: shoulders 58 cm; length at mid-back 134 cm; circumference at chest 128 cm.

Suit and coat, designed for the 1986-87 Autumn-Winter collection and shown in January 1986, both bear the label "Giorgio Armani - Via Borgonuovo 21 - Milano." The cotton shirt and silk tie were created for the same collection and shown in January '86 in combination with the suit. They bear the label "Giorgio Armani" and are preserved, together with suit and coat, in the Armani Archives in Milan. Most recent version of the "classical revisited" with variations on the theme, such as the coupling of the pale green shirt with the blue pinstripe, the shirt buttons in natural-coloured horn and the blue tint of the camel-hair. (*C.G.B.*)

Gianfranco Ferré

Long jacket in wool knit, made up of 35% lambswool, 34% alpaca, 22% kid mohair and 9% polyamide, in the colours of iron-grey and light grey which give the sateen knit an effect of mélange. Applied panels of soft leather and chamois cover the external part of the sleeve in the sequence, from bottom to top: cornflower blue chamois, yellowish orange chamois, reddish orange chamois, black leather; the black insert overlaps the one next to it, whereas the others bordered on each other. Label: "GIANFRANCO FERRÉ - Made in Italy." The jacket, designed by Ferré for his first collection of men's wear for the 1982-83 Autumn-Winter season, already displays the main characteristics that underlie his style: the use of primary colours, rarely blended in a pattern but set side by side, each one a separate shape or element, and the emphasis more on the volume of the garment than on its shape, revealed in this item by the treatment of the sleeves, especially at the shoulder. The black sweater belongs to the same collection while the black woollen trousers come from a more recent one. The jacket is preserved in the Ferré Archives in Milan. (*C.G.B.*)

Suit from the 1984-85 Autumn-Winter collection in somewhat "ginned" "Prince of Wales" combed wool. Numerous versions of the suit have been produced in different colours and fabrics. Photograph by Herb Ritts, taken in April 1984 for the 1984-85 Autumn-Winter advertising campaign. The colour positive is preserved in the Ferré Archives in Milan. (*C.G.B.*)

Coat partially lined in fur and with fur collar. Covert coating of 70% virgin wool and 30% cashmere, in which yarn dyed in grey, light blue and black has been used to produce a varying iron-grey colour. Musquash fur dyed grey and natural wolf fur.

Double-breasted model with wide lapels and collar shaped so that it can be closed right under the chin, with the plastron completely done up when the large fur collar and the half-lining of fur are not attached. Measurements: length at mid-back 136 cm; circumference at chest 122 cm, at bottom 168 cm. Label: "GIANFRANCO FERRÉ - Made in Italy." Owner: Ferré Archives in Milan.

The coat was designed for the 1985-86 Autumn-Winter collection, as was the blue pinstripe woollen suit, cotton shirt and silk tie. With fur collar and lining, it has a fairly traditional appearance, though an opulent one. But once they are removed, many details of the garment are revealed to be far from traditional, such as the very new geometrical shape of the collar, or extremely refined, such as the double box pleat at the back, with buttoned vent, or the chamois trimming, neither obvious nor garish, which recall the historical image of the dandy. (*C.G.B.*)

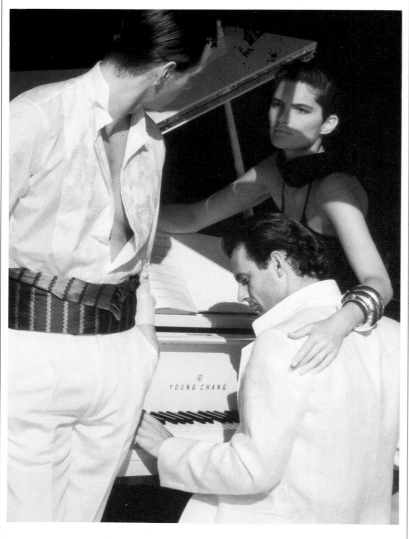

Evening suits from the 1986 Spring-Summer collection. Jacket in white linen. Shirt in white cotton gauze with shirt-front and cuffs in cotton embroidered with cotton (matt) and synthetic (shiny) thread in a pattern of volutes and waves. Trousers in white silk georgette. Sash in Jacquard weave silk, in a pattern of red spirals on a black ground.

In these recent suits, the use of raw silk, white on white embroidery and the introduction of shades of pink into the traditional black and white of evening wear, indicate the stylist's increasingly marked interest in the extremely refined and not very showy detail, almost a nostalgia for some of the long-past privileges of men's fashion. Photograph by Herb Ritts, taken in July 1985 for the 1986 Spring-Summer advertising campaign. The colour positive is preserved in the Ferré Archives in Milan. (*C.G.B.*)

Evening shoes for the winter: (In the foreground) Upper in black chamois leather; leather sole; black kid lining. Slipper model with high and straight toe-cap and triangular lateral inserts of elastic. Embroidered on toe-cap in matt black cotton cord: pattern of superimposed plaiting with the letter "F" at the centre. (In background) Upper in black chamois leather; leather sole, black kid lining. Slipper model with one-piece upper with low profiling at the instep. In the centre mechanically executed embroidery in matt black cotton and shiny black synthetic thread: dense and shiny floral patterns framing an "F" and a "IV" in matt thread.

The two models were designed for the 1986-87 Autumn-Winter collection. The inside of the shoes bears the label "GIANFRANCO FERRÉ - Made in Italy." Owner: Ferré Archives in Milan. (*C.G.B.*)

Drawing executed in black pencil and black and red felt pen, on paper. Folio of 42 × 29.5 cm. It depicts a suit of trousers and military-style double-breasted jacket underneath a coat, also double-breasted, that echoes the military features of the jacket. At bottom right can be seen the illegible signature. Jacket and coat were produced for the 1986-87 Autumn-Winter collection in cotton jersey, in the colours black and cream and various shades of blue, beige and green, with metal buttons. The drawing, preserved in the Ferré Archives in Milan, was executed by Gianfranco Ferré in the winter of 1985.

A preparatory design with the function of establishing the basic volumetric and formal characteristics of a suit. As in all Ferré's sketches, the trunk receives all the attention while the trousers are barely indicated. With respect to previous garments, this recent design, the realization of which has not yet been seen, appears simplified in its details, in the pattern of superimpositions and even in the materials employed, as if the stylist is moving towards a more rigorous formality in which refinement and preciosity of details and materials will be expressed in an increasingly more subtle manner. (*C.G.B.*)

Outfit made up of windcheater and cardigan with accessories (shirt, tie and scarf) created to accompany the outfit.

Windcheater: Jacquard knit in 50% virgin wool, 30% mohair and 20% polyamide. Pattern of horizontal bands of different widths in a variety of shades of green, pink, bordeaux and blue. Cardigan: sateen knit in 50% virgin wool, 30% mohair and 20% polyamide, solid light blue in colour. Shirt: Jacquard knit in 100% virgin wool, bouclé yarn. Pattern of "Regimental" stripes in alternating brick red and white. Scarf: double Jacquard knit executed with the same yarns, technique and colours as the windcheater. Pattern of undulating bands. The trousers belong to a more recent collection but are of the same type as those shown with the outfit. Label: with "Missoni - Made in Italy." Owner: Missoni Archives, at Sumirago (Varese).

The outfit was designed for the 1978-79 Autumn-Winter collection. One of the oldest complete examples of accessories to be found in the Missoni collection, it represents in a highly significant way what had been an established and successful style for many years: the article of knitwear, traditional symbol of practicality and casual wear. (*C.G.B.*)

Outfit made up of jacket and waistcoat with accessories (trousers, shirt, tie and hat) designed to accompany it. Jacket: Jacquard knit in 90% virgin wool and 10% polyamide, from which the dead nap has not been eliminated, and "cooked" after weaving. Pattern of the "flamboyant tracery" type with alternating layers of cognac, turquoise green, red, blue and beige that are repeated horizontally. Waistcoat: weaving, materials, pattern and colours are identical to those of the jacket, except for the absence of cooking. Trousers in 100% cotton corduroy, cognac colour, 100% wool shirt in checks ranging in shade from beige to brown and bow-tie in wool with pattern of multi-coloured checks but toned down in shade, as is the felt hat in dark green mélange. To all garments is attached a label with "MISSONI UOMO - Made in Italy" written on it in black, except for the hat which carries the label "Cappelleria ROSSI - Milano."

Shown as part of the 1985-86 Autumn-Winter collection, the outfit represents the Missonis' first experiment with the technique of cooked wool. The effect obtained is naturally that of a woven material rather than that of a knit and turns out to be particularly interesting when coupled with the waistcoat, the yarn, pattern, colours and treatment of which is identical except for the process of cooking. This creates an interesting contrast between *knit* and pseudo fabric. Owner: Missoni Archives at Sumirago (Varese). (*C.G.B.*)

257

Three scarves. (From the outside to the inside). Jacquard knit, 80% wool and 20% polyamide. Pattern of rectangles in rust red, dark green, blue and bordeaux, with internal squares and lines in black. Jacquard knit, 65% mohair and 35% polyamide. Design representing stylized greyhounds running along horizontal strips in which the following colour pattern combinations alternate: black/grey, black/burnt brown, black/cream. Jacquard knit, 43% mohair, 31% virgin wool, 26% polyamide. Two-ended braided pattern that runs vertically divided into horizontal strips by the change in colour of the ends of the braid every two intersections: green/blue, blue/red, red/green. Measurements respectively 180 × 65 cm; 200 × 50 cm; 180 × 45 cm. Label: "Missoni Uomo - Made in Italy." Owner: Missoni Archives at Sumirago (Varese). Designed by Ottavio Missoni for the 1986-87 Autumn-Winter collection.

For some years figured designs have been appearing alongside geometrical patterns in men's wear as well. But the innovative aspect of these scarves is the loose knit and the exaggerated proportions. This results in a new way of wearing the accessory: owing to its great width it will have to be draped rather than wrapped around the neck, but its lightness will allow it to create a voluminous halo. (*C.G.B.*)

Three pairs of socks, reaching to below the knee, made out of Jacquard knit, 80% wool and 20% polyamide.

(From left to right): Design of Greek frets and lozenges in cherry red and orange that alternate in a pattern of 4/2 on a cornflower blue ground. Design made up of three types of lozenge, in red and fuchsia, alternating in a pattern of 3/3 on a green ground. Three strips of turquoise dots alternating with a strip of rust coloured Greek frets on a mustard yellow ground. Missoni design for the 1986-87 Autumn-Winter collection manufactured and distributed by Malerba.

Label: "Missoni by Malerba - Made in Italy." Owner: Missoni Archives at Sumirago (Varese). (*C.G.B.*)

Suit made up of jacket and waistcoat with accesssories (trousers, shirt and tie) designed to accompany it. Jacket: twill weave fabric made out of 100% cotton yarn, with a pattern of squares and rectangles of different sizes in an irregular sequence of the colours red, iron grey, green, mustard yellow and cornflower blue on a light grey ground. Waistcoat: Jacquard knit, 46% linen, 24% cotton, 30% polyamide. Design made up of three different shapes of masks that alternate diagonally along horizontal strips, in green, cream, red, purple and black, on a black ground with a background pattern of zig-zags in cream, purple and green. Coal grey trousers in 100% linen, medium grey shirt in 100% linen and twill weave tie (50% wool, 50% cotton) in a pattern of multicoloured checks are exclusively produced for Missoni to the latter's design and in a variety of colours. Measurements of jacket: shoulders 49 cm, length at mid-back 83 cm; vest: shoulders 47 cm, length at mid-back 61 cm. Jacket and waistcoat carry the label "Missoni - Uomo - Made in Italy," while the label attached to the accessories merely reads "Missoni." Owner: Missoni Archives at Sumirago (Varese).

The suit, given the name "Dublino," in obvious reference to the chequered pattern of the jacket, was designed for the 1986 Spring-Summer season. The tendency to juxtapose woven fabrics with knitted ones, already visible in the collections of the two previous years, is here developed to the full.

The fabric is manufactured exclusively for Missoni to the latter's design by Marzotto. Photograph by Giovanni Gastel, taken for the 1986 Spring-Summer advertising campaign. (*C.G.B.*)

Gianni Versace

Trousers in chamois (foreground) and leather (background). Riding model with leggings laced up on the outside. Designed for the 1980-81 Autumn-Winter collection, the model was given the name "Cavallo" and was produced for the market in several different fabrics and colours.

Photograph taken by Francesco Scavullo in Spring 1980 for 1980-81 Autumn-Winter advertising campaign. The colour positive is preserved in the Versace Archives in Milan. (*C.G.B.*)

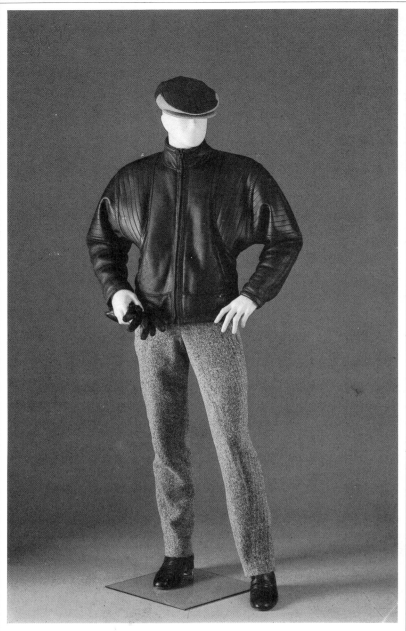

Outfit made up of sports jacket and trousers with accessories: cap, gloves and belt. Sport jacket: Sheepskin dyed black and turned inside out, black rubber and black soft leather. The rubber part is marked with "quilting" executed by laser. Trousers: 100% wool tweed, made out of white and grey yarn to produce a "grisaille" effect. Very close-fitting and "tight-waisted" model. The later effect is obtained through a band of five quilts made out of "schiumella" (synthetic fabric with one side, usually considered the "reverse," napped). Cap: Black rubber with "quilting" as in the jacket and red woollen cloth. Gloves: Black rubber with "quilting" as in the jack-

et, black soft leather, white 100% cashmere knit. Measurements of jacket 50 cm, length at mid-back 72 cm; trousers, length 110 cm. Label: "GIANNI VERSACE - Made in Italy," except the cap with label: "GIANNI VERSACE - Made in Italy by BORSALINO." Owner: private collection.

Designed for the 1983-84 Autumn-Winter collection, the outfit is highly representative of two of the most important tendencies underlying Versace's research: the decidedly untraditional style of men's trousers, and the use of unusual or new materials. These trousers forecast the formal scheme of recent collections with considerable degree of fullness at

the hips and thigh in striking contrast to the tight waistband and the very narrow bottoms. In this case, while sticking to the narrow waist and bottoms, the stylist has experimented with a "tight-waisted" form in which the light padding of the "graphic" and enwrapping part brings out the most virile quality of the male leg, the musculature. The model was in fact called "Muscolo." The trousers were coupled, at the show and in photographic advertisements, with the jacket which, since it is also close-fitting, returns to the theme of the "body revealed." The powerful impression of the shoulders is heightened by the great breadth of the sleeves at the armhole, only to fit tightly over

the muscles of the forearm and terminate in a powerful hand emphasized by the padded gloves. gloves.

The other line of research dear to Versace, can be detected here in the use of non-woven materials in clothing. Rubber has never been widely used since it is an amorphous material that cannot be texturized and one in which traditional stitching does not last long. These two problems were solved by the use of a technology that does not normally have anything to do with the field of fashion: the laser is in fact capable of texturizing rubber with "quilting" and ensures the grip of the stitching along the edges. (*C.G.B.*)

Suit and coat, with accessories. Suit: 100% virgin woollen cloth, in narrow black and medium grey stripes of equal width. Jacket: double-breasted model with very tight waist, while the skirts fall so as to leave a gap at the bottom. Trousers: model with tight waist and wide legs that narrow considerably towards the bottom. Attention is drawn to the waist by a very high waistband; two deep tucks give a notable degree of fullness to the upper part of the trousers in sharp contrast to the close-fitting shapes of the jacket. Coat: 100% virgin woolen cloth, in a pattern of bands with seven very thin black lines grouped together on a grey ground that forms narrower bands. Double-breasted model of fairly slim line accentuated by a half-belt made up of two segments that intersect before buckling. Shirt: patterned fabric (50% silk, 50% cotton) of the "Pékin" type with the following sequence: one ribbed strip in a cream colour/one smooth strip also in cream / one narrow stripe in black. Tie: 100% ribbed silk. "Regimental" type pattern. The suit and the coat were designed for the 1984-85 Autumn-Winter collection. The shirt and tie for the 1984-85 Autumn-Winter collection were manufactured in several variations. Measurements of jacket: shoulders 52 cm, length at mid-back 77 cm; trousers: length 120 cm; coat: shoulders 50 cm, length at mid-back 121 cm. All garments carry the label "GIANNI VERSACE - Made in Italy". Owner: Versace Archives in Novara. There is a remarkable coherence, quite rare in men's fashion, in the way the stylist has chosen the same weaves and the same colour combinations in the fabrics, in a pattern of variations on the theme of stripes and the colour grey which permeated the whole of that season's collection, for men and women, garments and accessories. (*C.G.B.*)

263

Suit and dust-coat with waist-coat. Suit: 100% linen in grey/light green with white pinstripes. During the finishing stage the cloth has been subjected to a special treatment that has made it permanently "wrinkled." Jacket: single-breasted model with a gap between the skirts, thanks to the "dress-coat" cut, producing an effect of slimness at the hips that is heightened by the bulkiness of the chest and wide shoulders. Trousers: model with narrow waist and wide legs that narrow considerably towards the bottom. The waist is made to stand out by a high waistband; two deep tucks give fullness to the legs which, very long and narrow at the bottom, flop over the feet. Dust-coat: fabric identical to that of the suit; fastenings in the raincoat style; very wide raglan sleeves. Waistcoat: mixed silk and synthetic fabric printed in bands of three white stripes very close together (0.5 cm) with interspaces in grisaille (3.5 cm). The suit and waistcoat were designed for the 1986 Spring-Summer collection and coupled in the July 1985 show. Shirt and tie, both in patterned silk, in rose-tinged shades of beige, come from the same collection. Measurements of jacket: shoulders 67 cm, length at mid-back 80 cm, circumference at chest 116 cm; trousers: length 115 cm; dust-coat: length at mid-back 110 cm; vest: length at mid-back 51 cm, shoulder tip length 71 cm. Label: "Gianni Versace - Made in Italy." Owner: Versace Archives in Novara.

The abundant and intentionally sagging forms of suit and dust-coat and the use of "wrinkled" linen give the outfit a rough and neglected air that is immediately belied by the "aplomb" of the waistcoat with its soft and sleek material and by the opulence of the patterned silk used for the shirt and tie. (*C.G.B.*)

Three versions of outfit made up of trousers, two cardigans worn one over the other, tie and Persian lamb busby. The photograph was taken by Beppe Caggi on the occasion of the January presentation of the 1986-87 Autumn-Winter collection. Owner: Versace Archives in Milan.

One of the recurrent themes in Versace's collections of women's wear in recent years is realized in full here for men as well: the highly repetitive geometrical design, in two colours, with tiny variations of proportion that create an optical effect of movement and/or confusion. As in the woman's collection for the same season the "optical" areas are rendered in black and white or white and yellow, whether printed or woven (shirts and ties), and in glossy materials (mercerized cotton and silk, along with metallic knit in the women's clothing). The visual impact of these optical patterns is softened by large areas of solid and bright colours that contrast with the black and white but are made out of soft and opaque material that absorbs light (here the wool knit, velvet in the collection of women's wear).

The drawing was executed by Werner at the beginning of 1986, after the garments had already been made for the January show. Hence it does not represent a creative stage, but is a sort of glorification of clothes that already exist and is to be used exclusively for advertising and promotion. (*C.G.B.*)

Ermenegildo Zegna

Drawing on paper in pencil, pen and gouache, in tones of grey, blue and brown. Folio 42 × 29.5 cm. It depicts a suit with double-breasted jacket, six buttons, "shirt-style" trousers, blue/grey pinstripes. On the left leg of the trousers is written "A. VANGORP '86." The garment was made for E. Zegna's 1986/87 Autumn-Winter collection out of flannel and 100% virgin wool worsted, in a variety of colours, solid or pinstripe. Owner: IN.CO. Archives, Novara (Gruppo E. Zegna S.p.A.), was executed in 1986 by Anna Maria Bernardoni Van Gorp to illustrate one of the three plastic patterns in this year's Zegna collection. (*C.G.B.*)

Summer suit. 100% wool worsted, in dark blue with very fine light-blue stripes. The suit is composed of a double-breasted jacket and fairly close-fitting trousers without darts at the waist, but cuffs at bottom. Measurements: waist 68 cm; length 110 cm. The cotton shirt, silk tie and purse have been produced in several different colours and patterns to accompany this and similar garments in the collection. Measurements of jacket: shoulders 52 cm, length at mid-back 80 cm, waist 70 cm; trousers: waist 68 cm, length 110 cm. Label: ".Z. ERMENEGILDO ZEGNA." Owner: E. Zegna Archives at Trivero (Vercelli).

The suit, made for the 1986 Spring-Summer collection, was produced in several different colours and even models, but the common feature is the type of fabric, created by E. Zegna after years of research aimed at coming up with a summer fabric that would be as light and cool as linen and as uncrushable as synthetic materials. The result is a fabric known as High Performance, made out of 100% Australian super wools, with combed and highly twisted yarn and natural methods of treatment, such as steam, to eliminate resins from the production cycle. Form the same reason, in making up the garments the rule followed is that of stitching all the fabrics on the inside and never using glues. In a season in which many stylists have gone in for the "wrinkled" appearance, Zegna came onto the market with the opposite, concentrating, as is her habit, on that area of the market that eludes the stylists, as well as ready-to-wear clothing. (*C.G.B.*)

Drawing on paper in pencil, pen and gouache, in the colours brown, purple, turquoise and lilac. Folio 42 × 29.5 cm. It depicts a double-breasted sports jacket, with four buttons and "shirtstyle" shoulders, in a pattern of brown checks within larger turquoise ones. On the left leg of the trousers is written "A. VANGORP '86."

The garment was made for the 1986 Spring-Summer collection out of mixed wool/silk or linen/silk fabric, with many variations in the proportions of the design and the colour. It was also produced for the 1986-87 Autumn-Winter collection in 100% virgin carded woollen fabrics, very soft to the touch, and in some cases with 30% cashmere wool, in many different colours and proportions of design. The drawing was executed in 1986 by Anna Maria Bernardoni Van Gorp to illustrate one of the three basic patterns in this year's Zegna collection. Owner: IN.CO. Archives, Novara (Gruppo E. Zegna S.p.A.). (*C.G.B.*)

Outfit made up of trousers, sweater and dust-coat, with scarf. Trousers: 100% wool worsted, of the *covert* type, woven out of yarn dyed brown, dark blue and light blue to produce a cognac colour with a mélange effect. 100% Bemberg artificial silk lining in the same colour. Sweater: 100% cashmere knit in cream colour. Knitted in broad vertical ribs. Dust-coat: 100% cashmere twill, in a "spike" design in the colours pearl grey and cream. 100% Scarf: carded wool twill, 70% virgin and 30% cashmere. Patterned in bands of different sizes each made up of two colours in the sequence: cognac, orange-purplish orange, purple-bluish purple, grey-bluish grey, cognac, etc. Measurements of trousers: waist 69 cm, length 110 cm; dust-coat: shoulders 51 cm, length at mid-back 124 cm; length of sleeve 64 cm. Scarf length 184 cm; width 30 cm. Label: ".Z. Ermenegildo Zegna." Owner: E. Zegna Archives at Trivero (Vercelli).

The common feature of these four items consists in the fact that all the stages of production, from selection of the flocks of wool to the design of the model and its manufacture, have been carried out by firms belonging to the Gruppo E. Zegna S.p.A. and therefore coordinated by a single system of research, from the choice of raw materials to the drawing-board and the finished product. (*C.G.B.*)

FASHION MAGAZINES: TWO DIFFERENT CASES

Stefania Ricci

The possibilities for research presented by an investigation of the periodical magazines published in Italy between 1960 and 1980 were infinite. Today there are a very high number of magazines available on the market with a publishing history of varying length behind them. An analysis that aimed to be, I will not say exhaustive, but at least adequate, would have required a great deal of time and a whole team of researchers.

Hence it has been found necessary to restrict the field to two sample publications, selected from among the weeklies and monthlies for their representative character and for the type of readership to which they are addressed, even though the differences are no longer so clear-cut as in the past.

Among the weeklies I have settled on *Amica*, both because it is one of the best-known magazines in Italy and has a current circulation that is among the highest and because it first came out at the beginning of the sixties, the period at which this investigation begins.

In the field of monthly publications, the choice fell on the Italian edition of *Vogue*, launched in November 1965. In fact it was unthinkable, in an investigation of fashion publications in Italy, however summary, to leave out of consideration what is considered throughout the world to be one of the most important magazines of this century and, among those still in existence, the one whose origins lie furthest back in the past. Those mentioned so far have been publications devoted to women's fashion and with a largely female readership. Those magazines that aim at a male readerhip deserve separate discussion. In recent years there has been a notable increase in the number of such publications, together with an improvement in their quality, in parallel with the commercial boom in men's fashion.

Once again it has seemed inevitable that the choice of a representative of these magazines should have fallen on the men's wear edition of *Vogue*, i.e. *L'Uomo Vogue*. In effect, out of all the publications specializing in this sector, it is the one most often consulted both by the average reader and by those active in the field. This is not the place to go into the history of the magazine, which has many points in common with magazine for women. I have considered it opportune to confine the analysis to a single year, 1980, as a moment of synthesis between two different approaches to magazines aimed at men and to fashion itself.

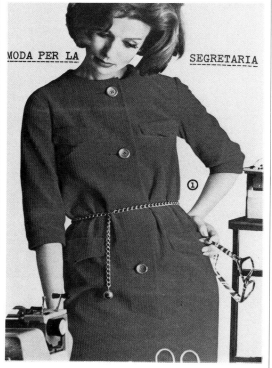

"Fashion for the secretary," in Amica, *December 2, 1962 (photo Mario Santana).*

Amica: A "Practical" Journal for Women

March 25, 1962, saw the launching of a new women's magazine, destined to achieve one of the highest levels of circulation in Italy: *Amica*, a weekly sister publication to *Il Corriere della Sera* dedicated to fashion and topical events.

The project was devised by Franco Sartori (then head of the Advertising and Development offices of the *Corriere*) and his vice, Mario Gallotti. The graphic layout was designed by Flavio Lucchini. Therefore a steering committee was formed made up of Enrico Gramigna, editor, and the two founders of the project Franco Sartori and Flavio Lucchini.

In order to grasp the public's attention and to face up to competition from long-established magazines, contributions were sought from specialists in the various sectors that go to make up the framework of this type of publication. Well-known journalists like Mila Contini, editor of *Grazia* as far back as 1940,[1] were called on for the editorial staff; Brunetta, one of the leading figures in Italian fashion illustration, was charged with providing the drawings, and in the first issue Dino Buzzati placed his pen at the service of the magazine's readers, offering them advice on how to do their hair and how to be beautiful and elegant, in accordance with the principle that the ultimate desire of the female public is that of being admired by men and envied by other women.[2]

Over the course of the twenty-year period under examination here, there have been changes in the weekly's format, the quality of its paper, its price and its contributors but, in spite of attempts to rationalize its lay-out, the basic structure has remained the same. Those changes which, at first glance, appear to be bound up with the very existence of the journal, were in reality part of a process that involved the whole of the fashion press and not just one particular magazine. It cannot be denied that the text of fashion reportages has, over the years, yielded more and more space to the photographic image, which has become the most important means of communication for the magazine. This evolution is not merely the consequence of a cultural choice made by *Amica*, but can be found in the majority of fashion publications.

The programme that Paolo Pietroni, chief editor of *Amica* since 1974, announced to its readers in the year following his appointment, follows a line that can be traced back, through the editorships of Gramigna, Zucconi, Alberti and Oriani, to the first appearance of the magazine. The essential characteristic on which *Amica* bases its approach and its difference from other publications is that of being a "practical" magazine, i.e. a magazine "that is not only attractive, agreeable, entertaining, well-informed about women's activities and committed to the struggle for the emancipation of women," but that is of "service" to women and that retains its usefulness with the passing of time.[3] If one takes a brief look at the tables of contents during the magazine's first year of publication, when it was under the editorship of Enrico Gramigna, one finds not only articles on fashion and beauty, which do not in fact take up the largest part of the magazine, but also sections of fiction and of book reviews, features on furnishing and antiques, and on cooking, together with columns of medical and legal advice. Such contents, which were professed to be written by experts, took on increasing importance over the course of time.

Rather than being exclusively concerned with fashion, *Amica* initially presented itself as an illustrated magazine, with the faces of actresses and singers on the cover,[4] and with secrets revealed inside. A good number of pages were devoted to gossip and to prominent figures in society, who opened up their homes to the magazine's reporters and made confession. Thus Paola di Liegi granted an interview to Mario Oriani in her castle of Belvedere[5] and Jacqueline Kennedy, symbol of the American woman, told the story of her meeting with and marriage to the President of the United States in episodes, as if in a novel. Assuring readers that "not all her clothes are created by a famous couturier" and that even she "buys from department stores," she was put forward as a new model for women to identify with.[6]

It should not be forgotten that *Amica* appeared at the beginning of an era of unrest and revolution: the sixties. *Amica* too found itself with a role to play in the dissemination of the new ideas, in a language that was within the reach of all. While the magazine continued to present the image of a narcissistic woman, preoccupied with her body and with the furnishings of her home, it did give space to debates and investigations into the most pressing of women's problems, from the crisis in matrimony in contemporary society[7] to the Ogino-Knaus method of birth control[8] and the abortion bill of 1975.[9]

A phenomenon like that of the birth of the mini-skirt and its widespread popularity among the young and not so young became the subject of a more thorough investigation, in which women in the street, doctors, priests and sociologists were asked questions of the type: "Cheerful piece of foolishness that will last a single summer or disturbing symptom of a world bent on change? Irresponsible challenge to tradition by the young or the first step towards a society with less and less concern for the moral aspect of fashion..."?[10]

It is important to answer one question first:

"*From the Brunetta notebook,*" *in* Amica, April 15, 1962.

Cover of Amica, *August 18, 1963.*

who are the readers of *Amica*? They form a heterogeneous group, made up of teenagers, to whom a section of the magazine called the "Clan of the very young" is dedicated, but above all of mature women, to whom the editors offer the cults of youth and freshness, proclaiming the freedom of the body and open-minded modes of behaviour, to be displayed even in the choice of clothes and their colours.[11] A largely middle-class readership, consisting partly of housewives, but mainly of working women, employed on the whole as office workers of one sort or another. It is revealing that *Amica* held a competition for secretaries, who made up the highest percentage of the magazine's readers during the first ten years of publication: run jointly with Remington Rand Italia, the competition offered as prizes to the "secretary of the year"[12] a trip by air to an exotic country or an original creation by the Sorelle Fontana, both of which were held to be symbols of a social status impossible to achieve on a modest office salary.

Amica also outlined an identikit of the ideal secretary:[13] a woman endowed with charm rather than perfect features, tidy in appearance rather than strikingly beautiful; she is recommended to avoid "architectural elaborations" in her hair-style, to use make-up of the "soap-and-water kind," and to wear sober clothes, of the sort specially designed by the fashion houses to be used by women who have to go out early in the morning, take the tram during the rush hour and stay tidy all day.

The increasing level of prosperity meant that interest in fashion also spread to those social classes that had previously been excluded from the purview of fashion and its clients. Indeed, it was realized that it was just this section of the public that the magazine tended to attract, justifying the policy towards advertising it adopted and the emphasis given to certain sectors, an approach that the magazine has retained to the present day.

For women who made their own clothes, *Amica* offered, on the initiative of the Singer company,[14] patterns designed by famous fashion houses and expert advice, in a weekly feature, on how to revamp a "demodé" dress,[15] or how to use tricks to transform and adapt an item of clothing for many different occasions.[16] Every two or three issues the magazine would carry a feature on knitting or crochet, including pull-out sections giving the measurements and explaining the stitches required. The slogan of "do-it-yourself" turned out always to be a valid one, attractive to those with limited financial resources, even when camouflaged under the name of "hobby."[17]

Such an approach makes it easy to explain the presence of articles like the one by Marta Schiavi in the spring of 1962 on fabrics used in fashion and on the instructions to be given to dressmakers, who still dominated the Italian market and who were prepared to copy the model of a famous designer from the pages of a magazine or from a fashion show.[18] Even the photographic illustrations were intended to reveal technical details of the clothing, with the aid of written descriptions of the structural elements, the material, the shape of the neck and the type of pleat. One can conclude that, in its early phase, the magazine was committed to a simple and practical kind of fashion, easy to wear, while reportages on French and Italian haute couture were of marginal importance, even when enlivened by Brunetta's graphics.[19]

Later on *Amica* followed the lead of other magazines, adapting its role to that of an informational and advertising vehicle for the industries connected with fashion. These supplied promotional material, regarding it as of fundamental importance that they should appear in the magazine. Articles on high fashion became necessary in order to lend prestige and credibility to the publication, and were regulated by the different seasonal collections, including those of Paris which were covered in collaboration with the French magazine *Elle*.[20]

In its attitude towards French fashion, one could still detect signs of reverential awe, but over the course of time the magazine became increasingly concerned with promoting the national product. This change in attitude is revealed by comments like the one to be found in an article on the autumn 1965 shows in Paris, which described the models presented as "undoubtedly beautiful clothes, but no more beautiful than in Italy."[21]

But *Amica's* efforts were largely concentrated on a sector of the market more within the reach of the public at large, that of prêt-à-porter which took on increasing importance at the beginning of the sixties. Not only did the magazine list the prices of all the clothes that were reproduced in photographs and the shops where they could be bought, but it carried a series of articles,[22] appearing at regular intervals, testifying to *Amica's* commitment to the new style in ready-to-wear clothing, which "has definitely improved (the standard of) its production by using fabrics very similar to those employed in haute couture and not infrequently making use of the same designers."[23]

This approach remained constant throughout the first decade of the magazine's publication. To some extent the gap was bridged that had hitherto divided the fashion weekly from the monthly, with its more sophisticated photography and language. This metamorphosis of the fashion weekly did not affect *Amica* alone, but was generally to be observed in all the other high-circulation magazines as they followed the evolution in women's taste that accompanied their cultural and social emancipation over the twenty-year period.

Thus if we analyze the language adopted over these two decades, we can find all the ingredients necessary to classify a verbal annotation as technical, informative, emphatic or evocative. It suffices to make a comparison between two captions, separated by twenty years in the history of the magazine, in order to

Sorpresa

dall'obbiettivo dopo il primo tuffo della giornata... Jean Shrimpton, il Gamberetto, nel più snello dei costumi bianchi: morbido e lucido, « nudo » dietro quasi più di un bikini... In fondo alla baia l'isola di Santorin vestita dei primi colori del mattino — una nebbiolina scintillante lilla e rosa... Costume da bagno di Rikki per Sport Trio, in nailon Antron, nailon Du Pont e Lycra. Nelle dodici pagine seguenti: pettinature di Ara Gallant con parrucche di capelli veri di Tovar Tresses.

Jean Shrimpton, portrayed with Jean Louis Sieff by Richard Avedon, wearing a bathing suit by Rikki for Sport Trio, in Vogue Italia, *May 1967.*

Willy Rizzo, Elsa Martinelli, in Vogue
Italia, *June 1967.*

get an idea of what had occurred. In December 1962 was announced "a romantic style that is on its way back; the high collar of black velvet closely fitting around the neck and brightened up in front by a paste brooch with pendent pearls."[24] The novelty for the close of the year conveyed a hint of far-off ages, but at the same time it was kept in strict relationship to the accessory reproduced in the illustration. Compare the comment made in a reportage on the use of silk fabrics in fashion from March 1983: "(Silk) is the reality behind an age-old myth. The legend of an intriguing lure. The desire to lose oneself in the effect of beauty." The word surpasses the object, becomes interpretation of its own dreams, of the ephemeral.[25]

If one goes on to examine the photographic features, it can be seen that in its early days the magazine favoured isolated pictures, coupling them at the most with a detail of the garment. At a later date the sequence of photographs, especially those of collections, was arranged so as to give the reader the impression of an imaginary parade staged for her benefit. Reportages that emerge from the studio and take the street, a café or a cruise-ship as their setting were still rare. When it did happen, the models were still posed and the dynamics of the scene were artificial.

Things were to change. Soon the style of the fashion photograph came to resemble that of the snapshot. The clothes began to bear witness to a way of being and behaving. Where photographs were organized into a sequence by the graphic designer, their succession was no longer determined by an established scheme, but composed in accordance with a narrative plot suggested by the title. Ideas were taken from the cinema or the theatre, as when *Amica* chose the panels of an imaginary stage in an old theatre in Portsmouth that was being used to put on a musical, *The Boyfriend*, as a setting for one of its own fashion features.[26] The effects and even the actual technique of film editing were imitated. The photographs of Henri Gissinger told a story, a story that was described as "quasi-American": "Her, him, the other. Brief love story in Hollywood style against the background of Our Home. Costumes: Yves Saint Laurent, Mila Schön, Valentino, Lancetti, Ungaro and other greats. Direction: the fashion of the fifties."[27]

"The Viewpoint of Vogue"

The first issue of the Italian edition of *Vogue* came out in November 1965, under the name of *Vogue/Novità* and the editorship of Lidia Tabacchi. This was part of the process of transformation, under way since 1962, of the Italian monthly *Novità* founded in 1950 by Emilia Rosselli Kunster but now managed in partnership with Condé Nast, the publishers of *Vogue America*.[28]

In her introduction to the new magazine, Tabacchi tended to emphasize its historical continuity with the former publication, which had set out be as international and accomplished as possible, not only on the level of journalism and

Elisabetta Catalano, Benedetta Barzini, in Vogue Italia, *January 1968.*

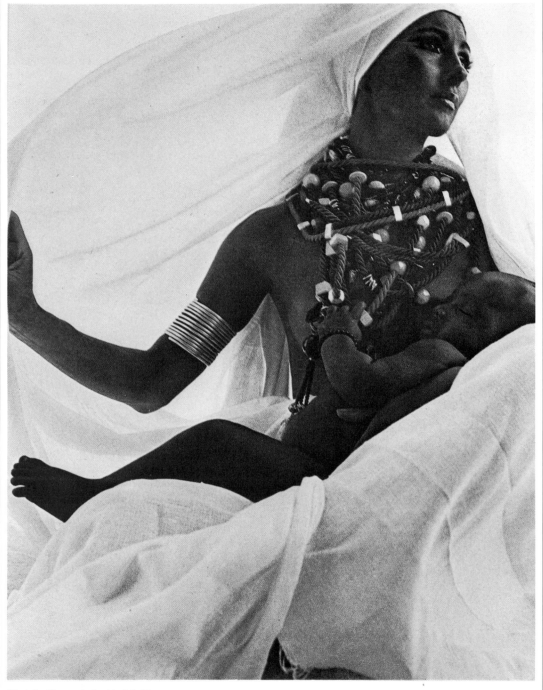

Photo by Gianpaolo Barbieri, in Vogue
Italia, *February 1969.*

photography, but also in its way of seeing fashion as a facet of style and design. From this point of view, it is easy to understand the position taken in features on furnishings and architecture, and in those dealing with art exhibitions and cultural events.

In a reportage entitled "To Be Ornamental," devoted to the Paris winter fashions, a comparison was drawn between the wealth of decoration in the new style and the ornamental world of Gustav Klimt.[29] This concept was reinforced by the photography of Norman Parkinson, one of the most celebrated of fashion photographers at an international level, who created montages out of the clothes and some of the Viennese artist's paintings. The refined approach taken to the photographs is matched by that of the language used to comment on them, full of references to early 20th-century symbolism. The readership at which the monthly is aimed is clearly represented by the aristocracy of breeding and culture and the upper middle class, which assumes a dual role with regard to the magazine, being its readers on the one hand and involving itself in the complex workings of the publication on the other. The members of "high society" become the protagonists of charity performances staged in *à la page* night-spots, of private views and of holidays in Sardinia, faithfully reported by the magazine. Sometimes some of the female readers belonging to the upper ranks of society allow their homes to be put on show, stand in as special models for a feature or, should they be engaged in some kind of working activity,[30] present their latest fashion creations or their boutiques. This has remained a constant feature of the magazine, even when it was purchased by Condé Nast. After a process of transformation both graphically and in content, promoted by Franco Sartori who had called in Flavio Lucchini as the new graphic designer, the monthly was rechristened *Vogue Italia* in November 1966. Franco Sartori, previously a contributor to *Amica* and *Novità*, was appointed as editor.

From this moment on the publication lost its Italian connotations in order to pursue the line followed by the foreign magazine. Of course a lot of space was given to Italian fashion, but sometimes the contents and images of the latter were repeated after a delay of several months, as in the case of Richard Avedon's famous photograph of Jean Shrimpton and Jean Louis Sieff, published in *Vogue America* in January 1967 and in *Vogue Italia* in May of the same year.[31] One thing that disappeared was advertising for cheap products outside the specific field of fashion, together with patterns and the explanations of how to use them to make a dress, the last trace of the original approach taken by *Novità*, as a useful and practical magazine.[32]

The journal grew still more refined. Carrying advertisements for the more important textile industries, leather and furs, cosmetics and anything connected with the sectors of fashion and beauty, which take up over half of the magazine,

Vogue tends to present itself as an indispensable source of information and a tool of consultation for specialists, whether producers or buyers. It is only in this section of the magazine that fashion is treated as a commercial product. For the rest it cannot be denied that the monthly aims to carry out a far-reaching cultural programme and to document the customs of the day, recording the most important news items, especially those with a cultural and sociological background, musical tendencies and artistic influences. Its contributors include famous names from the Italian cultural scene, names like Mario de Micheli, Dacia Maraini and Alberto Moravia.[33] There are features devoted to historical buildings, interior designers, architects and collectors.

The viewpoint of *Vogue* becomes clearer when one goes on the examine those pages that are devoted exclusively to high fashion. The underlying attitude, conveyed through the magazine's photography, text and type-face, is that fashion is a work of art. Emphasis tends to be laid on the formal aspect, design and the effects of style and dress on history.

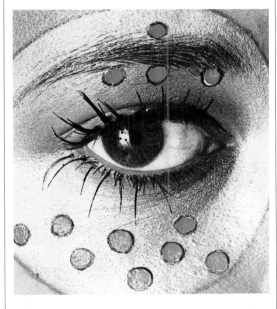

Fashionable artists are used by the magazine as models and leading stylists are presented according to a formula that is virtually identical to the one adopted by art critics when they discover new talent. As a mean of artistic expression, the historical past of fashion is examined. Its origins are sought, its influences analyzed and its cultural background defined, using methods of research that are not very different from the aforementioned ones adopted by a weekly like *Amica*, but using more refined instruments and a more dignified language. The latter draws on ideas, characters and even passages from literature, as in a 1968 article entitled "Hair Fantasy" that quotes a dialogue between Maxime Rude and her friend Baudelaire taken from the *Confidences d'un journaliste* of 1876.[34]

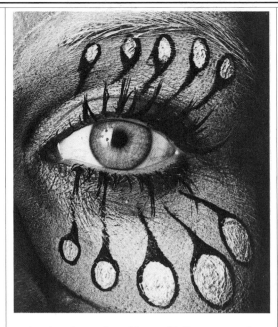

At the time when *Vogue Italia* appeared on the scene, the sixties were already drawing to a close. The social role of women had changed, as had their appearance, which was no longer founded on traditional aesthetic canons. Women identified with the adolescent bodies of Twiggy and Penelope Tree, consecrated by the camera of Richard Avedon.

Men in Vogue

It is worth emphasizing the fact that fashion publications aimed at men are a fairly recent development, especially with regard to the high levels of circulation achieved by this type of publication today. Fashion, especially since the 19th century, has always been considered a feminine prerogative, even on the many occasions when men's wear has assumed greater importance than that intended for women. In recent years there has been enormous growth in the former sector, with its output often exceeding that of women's clothing, in harmony with a change that has affected the entire social sphere. Attention to dress is no longer regarded as a sign of effeminacy and sexual ambiguity. On the contrary, it is something that is often willingly displayed.

Men's fashion first appeared in Condé Nast publications as a minor section of *Vogue Italia*, which as has been pointed out is a magazine aimed predominatingly at a female readership. The photographic illustrations were in no way outstanding and were accompanied by highly condensed descriptions of the colours and styles proposed by fashion designers. But little more than a year later, supplements to the magazine began to appear that were entirely devoted to men's wear. At the start only three of these came out in a year, then six, and finally they constituted an independent magazine, published on a regular monthly basis. The editor was still Franco Sartori, chief editor of *Vogue Italia*, but in reality responsibility for the new magazine

was left in the hands of Oliviero Toscani and Flavio Lucchini, who later became its editor.

The linguistic and photographic content of the periodical is the same as that of the women's magazine, as is the type of reader at which it is aimed, apart from the se. In the same way, space is given to up-to-date news of art and culture. The magazine also carries features on cooking and economics. To demonstrate how the two magazines run on parallel tracks, it is sufficient to cite an article entitled "Is Fashion Art?"[35] in which one finds the same ingredients as had appeared in *Vogue Italia*, only many years earlier.

Contemporaneously with a similar operation set in motion by the fashion houses, *Uomo Vogue*, as the new magazine was called, was initially concerned with giving a sense of individuality to men's wear, in order to disperse "the dense and sad crowd of 'men in grey'" as the magazine put it.[36]

An undoubted contribution to the evolution of this demand was made by the emergence of "unisex clothing" at the beginning of the sixties. The adoption of an identical wardrobe for men and for women was partly a reflection of a desire to demonstrate the social gains achieved by women in the world of men. But on the other hand it provided men with an excuse to wear women's furs and carry handbags,[37] to indulge their own narcissism and the pleasure of dressing up, without this casting any doubt on their virility. This was admitted in an article with the significant title "Lions in Furs": "... in 1967 two modes of conduct that, while excusable and even praiseworthy in women, had been regarded as serious flaws in men, became virtues: narcissism and exhibitionism. On those who know how to wear it properly, the fur bestows a sort of animal virility, composed of zest for life and contempt for the rules that exert an indisputable fascination."[38] The models used for this feature were top personalities from the world of Italian culture and industry: the sculptor Andrea Cas-

Photos by Irving Penn, in Vogue Italia, *October 1969.*

Valentino, 1986-87 Autumn-Winter collection, in Uomo Vogue, *July-August 1986.*

cella, Ettore Sottsass, chief designer of the electronics section of Olivetti, the publisher Giangiacomo Feltrinelli and the artist Lucio Fontana. In the editorial on masculine beauty, an attempt was made to refute any hint of ambiguity, by asserting that perfumes, creams and a suntan were indispensable instruments for those who wished to have Latin charm, to acquire a sense of confidence and to be successful, the traditional myths of the modern male as of that of the past.[39]

In order to overcome any prejudiced attitudes towards men's fashion, it was presented by occasional models during the early phase of the magazine's existence. These were selected from the most famous names in the worlds of entertainment, politics and art. Alternatively, ideal models were drawn from previous eras: "The men who made the century, but its fashion as well" as Isa Vercelloni wrote about Fidel Castro/Gagarin/Gropius/Gorky/Gide."[40] Even heads of state could find their way onto the cover, as did Mao Tse Tung for an issue that discussed the influence of China on fashion.[41] In the meantime, while the seductive role of women appeared to be threatened by the growth of feminism, men proposed turning the tables: "When a man gets under the skin, there is nothing to be done, you'll never get rid of him."[42]

In the light of what has been said about the early years of the magazine, let us take a look at what has changed and what has remained the same in the eighties, under the editorship of Cristina Brigidini. The structure of the magazine has not changed, even though the number of pages and of photographs has increased. The development of the magazine has coincided with that of "made in Italy," and this explains the increasing emphasis given to Italian fashion and its creators.[43]

On the walkways of *Uomo Vogue* continue to parade men who have achieved success in a variety of fields, whether artists like Andy Warhol[44] or the creators of fashion themselves, like Gianni Versace and his manager.[45] However there has been an increasingly strong shift towards the use of anonymous models. These have become the new symbols of identification, no longer represented by "playboys," but by agreeable and athletic young men, who dress with verve, are in love with speed, do "body building" and play tennis.[46]

The freedom to dress as one wishes also becomes the freedom to behave as one wishes, even to declare one's own sexual "deviation," without having it turn into a perversion: "... one can get married at the town hall or in church, but also on a steamboat at a height of three thousand metres or in a Las Vegas casino ('a marriage in five minutes'). The ideal couple, out of a romantic novel, consists of a blonde, very gentle 'her' and a serious, fascinating 'him.' But there is nothing to stop an exchange of rings between two strong men, an adolescent and a Valkyrie, or a neo-sultan and dozens of aspiring 'love slaves'..."[47]

1. C. Esposito, "Riviste italiane di Alta Moda 1940-1970," in *Il disegno dell'alta moda italiana 1940-1970*, vol. I, exhibition catalogue, Rome 1982, p. 70.
2. *Amica*, March 25, 1962, p. 70.
3. Ibidem, September 18, 1975, pp. 9-10.
4. Cover photograph in colour of Sofia Loren. Ibidem, March 25, 1962.
5. Ibidem, April 1, 1962, p. 15.
6. Ibidem, March 25, 1962, p. 11.
7. Ibidem, March 25, 1962, pp. 24-27.
8. Ibidem, August 18, 1963, pp. 13-15.
9. Ibidem, October 16, 1975, pp. 24-29.
10. Ibidem, July 31, 1966, pp. 22, 23.
11. Ibidem, March 25, 1962, pp. 33-46.
12. Ibidem, October 7, 1962, p. 31.
13. Ibidem, December 2, 1962, pp. 36-39.
14. Ibidem, March 25, 1962, p. 73.
15. Ibidem, October 7, 1962, p. 87.
16. Ibidem, November 11, 1962, pp. 54, 55.
17. Ibidem, October 14, 1962, p. 83.
18. Ibidem, April 8, 1962, pp. 32-49.
19. Ibidem, April 15, 1962, pp. 48, 49; January 26, 1964, pp. 32, 33; February 9, 1962, p. 39.
20. Ibidem, November 4, 1962, p. 39.
21. Ibidem, February 27, 1966, pp. 39-49.
22. Ibidem, October 21, 1962, pp. 40-51; December 16, 1962, pp. 30, 31.
23. Ibidem, January 12, 1964, pp. 26-75.
24. Ibidem, December 2, 1962, p. 53.
25. Ibidem, March 10, 1983, p. 53.
26. Ibidem, April 3, 1986, pp. 87-103.
27. Ibidem, July 2, 1981, pp. 200-211.
28. C. Esposito, op. cit., pp. 68, 69; V. Strukelj, "La forbice d'oro e l'industria della moda: Novità", in *Italian Fashion*, vol. I, Milan 1986, pp. 173-179.
29. *Vogue Novità*, November 1965, p. 71.
30. Ibidem, November 1965.
31. *Vogue Italia*, May 1967, pp. 54, 55.
32. Cf. C. Esposito, op. cit.; V. Strukelj, op. cit., p. 173.
33. *Vogue Italia*, January 1968; June 1969; December 1969.
34. Ibidem, January 1968, pp. 120, 121.
35. *Uomo Vogue*, February 1980, p. 472.
36. Ibidem, September 1967. Supplement to issue no. 195 of *Vogue Italia*, p. 55.
37. G. Dorfles, *Mode e Modi*, Milan 1979, pp. 159, 160.
38. *Uomo Vogue*, September 1967, pp. 58-65.
39. Ibidem, September 1967, p. 89.
40. I. Vercelloni, Ibidem, October 1970, pp. 174-179.
41. Ibidem, September 1975.
42. Ibidem, Autumn-Winter 1968/69, pp. 126, 127.
43. Ibidem, December-January 1980, p. 155.
44. Ibidem, June-July 1980, cover.
45. Ibidem, September 1980, pp. 548, 549, 614.
46. Ibidem, May 1980, p. 184.
47. Ibidem, October 1980, p. 306.

Giangiacomo Feltrinelli, portrait by Ugo Mulas, in Uomo Vogue, *September 1967.*

FASHION AND ART PHOTOGRAPHY

Lamberto Pignotti

What is it that fashion photography takes and makes its own, to what does it allude and refer, with what does it overlap and merge?

It is photography and it presents fashion: all too obvious. Any discussion of it presupposes an awareness of its characteristic features and its biographical data in the context of general photography; a prior familiarity with its particular range of subjects: clothes, underwear, footwear, dress accessories, jewellery... And since clothes, even in a photograph, make the man, one is immediately confronted by the social dimension with its allusions to the welter of ideologies and habits and class differences and generation gaps...

It was towards the end of the fifties that the kind of photography under examination here began to assume and develop those connotations on which its identity is still essentially based today. The fashionable image projected during this period was of a woman impeccably dressed, meticulously attractive, refined in the highest degree, agreeably languid, enticingly merry and even dynamic and tangible, but in the end distant, indeed remote, or rather inaccessible. The fact is that up until then the fashion photograph had primarily been a portrait of fashion itself, a fashion that was predominantly "high" fashion, aimed at the "upper" middle class. Rather than clothing for everyday life what was being proposed – and portrayed – was the dress for cerimonial occasions or society events.

Then the idea of fashion began to change, and with it the fashion photograph. Haute couture gave way to prêt-à-porter, couturiers to stylists. The clothing industry became an increasingly complex and ramified phenomenon, capable of modifying habits, modes of behaviour, expressions and languages on a vast scale. In the sector in which we are specifically interested, the dignified black-and-white photograph was driven from the pages of magazines, to be replaced by intrusive ones in colour, often intent on catching the reader's eye in the same way as an advertising image.

The imagery used in fashion photography became increasingly articulate over the course of the sixties. The repertory of images drawn on gradually assumed the characteristics of a complex "visual language" which, by way of the various cross-references that relate this genre of photography to the realm of words, aimed to present itself and to be read as a "verbo-visual language."

Barry McKinley, model by Alberta Ferretti, in Vogue Italia, *March 1983.*

It was during this period that greater freedom of movement and a more three-dimensional quality was granted to the photographic model: from this time on, she almost always had a precise identity. And she drew nearer, indeed merged with the observer: the cover girl, the superstar model, became more natural but also more aggressive; she was more unconventional but also more sensual. The tendency now was not towards contemplation, but towards astonishment; the portrait-style pose was replaced by the theatrical gesture or the film image. Rather than documenting fashion, the photograph became a promotional vehicle and a spectacular performance.

For some time the photographic model had been regarded not so much as a mannequin as an actress. Many centuries seem to have passed, and not a mere fifty years, since the famous Parisian couturier Paul Poiret interrupted a reporter who wished to interview one of his models with the following eloquent statement: "Don't ask her anything. It is as if she were not there."

During the sixties the cover girl or top model was transformed from a romantic but platonic idea, from a poetic but presumably asexual creature, into one of the most tangible symbols of sexuality. The scene as suddenly rocked by the enigmatic and protean beauty of Jean Shrimpton, or the sharp and dynamic beauty of Twiggy. These were the days of Veruschka's legendary seductiveness and of the provocative eroticism of Donyale Luna and Penelope Tree; it was also the time of the irresistible lure of women like Marisa Berenson and Benedetta Barzini. The same decade would see other heroines make their way across the stage: Lauren Hutton, Dalila Di Lazzaro, Margaux Hemingway, René Russo, Jerry Hall...

That the model should really, and not just symbolically, turn into an actress – and to be more precise a film star – had already happened: the most famous cases are those of Grace Kelly and Audrey Hepburn. But it was over the course of the seventies and the early eighties that such transformations became more common and even customary. Kelly Le Brock became *The Woman in Red*, Kim Basinger was seen in the film *Never Say Never*, Michelle Pfeiffer starred in *All in One Night* and Lori Singer appeared in *Fame*. If the versatile, ubiquitous Isabella Rossellini is shooting a film one day, then the next she is posing for a magazine cover, and vice versa.

Albert Watson, Pancaldi & B. campaign, in
Donna, *March 1986.*

Max Vadukul, original by Gianfranco Ferré,
in Vogue Italia, *October 1985.*

As in the realm of the visual arts, the model of beauty turns out to be predominantly – indeed overwhelmingly – female in the sphere of fashion photography. Yet among the multitude of models, whose numbers have increased remarkably in the last few years, there seems to be no sign of the equivalent of a Jean Shrimpton or a Kelly Le Brock.

Rather than the performers, it is of course the creators – the photographers, in this case – who should take credit for the linguistic shift that we are outlining in brief. It is a shift that has led to the stylistic significance and unmistakable identity of fashion photography that now distinguishes it from the general mass of messages churned out by today's image-based civilization. Among those who have made a major contribution to revolutionizing the grammar of imagery in this sector, Richard Avedon has an undoubted claim to being in the first rank. He began his career in France, working for *Harper's Bazaar* from 1945-65 and then moving on to *Vogue*. Avedon's model – white or black, mischievous or sad, chastely erotic or morbidly ingenuous – gets angry, plays, cries, sulks, winks, beguiles or gazes boldly and provocatively into the observer's face. Avedon favours the hyperrealistic image, where light is used to reveal wrinkles on the face, veins on the hands, the hollows of the armpits and the muscles of the legs. He claims that he does not like beauty that is polished, but beauty that is experienced and worn.

Another brilliant photographer whose work has contributed to the new stylistic direction taken by this genre is without doubt Helmut Newton, whose pictures began to appear in *Vogue* towards the end of the fifties. They are images that gently assail the eye: voluptuousness is tempered by irony, perversity shades into lyricism. Newton's models break all the rules: they fly like Batman or sit in front of men with their legs spread wide, wear very high-necked dresses or expose their buttocks to the open air while seated on a fur, but without ever straying into immoderation.

For over thirty years Guy Bourdin has also been producing fashion photographs that are at one and the same time highly characteristic and innovative. His models look rather like objects from a still life, but their charge of sexuality – "metaphysical" but perverse too – is emphasized by relating it to everyday acts of violence.

Dazzling lights or dim ones, sumptuous settings or exotic landscapes, aggressive colours or alluring tones, gloomy atmospheres or delightful locations, theatrical back-drops or brazen reality: all these and much more certainly form part of the range of contrivances that go to make up the personality of a fashion photographer. But such a personality is determined primarily by the image of woman that he manages to put across.

Chris Von Wangenheim for example has long conveyed this image by means of details that communicate particular, and sometimes unpleasant tactile sensations: the face and hands of a naked girl sink into the muzzle of a horse; a little foot cased in a golden shoe with a stiletto heel shatters a television screen. Arthur Elgort's models, sometimes a little off balance or suspended in the air, look like typical "fiancées" photographed in charming spots on a Sunday. But Elgort's snapshots are highly sophisticated. Also sophisticated, however they may appear to be out of focus because of movement, are the photographs of Oliviero Toscani that portray another unknown face, that of the "lady next door."

Less definable and corporeal, and more abstract and ideal, appear at first sight the splendid photographs of women taken by a woman, Deborah Turbeville. Here the photography deliberately takes its inspiration from the world of painting, merging pre-Raphaelite traits with symbolist visions. The women may look ethereal and ideal, but in huge and opulent mirrors they reflect anxieties, bounce off desires, transmit voluptuousness...

A different example of links with painting can be found in the pictures of another female photographer, Sarah Moon. At times her women's faces communicate an agonizing distress, immersed in shadows shot through with a luminous dust that makes one think of an almost pointilliste intent, of a Neo-Impressionist influence reinterpreted in terms of "art déco." In contrast to the discreet chiaroscura of Moon is the distinctly gloomy vision of Rebecca Blake: her models flaunt – or rather throw in the observer's face – naked and dazzling detail in luxurious but grim, forbidding and mysterious surroundings. The vibrant beauty of these women has a funereal fixity, their lasciviousness that of the horror film.

Once again we are obliged to face the fact that the image of fashion, and consequently that of the fashion photograph, is the image of woman. The contribution made by the male image – notwithstanding the fact that a variety of publications have appeared in recent years that are specifically intended for men, and in spite of the fact that ever since the sixties successful artists, gallery-owners, publishers and writers have been prepared to act as occasional models – has been highly marginal and not particularly emblematic. In the field that we are concerned with photographers have deliberately and primarily aimed at bringing to light, drawing attention to, revealing and almost squeezing dry a particular feature – perhaps a neglected, misunderstood, undervalued, remote or potential one – of feminine beauty, understood in the broad sense. Sometimes this is done with refined discretion as in the work of Gianpaolo Barbieri, whose models – caught as if in a film still pregnant with meaning or surprised like a long-desired object in a shop window – tend to establish a relationship of complicity with the observer. At others with sophisticated effrontery as in the photographs of Alan Kaplan, who sets a "Venus in furs" in a garage or flings the

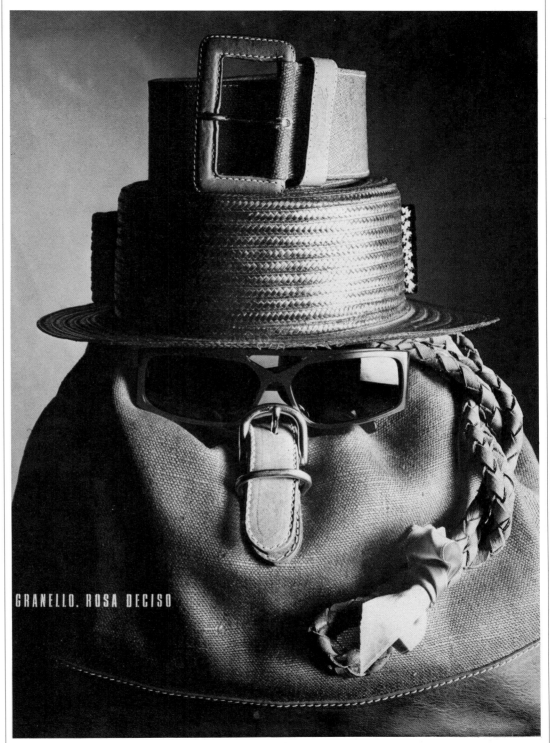

GRANELLO. ROSA DECISO

Photograph by Giovanni Gastel for Granello, in Donna, *March 1986.*

Art Kane, photograph by Harper's Bazaar, *January 1980.*

magnificently clothed body of a beautiful woman on top of a heap of rubbish. Kaplan's concupiscence is not reminiscent of the news photograph but of the theatrical image.

With an eye to the photomontage of the early 20th century – but with a lyrical flavour – and a propensity for the kind of "making-up" developed in the sixties by a certain kind of pop art – but reinterpreted in a languid style – Barry Lategan outlines dreamlike and inaccessible women in photographic features that resemble recordings of unpredictable performances. Peter Knapp too is influenced by the stylistic features of pop art, although he blends them with hints of the Bauhaus: his models, who look as though they were conceived in a laboratory and are set against back-drops out of science fiction, freeze one with their gaze. David Bailey seems to have been equally influenced by pop art, but his models have a more accessible seductiveness and an aggressivity that is more suggested than real.

The rapport between fashion photography and painting – sometimes in its more comprehensive or "classical" sense, at others in that of its various 20th-century and current movements – used as a fundamental reference or a guiding thread is markedly present in the photographs by the above-mentioned David Bailey that make up a feature published in the February 1980 edition of *Vogue Italia*. The vegetation in the background is painted; the eyes and lips of the model are made to stand out by their colour, which appears to be the result of retouching. There is a strident hint of violence; there is, as mentioned in the earlier brief description of this photographer, a vague reference to the pop matrix. In fact, Bailey got his training in the sixties, at the same time as Warhol. But pictorial effects are often sought after in fashion photography: in general by imitating the brush-stroke that is gently passed over or thickly laid onto the surface of the canvas. As we have seen, both Deborah Turbeville and Sarah Moon have carried out masterly experiments with such an effect. It has been recently and originally revived by Tiziano Magni in a number of his fascinating "portraits" published in the April 1986 issue of *Harper's Bazaar Italia*.

The vast majority of fashion photographs are "portraits." Fashion magazine covers are, almost by right. It is not rare for the form of the subject, the pose, the attitude, the gaze, to refer in some way to or even to be openly copied from the pictorial genre of the portrait. Perhaps the portrait of a woman in white drapes discreetly parted in the rear by an innocent breeze, as photographed by Barry McKinley for *Vogue Italia*, March 1983, is more romantic than classical ("romantic-sexy"), but the portrait of woman by Albert Watson that appeared in *Donna*, March 1986, is decidedly classical in its approach.

If the "portrait" genre, at times directly borrowed from the representational schemes of painting, is the one most frequently encountered in fashion photography, there is no lack of other genres such as the "still life" and the "landscape." In general the former serves to reveal to the eye of the beholder a composition of dress accessories, a blend of printed silk drapes, a tangle of multi-coloured hanks of wool, a plethora of jewellery, a deluge of precious stones... One might also add the ironic "still life" in the manner of Arcimboldo – a composition in pink made up of a bag, a pair of sunglasses, a hat and a belt – by Giovanni Gastel that appeared in the above-mentioned issue of *Donna*.

In fashion photography, "landscape" should be understood as the background. It ranges from the traditional one of painting, with trees, expanses of water and the sky, to more or less urbanized landscapes and vaguely or decidedly exotic ones. A photograph like the one by Renato Grignaschi, published in the March 1983 edition of *Vogue Italia*, blends together just about all these types of landscape. On the other hand, the landscape cum back-drop of Max Vadukol's photograph in *Vogue Italia*, October 1985, is more typically urban. An example of a back-drop cum landscape is provided with equal irony in the photograph by Barry Lategan in the March 1980 issue of *Vogue Italia*. So far we have been discussing a number of necessarily summary references by fashion photography to "traditional" painting and a degree of paradigmatic parallelism with its fundamental genres. However other links may be found if we shift our attention from the sphere of classical and figurative art to that of 20th-century experimentalism. Even fashion photography, through its structural articulations and compositional patterns, can tend towards abstraction, or the metaphysical, surreal, and so on. A reference to emotional abstractionism can be found for example in a photograph by Franco Bottino in *Harper's Bazaar Italia*, April 1986, that brings together, perhaps with a nod in the direction of a certain Prampolini, printed silks, lettuce leaves and a loaf of French bread. Geometrical and rational abstraction and a hint of the Bauhaus can be found in a photograph by Franco Franceschi, in *Vogue Italia*, March 1983, that sets the profile of a standing model against the contrasting backgrounds of a circle and a rectangle.

This kind of photography very frequently demonstrates a marked interest in the visualization of movements: the prototype to which it then resorts in a particular phase of futurism, that of photodynamism in the style of Bragaglia. There is certainly no shortage of examples. Let us take a fairly recent one by Fabrizio Ferri (*Donna*, March 1986), in which the stillness of the model in the centre and the fixity of her gaze are emphasized by their contrast with the girls that are moving around her.

Another photograph by David Bailey illustrating a feature in *Vogue Italia*, December 1984 has a structure that sets it somewhere

Photograph by David Bailey, in Vogue Italia, *December 1984.*

between the enigmatic impression of the metaphysical picture and the irreverent irony of Dada photomontage: the half-length portrait of the model handled in delicate tones of pink and violet is posed in the same way as a sculpture standing on a column.

Again surrealistic composition, with the magical and oneiric atmosphere that is characteristic of it, is frequently encountered in the iconographic structure of the fashion photograph. As an example of this we might point to

reinterpreted – to the structural and compositional forms of traditional and avant-garde painting. On the contrary, this photographic genre displays a special interest in dramatic idioms of representation: cinema, theatre, happenings, performances, dance...

A frame from a film with realistic connotations – to pick one of a multitude of examples – was certainly the model for the picture of a woman, portrayed in the bathroom with a cigarette between her lips and a bathrobe at

Cinema with a hint of exoticism and theatre that tends towards the absurd – the figurative approach has the fixity of the metaphysical and the conceptualism of certain recent forms of drama – come together in the structure of a photograph by Alberta Tiburzi, published in the January 1985 issue of *Harper's Bazaar Italia*, in which from a predominantly black back-drop, pierced by an opening that gives a glimpse of distant lands, emerge three mysterious women dressed in black and white.

Alberta Tiburzi, advertising for Callaghan,
in Harper's Bazaar Italia, *January 1980.*

a feature by Art Kane, published in *Harper's Bazaar Italia*, January 1980, on a stated theme, "Beauty and the Beast." This "classic" theme of both pictorial representation and this genre of photography is handled here by portraying the reactions, from the grotesque to the terrorized, of a model in an empty room confronted by a frog that gradually grows to gigantic proportions. The relations between fashion photography and art are not confined to allusions – obviously altered, readapted and

her feet, watching over her young son playing in the bathtub: this photograph by Charlotte March appeared in the October 1985 issue of *Vogue Italia*.

A cut from a film and at the same time an allusion to a theatrical scene can be met with in a photograph by Gianpaolo Barbieri in *Vogue Italia*, February 1980: the "actor" reflected standing up in the mirror of an opulent room stares intensely at the "actress" who, seated, is gazing elsewhere with vague longing.

In the very wide range covered by his work, Richard Avedon has often experimented with effects of a theatrical nature. Current forms of drama seem to be the inspiration behind a feature of his that appeared in *Harper's Bazaar Italia* in January 1980, in which a group of models of both sexes seem to be trying out expressive situations that fall somewhere between mime and performance art.

The fashion photographer may have an extremely direct, immediate and deliberate relationship with the art world. He may, for instance, be involved in a parallel aesthetic research that leads to his work being exhibited in avant-garde galleries. A case in point is that of Peter Knapp, who has for some time combined his career as a fashion photographer with that of a painter. Fairly recently, he has also exhibited a series of conceptual photographs of the blue sky at midday, taken from seventy-five different locations. It is natural that an analytical experimentalism of this kind should also be reflected in his more specifically professional activity.

It is fairly commonplace, in the different fields of aesthetic expression, to come across the artist who perceives the present in gloomy terms, especially when he compares it with the more brilliant colours of the past. This is particularly true of the genre under examination. Even such a great photographer as Helmut Newton has declared in an interview – of two, or perhaps three years ago – that fashion photography had sunk to the lowest level in its entire history. And an undisputed master of this artistic medium, the almost eighty-year old Horst P. Horst who is still producing sound work, when specifically asked about this some time afterwards, expressed his agreement with Newton. In fact he was even more critical of the commercial exigencies that dominate everything else, limiting freedom and the possibilities for research. Horst went on to say that while the idea of abandoning one's studies and going out into the streets to create naturalistic and realistic images had been revolutionary in the sixties, photographs in movement with the model running or jumping cannot help but turn into a very boring stereotype.

It would be pointless to pretend that there are no commercial limitations, no conditions imposed by the requirements of the advertising industry and no standardization of style. However, once all this has been realized and admitted, are complaints of this kind entirely appropriate? It ought to be obvious – even to the protagonists of this medium of expression – that the fashion photograph cannot be immune to the laws of the market, that it is subject to its own more or less direct patronage, that in short it cannot claim to be a field of "pure" art... In any case, where is the art so "pure" that it is not subject to conditioning? It would not be a bad thing if, before complaining, some of these photographers took a look at one of the texts put out by the school of Frankfurt.

After all fashion photographers – whose image has been presented for some time as an enviable symbol, eccentric and of almost star quality, of modernity in films, soap operas, television advertisements and video-clips – can be counted among those artists who have the greatest freedom to impose their own original and innovative aesthetic style. Their clients are often prepared to give them carte blanche, expecting them to be daring and allowing even for their more extravagant caprices.

Richard Avedon, Gianni Versace campaign, in Harper's Bazaar Italia, *January 1980.*

THE GARMENT AND THE BODY
THE BODY AND THE FIGURE

Gianfranco Ferré, Emilio Tadini

The Garment and the Body

Similarities and Differences Between Fashion and Design

If design is the act of transformation that leads from the conception of an idea to the object itself, then it clearly applies to fashion. In this sense the creation of fashion is a process of design: in both spheres, in fact, phases of transformation, modes and means of expression proceed in parallel. Both involve research into form, material and the decoration of material, invention, the creative act, expression through words and drawings, ergonometric checks and the limitations of industrial resources. Even the relationship between conception, design and production is absolutely the same. Only the means of expression changes.

Given these premises, a negative parallel may also emerge: certain ways of distorting the design of clothing correspond to certain examples of distortion in the approach to designing furniture. If one then considers that the small production run of an item of clothing runs in parallel to the larger scale one of a piece of furniture, then even the problem of repetitivity through variants – a supposed difference between the two fields – seems to me to be a false one. After all I have to go through it every six months for at least 500 items: I have to come up with many more simplifications than the designer of a radio and, in addition, I do it on a much shorter time scale. I also feel that the relationship between architecture and fashion is a very close one: apparently architecture is hard and clothes are soft. But even though clothes are soft, I am designing for something hard and definite, the human body. Moreover, when I design clothes for men or for women, I always have a precise typology in mind, just as an architect does when he plans houses with a particular space and function.

For a Designer of Clothing

I see the road of specialization and creativity as being increasingly necessary to the fashion designer, whether it is applied to production on a pseudo-artisan level or on a mass scale, backed up by the constant stimulation of research.

The time of improvisation and spontaneity is over. Instead of a vague and impromptu creator, I believe in a rigorous and controlled designer. I spurn half-measures and am opposed to inventions for their own sake. This is partly because I feel that there is little left to be invented as far as clothing is concerned: on the contrary the work of the stylist has become one of moulding all that has already been done into new forms. The conditions under which a designer of clothes is obliged to work are those of an individual design that is modified and grows through the methods and possibilities for assembly provided by technology. At the base a personal intuition, then the interventions that determine the transformation of the original material, bound up with a choice of image or with particular developments that occur during the phase of transformation: the whole dependent on the industrial resources that permit reproduction on a large scale.

Methodology

When I think of an item of clothing, an accessory, or the like, in general whenever I think about something that will eventually go on show and be manufactured, I think of it as a *unique fact*; I visualize it a priori, imagining it on "stage," whether that of a fashion show or of ordinary life, but without ever forgetting that the garment is intended for mass production. This involves a series of estimates, in terms of consumption, costs and image, that in turn depend on a very large-scale structure – manufacturers, distribution channels, targets and promotions. In any type of design that I carry out, there is always a prior unification of all the phases of transformation, one which depends on the structural pattern of the individual company to which decisions taken during the process of transformation have to be entrusted.

Each collection requires study, research into materials, design, realization of the prototype, presentation and creation of the image. For all this I turn to my closest collaborators, to the technical experts of the manufacturing companies and to experts in communication and marketing. Each link in the chain requires very careful control.

When I think of a garment I never picture it as motionless, draped over a hanger or a dummy, but I imagine it in movement, worn by someone walking. At the same time my training in geometry, refined by influences coming out of my knowledge of Oriental methods of design (origami and its derivative forms of assembly, which can also be found in cultures like that of India), leads me to make immediate transpositions in design, as a primary approach to geometric solutions, which are the real matrix in the creation of an item of clothing. But the moment of conception of that item also involves intentions, and these are perhaps the more dominant matrices, derived from my personal "credos" that are in continual evolution, such as the importance of gesture and movement, the more or less balanced presence of colour and its conceptual significance, and at times poetic suggestiveness. I have a great belief in everything that is personally put together, prepared and tried out, without the taboo of starting out from the maximum of elementariness and simplicity in order to obtain even the greatest of effects. For instance I make the models for belts and shoes myself, pressing the paper, cutting the cardboard: I came up with the double belts, rounded off at the hips, by elaborating the shape of a truncated cone. I like to mould, to give the final touch. It is often then, by completely overturning the directions of the design, that unusual effects are obtained. For me designing women's clothing is a studied but instantaneous gesture, that I do with spontaneity. Designing for men, in my view, means putting a spontaneous idea down on paper and then subjecting it to an intense process of examination, pruning it down and reducing it to basic elements by the yardstick of those who belong to the male sex. In fact, believing firmly in the difference, necessary and vital, between the sexes, I mentally split my approach to design: designing for women puts me in situations of antithesis, of necessary intuitions and interpretative fantasies that are wide-ranging and often more poetical. Designing for men always has an immediate and natural check on it, and is therefore a slower and more stepped process.

I am a firm believer in individual choices and capacities of interpretation. I am also fond of a certain kind of disobedience to which women are less prone than men: breaking the rules by wearing a light blue shirt is the sort of thing I mean. Yet I believe men have to be re-educated not to be boring and to remember that their aesthetic history has been a brilliant one, from the black dress-coat to the red or green waistcoat. As for the pleasure of touching and trying on, I can say that I wear the clothes I design for men, which I make even in size 50, even when they are not my size, because I like to find out what they feel like.

I see man as an anomalous planet, picturing him as a rectangle to which sprouts are attached: each of these is part of him and cannot be cut off. This can be expressed through the salvage of an old shirt that is regarded with

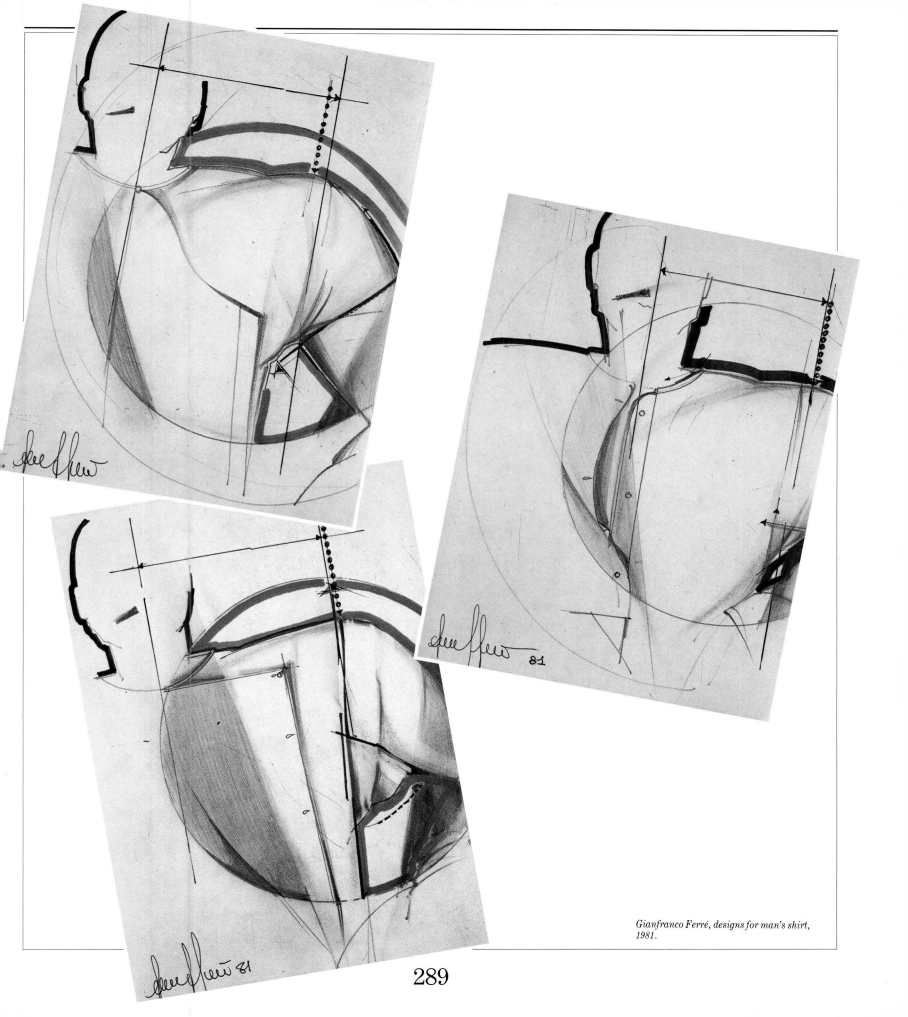

Gianfranco Ferré, designs for man's shirt, 1981.

the same affection as a forgotten sentiment, through the sports jacket that has the right to be threadbare.

The Design Route and Its Surroundings

At this point a theoretical statement is necessary the creative act determines the shape of the design, i.e. of the collection; the basis of transformation determines the typology of the product; the technology of transformation determines the finished product. On these premises is

three-dimensional product. A fundamental example of this is the use of the spiral, a pattern I hold dear. From time to time I apply it to different functions, from the collar of a garment to the belt and so on.

At the root of every design stands a particular expressive intent: if I need a fabric, it will be that one and no other; if the pleat has to fall in a certain way, it will be sewn over and over again until the right result is obtained; if there is an optimum size for the lapel, it will be that

rhythm is different and the technique of tailoring acquires precision. It is important to get a grasp of the technique of ergonometry, i.e. of movement within the clothes.

If on the one hand dream, imagination and tension are constantly called on to give an article of clothing the impression it must convey even when hanging in the shop, on the other there is and has to be a constant search for the solution to technical problems. A "dart," for example, is the traditional way to give roundness

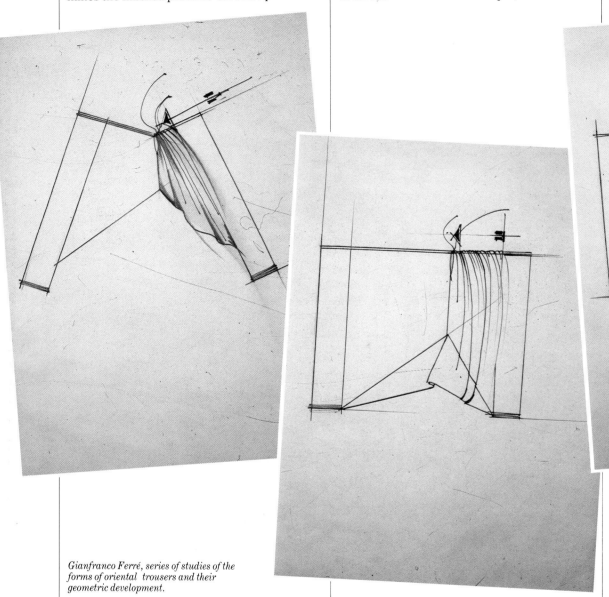

Gianfranco Ferré, series of studies of the forms of oriental trousers and their geometric development.

based the route taken in designing the garment and/or the accessory. The construction of an item of clothing consists in designing something that can be reproduced by mechanical means: this involves being familiar with the field, the resources and the equipment. At the outset clothes are made up of flat shapes, which are built up to respond to precise ergonometric requirements. Here is involved an awareness of the development in space of shapes that are originally two-dimensional but that turn into a

and not a centimetre more or less.

I have the habit, or the mannerism as some call it, of designing in plan, i.e. of designing clothes in the same way as one designs architecture. Once the fashion-sketch has been executed, which helps me to get an idea of my style, I carry out the process of transferring the models from paper to the factory by drawing plans of them, taking particular care over sections – a sleeve, a buttonhole, etc. This facilitates the work of the pattern makers. The

to a rectangle of flat cloth. Yet the same problem can be solved by inventing a series of new forms. Personally, by training and by inclination, I tend to prefer elementary geometric shapes that can be elaborated. The majority of my collections are based on the spatial extension of geometric shapes. Introduced as pure forms, they are modified according to the type and area of application. The formal solution is always closely connected to the material, which is selected on the basis of its suitability to the sought-after form. I must say, however, that the choice of the kind of shapes to be used in a collection often depends on influences that, slowly accumulating, create an imaginary physical landscape in my mind, the landscape through which I am travelling at the time. Parallel to the initial conception of the object comes exploration in the field of fabrics: I have wonderful and productive relationships with the textile manufacturers. I can never manage to ask for a red or a yellow, but only to describe the sensations that I want to obtain. At

some accuracy. I am attracted both by innovations arising out of the application of industrial technology to weaving – wefts and warps and decorations that derive from the machine and not from the imagination – and by the classic fabrics that will always be a part of the way men and women dress. At this stage it is very important to get the right blending, so as to produce a colder or a warmer effect, on which the final appearance of the fabric will depend. I have revived traditional fabrics such as cavallery, usually adopted for military great coats,

become constant landmarks on the route towards the creation of a collection. One example is *tradition*. I feel that situations can be changed completely only if the charm of the past is retained unaltered. I will explain this: if one produces a straight skirt, which is a revival, it is enough to give it modern proportions, putting above it a very loose blouse. If one uses high heels by day and low ones at night, one has already carried out, using well-known systems, a modern operation. In any case, classicism is, in my view, an architrave in the design

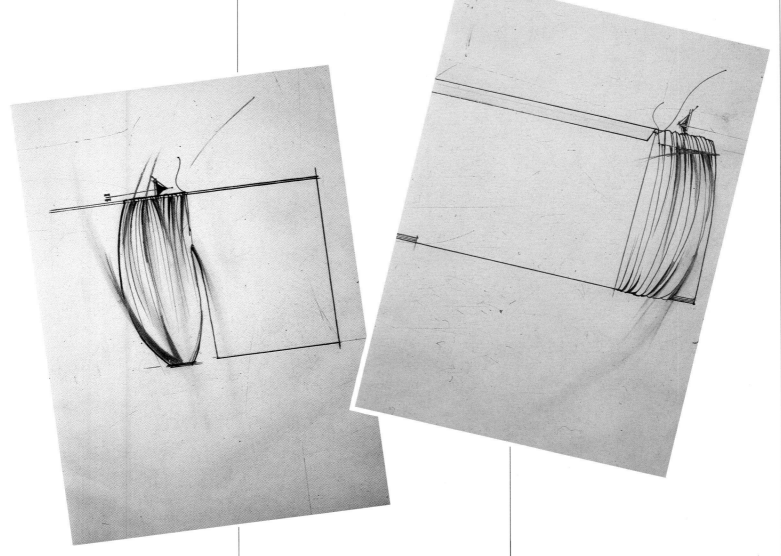

this stage the textile manufacturer has little to contribute, merely saying whether this or that fabric can be made in this or that colour. The work proceeds along the paths of experimentation and technology, until the definitive result is obtained. For technical reasons, this reaches me only a few days before the shows are due to be held. Hence much of the work is carried out with fabrics that do not match the ones that will eventually be used. This makes it necessary to be able to picture the final result with

overcoats in wool and cotton and the herringbone pattern known as "caledon." The same criterion of selection holds for the choice of colours in a collection: apart from the basic ones – black and white and the classic shades, with which I have a sort of love affair – I make little use of patterns. Where I do they have to be designed for the purpose, perennial in their appeal and include some bright colours, always clean and sharp.

There are some points of reference that have

of clothing. Following my line of research, I find myself slowly stabilizing certain themes, which I keep returning to. Apart from changes in colour, certain forms remain analogous to those of my past which, besides, is recent for man. I believe it to be a virtue to recognize that a number of essential forms are, in a way, not subject to fashion. On the other hand one saves oneself from obsessivity only if one never "bluffs." In men's fashion, in particular, creativity has to be filtered through more care-

Gianfranco Ferré, trouser suit from the 1982-83 Autumn-Winter collection of women's wear.

fully weighed means of expression. It is a subtle kind of experimentation, that requires a precise logic and unobtrusive forms: trousers, for instance, will always be trousers. Yet it is possible to invent different pockets, materials and stitching that do not upset gestures and habits, but which provide greater comfort, which is after all the final objective. Every design has its aspect of research, whose roots reach down into the soil of personal, emotional, geographical and cultural references. They are what are usually described as sources or themes of inspiration: I discover them all over the place, when travelling, at exhibitions, in the pages of magazines and, of course, in architecture.

Among these influences, but perhaps the one with greatest force and intensity, is my prolonged experience of working in India. It has led and still leads me to formulate a precise interpretation of the relationship between man, environment, clothing and his forms of expression. It has been an exceptional experience that has taught me that clothing is a design made up of elementary forms. Assembled by different techniques, they take on a physical character of their own which I call "appearance." This is bound up with the importance that the designer gives to the characteristics of his resources, i.e. material and use, which is nothing but the final interpretation made by whoever applies it. There is nothing more perfect than the "kurta," the most traditional of Indian shirts, made out of cotton with a strip of a collar, unbuttoning only halfway down the shirt front, fine side pockets concealed in the stitching, a length that extends below the hips and slits in the sides to allow the wearer to sit comfortably.

For functionality there is no rival to the "lungi," those wonderful breeches made out of a rectangular, absolutely elementary piece of cloth – I do not tire of saying it – held up by a waistband, without any superfluous cuts, allowing the maximum of freedom in the way it is worn. If I worked as an architect, I would draw an analogy with the chopping knife in the field of spontaneous design, or with the "Naskaloris" in the field of anonymous technical design.

Fashion and the Living Object

There is design in fashion too, only that at a certain point its place is taken by man, whose interpretation of it transforms the garment into a living object. The fashion design has to come to terms with a reality that is sometimes impalpable, a reality in which one speaks only of modes of behaviour, of slow or rapid metamorphoses, of ebbs and flows. The job was once a much simpler one: the couturier dictated what was "in or out." Today fashion has to interpret needs. The stylist is not responsible for persuading people to be elegant. In my opinion, elegance is the relation between a person and the outside world, between himself and his own behaviour. Clothing can be an ally, but it is never elegant in and of itself.

The article of clothing possesses values that emerged during the process of its creation: they are those suggestions that set up a relationship of exchange with its wearer. The object comes alive precisely because it is changed by the person who uses it. The clothing adapts itself to the body, giving it some qualities and taking on others. The fact that these qualities exist and continue to be there means that there is no time limit on the garment, apart from that natural one of its own wear and tear.

The attitude of the user and that of the object used are so peripatetic that they create an uninterrupted life of their own.   *G.F.*

The Body and the Figure

Do you remember them, those scenes from certain films in the old days, when the hero accompanied his woman to a highly luxurious fashion house and the two settled comfortably on a couch, with legs crossed, while a lady, rather elderly but very much on the ball, perched elegantly on the edge of a nearby armchair, showing them the models with an aristocratic air? The mannequins passed along the carpet, one after the other, with hand on hip, and the woman said "That one!," pointing to an evening dress, and everyone smiled through the cigarette smoke, even the spectators concealed in the dark of a suburban cinema amidst the smell of lysoform and other things. That, in any case, was one idea of fashion. Indeed, in those days it was probably *the* Idea of Fashion. Something was communicated, from above. A message. A model. Not "be like this!" or "this is how you ought to be!" Rather a "this is what they're like – up there!," a slightly prevaricatory, and indisputable statement – but for this very reason also fairly reassuring.

Every discussion of fashion – it seems to me – eventually leads to that rather fundamental matter that could be described as "The question of body and figure." What is the figure? It is probably very difficult to answer this question. Just as it seems very difficult to answer the question "What is the body?" – even though it looks like a very easy one at first sight. (But the fact is that an anatomical description is good only for a dead body. And which body is a dead body? Another complicated question...) So, let us get back to the first one. Very vaguely, one might try to answer it by saying that figure is everything that renders a body "communicable" – that in a way transforms it into a message, into comprehensible information. (Which could also mean: figure is everything that allows us, after having seen it, to imagine a body – to turn it, literally, into an image). And to bring more grist to the mill of this discussion, I could also refer to the argument of the nudists. They insist on nature, on naturalness. But does not naturalness in the pure state imply what could be described as a drastic reduction in the quantity and quality of information? If they do not speak, two naked people can only act. Two people wearing clothes com-

Gianfranco Ferré, suit from the 1985 Spring-Summer collection of women's wear.

Gianfranco Ferré, coat from the 1986-87 Autumn-Winter collection of women's wear.

municate a lot of things to each other merely by looking and being looked at. Which means a sort of increase in the output of languages.

So: figure as what a body "signifies." And clothing, of course, as something that is on the side of the figure. And just as the bedsheet *is* the ghost, in particular circumstances, not all that infrequent at that, clothes may be the only thing capable of lending solidity to a body, a person, to the famous subject – hesitant and so docile in offering itself for multiplication, for "technical reproducibility." (I am reminded of myself, sometimes, in the mirror...) One might even say that the emblem of fashion is just this sheet turned into a ghost. (Does not the habit, in "mental habit," refer to a mode of dress?). And as a thing is not united to its name by a word, but by a sound and a concept, clothing does not unite a (visual) definition to a body, but an image to what is called "a person." (Hence this could even become a "Discussion of the body, the person, the figure," or at least hint at such a discussion which would have, undoubtedly, an importance of its own).

They are so important in our world, figures! They literally substitute for the body. And there is no question about them being more manageable. More than perfect tools. Does it not look, at times, as if our bodies are limited to watching, from the depths of some dark cinema hall, the wonderful adventures of all these unbridled figures? They stir unfathomable depths and produce front-page headlines, those figures. On stage, they move immense masses around. They act out feelings, passions and collective psychoses. They know how to make love and war; they even seem to be able to dream. Think of those figures, for instance, that pass in swarms across our television screens. Gestures – and clothes, certainly. And where the devil are the bodies that are supposed to match this type of figure? But what does it matter? Absolutely nothing. Those figures are more than enough. We think about them, go on talking about them... And in the end it is we who move and go and live in their world made out of nothing. And we treat its shadows as though they were the most solid thing in the world.

I was talking about the fashion houses of the old days – as they were in the old films and more or less as I believe they were in reality. Some figure came down from above. It was not even that it was put forward as a model. It showed itself and that is all – which was and had to be enough for the timorous curiosity of the many. Then things changed. Incidentally, an early change in the idea of fashion may have come with the rise of gossip columns – and there must be a connection somewhere. Horrifying, certainly, all that gossip. What they were doing up there... great things and paltry ones – even dirty tricks. All in very bad taste, of course. But the gods on high emerged, had to emerge from the sumptuous shadow that had sheltered them up till that time. The gods, and those vicarious figures of theirs represented by certain personalities of the cinema. Privacy was dead, surrounded by flocks of greedy, bald-headed vultures and by noisy sheets of newspaper. They were compelled to display themselves, the social demigods, in the disastrous light of the illustrated magazines, in the catastrophic black and white of the cinema newsreels. I am not of course trying to claim that the gossip column was the monstrous form of some "democratic" attitude. But it is certain that, by dint of their being flaunted any old how, the great models ended up revealing the abundant dose of nothing out of which they were made – all that puffed up, pathologically turgid normality of theirs... Whether their numberless admirers – the adepts in the cult of the "stars" realized it or not.

Thus, Fashion Shows began to appear in the newsreels. Immoderate, they seemed. There were characters with a very bizarre appearance... "The couturiers!" it was said. Not "the stylists." There were men, for instance, who looked a bit effeminate, with big rings on their fingers and small in stature... Issuing from the screen in vulgar declamatory voices, the commentators were free and easy with the double entendres of classical comedy – but debased by petit bourgeois cunning. In the cinemas, people laughed uproariously. They yelled atrocious jokes in response. (There was a time when people screamed for no reason in the packed suburban cinemas: we were surrounded by hosts as boisterous as they were harmless, amid dense clouds of smoke. Now – have you noticed? – a mortuary. A perpetual, indolent "no comment" stagnates in the clear air of the half-empty stalls...). But the fashion shows were quite a different thing from the fashion houses of the past. The figures – and the figures of those clothes – became more approachable. Then, seamstresses, copying and recopying and persisting in errors that were really symptoms of their class outlook (if I say "group" or "social," does it sound better?); seamstresses, as I was saying, reduced the creations, however solemn, to the vernacular. And this was, more or less, the Second Age.

At the beginning of the Third Age, in my view, came what is referred to as 1968. The heavens open up – no? Isn't that almost a blasphemy? And even critically – "from the critical point of view," as people used to say – it must be, in all likelihood, completely mistaken. "But no, not in the least! Don't you realize that these are old arguments? So dated! And then, come on, this point of view from the seats of a cinema – and not even a first run one... All that was needed, now, was 1968!" It has almost become a dirty word, 1968. One of those that must not be pronounced at any cost. In that case, what I am writing will at least give somebody the opportunity to get authoritatively to his feet and refute, clarify, make the right quotations... That may be. But no-one will get out of my head the conviction that in those years something changed in the idea of the figure – as well as the idea of the body, of course, and the idea of the person. And the idea of clothing too. Confused changes, without a doubt. I can still hear them, amid caricatures of crisis and bonzai-apocalypses, those vacuous prophesies proclaimed in public by terrible affected voices from microphones and megaphones, echoing... Prophesy mixed up with terror... Of course, one heard an awful lot of rubbish, and saw people wandering around in horrible disguises. Why not? But in the meantime it was during those years that people in Italy and throughout the world began to think that luxury (that loathsome word!) was not after all an indispensable ingredient in any recipe for fashion. And also began to realize that the storehouses of ideas that could be drawn on to invent new forms of clothing were much richer and more numerous than had previously been thought. (And to think that, at the same time, History-as-Progress was lying at its last gasp on those pavements: amid a crowd of extras, with miss-matched clothing, who would have sworn to the opposite. Of course, a confused hodge-podge like that could not last forever. But perhaps something had changed forever.

There may have been stylists, in Italy, who had anticipated it all some years earlier. Perhaps. But I think that the new Italian fashion, in so far as it can be regarded as an organic whole, was born out of the ingeniousness of a few people who knew how to interpret a number of small truths that had been multiplied beyond belief in the speeches, parades and public exhibitions of the years around 1968. (I have used the word interpret, but I would like to blur its meaning. One can interpret something without having a precise plan in one's head – without knowing exactly what one is doing. But isn't that a bit like what we usually call "creating"?) And then, of course, there were those who have "reacted" to 1968 and to its figures – but who naturally would not have been able to become what they were without 1968. And there are a lot of them, really a lot.

It is going too far to speak of cynicism. But what I think came into play here was that attitude – which we might venture to describe as typically Italian – of formalizing absolutely everything, off-hand, of resolving everything into some image, into the irresponsibility of an irresponsible figure. Endemic national ills are founded on this attitude. And highly evident horrors stem from it. But perhaps something survives, in spite of all. Some molecule of lightness. A nothing – perhaps just a way of conceiving the shape of a garment, of wearing it...

Woe betide stylists who sociologize! And above all, woe betide the serious. They will end up embalmed, in some revolting Wax Works, amidst terrifying dummies of Real Ladies and Gentlemen. If it were up to me I would preserve those who, biased towards the gratuitous, save, preserve and nourish, perhaps even without being aware of it. Some miniscule collective desire – shadow of a shadow, and highly concrete... The ones who are there – on purpose and by chance – to represent fluctuating states of mind, things resembling desires, or vanities, nostalgias, illusions... (The illusion, of course, of beauty, the deluded wish to achieve it; which is revealed, and how, not only in our wardrobes, but in every corner of our houses – indicated even by some repulsive trace of vulgarity...). Perhaps the new Italian fashion was born precisely because someone was smart enough to look around him, and then give in to the desire to invent something that was new and at the same time already familiar, in some way, to everyone. (To give an example, is there not the archetype of the Planetary Gypsy, who went wandering impetuously round the world in 1968, may not that very image underlie certain loose-fitting knitted dresses made by Missoni later on – with their excessive and rambling shapes, cheerful sumptuousness and warm and graceful bombast? Or another one: may not the revival of jeans be the symptom of a mild nostalgia for the old days?).

Fashion is ephemeral, the forms of clothing are transient. But the bodies inside those clothes, what are they, eternal? The language of fashion is a language that changes rapidly – even though its function is in reality one of the most stable things that it is possible to imagine. We should go on trying to understand it, that language. We should go on trying to understand what it is saying. Hieroglyphs to be deciphered? Rather an enormous, mobile text, open to the eyes of all, to millions of eyes that look at it without reading it or that follow it word by word. It speaks of many things, that text. Of desires, as I have tried to show, of wishes, regrets, of certain worries. But also of social wiles. Even of cold calculation. Let us pretend that it is like in some sort of fable. A small, obscure and vulnerable truth and a brazen lie bristling with claws and teeth. And the two meet, touch one another. With something that is born out of them – out of both of them, I would say, out of that union. However monstrous the thing may seem to the Ethicist and the Aesthetician. (Good heavens, I am struck by a thought: it can't be art that I'm talking about?)

There is a point in fashion, in fact, where truth and falsehood come into some kind of contact. That is the interesting point. For those who make fashion – and can allow themselves to use their intuition. For those who use fashion – heedlessly, without thinking about it. And perhaps even for those who have something to say about fashion. Talk about it, I say. Speak about it as a sort of category – suspended between identity and alterity, let's say – and at the same time as a phenomenon. (A real theoretical virtuosity – don't you think?) And above all for those who know how to talk about fashion as an authentic quotidian fever, as a daily mass hallucination. That would be really interesting. Not like these disorderly and digressive ramblings. *E.T.*

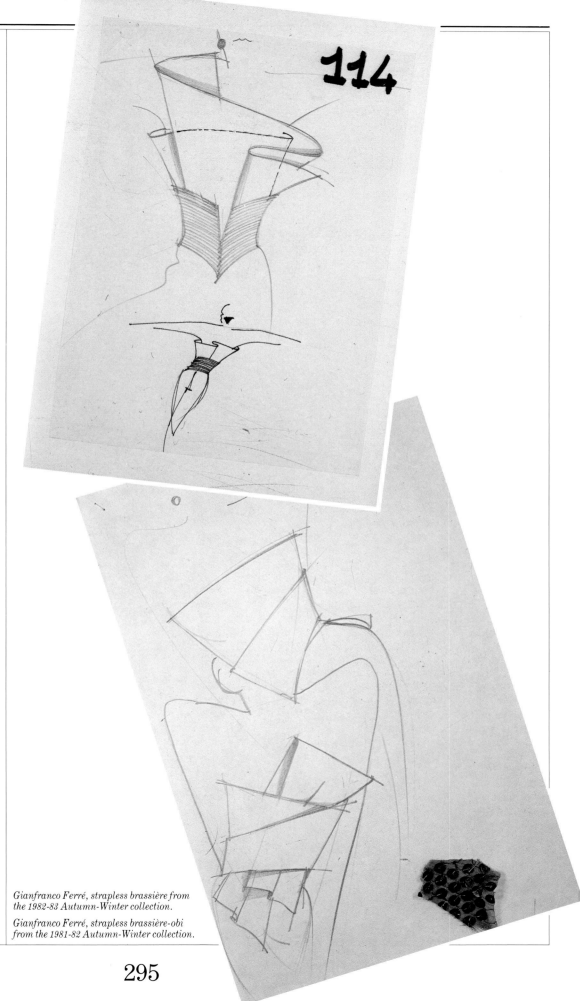

Gianfranco Ferré, strapless brassière from the 1982-83 Autumn-Winter collection.

Gianfranco Ferré, strapless brassière-obi from the 1981-82 Autumn-Winter collection.

Appendices

Bibliography

The reader is referred to the notes at the end of each chapter for specific bibliographical references. In addition to the authors cited therein, the following sources have been consulted:

AA.VV., *The Psychology of Man's Clothing*, Novara n.d.

M.V. Alfonsi, *Leaders in Fashion*, Bologna 1983.

G. Amato, "Sembrava che tutto dovesse cambiare," in *Enciclopedia politica dell'Italia dal 1946 al 1980*, cap. 7, supplement to *L'Espresso*, Roma 1980.

Amica, December 16, 1962, pp. 32, 33; September 1, 1963, p. 52; no. 40, 1964; October 11, 1964, pp. 44-61; February 2, 1966, p. 39; November 28, 1966, pp. 46-55; no. 66, 1966, p. 61; February 3, 1970, p. 33; October 16, 1971; September 4, 1975, pp. 44-60; November 14, 1985, p. 93.

Ars sutoria, a. V., no. 13, 1952; a. XI, no. 45, 1959; a. XX, no. 83, 1968.

E. Babtz, *Fiorucci the Book*, Another Harlin Quist Book, New York 1980.

R. Barthes, *Sistema della moda*, Turin 1967.

N. Branzi, *Fiorucci presenta vestiti per un anno*, Milan 1976.

G. Butazzi, "Il panno di lana ricamato nella moda maschile," in *I tessili antichi e il loro uso, atti del III Convegno CISST*, Turin 1986, pp. 288-294 (includes bibliography).

"Calzatura" (sub-entry), in *Enciclopedia Italiana di Scienze*, Lettere ed Arti, Istituto Giovanni Treccani, Vol. VIII, Milan 1930.

Carta della moda maschile 1958-1959, Rome 1959.

M. Cataldi Gallo, "Cenni sulla moda maschile nel XIX secolo," in *Fortune della seta*, exhibition catalogue, Milan 1986.

M. Cisario, in *Petronio*, a. XXII, no. 181, 1968, p. 70.

Corriere della Sera, November 13, 1965 (interview with Jole Veneziani by Brunetta).

A. Detheridge, "L'alta sartoria nella tradizione. In cerca della giusta misura," in *Vogue Italia*, March 1981, p. III.

F. Di Castro (ed.), *Moda e ritratto, Fotografi per una linea italiana*, catalogue, Istituto Nazionale per la Grafica-Calcografia, February 10-March 31, 1982, Rome 1982.

F. Di Castro, "Fotografi per una linea italiana," in *Il disegno dell'alta moda italiana 1940-70*, Vol. II, Rome 1982, pp. 15, 16, no. 2.

Fiorucci, relazioni e bilanci annuali dal 1974 al 1982; production catalogues 1984 and 1985.

L. Gonzales (ed.), "Le novità della moda componibile," in *Amica* no. 40, 1971, p. 49.

N. Hall Duncan, *Histoire de la photographie de mode*, Paris 1978.

J. Laver, *Costume and Fashion*, 1985, pp. 270 seqq.

R. Levy Pisetsky, *Storia del costume in Italia*, Vol. V, Milan 1969.

C. McDowell, *McDowell's Directory of Twentieth Century Fashion*, Frederick Muller, 1974.

Il Maestro Sarto Italiano, a. IV, no. 1, 1964.

E. Miscia, "Come si riconosce il gran sarto," in *Il Maestro Sarto Italiano*, a. XVIII, no. 3, 1975, p. 66.

G. Moncalvo, *Milano no. Dizionario dei milanesi da buttare via*, Milan 1977.

A. Mulassano, "L'alta moda alla ricerca di una difesa dai jeans," in *Corriere della Sera*, July 15, 1973.

A. Mulassano, *The Who's Who of Italian Fashion*, Florence 1979.

G. Pent Fornengo, *L'industria italiana dell'abbigliamento*, Bologna 1978.

L. Pignotti, *Fra parola e immagine*, Padua 1972.

L. Pignotti, E. Mucci, *Marchio & femmina. La donna inventata dalla pubblicità*, Florence 1978.

L. Pignotti, S. Stefanelli, *La scrittura verbo-visiva. Le avanguardie del Novecento tra parola e immagine*, Milan 1980.

L. Pignotti, "La moda in *Vogue*," in *D'Ars*, no. 94, December 1980.

L. Pignotti, "Per una indagine sulla foto di moda," in *Terzo occhio*, no. 24, March 1982.

L. Pignotti, "Per una iconografia della foto di moda," in *D'Ars*, no. 100, December 1982.

PM, March 1985 (article entitled "I camiciai").

A.C. Quintavalle, "Il pelo e la pelle. Per una mitologia," in *Un percorso di lavoro Fendi-Karl Lagerfeld*, Rome 1985.

G. Ragone (ed.), *Sociologia dei fenomeni di moda*, Milan 1976.

G. Reanda, *L'evoluzione della moda maschile dal 1800 ai nostri giorni*, Rome s.d., p. 38.

S. Romano, *Storia d'Italia dal Risorgimento ai nostri giorni*, Milan 1977, p. 256.

P. Sealfon (ed.), "Tavola rotonda sulla fotografia di moda," in *Zoom*, no. 3, January 1981.

T. Veblen, *La teoria della classe agiata*, Turin 1949.

G. Vergani, "Intervista a Elio Fiorucci," in *Playboy*, February 1975.

L'Uomo Vogue, December 1979-February 1980, p. 97.

Vogue Italia, January 1968, pp. 49, 66-67; February 1969, p. 51; March 1969, pp. 240, 241; May 1970, p. 46; April 1971, p. 137; July-August 1973, pp. 109-112; July-August 1976, pp. 158, 159; January 1980, pp. 198-200; April 1981, pp. 246-259.

Acknowledgments

The editors and authors wish to express their grateful appreciation to the fashion houses and firms for having granted them permission to consult collections and archives; they are particularly grateful to Omar Calabrese; Franco Sartori, editor of *Vogue*, and *Harper's Bazaar* and *Donna*, for their contribution of illustrative material. The editors further thank the Commune of Milan, particularly Elio Quercioli. Almax International at Mariano Comense kindly contributed by lending the mannequins.

Authors of the chapter *Clothing Manufacturers in the Sixties: Between Crisis and Innovation* are particularly indebted, for information provided on individual firms and magazines, to the late Antonio Alberti, for *Amica*; F. Balduzzi and G. Callegari, for Unimac; to G. C. Bussola, for Marzotto; A. Maramotti, for Max Mara; Signora Martina, for Gruppo Finanziario Tessile.
The author of the article *Anti-Fashion. Milanese Examples* extends her thanks to all of those who, through discussions, kindly offered her highly useful information in the structuring of her text. She particularly thanks Gabriella Barassi, Nuccia Fattori, Elio Fiorucci, Ersilia Fiorucci, Gherardo Frassa, Vittoria Lombardini, Franco Marabelli, Bruno Marturini, Elda Merlini, Mario Morelli, Cristina Rossi, Alberto Tonti, and all persons who contributed in the research of original clothing and material, mainly Patrizia Ascari, Fabrizia Baldissera, Ottavia Bassetti, Nicoletta Bocca, Valentina Crepax, Luisa Gnecchi, Agneta Holst, Daniela Travaglio, Alessandra Zanuso, Ornella Zanuso.
The authors of the chapter *Stylism in Women's Fashion* thank all of those who, through their precious efforts, were helpful during their research including: Renato Agostini, Rita Airaghi, Rosanna and Silvana Armani, Angelo Azzena, Beppe Barani, Wanda Bernasconi, Patrizia Biffi, Gisella Borioli, Paola Brambilla, Cristina Brigidini, Donatella Brunazzi, Giuliana Camerino, Alice Canali, Alfa Castaldi, Elisabetta Catalano, Jean Baptiste Caumont, Fiore Crespi, Giuseppe Della Schiava, Anna Domenici, Gimmo Etro, Fashion Institute of Technology, New York, Mario Ferrari, Gianfranco Ferré, Edgarda Ferri, Fabrizio Ferri, Ada Fin, Gabriella Forte, Paola Fumagalli, Carla Gabetti, Giovanni Gastel, Tania Giannesin, Romeo Gigli, Luisella Giraudo, Federica Inghilleri, Madina Iuris, Claudio La Viola, Donata Lo Bue Lemos, Silvano Malta, Mariuccia Mandelli, Marina Mascazzini, Enrica Massei, Rossella Mauri, Milva, Carla Mocenigo, Bianca Montanari, Emanuela di Montezemolo, Gigi Monti, Franco Moschino, Adriana Mulassano,

Irene Pantone, Luciano Papini, Alberto Peretti, Maria Pezzi, Anna Piaggi, Pierpaolo Pieri, Lee Pring, Giulia Re, Gianni Ricci, Paolo Rinaldi, Marco Rivetti, Cinzia Ruggeri, Ken Scott, Giancarlo Solanga, Vittorio Solbiati, Luciano Soprani, Nanni Strada, Studio Nando Miglio, Romano Sudati, Gian Marco Venturi, Gianni Versace, Maria Cristina Vimercati, Emy Vincenzini, Luciano Zanini, Antonella Zunino.
The author of *The Reaction of Roman High Fashion* gratefully thanks Serena Angelini, Francesca Bonetti and Orsetta Leonardi for their valuable contributions to the realization of the text.
The authors of *Men and Fashion: Classic Tailoring* thank all of those who have offered valuable information, especially Anna Maria Cavagna from the company of the same name in Turin, employees of the Casa del Guanto in Turin, the Cream Company in Genoa, Albertini in Milan, Ugo Fulco in Turin and Giuseppe Gatto in Rome; Vito Artioli and Gisella Buffoni, from P.B.F. Fashion Initiatives in Milan.
The author of *Stylism in Men's Fashion* is especially grateful to Migia Bianchi, from Ermenegildo Zegna Spa; to Angelo Azzena, from Gianni Versace Srl; to Rita Airaghi, from Gianfranco Ferré Srl.

Photographs: Giò Belli (pp. 36 left, 37), André Carrara (p. 39), Roland di Centa (pp. 34, 36 right), Giorgio Como, Rome (p. 220), Giovanni Lunardi (p. 35), Mario Santana (pp. 32, 270).
Photographs shot in the posing-room are by Studio A.D.V., Genoa (pp. 219, 220, 222), Fashion Institute of Technology, New York (p. 120), Fratelli Grazzani, Milan (pp. 38, 40, 41, 47, 52, 53, 55, 56, 57, 58, 59, 60, 61, 62, 63, 103, 104, 105, 106, 107, 108, 109, 110, 111, 112, 113, 114, 115, 116, 117, 118, 119, 121, 122, 123, 124, 125, 126, 127, 128, 129, 130, 131, 132, 133, 134, 135, 136, 137, 138, 139, 140, 141, 142, 143, 144, 145, 146, 147, 148, 149, 150, 151, 152, 153, 154, 155, 156, 157, 158, 159, 160, 161, 162, 163, 164, 165, 166, 167, 168, 169, 170, 171, 172, 173, 174, 199, 200, 201, 202, 203, 204, 205, 206, 208, 216, 221, 223, 224, 225, 226, 227, 228, 229, 230, 238, 239, 245, 247, 248, 250, 251, 253, 254, 256, 257, 258, 259, 260, 262, 263, 264, 267, 269).

Printed on behalf of Edizioni Electa
by Fantonigrafica, Venice